WAY

Peterson's

**DO NOT REMOVE
CARDS FROM POCKET**

Copyright © 1994 by Peterson's Guides, Inc.

Previous editions © 1991, 1992, 1993

Data on technology companies © 1994 by Corporate Technology
Information Services, Inc. This material is compiled and
copyrighted by Corporate Technology Information Services,
Incorporated, Woburn, Massachusetts. All rights reserved.

ISSN 1064-1769
ISBN 1-56079-402-X

Printed in the United States of America

10 9 8 7 6 5 4 3 2 1

Contents

Low-Tech Jobs at High-Tech Companies

Richard Thau

It has become almost axiomatic that workers must possess a multitude of skills in order find employment in today's work force. Indeed, small to mid-size companies, where most of the growth in employment is occurring, require staff that can handle a variety of disparate tasks.

But what happens when these types of companies — specifically hi-tech ones — grow, and grow quickly? Do CEOs still do the bookkeeping? Are presidents handling all of the personnel requirements? Or do they find qualified professionals to pick up these responsibilities?

The answer is that these firms increasingly find themselves turning to non-technical personnel to handle their ever-increasing business responsibilities. However, hiring is usually done sparingly, only when firms are pressed against the wall by clients or changes in the business climate.

As the director of personnel for one medical products company put it, "When you're smaller, you have people who wear a lot of different hats. As you grow, you don't have time to have people wear so many hats."

Successful high-tech companies, many of which have grown phenomenally fast over the last several years, have come increasingly to find that they must turn to specialists in personnel, accounting, marketing and advertising to handle the non-technical aspects of their businesses. Data compiled by the Bureau of Labor statistics support this assertion.

Between the years 1990 and 2005, assuming moderate economic growth, BLS says the percentage of "marketing, advertising and public relations managers" in the "Computer and Office Equipment" category will grow from 1.08 percent of that category's work force to 1.24 percent. The same types of employees working in "Electrical and Other Electronic Equipment" will grow from 0.74 percent to 0.98 percent. At "Measuring and Controlling Devices" firms, marketing, advertising and public relations managers will grow from 1.53 percent to 1.91 percent of the total.

Interestingly, the U.S. Department of Labor estimates that the aggregate work forces in each of these industries will suffer net decreases in employees. The most obvious explanation is that jobs are moving overseas. But as Cheryl Turner, a manpower development specialist at the Department of Labor puts it, "Support services are moving much, much faster than technical jobs are. It's largely as a result of technology. As manufacturing becomes more automated, you need fewer people doing that."

"Computer and Office Equipment" firms, for example, are slated to decline by 61,800 net jobs. "Electric and Other Electronic" will lose 105,900 jobs. And "Measuring and Controlling Devices" will see 62,900 disappear.

But for the purposes of this analysis, it might be valuable to discount this aspect of the projection, since it counts all existing companies — both strong and weak. Aggressive start-up companies, such as the ones listed in this book, will most likely continue to thrive in the U.S. And as they do, they will continue to need support specialists.

One company that has been growing its non-technical work force is Columbia Analytical Services in Kelso, Washington. Alicia Pulaski, the company's human resources manager, says that her firm adheres to a strict 3.3 to 1 ratio of technical to non-technical employees. She says, "It's a goal we've set and it's an industry standard."

What happened to her company is typical of high-tech firms: "We went through a great growth spurt in 1990 and 1991, adding a lot more people [indiscriminately] as opposed to being more consistent." Since then, she reports, "We've been fairly conservative" in hiring support specialists, sometimes letting the ratio grow to 4:1 or 5:1.

Where the greatest amount of recent hiring has occurred is in the sales department, because that is the place it is needed most. "In the last year or so, it seems like the environmental industry has leveled out," Pulaski says. "We had to look for areas we could expand on. That's why we added salespeople. Before, we didn't have salespeople. We just managed the work that came in."

Similarly, 200-employee Columbia Analytical Services hired computer people once the status quo no longer remained sustainable. "We were not standardized," Pulaski recalls of the recent past. Meanwhile, "clients wanted electronic delivery of reports." Needing to meet these clients' demands, the company simultaneously chose to standardize the software it used.

At other companies, the prevailing mindset is averse to hiring an ever growing percentage of non-technical workers. The goal at Norand Corp., a computer hardware and software company in Cedar Rapids, Iowa, is to "slow or stop administrative expenses" from growing, says Personnel Director Mike Wakefield. Where there is growth in non-technical positions, it is confined at Norand mainly to the finance department.

At Loveland, Colorado-based Hach Co., Vice President of Human Resources Randall Petersen boasts, "We've been able to reduce the amount of support staff through efficiencies and out-sourcing." Proportionately, he notes, "more technical [than non-technical] people are being hired all the time." Hach employees 900 people.

Even more averse to support specialists is SunGard Investment Systems of Hinsdale, Illinois. There, Vice President of Finance Margaret Sage says that in her 11 years with the company, "We've increased administrative staff by one part-time person," raising this segment of the staff total to nine. In the same time, technical staff has "probably doubled." How does the company do it? "We don't have secretaries" and "everyone knows WordPerfect."

One illustrative trend in the hiring of personnel in high-tech companies is found in an ongoing study of biotech firms in Massachusetts.

Robard Williams, a research associate at the Center for Labor Market Studies at Northeastern University, where the study is being conducted, says that "at the basic level," the intention of fledgling biotech firms is to "keep the administrative side as small as possible to keep resources focused on research and development. You don't see a lot of middle management."

However, "when they move over to manufacturing, you see greater levels of middle management."

In the larger picture, then, the following course emerges: success followed by growth, and growth controlled by specialization. When this phenomenon occurs, some new blood inevitably circulates to maintain business order. And the clotting agent, which prevents firms from hemorrhaging money, is the non-technical employee.

Richard Thau is a freelance business writer from New York City.

The Thriving
Technology Industry

Andrew Campbell
President
CorpTech Information Services, Inc.

Manufacturers and developers of technology products constitute the most successful business segment in the country today, the one major area that has expanded consistently over the past decade. With every facet of industry, commerce, and government looking to them to solve problems of productivity and competitiveness, technology companies are creating our tomorrow, and many analysts anticipate that this will be the sector that leads the economy back to prosperity.

Although many large technology manufacturers are experiencing considerable difficulty, small and midsize companies have been better able to adapt to changing demands and consequently have been riding a steady wave of expansion. Technology manufacturers with under 1,000 employees now represent over 20 percent of durable goods manufacturing employment, and, in 1993, this was the strongest sector of the economy.

The next year promises to be even more exciting. Between January and March 1994 CorpTech surveyed 2,750 emerging technology manufacturers with under 1,000 employees. These firms projected a combined job growth rate of 4.31 percent during the following year, with one in six expecting to grow at over 25 percent. The graph on the next page gives the growth projections broken down by industry.

Over 90,000 Jobs Created

The 2,000 firms listed in *Peterson's Hidden Job Market* were selected from a unique database of 36,000 technology manufacturers and developers created by Corporate Technology Information Services, Inc. (CorpTech),

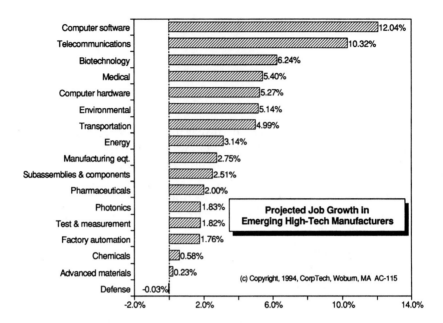

Computer software	12.04%
Telecommunications	10.32%
Biotechnology	6.24%
Medical	5.40%
Computer hardware	5.27%
Environmental	5.14%
Transportation	4.99%
Energy	3.14%
Manufacturing eqt.	2.75%
Subassemblies & components	2.51%
Pharmaceuticals	2.00%
Photonics	1.83%
Test & measurement	1.82%
Factory automation	1.76%
Chemicals	0.58%
Advanced materials	0.23%
Defense	-0.03%

Projected Job Growth in Emerging High-Tech Manufacturers

(c) Copyright, 1994, CorpTech, Woburn, MA AC-115

one of the country's leading suppliers of information on the high-tech industry. These are the firms with under 1,000 employees that added the most employees during the survey year. In fact, these 2,000 companies expanded their combined work force by 26 percent in the past year, creating over 93,000 new jobs!

These are not just technical jobs that are being created. Expanding firms need people in all areas and at all levels of experience—from sales to clerical, from manufacturing to accounting, and from entry level to senior management. This is the hidden job market.

How Does CorpTech Collect Its Information?

CorpTech has assembled the country's most comprehensive source of information about technology companies. It tracks over 36,000 technology manufacturers and developers with a unique five-stage research and checking process:

1. New and emerging firms are identified through local economic development groups, trade associations, the trade press, and other technology companies. Each is then entered into a central database.

2. Each new company is interviewed by phone for information on over 100 data elements, which are then entered into the database to form a comprehensive profile.

3. The profile is checked by sophisticated software and printed. Any errors detected are flagged on the printout.

4. The printed profile is edited by senior staff, and corrections are made to the database.

5. A copy of the edited profile is mailed to the firm for verification, and any corrections are added to the database.

Steps 2 through 5 are repeated each year for each company to ensure the currency and accuracy of the database, which has been continuously refined for nine years at an investment of over $4 million.

What Information Can You Find in This Book?

The companies listed in this book are arranged alphabetically by state. Most profiles include:

- Company name and address
- Year the company was founded
- Number of employees
- Annual sales revenue in the survey year
- The technology industries in which the company is active
- Number of employees added in the year prior to CorpTech's latest interview
- Percentage of growth, based on the previous year's employee number
- Contact name and title (usually the executive responsible for the personnel function or the chief executive officer)
- Telephone and fax numbers

The Hidden Job Market Technology Manufacturers
Sales and Employee Analysis by Primary Industry

Primary Industry	Firms #	Firms %	Sales $m	Sales %	Empl #	Empl %	Sales /Emp	Growth LstY	Growth NxtY
Factory Automation	110	5.5%	$18,075	4.7%	18,025	5.1%	$127,286	25.9%	4.7%
Biotechnology	72	3.6%	$10,877	2.8%	12,047	3.4%	$97,585	29.0%	10.8%
Chemicals	32	1.6%	$15,980	4.2%	7,748	2.2%	$227,842	14.7%	2.5%
Computer Hardware	192	9.6%	$49,451	13.0%	31,441	8.9%	$177,881	29.9%	11.0%
Defense	40	2.0%	$6,084	1.6%	9,794	2.7%	$116,948	25.1%	8.9%
Energy	46	2.3%	$6,384	1.6%	6,375	1.8%	$150,154	19.4%	7.0%
Environmental	116	5.8%	$14,569	3.8%	17,863	5.0%	$116,129	27.7%	6.8%
Manufacturing Eqp	79	3.9%	$15,413	4.0%	16,723	4.7%	$109,539	23.8%	6.4%
Advanced Materials	67	3.3%	$11,755	3.1%	9,796	2.7%	$156,375	20.4%	4.4%
Medical	117	5.8%	$21,504	5.6%	21,583	6.1%	$117,409	25.9%	6.0%
Pharmaceuticals	66	3.3%	$15,706	4.1%	15,004	4.2%	$140,928	32.1%	5.9%
Photonics	33	1.6%	$5,414	1.4%	5,327	1.5%	$115,972	24.6%	9.3%
Computer Software	424	21.2%	$67,172	17.7%	66,751	19.0%	$123,010	35.7%	14.9%
Subassemblies & Components	249	12.4%	$46,729	12.3%	47,590	13.5%	$106,332	21.7%	6.0%
Test & Measurement	68	3.4%	$7,919	2.0%	11,184	3.1%	$123,385	17.6%	5.2%
Telecommunications	170	8.5%	$45,057	11.9%	30,780	8.7%	$151,282	30.6%	15.5%
Transportation	41	2.0%	$3,906	1.0%	5,803	1.6%	$119,546	21.3%	6.9%
Not primarily high-tech	78	3.9%	$16,276	4.3%	17,240	4.9%	$137,860	27.5%	4.7%
	2,000	100.0%	$378,270	100.0%	351,074	100.0%	$132,179	26.7%	8.8%

Notes: **Sales/Employee** is a national average. **Growth** is based on employee growth reported by firms with under 1,000 employees. **LstY** is for the year prior to their interview, **NxtY** is their projected growth for the year following the interview.

Source: CorpTech, Woburn, MA (800) 333-8036

The company listings are followed by two indexes. The **Industry Index** lists the companies in this book according to the industry or industries in which they are active, along with their state and the page number of their profile. The eighteen categories of technology industry used are as follows:

- Advanced Materials
- Biotechnology
- Chemicals
- Computer Hardware
- Computer Software
- Defense
- Energy
- Environmental
- Factory Automation
- Holding Companies
- Manufacturing Equipment
- Medical
- Pharmaceuticals
- Photonics
- Subassemblies and Components
- Telecommunications
- Test and Measurement
- Transportation

The Hidden Job Market
Technology Industries Ranked by Total Job Growth

#	Jobs	Industry	Firms
1	11,138	Computer Software	424
2	6,169	Telecommunications	170
3	4,091	Computer Hardware	192
4	3,720	Subassemblies & Components	249
5	1,694	Medical	117
6	1,606	Environmental	116
7	1,350	Biotechnology	72
8	1,203	Manufacturing Equipment	79
9	1,033	Defense	40
10	974	Factory Automation	110
11	956	Pharmaceuticals	66
12	755	Advanced Materials	67
13	730	Test & Measurement	68
14	728	Energy	46
15	606	Photonics	33
16	602	Transportation	41
17	280	Chemicals	32

Employment at technology manufacturers with under 1,000 employees where the home office is in this area. Jobs = new technology manufacturing jobs projected for the 12 months following the survey.
Source: CorpTech, Woburn, MA (800) 333-8036

The **Company Index** lists companies alphabetically, giving their state and the page number on which their detailed information appears.

The 20 Fastest Growing Hidden Job Market Companies
Technology Producers Ranked by Projected Job Growth

#	Jobs	Company	City	Phone	Main high-tech activity	Sales($m)
1	500	Platinum Software Corp.	Irvine, CA	(714) 727-1250	Computer Software	$39
2	250	ALLTEL Mobile Communications, Inc.	Little Rock, AR	(501) 661-8500	Telecommunications	$110 e
3	250	Mastech Systems Corporation	Pittsburgh, PA	(412) 279-6400	Computer Software	$25-50
4	242	IDB Communications Group, Inc.	Culver City, CA	(213) 870-9000	Telecommunications	$311
5	200	Nano Pulse Industries, Inc.	Brea, CA	(714) 529-2600	Telecommunications	$9.0
6	175	Integrated Medical Systems, Inc.	Golden, CO	(303) 279-6116	Computer Software	$14 e
7	170	NCI Information Systems, Inc.	Mc Lean, VA	(703) 903-0325	Computer Software	Declined
8	170	IWI	San Jose, CA	(408) 923-0301	Telecommunications	Declined
9	155	Commonwealth Communication, Inc.	Wilkes-Barre, PA	(717) 820-5000	Telecommunications	$19
10	150	Harris Corp. / Air Traffic Control Systems Division	Melbourne, FL	(407) 727-4000	Telecommunications	$125
11	150	Genetics Institute, Inc.	Cambridge, MA	(617) 876-1170	Biotechnology	$88
12	150	Seer Technologies, Inc.	Cary, NC	(919) 380-5000	Computer Software	$50
13	148	On Command Video, Inc.	Santa Clara, CA	(408) 496-1800	Telecommunications	$20 e
14	130	Crystal Semiconductor Corp.	Austin, TX	(512) 445-7222	Subassemblies & Components	$100
15	125	Aspect Telecommunications Corp.	San Jose, CA	(408) 441-2200	Telecommunications	$105
16	125	Curative Technologies, Inc.	East Setauket, NY	(516) 689-7000	Pharmaceuticals	$31
17	125	MEVATEC	Huntsville, AL	(205) 890-8000	Defense	$15
18	125	Unified Systems Solutions	Mountain Lakes, NJ	(201) 402-2333	Computer Software	$4.5
19	125	AER Energy Resources, Inc.	Smyrna, GA	(404) 433-2127	Energy	$0
20	120	Systems Research and Applications Corp.	Arlington, VA	(703) 558-4700	Manufacturing Equipment	$66

Based on employment at emerging technology manufacturers with under 1,000 employees. **Jobs** = number of new technology manufacturing jobs projected for the 12 months following the survey. **e** = estimated, **p** = parent.
Source: CorpTech, Woburn, MA (800) 333-8036

The **Metropolitan Area Index** lists companies by the major metropolitan areas in which they are located. If your job search is focused on a particular region, you should start your research in this section.

Top 20 Hidden Job Market Cities
Ranked by Projected High-Tech Job Growth

#	Jobs	City	Firms	Main high-tech activity	Jobs
1	3,339	San Jose, CA	284	Subassemblies & Components	748
2	3,108	San Diego, CA	311	Computer Hardware	605
3	2,610	Houston, TX	438	Energy	764
4	2,075	New York, NY	218	Computer Software	948
5	1,911	Dallas, TX	264	Computer Software	655
6	1,809	Pittsburgh, PA	283	Computer Software	612
7	1,714	Sunnyvale, CA	202	Telecommunications	579
8	1,696	Minneapolis, MN	176	Subassemblies & Components	318
9	1,676	Chicago, IL	195	Subassemblies & Components	290
10	1,655	Santa Clara, CA	197	Subassemblies & Components	504
11	1,626	Atlanta, GA	135	Computer Software	968
12	1,554	Irvine, CA	177	Computer Hardware	417
13	1,382	Waltham, MA	128	Computer Software	612
14	1,333	Saint Louis, MO	145	Factory Automation	188
15	1,332	Mountain View, CA	133	Computer Software	531
16	1,321	Cambridge, MA	174	Computer Software	703
17	1,312	Rockville, MD	114	Computer Hardware	395
18	1,263	Austin, TX	240	Subassemblies & Components	294
19	1,017	Hauppauge, NY	56	Telecommunications	325
20	970	Rochester, NY	77	Test & Measurement	150

Based on employment at firms with under 1,000 employees where the home office is in the city. **Jobs** = number of new technology manufacturing jobs projected for the 12 months following the survey. **Main high-tech activity** = largest of 17 segments by employment; .... **Jobs** = new jobs projected within the main activity.

Source: CorpTech, Woburn, MA (800) 333-8036

Using the Book to Your Advantage

This book has been developed to assist in all three phases of the job-hunting process:

1. Identifying potential employers
2. Persuading a potential employer that you are a good applicant
3. Convincing a potential employer that you would be a good employee

Identifying Potential Employers

For a company to be regarded as a potential employer, it must currently be hiring new staff, be in a location where you wish to work, and be an employer of people with your skills at your income level. No approach will guarantee success, but the following steps will help you identify potential employers.

1. *Concentrate on growing companies.* Simply by using this book, you have an advantage over other job seekers. The 2,000 firms profiled are those that have added the most new jobs in the past year in the most dynamic sector of the country's economy.

2. *Find companies in your area.* Turn to your state in the book where the companies are listed alphabetically by name. Use the **Metropolitan Area Index** to find companies in specific areas within states.

3. *Find companies active in your industry.* If your job skills are specific to a particular industry, turn to the **Industry Index**. Firms active in specific

areas of industry are listed alphabetically, with a page number directing you to their detailed description.

4. *Use the press.* Read the business section of your local paper and the regional and national business press. Look for stories about firms that are doing well. Notice which companies have just won a major contract, opened a new manufacturing plant, or are simply growing rapidly. When you find one that sounds interesting, look for it in the **Company Index**; if it is listed, the index will direct you to its profile.

Once you have found a firm that you would like to approach, call its sales department and request company literature. When this arrives, scan it to gain an overview of the company's products, noting questions that occur to you. If you are still interested, memorize the main facts—number of employees, growth, annual sales, and industries in which the company is active. (For the firms listed in *Peterson's Hidden Job Market 1995,* all of this information is featured.) Now you are ready to make contact.

Persuading a Potential Employer That You Are a Good Applicant

Remember that companies receive job applications every day. Your task is to make your application stand out from the pack so that you get an interview. The good news it that 95 percent of job applications are poorly prepared, and yours won't be among them if you take this advice:

- Don't mail out a form letter to dozens of firms.
- Don't enclose a poorly copied resume—in fact, don't enclose a resume at all. The task at this phase is to get in the door, not to get hired. The more you say about yourself, the more reasons the employer will have to cross you off the list before ever meeting you.
- Don't apply to a company unless you can think of several reasons you would be of value. Consider the job for which you are applying, and write down the skills and experience it requires. Then note your own skills and experience as they relate to the employer's needs. If your skills and experience are strong, make sure you communicate this to the company. If they are not, think about another job. If *you* can't think of some good reasons why you should be hired, it is certain the company won't either!

On the positive side, there are a number of things you can do to advance your application:

- Make a personal approach to a named executive, not just to a department. (The listings in this book usually give the name of the personnel director or CEO.)
- Make your initial contact a telephone call rather than a letter.

- Make sure you are sufficiently prepared *before* making your approach.
- Explain in as few words as possible what you have to offer the company, emphasizing your past accomplishments rather than future goals. The world is full of dreamers with goals, but companies hire people to do a job, and your list of actual accomplishments is your best selling tool. Even if you are looking for your first job, you should be able to cite accomplishments in community or leisure activities that demonstrate your ability to define a goal and work to achieve it.
- If you choose to approach the executive in writing, call first to double-check his or her name, title, and address and make sure that the person is still in the same position. Make your letter brief, and design it to get yourself in the door only. There must be no typing or spelling errors. The letter should be perfect and attractively laid out. Use a word processor with a good printer if you have them, or enlist the aid of a friend or professional who does. You will be judged by the impression the letter makes.
- If you phone as suggested, rehearse your technique with a friend until you know without thinking what you will say to a variety of responses, from "He's not in" to "We aren't hiring" to "Put your resume in the mail" to "Why should I see you?"
- Whether you call or write, use your knowledge of the firm's products to explain why you think that you would be of value to the company, and request an interview.

Convincing a Potential Employer That You Would Be a Good Employee

Take the sales literature you received to the interview together with the list of questions you compiled. Make a point of asking your questions as early in the interview as possible, showing the interviewer that you are serious and interested. Refer to the job analysis you made, and ask if this accurately defines the skills and experience required — this demonstrates that you have made an effort to see the job from the employer's perspective, a valuable quality. The answers you receive to these questions will allow you to present yourself in a way that is relevant to the company's needs.

In interviewing hundreds of job applicants over many years, I have found that most interviewees have little or no knowledge of the companies to which they apply. This comes across as a lack of interest. Those few who take the modest amount of time needed to do the kind of research described stand out head and shoulders above the rest. They are not simply *claiming* competence, they are *demonstrating* it! And remember that the interviewer has a hard job — to choose the best applicant. Make that job easier by showing exactly what you have to offer in terms of accomplishments and a proven willingness to work hard.

Competing for Jobs in the Information Age

Richard A. Shinton
Director of Human Resources
Exabyte Corporation

Welcome to the information age. We live in a fascinating new world, one in which the workplace has changed forever. As we approach the on-ramp to an information superhighway leading who knows where, there's a PC on every desk, and now almost all of those PCs are connected to a network. High-tech used to mean the computer industry — not anymore. High-tech has reached into every job, every company. It is simply a way of business life.

Today's job seekers face the challenge of adapting to and excelling in a world that never slows its pace. Daunting? Yes. But the information revolution has spawned more creative opportunities than ever before in the American workplace. Entire industries — biotechnology, for example — spring to life seemingly overnight. Entrepreneurs spin off companies that grow, thrive, and vanish like summer thunderstorms.

We live in an economic world that was unimaginable just a few decades ago. Industry has changed. The workforce has changed. You are being asked to bring greater capabilities to jobs — even entry-level personnel must know several word-processing packages. And, ironically, these jobs are inherently less secure, but that's just the nature of the high-tech environment. What all of this does is place the responsibility for a successful career back where I believe it has belonged all along: on you, the employee.

The idea of remaining with one company all the way to retirement is fading fast, as it should. It's a fallacy that any company can determine what is best for you as a person. And while this instability and demand for employee responsibility can create some difficulties, I believe the benefits are far greater. Employees now find themselves in jobs that allow for continuous learning, even at the higher levels of management. Although I've been a human resources professional for more than fifteen years, every day I come into contact with a new software package or create a flexible benefits package to reflect the diverse nature of today's corporate payroll — from single mothers to head-of-household fathers. One size no longer fits all. This means that life in the company will never be as easy as it once was.

Or as stifling.

Put Technology to Work for You—But Don't Forget . . .

So how do you keep up? You work with these changes, and you uncover opportunities. You make technology work for you. Start with the job search itself. The world is smaller now. You're not limited by geographic concerns. Your resume can be in a distant human resources office in just seconds, thanks to the fax machine and the modem. Master these modern-day tools. Harness them and use them in your search. If you have a PC at home, use it to learn software packages that will prove helpful in the industries you've targeted. Keep expanding.

Apply technology to show creativity even as part of your job-search process. I've seen graphic artists include diskettes with a brief software slide show of their work. Confirm receipt of your resume through the use of electronic mail. Show that you know how to put technology to work for you. Use it to separate yourself from the pack — that's exactly what employers want. But, as always, be careful to avoid gimmickry. Sell yourself the same way you would sell one of your ideas on the job.

You must also be aware that today's employers are often looking beyond your specific skill set. As someone who has overseen hiring through periods of tremendous growth, I know we can't afford to bypass creative, dynamic people just because they lack experience in one certain area. We look for people who show confidence that they can learn whatever they need to learn. You can demonstrate this confidence by familiarizing yourself — familiarizing, not necessarily becoming an expert — with the tools of business. Show that you understand the concepts of word-processing, database, and spreadsheet software, that you have an idea about how these packages help make a business more effective. Skill is nothing but the implementation of talent. I believe that we're all born with the same amount of talent and that we have an unlimited capacity to learn. Take the talent you were born with, and turn it into something employers can use. And let them know about it.

But don't let your view get too sidetracked by technology. In the end we always come back to the basics, even in the high-tech arena. There's no substitute for hard work. You may dazzle prospective employers with your application of technology, but their interest will only last as far as a phone call if you haven't build a reputation as a quality contributor to the teams you've worked with in the past. You need to be reliable. Go to work on time. Go to work every day. And once you're there, accept responsibilities. You're not going to get ahead by picking and choosing projects. Take charge of what needs to be done and *do it*. That's how you build a name as an effective person. Does that mean harder work and more hours? Probably so. Does it mean you'll always get real-time rewards for your efforts? Probably not. But in the end you'll come out ahead because that reputation as a make-it-happen player will precede you wherever you go.

What it boils down to is this: the same thing that made people successful in the 1920s makes people successful in the 1990s. There's no substitute for getting the job done.

Employees and Employers: A New Relationship

No other time in history has given the job seeker so many options. And the high-tech world takes those options to the extreme. Do you want to be part of a startup team, or are you looking for something more established? Do you want a loosely structured environment where you essentially manage yourself, or do you prefer a solid chain of command where you work closely with managers and supervisors? There's something out there for everyone. The first step to finding a position that's right for you is recognizing that you have some power and responsibility in the job-search process.

Determine what it is you want. Not just from a job, but from your life. You need to go through some sort of self-examination before throwing yourself into the market. Figure out what is important to you personally, because work isn't all that different. I'll often ask people, "What do you have fun doing? What is the most fun you ever had at work?" It's vital that you *know* these things, not just that you have an answer.

Then learn about the companies with which you hope to work. This comes back to putting technology to work for you — it's easy to find basic information about companies. Look at the information you uncover from two sides. First, does this company fit your desired profile, whether through its financial outlook, management styles, or kinds of jobs and growth opportunities? You'll find yourself much more effective when you are competing for a position you truly desire. Second, know what the company actually does. Human resources personnel don't expect you to be a walking encyclopedia about their company, but if you've taken the time to send in a resume, you should at least know what business they're in. By not knowing the basics, you paint an all-too-real — at not very appealing — picture of the kind of employee you will be.

This book is called *Peterson's Hidden Job Market.* I like that, because there are markets — especially today — that you must uncover for yourself. We've come through a difficult time in American business recently. People have been through layoffs and have gotten caught in downsizing. But once again, every crisis creates opportunity. Don't base your strategy on panic, saying "I've got to find a job right now." Instead, think about the options. You could work for a temporary agency while you plan your job search. Many companies now use consultants and contract groups. Take care of your physical needs, and put some time into building a plan that works for you.

Finally, never let yourself become complacent, even when you've won the perfect job. It comes back to taking responsibility for your life. You can be loyal to your employer and, at the same time, think about your future. Understand the high-technology trade-off: excitement and creativity for traditional security. You always have to have a plan. It's your own insurance policy.

Communicate, Communicate, Communicate

To get what you want from a job, you need to let people know exactly what you want. Make it clear during the interviewing process, during the negotiation process, and, most of all, once the work has commenced. The "hidden" job usually isn't very far from a job you already have.

Some companies, like Exabyte, sponsor employee-education programs on everything from software packages to personality dynamics. If you find something that interests you, learn all you can about it, and let your enthusiasm shine through in your work, your resume, and your interviews. The best positions are those that are created. Play a role in that process. Sell yourself and your talent/skills package. Innovation is the crux of all high-tech industries. Make yourself and your work visible. Make your voice heard. Drive your ideas into every part of your professional life.

One of the most exciting aspects of today's corporations is their focus on team building and teamwork. More and more companies are forming Total Quality Management programs or employee-action teams as a way of empowering employees. Volunteer for teams focusing on areas in which you're interested. These teams often report directly to the president or to other executives in the corporation. One of the best ways to tap into unseen opportunity is to make yourself visible to those at the top levels. Never turn down a chance to do this. At Exabyte, we've tried to give every employee an opportunity to be heard by holding a monthly breakfast where a group of 10 or so employees meets with the CEO. Don't view such events as useless gestures. The reason management does this is because they *really do* want to hear what's on your mind. Tell them! Let someone know if your job has become less challenging than you would like. Propose a project of your own design and offer to lead it. Make it happen and see what transpires. *The job you've always wanted just may be the one you already have.*

Follow the time-proven methods of networking. Join professional organizations and make yourself available to serve on event or program committees. You'll meet countless people who have made it to where you're trying to go. Knock them out with your energy and creativity. Be open to all possibilities. Who knows what could transpire through a casual contact?

Finally, throughout my years of experience I have found that all successful people share one trait, and it's something that anyone can master: *learn to change ideas into action.* By doing this you become more than an asset. You become a vital force — a hot commodity, so to speak. This trait will come out in interviews. It will come out in your current job. It will come out in any conversation where your name arises.

In today's competitive and high-tech world, you just don't have the option of showing up every day for forty years and then collecting a gold watch and a pension. You've got to carve your own niche. You've got to meet management on its own level, with your hand extended and your grip firm. Find the ways to do this, and you'll find all the opportunities you once thought were hidden.

Richard A. Shinton heads the human resources department at Exabyte Corporation. He was the first member of this department in 1988, when Exabyte had just a handful of employees. Now he oversees the department, maintaining responsibility for more than 1,100 employees.

Exabyte Corporation of Boulder, Colorado, designs, manufactures, and markets tape backup subsystems to a worldwide customer base. Founded in 1985, the company has shipped nearly half a million subsystems to date. Exabyte reported more than $287 million in revenue in 1992.

The 2,000 Fastest-Growing High-Tech Companies in the United States

Alabama

Adtran, Inc.
901 Explorer Blvd.
Huntsville, AL 35806

Founded 1986
Total employees 340
Annual sales $57 million
Industry
  Telecommunications
Growth Openings in past
  year 90; percentage
  growth 36%
Contact
Mark Smith, President
Tel 205-971-8000
Fax 205-937-8699

Applied Research, Inc.
6700 Odyssey Dr.
Huntsville, AL 35806

Founded 1980
Total employees 265
Industry Defense
Growth Openings in past
  year 65; percentage
  growth 32%
Contact
Keith Frost, Personnel
  Manager
Tel 205-922-8600
Fax 205-922-8601

CMS Research Corp.
200 Chase Park South,
  Suite 100
Birmingham, AL 35244

Founded 1986
Total employees 41
Annual sales $4.3 million
Industry Environmental
Growth Openings in past
  year 16; percentage
  growth 64%
Contact
Gary Sides, President
Tel 205-733-6900
Fax 205-733-6919

**Continental Conveyor
and Equipment Co.**
4th Ave. South
Winfield, AL 35594

Founded 1959
Total employees 500

Annual sales $63 million
Industry Factory
  Automation
Growth Openings in past
  year 100; percentage
  growth 25%
Contact
C.E. Bryant, President
Tel 205-487-6492
Fax 205-487-4233

CPSI
6600 Wall St.
Mobile, AL 36695

Founded 1979
Total employees 140
Annual sales $14 million
Industry Computer
  Software
Growth Openings in past
  year 50; percentage
  growth 55%
Contact
Dr. Dennis Wilkins, Ph.D.,
  President
Tel 205-639-8100
Fax 205-639-8100

Decatur Cylinders, Inc.
1112 Brooks St.
  Southeast, PO Box 2068
Decatur, AL 35602

Founded 1981
Total employees 70
Annual sales $6 million
Industry Subassemblies
  and Components
Growth Openings in past
  year 15; percentage
  growth 27%
Contact
Mike Lothspeich,
  President/COO
Tel 205-350-2603
Fax 205-351-1264

**M&M Chemical and
Equipment Co., Inc.**
1229 Valley Dr.
Attalla, AL 35954

Founded 1976
Total employees 100
Annual sales $10 million
Industry Environmental
Growth Openings in past
  year 50; percentage
  growth 100%

Contact
John Roberts, President
Tel 205-538-3800

Marathon Equipment Co.
PO Box 1798
Vernon, AL 35592

Founded 1965
Total employees 468
Annual sales $49 million
Industry Environmental
Growth Openings in past
  year 78; percentage
  growth 20%
Contact
Gordon Fenner, Chief
  Executive Officer
Tel 205-695-9105
Fax 205-695-7250

MEVATEC
1525 Perimeter Pkwy.,
  Suite 500
Huntsville, AL 35806

Founded 1985
Total employees 200
Annual sales $14.5 million
Industry Defense
Growth Openings in past
  year 115; percentage
  growth 135%
Contact
Ms. Nancy Archuleta,
  President/CEO
Tel 205-890-8000
Fax 205-890-0000

Sirsi Corp.
110 Walker Ave.
Huntsville, AL 35801

Founded 1980
Total employees 52
Industry Computer
  Software
Growth Openings in past
  year 18; percentage
  growth 52%
Contact
James J. Young, President
Tel 205-536-5881
Fax 205-536-8345

Techsonic Industries, Inc.
3 Humminbird Ln.
Eufaula, AL 36027

Founded 1973
Total employees 300
Annual sales $34 million
Industries Test and
Measurement,
Transportation
Growth Openings in past
year 50; percentage
growth 20%
Contact
Jim Balkcom, Chief
Executive Officer
Tel 205-687-6613
Fax 205-687-4272

Thermal Components, Inc.
2760 Gunter Park West,
PO Box 3253
Montgomery, AL 36193

Founded 1969
Total employees 305
Annual sales $53 million
Industries Energy,
Holding Companies,
Subassemblies and
Components
Growth Openings in past
year 33; percentage
growth 12%
Contact
John Marshall, President
Tel 205-277-1810
Fax 205-277-3681

VME Microsystems International Corp.
12090 South Memorial
Pkwy.
Huntsville, AL 35803

Founded 1983
Total employees 156
Industries Computer
Hardware,
Telecommunications
Growth Openings in past
year 26; percentage
growth 20%
Contact
Ms. Faye Robinson,
Human Resources
Administrator
Tel 205-880-0444
Fax 205-882-0859

XANTE Corp.
2559 Imogene St.
Mobile, AL 36606

Founded 1988
Total employees 90
Annual sales $16 million
Industry Computer
Hardware
Growth Openings in past
year 17; percentage
growth 23%
Contact
Robert Ross, President
Tel 205-476-8189
Fax 205-476-9421

Arizona

Active Noise and Vibration Technologies, Inc.
4824 South 40th St.
Phoenix, AZ 85040

Founded 1987
Total employees 75
Industries Environmental,
Transportation
Growth Openings in past
year 40; percentage
growth 114%
Contact
Bob Bosserman, Chief
Executive Officer
Tel 602-470-0020
Fax 602-470-1780

Anasazi, Inc.
7500 North Dreamy Draw
Dr., Suite 120
Phoenix, AZ 85020

Founded 1980
Total employees 160
Industries Computer
Software,
Telecommunications
Growth Openings in past
year 40; percentage
growth 33%
Contact
Angela Biezer, President
Tel 602-870-3330
Fax 602-861-7687

Arizona Instrument Corp.
PO Box 1930
Tempe, AZ 85280

Founded 1987
Total employees 105

Annual sales $12 million
Industries Factory
Automation, Test and
Measurement
Growth Openings in past
year 30; percentage
growth 40%
Contact
Ms. Sue Berry, Corporate
Secretary
Tel 602-731-3400
Fax 602-731-3434

Avalon Software, Inc.
3716 East Columbia Dr.
Tucson, AZ 85714

Founded 1976
Total employees 100
Annual sales $10 million
Industry Computer
Software
Growth Openings in past
year 40; percentage
growth 66%
Contact
Gary Gibson, President
Tel 602-790-4214
Fax 602-750-0822

Continental Circuits Corp.
3502 East Roeser Rd.
Phoenix, AZ 85040

Founded 1973
Total employees 875
Annual sales $70 million
Industry Subassemblies
and Components
Growth Openings in past
year 18; percentage
growth 2%
Contact
Michael Flatt, President
Tel 602-268-3461
Fax 602-268-0208

Dynaco Corporation
1000 South Priest Dr.
Tempe, AZ 85283

Founded 1989
Total employees 177
Annual sales $18.5 million
Industry Subassemblies
and Components
Growth Openings in past
year 47; percentage
growth 36%
Contact
Ms. Jane Petri, VP of
Human Resources &
Administration
Tel 602-968-2000
Fax 602-921-9830

EFData Corp.
2105 West 5th Pl.
Tempe, AZ 85281

Founded 1985
Total employees 350
Annual sales $45 million
Industries Energy,
Subassemblies and
Components,
Telecommunications
Growth Openings in past
year 150; percentage
growth 75%
Contact
Robert Fitting, Chief
Executive Officer
Tel 602-968-0447
Fax 602-921-9012

ESH, Inc.
3020 South Park Dr.
Tempe, AZ 85282

Founded 1983
Total employees 75
Annual sales $9.4 million
Industry Factory
Automation
Growth Openings in past
year 15; percentage
growth 25%
Contact
Dennis Gauthier, President
Tel 602-438-1112
Fax 602-431-9633

**Fresh Test Technology
Corporation**
1478 North Tech Blvd.,
Suite 101
Gilbert, AZ 85234

Founded 1985
Total employees 63
Annual sales $7.9 million
Industry Factory
Automation
Growth Openings in past
year 33; percentage
growth 110%
Contact
Grady Brown, Manager of
Human Resources
Tel 602-497-4200
Fax 602-497-4242

Inter-Tel, Inc.
7300 West Boston St.
Chandler, AZ 85226

Founded 1969
Total employees 615
Annual sales $84 million
Industry
Telecommunications

Growth Openings in past
year 41; percentage
growth 7%
Contact
Steve Mahaylo, President
Tel 602-961-9000
Fax 602-961-1370

Lion Industries, Inc.
PO Box 980
Snowflake, AZ 85937

Founded 1982
Total employees 50
Industries Advanced
Materials, Chemicals
Growth Openings in past
year 20; percentage
growth 66%
Contact
Charles McQueeny,
President
Tel 602-536-7171
Fax 602-536-2410

**Microsemi Corp.,
Scottsdale Division**
8700 East Thomas Rd.,
PO Box 1390
Scottsdale, AZ 85252

Founded 1982
Total employees 350
Annual sales $23.4 million
Industry Subassemblies
and Components
Growth Openings in past
year 20; percentage
growth 6%
Contact
Ms. Lorraine Greager,
Personnel Manager
Tel 602-941-6300
Fax 602-947-1503

Microtest, Inc.
4747 North 22nd Str.
Phoenix, AZ 85016

Founded 1984
Total employees 160
Annual sales $22.14
million
Industries Factory
Automation,
Telecommunications
Growth Openings in past
year 50; percentage
growth 45%
Contact
Richard G. Meise, CEO/
President
Tel 602-942-6400
Fax 602-952-6604

Simula, Inc.
10016 South 51st St.
Phoenix, AZ 85044

Founded 1975
Total employees 235
Annual sales $18 million
Industries Advanced
Materials, Transportation
Growth Openings in past
year 35; percentage
growth 17%
Contact
Ms. Linda Burson,
Personnel Manager
Tel 602-893-7533
Fax 602-893-8643

Spectrum Astro, Inc.
1440 North Fiesta Blvd.
Gilbert, AZ 85234

Founded 1988
Total employees 60
Industries Subassemblies
and Components,
Telecommunications,
Transportation
Growth Openings in past
year 30; percentage
growth 100%
Contact
W. David Thompson,
President
Tel 602-892-8200
Fax 602-892-2949

Syntellect, Inc.
15810 North 28th Ave.
Phoenix, AZ 85023

Founded 1984
Total employees 220
Annual sales $43.67
million
Industries Holding
Companies,
Telecommunications
Growth Openings in past
year 40; percentage
growth 22%
Contact
Thomas Mayer, COB/CEO
Tel 602-789-2800
Fax 602-789-2899

Three-Five Systems, Inc.
10230 South 50th Pl.
Phoenix, AZ 85044

Founded 1985
Total employees 650
Annual sales $20 million
Industries Computer
Hardware, Photonics

Growth Openings in past year 249; percentage growth 62%
Contact
David R. Buchanan, COB/President/CEO/ Treasurer
Tel 602-496-0035
Fax 602-496-0168

Tri-Tronics, Inc.
1650 South Research Loop, PO Box 17660
Tucson, AZ 85710

Founded 1968
Total employees 130
Annual sales $11 million
Industry Medical
Growth Openings in past year 30; percentage growth 30%
Contact
Bob Thomisak, Chief Executive Officer
Tel 602-290-6000
Fax 602-722-9000

Universal Navigation Corp.
3260 East Lardo Rd.
Tucson, AZ 85706

Founded 1975
Total employees 135
Annual sales $15 million
Industry Transportation
Growth Openings in past year 35; percentage growth 35%
Contact
Hubert L. Naimer, President/CEO
Tel 602-295-2300
Fax 602-295-2395

Universal Propulsion, Inc.
25401 North Central Ave.
Phoenix, AZ 85027

Founded 1960
Total employees 200
Industry Transportation
Growth Openings in past year 17; percentage growth 9%
Contact
Harold G. Watson, President/General Manager
Tel 602-869-8067
Fax 602-869-8176

Viasoft, Inc.
3033 North 44th St., Suite 101
Phoenix, AZ 85018

Founded 1983
Total employees 180
Annual sales $20 million
Industry Computer Software
Growth Openings in past year 20; percentage growth 12%
Contact
LeRoy Ellison, CEO
Tel 602-952-0050
Fax 602-840-4068

Arkansas

ALLTEL Mobile Communications, Inc.
10825 Financial Pkwy., Suite 401
Little Rock, AR 72211

Founded 1960
Total employees 850
Annual sales $110 million
Industry Telecommunications
Growth Openings in past year 450; percentage growth 112%
Contact
Carrol McHenry, President
Tel 501-661-8500
Fax 501-661-8599

Babcock & Wilcox Co., Struthers Thermo-Flood
8900 Fourche Dam Pike
Little Rock, AR 72206

Founded 1971
Total employees 275
Annual sales $36 million
Industries Energy, Subassemblies and Components
Growth Openings in past year 64; percentage growth 30%
Contact
Ron Fair, Human Resources Manager
Tel 501-490-2424
Fax 501-490-1414

Pel-Freez Rabbit Meat, Inc.
PO Box 68
Rogers, AR 72757

Founded 1911
Total employees 150
Annual sales $14 million
Industry Holding Companies
Growth Openings in past year 15; percentage growth 11%
Contact
David Dubbell, President
Tel 501-636-4361
Fax 501-636-4282

Uniforce Technologies, Inc.
East 5th and Hemlock, PO Box 5786
North Little Rock, AR 72119

Founded 1981
Total employees 90
Annual sales $10 million
Industry Transportation
Growth Openings in past year 15; percentage growth 20%
Contact
Kenneth N. Burks, President/CEO
Tel 501-945-3283
Fax 501-945-3935

California

ABB Systems Control Co., Inc.
2550 Walsh Ave.
Santa Clara, CA 95051

Founded 1968
Total employees 160
Annual sales $18 million
Industry Computer Software
Growth Openings in past year 20; percentage growth 14%
Contact
Ms. Mimi Henninger, Manager of Human Resources
Tel 408-988-3200
Fax 408-987-6066

Ablestik Laboratories
20021 Susana Rd.
Rancho Dominguez, CA
90221

Founded 1961
Total employees 200
Industry Advanced
Materials
Growth Openings in past
year 25; percentage
growth 14%
Contact
Ms. Suzi Olvera,
Personnel Manager
Tel 310-764-4600
Fax 310-764-2545

**Access Health
Marketing, Inc.**
11020 White Rock Rd.
Rancho Cordova, CA
95670

Founded 1988
Total employees 225
Annual sales $12 million
Industry Computer
Software
Growth Openings in past
year 95; percentage
growth 73%
Contact
Ken Plumlee, President
Tel 916-851-4000
Fax 916-852-3890

Accolade, Inc.
5300 Stevens Creek Blvd.,
Suite 500
San Jose, CA 95129

Founded 1984
Total employees 110
Annual sales $12 million
Industry Computer
Software
Growth Openings in past
year 25; percentage
growth 29%
Contact
Alan R. Miller, COB/
President/CEO
Tel 408-985-1700
Fax 408-246-1282

Accom, Inc.
1490 O'Brien Dr.
Menlo Park, CA 94025

Founded 1988
Total employees 75
Annual sales $10 million
Industry
Telecommunications

Growth Openings in past
year 25; percentage
growth 50%
Contact
Junaid Sheikh, COB/
President
Tel 415-328-3818
Fax 415-327-2511

ACIUS, Inc.
10351 Bubb Rd.
Cupertino, CA 95014

Founded 1987
Total employees 85
Industry Computer
Software
Growth Openings in past
year 50; percentage
growth 142%
Contact
Ms. Pat Cohen-Hadria,
Director of Personnel
Tel 408-252-4444
Fax 408-252-0831

**ACS Communications,
Inc.**
250 Technology Cir.
Scotts Valley, CA 95066

Founded 1976
Total employees 140
Annual sales $19 million
Industry
Telecommunications
Growth Openings in past
year 20; percentage
growth 16%
Contact
Ms. Jan Peterson, Director
of Personnel
Tel 408-438-3883
Fax 408-438-7730

ACTEL Corp.
955 East Arques Ave.
Sunnyvale, CA 94086

Founded 1985
Total employees 203
Annual sales $44 million
Industry Subassemblies
and Components
Growth Openings in past
year 53; percentage
growth 35%
Contact
Ms. Michelle Begun, VP of
Human Resources
Tel 408-739-1010
Fax 408-739-1540

Activision, Inc.
11440 San Vicente Blvd.,
Suite 300
Los Angeles, CA 90049

Founded 1979
Total employees 65
Annual sales $20.3 million
Industry Computer
Software
Growth Openings in past
year 35; percentage
growth 116%
Contact
Robert Kotick, COB/CEO
Tel 310-207-4500
Fax 310-820-6131

Acucobol, Inc.
7950 Silverton Ave., Suite
201
San Diego, CA 92126

Founded 1988
Total employees 75
Annual sales $8.7 million
Industry Computer
Software
Growth Openings in past
year 20; percentage
growth 36%
Contact
Dr. Pamela Coker, Ph.D.,
President
Tel 619-689-7220
Fax 619-566-3071

Adobe Systems, Inc.
1585 Charleston Rd.
Mountain View, CA 94039

Founded 1982
Total employees 887
Annual sales $265.9
million
Industry Computer
Software
Growth Openings in past
year 184; percentage
growth 26%
Contact
Ms. Rebecca Guerra,
Director of Human
Resources
Tel 415-961-4400
Fax 415-961-3761

**Advanced Computer
Communications**
10261 Bubb Rd.
Cupertino, CA 95014

Founded 1987
Total employees 118
Annual sales $16 million

Industries Computer
Hardware,
Telecommunications
Growth Openings in past
year 23; percentage
growth 24%
Contact
Ms. Colleen Devlin,
Human Resources
Manager
Tel 408-864-0600
Fax 408-446-5234

**Advanced Management
Technologies**
2723 Crow Canyon Rd.,
Suite 101
San Ramon, CA 94583

Founded 1981
Total employees 40
Annual sales $1.7 million
Industry Computer
Hardware
Growth Openings in past
year 25; percentage
growth 166%
Contact
Ms. Gloria Burola, Vice
President
Tel 510-820-0644
Fax 510-820-1559

**Advanced Membrane
Technology, Inc.**
10350 Barnes Canyon Rd.
San Diego, CA 92121

Founded 1983
Total employees 125
Annual sales $12 million
Industries Biotechnology,
Test and Measurement
Growth Openings in past
year 35; percentage
growth 38%
Contact
Cheng Lee, President
Tel 619-457-4488

Advanced Technology
47341 Bayside Pkwy.
Fremont, CA 94538

Founded 1976
Total employees 30
Industries Advanced
Materials, Computer
Hardware, Manufacturing
Equipment
Growth Openings in past
year 18; percentage
growth 150%

Contact
Arthur Barufka, VP of
Finance
Tel 510-249-1144
Fax 510-249-1150

**Advanced Tissue
Sciences, Inc.**
10933 North Torrey Pines
Rd.
La Jolla, CA 92037

Founded 1986
Total employees 115
Industry Medical
Growth Openings in past
year 45; percentage
growth 64%
Contact
Arthur J. Benvenuto,
COB/President/CEO
Tel 619-450-5730
Fax 619-450-5703

**Advantage Memory
Corp.**
66 Argonaut, Suite 160
Aliso Viejo, CA 92656

Founded 1991
Total employees 50
Industry Computer
Hardware
Growth Openings in past
year 25; percentage
growth 100%
Contact
John Harriman, President
Tel 714-707-5299
Fax 714-707-5493

Advent Software, Inc.
301 Brannan St., 6th Floor
San Francisco, CA 94107

Founded 1983
Total employees 140
Annual sales $16 million
Industry Computer
Software
Growth Openings in past
year 50; percentage
growth 55%
Contact
Ms. Stephanie DiMarco,
President
Tel 415-543-7696
Fax 415-543-5070

Affymax N.V.
4001 Miranda Ave.
Palo Alto, CA 94304

Founded 1988
Total employees 239

Annual sales $13.5 million
Industry Holding
Companies
Growth Openings in past
year 30; percentage
growth 14%
Contact
Alejandra Zaffaroni,
COB/CEO/Managing
Director
Tel 415-496-2300

**Agouron
Pharmaceuticals, Inc.**
10350 North Torrey Pines
Rd., First Fl.
La Jolla, CA 92037

Founded 1984
Total employees 181
Annual sales $9.97 million
Industries Biotechnology,
Pharmaceuticals
Growth Openings in past
year 51; percentage
growth 39%
Contact
Ms. Pat Moses, Associate
Director of Human
Resources
Tel 619-622-3000
Fax 619-622-3298

**Akashic Memories
Corporation**
305 West Tasman Dr.
San Jose, CA 95134

Founded 1982
Total employees 900
Annual sales $140 million
Industry Computer
Hardware
Growth Openings in past
year 248; percentage
growth 38%
Contact
Yoshiki Takemura,
President/CEO
Tel 408-944-9080
Fax 408-944-9150

ALANTEC
70 Plumeria Dr.
San Jose, CA 95134

Founded 1987
Total employees 75
Annual sales $10 million
Industries Factory
Automation,
Telecommunications
Growth Openings in past
year 35; percentage
growth 87%

Contact
George Archuleta,
President
Tel 408-955-9000
Fax 408-955-9500

Alliance Pharmaceutical Corp.
3040 Science Park Rd.
San Diego, CA 92121

Founded 1983
Total employees 180
Annual sales $2 million
Industries Advanced
Materials, Chemicals,
Pharmaceuticals
Growth Openings in past
year 58; percentage
growth 47%
Contact
Duane Roth, President/
COB/CEO
Tel 619-558-4300
Fax 619-558-3625

Alliance Semiconductor Corp.
1930 Zanker Rd.
San Jose, CA 95112

Founded 1985
Total employees 40
Annual sales $3.9 million
Industry Subassemblies
and Components
Growth Openings in past
year 22; percentage
growth 122%
Contact
N. Damodar Reddy,
President
Tel 408-436-1860
Fax 408-436-1864

Alpha Systems Lab, Inc.
2361 McGaw Ave.
Irvine, CA 92714

Founded 1990
Total employees 80
Annual sales $40 million
Industry Computer
Hardware
Growth Openings in past
year 50; percentage
growth 166%
Contact
Ms. Rose Hwang,
President
Tel 714-252-0117
Fax 714-252-0887

Alps Electric (U.S.A.), Inc.
3553 North First St.
San Jose, CA 95134

Founded 1976
Total employees 859
Annual sales $296 million
Industries Computer
Hardware,
Subassemblies and
Components
Growth Openings in past
year 41; percentage
growth 5%
Contact
John Pepper, VP of
Human Resources
Tel 408-432-6000
Fax 408-432-6035

Altera Corp.
2610 Orchard Pkwy.
San Jose, CA 95134

Founded 1983
Total employees 475
Annual sales $107 million
Industries Computer
Software, Subassemblies
and Components
Growth Openings in past
year 23; percentage
growth 5%
Contact
Ms. Sandy Scarsella, VP
of Human Resources
Tel 408-894-7000
Fax 408-954-8186

American Turnkey
3601 South Harbor Blvd.,
Suite 200
Santa Ana, CA 92704

Founded 1985
Total employees 60
Annual sales $9.8 million
Industries Computer
Hardware, Computer
Software, Factory
Automation
Growth Openings in past
year 20; percentage
growth 50%
Contact
Boris N. Reznik, COB/
CEO
Tel 714-557-9050
Fax 714-557-9056

AMP Incorporated, Kaptron
2525 East Bay Shore Rd.
Palo Alto, CA 94303

Founded 1973
Total employees 75
Annual sales $5.2 million
Industries Photonics, Test
and Measurement,
Telecommunications
Growth Openings in past
year 25; percentage
growth 50%
Contact
Dr. Narinder Kapany,
Ph.D., President
Tel 415-493-8008
Fax 415-493-8924

Amtec Engineering Corp.
2749 Saturn St.
Brea, CA 92621

Founded 1958
Total employees 100
Industry Manufacturing
Equipment
Growth Openings in past
year 59; percentage
growth 143%
Contact
Robert Underwood,
President
Tel 714-993-1900
Fax 714-993-2419

Amylin Pharmaceuticals, Inc.
9373 Towne Centre Dr.,
Suite 250
San Diego, CA 92121

Founded 1987
Total employees 130
Industries Medical,
Pharmaceuticals
Growth Openings in past
year 30; percentage
growth 30%
Contact
Ted Greene, COB/CEO
Tel 619-552-2200
Fax 619-552-2212

Antec, Inc.
2859 Bayview Dr.
Fremont, CA 94538

Founded 1986
Total employees 100
Annual sales $27 million
Industries Computer
Hardware,
Subassemblies and
Components

Growth Openings in past year 30; percentage growth 42%
Contact
Andrew Lee, President
Tel 510-770-1200
Fax 510-770-1288

Application Group, Inc.
200 Pine St., Suite 800
San Francisco, CA 94104

Founded 1978
Total employees 200
Annual sales $25 million
Industries Computer Hardware, Computer Software
Growth Openings in past year 90; percentage growth 81%
Contact
Ms. Peggy Negus, Personnel Manager
Tel 415-421-1627
Fax 415-765-5200

Applied Immune Sciences, Inc.
5301 Patrick Henry Dr.
Santa Clara, CA 95054

Founded 1984
Total employees 164
Annual sales $1.54 million
Industry Medical
Growth Openings in past year 64; percentage growth 64%
Contact
Dr. Thomas Okarma, President/CEO
Tel 408-492-9200
Fax 408-980-5888

Applied Micro Circuits Corp.
6195 Lusk Blvd.
San Diego, CA 92121

Founded 1979
Total employees 275
Annual sales $39 million
Industry Subassemblies and Components
Growth Openings in past year 25; percentage growth 10%
Contact
Albert Martinez, President
Tel 619-450-9333
Fax 619-450-9885

Applied Signal Technology, Inc.
160 Sobrante Way
Sunnyvale, CA 94086

Founded 1984
Total employees 430
Annual sales $51 million
Industries Defense, Telecommunications
Growth Openings in past year 43; percentage growth 11%
Contact
Ms. Diane Cusano, Human Resources Director
Tel 408-749-1888
Fax 408-738-1928

Aptech Engineering Services, Inc.
1282 Reamwood Ave.
Sunnyvale, CA 94089

Founded 1979
Total employees 85
Annual sales $9.4 million
Industry Energy
Growth Openings in past year 15; percentage growth 21%
Contact
Geoffrey R. Egan, President
Tel 408-745-7000
Fax 408-734-0445

Aquatec Water Systems, Inc.
2259 Via Burton St.
Anaheim, CA 92806

Founded 1986
Total employees 40
Annual sales $5.5 million
Industries Environmental, Subassemblies and Components, Test and Measurement
Growth Openings in past year 15; percentage growth 60%
Contact
Thomas Barnes, President
Tel 714-535-8300
Fax 714-776-7867

Ardrox, Inc.
16961 Knott Ave.
La Mirada, CA 90638

Founded 1984
Total employees 125
Industries Chemicals, Factory Automation

Growth Openings in past year 43; percentage growth 52%
Contact
Sam Currie, President
Tel 714-739-2821
Fax 714-670-6480

Artecon, Inc.
2460 Impala Dr.
Carlsbad, CA 92008

Founded 1984
Total employees 70
Annual sales $25.4 million
Industry Computer Hardware
Growth Openings in past year 15; percentage growth 27%
Contact
Ms. Pamela Lambert, Director of Human Resources
Tel 619-931-5500
Fax 619-931-5527

Asante Technologies, Inc.
821 Fox Ln.
San Jose, CA 95131

Founded 1988
Total employees 175
Annual sales $19 million
Industry Telecommunications
Growth Openings in past year 35; percentage growth 25%
Contact
Ralph Dormitzar, CEO/President
Tel 408-435-8388
Fax 408-734-4864

Ascend Communications, Inc.
1275 Harbor Bay Pkwy.
Alameda, CA 94501

Founded 1988
Total employees 70
Annual sales $9.6 million
Industry Telecommunications
Growth Openings in past year 35; percentage growth 100%
Contact
Robert Ryan, President
Tel 510-769-6001
Fax 510-814-2300

Ascent Logic Corp.
180 Rose Orchard Way,
Suite 200
San Jose, CA 95134

Founded 1986
Total employees 110
Annual sales $12 million
Industry Computer
Software
Growth Openings in past
year 25; percentage
growth 29%
Contact
Thomas Little, President/
CEO
Tel 408-943-0630
Fax 408-943-0705

Ashtech, Inc.
1170 Kifer Rd.
Sunnyvale, CA 94086

Founded 1987
Total employees 140
Annual sales $36 million
Industries
Telecommunications,
Transportation
Growth Openings in past
year 32; percentage
growth 29%
Contact
Javad Ashjaee, President
Tel 408-524-1400
Fax 408-524-1500

**ASI Systems
International, Inc.**
326 West Katella Ave.,
Suite 4K
Orange, CA 92667

Founded 1967
Total employees 83
Annual sales $6 million
Industry Computer
Software
Growth Openings in past
year 18; percentage
growth 27%
Contact
Tom Gilbert, President
Tel 714-744-1594
Fax 714-744-4794

**Aspect
Telecommunications
Corp.**
1730 Fox Dr.
San Jose, CA 95131

Founded 1985
Total employees 500
Annual sales $105 million

Industry
Telecommunications
Growth Openings in past
year 148; percentage
growth 42%
Contact
Ms. Shelley Brown, VP of
Human Resources
Tel 408-441-2200
Fax 408-441-2261

Astro Sciences Corp.
9238 Deering Ave.
Chatsworth, CA 91311

Founded 1982
Total employees 50
Annual sales $11.01
million
Industry Holding
Companies
Growth Openings in past
year 25; percentage
growth 100%
Contact
Arnold C. Lubash,
President/CEO/CFO
Tel 818-709-1778
Fax 818-882-1424

Asymtek
1949 Palomar Oaks Way
Carlsbad, CA 92009

Founded 1983
Total employees 75
Annual sales $9.2 million
Industries Factory
Automation, Test and
Measurement
Growth Openings in past
year 15; percentage
growth 25%
Contact
Philip Maiorca, VP of
Research and
Development
Tel 619-431-1919
Fax 619-431-2678

AT&T EO
919 East Hillsdale Blvd.,
Suite 400
Foster City, CA 94404

Founded 1987
Total employees 185
Annual sales $21 million
Industry Computer
Software
Growth Openings in past
year 55; percentage
growth 42%

Contact
Alain Rossman, President/
CEO
Tel 415-345-7400
Fax 415-345-9833

**Athena Neurosciences,
Inc.**
800 Gateway Blvd.
South San Francisco, CA
94080

Founded 1986
Total employees 154
Annual sales $7.0 million
Industry Pharmaceuticals
Growth Openings in past
year 30; percentage
growth 24%
Contact
John Groom, President/
CEO
Tel 415-877-0900
Fax 415-877-8370

Athens Corp.
1922 Avenida Del Oro
Oceanside, CA 92056

Founded 1985
Total employees 85
Annual sales $9.9 million
Industry Manufacturing
Equipment
Growth Openings in past
year 35; percentage
growth 70%
Contact
Robert Corey, President/
CEO
Tel 619-758-0994
Fax 619-758-7518

Atwork Corp.
2150 Trade Zone Blvd.,
Suite 201
San Jose, CA 95131

Founded 1980
Total employees 150
Annual sales $25 million
Industry Computer
Software
Growth Openings in past
year 25; percentage
growth 20%
Contact
Michael Warner, President
Tel 408-263-1080
Fax 408-263-1240

AUDRE, Inc.
11021 Via Frontera
San Diego, CA 92127

Founded 1983
Total employees 60
Annual sales $2.3 million
Industry Computer
Software
Growth Openings in past
year 28; percentage
growth 87%
Contact
Ms. Lisa Howell, Human
Resources Manager
Tel 619-451-2260
Fax 619-451-0267

AuraVision Corp.
47885 Fremont Blvd.
Fremont, CA 94538

Founded 1992
Total employees 30
Annual sales $2.9 million
Industry Subassemblies
and Components
Growth Openings in past
year 15; percentage
growth 100%
Contact
Steve Chan, Chief
Executive Officer
Tel 510-440-7180
Fax 510-438-9350

Auspex Systems, Inc.
5200 Great American
Pkwy.
Santa Clara, CA 95054

Founded 1987
Total employees 306
Annual sales $73.5 million
Industry
Telecommunications
Growth Openings in past
year 126; percentage
growth 70%
Contact
Laurence B. Boucher,
President
Tel 408-492-0900
Fax 408-492-0909

Balboa Instruments, Inc.
1611 Babcock St.
Newport Beach, CA 92663

Founded 1979
Total employees 40
Annual sales $4.7 million
Industry Test and
Measurement

Growth Openings in past
year 18; percentage
growth 81%
Contact
Ms. Barbara Holloway,
Controller
Tel 714-645-3201
Fax 714-645-0156

Baron-Blakeslee, Inc.
1500 West 16th St.
Long Beach, CA 90813

Founded 1933
Total employees 60
Industry Factory
Automation
Growth Openings in past
year 40; percentage
growth 200%
Contact
Joel Rodgers, President
Tel 310-491-1228
Fax 310-491-1091

BARRA, Inc.
1995 University Ave.
Berkeley, CA 94704

Founded 1975
Total employees 300
Annual sales $39.24
million
Industry Computer
Software
Growth Openings in past
year 28; percentage
growth 10%
Contact
Ms. Ramona Nicholson,
Personnel Manager
Tel 510-548-5442
Fax 510-548-4374

bd Systems, Inc.
385 Van Ness Way, Suite
200
Torrance, CA 90501

Founded 1981
Total employees 150
Annual sales $11 million
Industries Computer
Hardware, Computer
Software, Defense,
Manufacturing Equipment
Growth Openings in past
year 40; percentage
growth 36%
Contact
Ms. Clarisa F. Howard,
President
Tel 310-618-8798
Fax 310-212-0753

**Bell Atlantic Healthcare
Systems, Inc.**
300 Drakes Landing, Suite
1000
Greenbrae, CA 94904

Founded 1984
Total employees 140
Annual sales $19 million
Industry
Telecommunications
Growth Openings in past
year 40; percentage
growth 40%
Contact
Michael Lake, President
Tel 415-925-0121
Fax 415-925-4610

**BioSource International,
Inc.**
887 Mitten Rd.
Burlingame, CA 94010

Founded 1979
Total employees 50
Annual sales $4 million
Industries Biotechnology,
Chemicals, Medical
Growth Openings in past
year 20; percentage
growth 66%
Contact
Jim Chamberlain, COB/
CEO/President
Tel 415-692-4015
Fax 415-692-9004

Biotrack, Inc.
1058 Huff Ave.
Mountain View, CA 94043

Founded 1984
Total employees 150
Annual sales $16 million
Industry Medical
Growth Openings in past
year 25; percentage
growth 20%
Contact
Bill Dippel, President
Tel 415-965-7400
Fax 415-965-0439

**Bird Medical
Technologies, Inc.**
1100 Bird Center Dr.
Palm Springs, CA 92262

Founded 1984
Total employees 421
Annual sales $44 million
Industry Holding
Companies

Growth Openings in past
year 146; percentage
growth 53%
Contact
Felix (Phil) T. Troilo,
COB/CEO
Tel 619-778-7200
Fax 619-778-7301

Bit Software, Inc.
57987 Fremont Blvd.
Fremont, CA 94538

Founded 1983
Total employees 50
Annual sales $5.8 million
Industry Computer
Software
Growth Openings in past
year 15; percentage
growth 42%
Contact
Jon Wan, President
Tel 510-490-2928
Fax 510-490-9490

**Broderbund Software,
Inc.**
500 Redwood Blvd., PO
Box 6121
Novato, CA 94948

Founded 1980
Total employees 375
Annual sales $75.1 million
Industry Computer
Software
Growth Openings in past
year 75; percentage
growth 25%
Contact
Doug Carlston, COB/CEO
Tel 415-382-4400
Fax 415-382-4665

Brooktree Corp.
9868 Scranton Rd.
San Diego, CA 92121

Founded 1981
Total employees 565
Annual sales $92 million
Industry Subassemblies
and Components
Growth Openings in past
year 12; percentage
growth 2%
Contact
Robert W. Zabaronick, VP
of Human Resources
Tel 619-452-7580
Fax 619-452-1249

BusLogic, Inc.
4151 Burton Dr.
Santa Clara, CA 95054

Founded 1988
Total employees 95
Annual sales $15 million
Industries Computer
Hardware, Computer
Software
Growth Openings in past
year 45; percentage
growth 90%
Contact
Jesse Chen, President
Tel 408-492-9090
Fax 408-492-1542

Caere Corp.
100 Cooper Ct.
Los Gatos, CA 95030

Founded 1973
Total employees 180
Annual sales $29 million
Industries Computer
Hardware, Computer
Software
Growth Openings in past
year 25; percentage
growth 16%
Contact
Ms. Blanche M. Sutter, VP
of Finance/CFO
Tel 408-395-7000
Fax 408-354-2743

California Amplifier, Inc.
460 Calle San Pablo
Camarillo, CA 93012

Founded 1981
Total employees 300
Annual sales $20.63
million
Industries Subassemblies
and Components,
Telecommunications
Growth Openings in past
year 50; percentage
growth 20%
Contact
Ms. Jackie Sheehan,
Personnel Director
Tel 805-987-9000
Fax 805-987-8359

**Canary Communications,
Inc.**
1851 Zanker Rd.
San Jose, CA 95112

Founded 1987
Total employees 60
Annual sales $8.2 million

Industry
Telecommunications
Growth Openings in past
year 20; percentage
growth 50%
Contact
Vinh Tran, President
Tel 408-453-9201
Fax 408-453-0940

Cardiometrics, Inc.
645 Clyde Ave.
Mountain View, CA 94043

Founded 1985
Total employees 150
Industry Medical
Growth Openings in past
year 80; percentage
growth 114%
Contact
Ms. Kathy Morales,
Director of Personnel
Tel 415-961-6993
Fax 415-961-8753

Catalina Marketing Corp.
721 East Ball Rd.
Anaheim, CA 92805

Founded 1983
Total employees 285
Annual sales $51.71
million
Industries Computer
Hardware, Computer
Software
Growth Openings in past
year 114; percentage
growth 66%
Contact
Tommy Greer, Chief
Executive Officer
Tel 714-956-6600

**C-Cube Microsystems
Corp.**
1778 McCarthy Blvd.
Milpitas, CA 95035

Founded 1988
Total employees 100
Annual sales $16 million
Industry Computer
Hardware
Growth Openings in past
year 20; percentage
growth 25%
Contact
Allen Hunt, Director of
Human Resources
Tel 408-944-6300
Fax 408-944-6314

Celeritek, Inc.
617 River Oaks Pkwy.
San Jose, CA 95134

Founded 1985
Total employees 318
Annual sales $31 million
Industry Subassemblies
and Components
Growth Openings in past
year 42; percentage
growth 15%
Contact
Tamer Husseini, COB/
President
Tel 408-433-0335
Fax 408-433-0991

Cell Genesys, Inc.
322 Lakeside Dr.
Foster City, CA 94404

Founded 1988
Total employees 73
Industry Biotechnology
Growth Openings in past
year 29; percentage
growth 65%
Contact
Stephen A. Sherwin, MD,
COB/President/CEO
Tel 415-358-9600
Fax 415-358-0803

Cerplex, Inc.
3332 East La Palma Ave.
Anaheim, CA 92806

Founded 1990
Total employees 180
Annual sales $12 million
Industries Computer
Hardware, Medical
Growth Openings in past
year 88; percentage
growth 95%
Contact
Ted Wisniewski, President
Tel 714-632-2600
Fax 714-632-2619

**Chaparral
Communications, Inc.**
2450 North First St.
San Jose, CA 95131

Founded 1980
Total employees 185
Annual sales $40 million
Industry
Telecommunications
Growth Openings in past
year 25; percentage
growth 15%

Contact
Robert R. Taggart, Chief
Executive Officer
Tel 408-435-1530
Fax 408-435-1429

ChemTrack, Inc.
929 East Arques Ave.
Sunnyvale, CA 94086

Founded 1985
Total employees 120
Annual sales $6.7 million
Industry Medical
Growth Openings in past
year 30; percentage
growth 33%
Contact
Dr. Prithipal Singh, Chief
Executive Officer
Tel 408-773-8156
Fax 408-773-1651

**Cherokee International,
Inc.**
2841 Dow Ave.
Tustin, CA 92680

Founded 1979
Total employees 400
Annual sales $39 million
Industry Subassemblies
and Components
Growth Openings in past
year 50; percentage
growth 14%
Contact
Ganpat I. Patel, President
Tel 714-544-6665
Fax 714-838-4742

Clarion Corp. of America
661 West Redondo Beach
Blvd.
Gardena, CA 90247

Founded 1964
Total employees 300
Industry
Telecommunications
Growth Openings in past
year 30; percentage
growth 11%
Contact
Ms. P.P. Garcias, Manager
of Personnel and
Administration
Tel 310-327-9100
Fax 310-327-1999

Claris Corp.
5201 Patrick Henry Dr.
Santa Clara, CA 95052

Founded 1987
Total employees 600

Annual sales $104 million
Industry Computer
Software
Growth Openings in past
year 50; percentage
growth 9%
Contact
Mike Ahern, VP of Human
Resources
Tel 408-987-7000

Clary Corp.
1960 South Walker Ave.
Monrovia, CA 91016

Founded 1939
Total employees 75
Annual sales $13 million
Industries Energy,
Subassemblies and
Components
Growth Openings in past
year 25; percentage
growth 50%
Contact
Donald G. Ash, President
Tel 818-359-4486
Fax 818-305-0254

Claude Laval Corp.
1365 North Clovis Ave.
Fresno, CA 93727

Founded 1980
Total employees 100
Annual sales $10 million
Industry Environmental
Growth Openings in past
year 20; percentage
growth 25%
Contact
Claude Laval, President
Tel 209-255-1601
Fax 209-255-8093

**CLONTECH
Laboratories, Inc.**
4030 Fabian Way
Palo Alto, CA 94303

Founded 1984
Total employees 100
Annual sales $9.6 million
Industries Biotechnology,
Chemicals, Computer
Software
Growth Openings in past
year 20; percentage
growth 25%
Contact
Ms. Hensl Lise, Personnel
Manager
Tel 415-424-8222
Fax 415-424-1064

CMD Technology, Inc.
1 Vanderbilt
Irvine, CA 92718

Founded 1986
Total employees 105
Annual sales $10 million
Industry Computer
Hardware
Growth Openings in past
year 25; percentage
growth 31%
Contact
Simon Huang, President
Tel 714-454-0800
Fax 714-455-1656

CMSI, Inc.
1900 Main St., Suite 310
Irvine, CA 92714

Founded 1970
Total employees 520
Annual sales $50 million
Industries Computer
Hardware, Computer
Software
Growth Openings in past
year 138; percentage
growth 36%
Contact
Michael S. Wall, President
Tel 714-863-3011
Fax 714-474-8581

Cohu, Inc.
PO Box 85623
San Diego, CA 92186

Founded 1957
Total employees 521
Annual sales $54.3 million
Industry Holding
Companies
Growth Openings in past
year 21; percentage
growth 4%
Contact
Ms. Linda Jacobson,
Personnel Manager
Tel 619-277-6700
Fax 619-277-0221

Collagen Corp.
2500 Faber Place
Palo Alto, CA 94303

Founded 1975
Total employees 300
Annual sales $50 million
Industries Biotechnology,
Medical
Growth Openings in past
year 60; percentage
growth 25%

Contact
Ms. Deborah Berard, VP
of Human Resources
Tel 415-856-0200
Fax 415-856-1430

Com Stream
10180 Barnes Canyon
Rd., PO Box 6005
San Diego, CA 92121

Founded 1993
Total employees 350
Annual sales $101 million
Industry
Telecommunications
Growth Openings in past
year 109; percentage
growth 45%
Contact
Ronald Derry, President
Tel 619-458-1800
Fax 619-552-0488

Comair Rotron, Inc.
2675 Custom House Ct.
San Ysidro, CA 92173

Founded 1947
Total employees 800
Annual sales $78 million
Industry Subassemblies
and Components
Growth Openings in past
year 46; percentage
growth 6%
Contact
Ms. Mary Talley, Director
of Human Resources
Tel 619-661-6688
Fax 619-661-6057

Comdisco Systems, Inc.
919 East Hillsdale Blvd.
Foster City, CA 94404

Founded 1969
Total employees 130
Industry Computer
Software
Growth Openings in past
year 40; percentage
growth 44%
Contact
Dr. William C. Newman,
VP of Research and
Development
Tel 415-574-5800
Fax 415-358-3601

**Communication
Intelligence Corp.**
275 Shoreline Dr., 6th Fl.
Redwood Shores, CA
94065

Founded 1981
Total employees 95
Annual sales $2.6 million
Industries Computer
Hardware, Computer
Software
Growth Openings in past
year 35; percentage
growth 58%
Contact
James Dao, President/
CEO/COB
Tel 415-802-7888
Fax 415-802-7777

**Compass Design
Automation, Inc.**
1865 Lundy Ave.
San Jose, CA 95131

Founded 1991
Total employees 330
Annual sales $38 million
Industry Computer
Software
Growth Openings in past
year 90; percentage
growth 37%
Contact
Dieter Mezger, President
Tel 408-433-4880
Fax 408-433-7977

Compression Labs, Inc.
2860 Junction Ave.
San Jose, CA 95134

Founded 1976
Total employees 360
Annual sales $107.8
million
Industry
Telecommunications
Growth Openings in past
year 18; percentage
growth 5%
Contact
Ms. Bonnie Nunke, VP of
Human Resources and
Administration
Tel 408-435-3000
Fax 408-922-5429

Compton's NewMedia, Inc.
2320 Camino Vida Roble
Carlsbad, CA 92009

Founded 1983
Total employees 170
Annual sales $35 million
Industry Computer
Software
Growth Openings in past
year 100; percentage
growth 142%
Contact
Ms. Teresa Stephenson,
Manager of Human
Resources
Tel 619-929-2500
Fax 612-929-2511

Computer Intelligence InfoCorp
3344 North Torrey Pines
Ct.
La Jolla, CA 92037

Founded 1969
Total employees 500
Annual sales $82 million
Industry Computer
Hardware
Growth Openings in past
year 100; percentage
growth 25%
Contact
Bob Brown, President
Tel 619-450-1667
Fax 619-452-7491

Consolidated Engineering Laboratories, Inc.
4464 Willow Rd., Suite C
Pleasanton, CA 94588

Founded 1985
Total employees 150
Industries Advanced
Materials, Environmental
Growth Openings in past
year 50; percentage
growth 50%
Contact
Gary M. Cappa, President/
CEO
Tel 510-460-5100
Fax 510-460-5118

Contour Software, Inc.
1129 Dell Ave.
Campbell, CA 95008

Founded 1982
Total employees 115
Industry Computer
Software

Growth Openings in past
year 45; percentage
growth 64%
Contact
Scott Cooley, President
Tel 408-370-1700
Fax 408-370-0366

COR Therapeutics, Inc.
256 East Grand Ave.
South San Francisco, CA
94080

Founded 1988
Total employees 88
Industries Medical,
Pharmaceuticals
Growth Openings in past
year 45; percentage
growth 104%
Contact
Vaughn M. Kailian,
President/CEO
Tel 415-244-6800
Fax 415-244-9208

Cornerstone Imaging, Inc.
1990 Concourse Dr.
San Jose, CA 95131

Founded 1986
Total employees 84
Annual sales $23.15
million
Industry Computer
Hardware
Growth Openings in past
year 34; percentage
growth 68%
Contact
Thomas T. van Overbeek,
President
Tel 408-435-8900
Fax 408-435-8998

Corvas International, Inc.
3030 Science Park Rd.
San Diego, CA 92121

Founded 1987
Total employees 80
Annual sales $10 million
Industry Pharmaceuticals
Growth Openings in past
year 17; percentage
growth 26%
Contact
Dr. David Kabakoff, Ph.D.,
President/COO
Tel 619-455-9800
Fax 619-455-7895

CrystalGraphics, Inc.
3110 Patrick Henry Dr.
Santa Clara, CA 95054

Founded 1986
Total employees 100
Annual sales $11 million
Industry Computer
Software
Growth Openings in past
year 50; percentage
growth 100%
Contact
Dennis Ricks, President/
CEO
Tel 408-496-6175
Fax 408-496-0970

CTX International, Inc.
20530 Earlgate St.
Walnut, CA 91789

Founded 1984
Total employees 50
Annual sales $8.2 million
Industry Computer
Hardware
Growth Openings in past
year 25; percentage
growth 100%
Contact
Y.C. Liu, President
Tel 909-595-6146
Fax 909-595-6293

Cylink Corp.
310 North Mary Ave.
Sunnyvale, CA 94086

Founded 1984
Total employees 160
Annual sales $22 million
Industries Subassemblies
and Components,
Telecommunications
Growth Openings in past
year 35; percentage
growth 28%
Contact
Lewis Morris, President/
CEO
Tel 408-735-5800
Fax 408-720-8294

Dainippon Screen Engineering of America, Inc.
3700 West Segerstrom St.
Santa Ana, CA 92704

Founded 1943
Total employees 60
Annual sales $50 million
Industries Computer Hardware, Manufacturing Equipment, Photonics
Growth Openings in past year 20; percentage growth 50%
Contact
S. Araki, President
Tel 714-546-9491
Fax 714-751-7826

Dako Corp.
6392 Via Real
Carpinteria, CA 93013

Founded 1979
Total employees 80
Annual sales $7.7 million
Industries Biotechnology, Medical
Growth Openings in past year 40; percentage growth 100%
Contact
Viggo G. Harboe, President
Tel 805-566-6655
Fax 805-566-6688

Dataworks Corp.
5910 Pacific Center Blvd., Suite 300
San Diego, CA 92121

Founded 1977
Total employees 100
Annual sales $12 million
Industry Computer Software
Growth Openings in past year 25; percentage growth 33%
Contact
Stuart Clifton, President
Tel 619-546-9600
Fax 619-546-9777

Davidson & Associates, Inc.
19840 Pioneer Ave., PO Box 2961
Torrance, CA 90503

Founded 1984
Total employees 300
Annual sales $58.57 million

Industries Computer Software, Holding Companies
Growth Openings in past year 30; percentage growth 11%
Contact
Ms. Jan Davidson, President
Tel 310-793-0600
Fax 310-793-0601

Delfin Systems
3000 Patrick Henry Dr.
Santa Clara, CA 94089

Founded 1984
Total employees 156
Annual sales $25 million
Industries Computer Hardware, Computer Software, Telecommunications
Growth Openings in past year 41; percentage growth 35%
Contact
Ms. Pat Yanez, VP of Human Resources and Administration
Tel 408-748-1200
Fax 408-748-1140

Delrina (U.S.) Corp.
6830 Via Del Oro, Suite 240
San Jose, CA 95119

Founded 1988
Total employees 500
Annual sales $58 million
Industry Computer Software
Growth Openings in past year 24; percentage growth 5%
Contact
Dennis Bennie, Chief Executive Officer
Tel 408-363-2345
Fax 408-363-2340

Delta Design, Inc.
5775 Kearny Villa Rd.
San Diego, CA 92123

Founded 1959
Total employees 375
Annual sales $35 million
Industries Factory Automation, Manufacturing Equipment, Test and Measurement

Growth Openings in past year 175; percentage growth 87%
Contact
Ms. Susan Hane, Director of Personnel
Tel 619-292-5000
Fax 619-277-7884

DeltaPoint, Inc.
2 Harris Ct., Suite B1
Monterey, CA 93940

Founded 1989
Total employees 55
Annual sales $6.3 million
Industry Computer Software
Growth Openings in past year 25; percentage growth 83%
Contact
Ray Kingman, President
Tel 408-648-4000
Fax 408-648-4020

Deposition Technologies, Inc.
4540 Viewridge Ave.
San Diego, CA 92123

Founded 1978
Total employees 100
Industry Energy
Growth Openings in past year 25; percentage growth 33%
Contact
John Robinson, President
Tel 619-576-0200
Fax 619-571-3605

Desalination Systems, Inc.
1238 Simpson Way, Suite A
Escondido, CA 92029

Founded 1967
Total employees 250
Annual sales $24 million
Industries Biotechnology, Environmental, Test and Measurement
Growth Openings in past year 40; percentage growth 19%
Contact
Ms. Thea Matlock, Personnel Manager
Tel 619-746-4995
Fax 619-747-8253

Destiny Technology Corp.
3255 Scott Blvd., Bldg. 1, Suite 201
Santa Clara, CA 95054

Founded 1982
Total employees 100
Annual sales $9.7 million
Industries Computer Software, Subassemblies and Components
Growth Openings in past year 20; percentage growth 25%
Contact
Gary Cheng, President
Tel 408-562-1000
Fax 408-562-1010

Devices for Vascular Intervention, Inc.
595 Penobscot Dr.
Redwood City, CA 94063

Founded 1984
Total employees 526
Annual sales $57 million
Industry Medical
Growth Openings in past year 206; percentage growth 64%
Contact
Alan Will, President
Tel 415-361-1444
Fax 415-364-2889

Dexter Corp., Dexter Electronic Materials Division
15051 East Don Julian Rd.
City of Industry, CA 91746

Founded 1767
Total employees 600
Annual sales $130 million
Industries Advanced Materials, Subassemblies and Components
Growth Openings in past year 18; percentage growth 3%
Contact
Ronald Benham, President
Tel 818-968-6511
Fax 818-336-0160

Diamond Computer Systems, Inc.
1130 East Arques Ave.
Sunnyvale, CA 94086

Founded 1981
Total employees 80
Annual sales $74 million

Industry Computer Hardware
Growth Openings in past year 15; percentage growth 23%
Contact
Chong-Moon Lee, President/CEO
Tel 408-736-2000
Fax 408-730-5750

Diamond Flower Instruments, Inc.
135 Main Ave.
Sacramento, CA 95838

Founded 1986
Total employees 120
Industry Computer Hardware
Growth Openings in past year 50; percentage growth 71%
Contact
Rocky Liu, Chief Executive Officer
Tel 916-568-1234
Fax 916-568-1233

Digicom Systems, Inc.
188 Topaz St.
Milpitas, CA 95035

Founded 1987
Total employees 85
Annual sales $11 million
Industry Telecommunications
Growth Openings in past year 15; percentage growth 21%
Contact
Gwong Lee, President
Tel 408-262-1277
Fax 408-262-1390

Digidesign, Inc.
1360 Willow Rd., Suite 101
Menlo Park, CA 94025

Founded 1983
Total employees 130
Industries Computer Hardware, Computer Software, Telecommunications
Growth Openings in past year 50; percentage growth 62%
Contact
Peter Gotcher, CEO/President/Founder
Tel 415-688-0600
Fax 415-327-0777

Digimedics Corp.
280 Technology Cir.
Scotts Valley, CA 95066

Founded 1976
Total employees 50
Annual sales $5.8 million
Industry Computer Software
Growth Openings in past year 18; percentage growth 56%
Contact
John Frieberg, CEO/CFO
Tel 408-438-4735
Fax 408-438-8422

Digital Link Corp.
217 Humboldt Ct.
Sunnyvale, CA 94089

Founded 1985
Total employees 127
Annual sales $22.5 million
Industry Telecommunications
Growth Openings in past year 27; percentage growth 27%
Contact
Ms. Vinita Gupta, CEO/COB
Tel 408-745-6200
Fax 408-745-6250

Digitalk, Inc.
5 Hutton Center Dr.
Santa Ana, CA 92798

Founded 1983
Total employees 95
Annual sales $11 million
Industry Computer Software
Growth Openings in past year 30; percentage growth 46%
Contact
Douglas Wride, Vice President/CFO
Tel 714-513-3000
Fax 714-513-3100

Diversified Software Systems, Inc.
18630 Sutter Blvd.
Morgan Hill, CA 95037

Founded 1978
Total employees 70
Annual sales $8.1 million
Industry Computer Software
Growth Openings in past year 25; percentage growth 55%

Contact
Lowell L. Sando, COB/
CEO
Tel 408-778-9914
Fax 408-776-0382

**Dura Pharmaceuticals,
Inc.**
5880 Pacific Center Blvd.
San Diego, CA 92121

Founded 1981
Total employees 186
Annual sales $15.8 million
Industries Medical,
Pharmaceuticals
Growth Openings in past
year 36; percentage
growth 24%
Contact
Rich Everett, Human
Resources Director
Tel 619-457-2553
Fax 619-457-2555

**Dynamic Instruments,
Inc.**
3860 Calle Fortunada
San Diego, CA 92123

Founded 1980
Total employees 125
Annual sales $15 million
Industries Factory
Automation, Holding
Companies, Test and
Measurement
Growth Openings in past
year 25; percentage
growth 25%
Contact
Hugh Ness, President
Tel 619-278-4900
Fax 619-278-6700

Earth Technology Corp.
100 West Broadway, Suite
5000
Long Beach, CA 90802

Founded 1970
Total employees 450
Annual sales $55 million
Industry Environmental
Growth Openings in past
year 22; percentage
growth 5%
Contact
Ms. Diana C. Creel,
CEO/President
Tel 310-495-4449
Fax 310-426-0666

Edify Corp.
2840 San Thomas Expwy.
Santa Clara, CA 95051

Founded 1989
Total employees 65
Annual sales $7.5 million
Industry Computer
Software
Growth Openings in past
year 15; percentage
growth 30%
Contact
Jeffrey Crowe, President
Tel 408-982-2000
Fax 408-982-0777

Electro Pneumatic Corp.
3016 Kansas Ave.
Riverside, CA 92507

Founded 1970
Total employees 135
Annual sales $15 million
Industry Transportation
Growth Openings in past
year 24; percentage
growth 21%
Contact
Ms. Karen Whiteside,
Human Resources
Manager
Tel 909-784-0410

Electronic Arts
1450 Fashion Island Blvd.
San Mateo, CA 94404

Founded 1982
Total employees 999
Annual sales $300 million
Industries Computer
Software, Holding
Companies
Growth Openings in past
year 83; percentage
growth 9%
Contact
Lawrence F. Probst,
President/CEO
Tel 415-571-7171
Fax 415-570-5137

Electronic Solutions
6790 Flanders Dr.
San Diego, CA 92121

Founded 1974
Total employees 250
Industries Computer
Hardware, Factory
Automation,
Subassemblies and
Components

Growth Openings in past
year 150; percentage
growth 150%
Contact
Ms. Sheilah Hernandez,
Director of Human
Resources
Tel 619-452-9333
Fax 619-452-9464

**Electronics for Imaging,
Inc.**
2855 Campus Dr.
San Mateo, CA 94403

Founded 1989
Total employees 154
Annual sales $53.7 million
Industry Computer
Software
Growth Openings in past
year 28; percentage
growth 22%
Contact
Efi Arazi, President
Tel 415-286-8600
Fax 415-286-8686

ELMA Electronic Inc.
44350 Grimmer Blvd.
Fremont, CA 94538

Founded 1986
Total employees 70
Annual sales $8.8 million
Industries Computer
Hardware, Factory
Automation,
Subassemblies and
Components
Growth Openings in past
year 20; percentage
growth 40%
Contact
Fred Ruegg, President
Tel 510-656-3400
Fax 510-656-3783

ENCAD, Inc.
6059 Cornerstone Ct.
West
San Diego, CA 92121

Founded 1981
Total employees 130
Annual sales $23 million
Industry Computer
Hardware
Growth Openings in past
year 45; percentage
growth 52%
Contact
David Purcell, President
Tel 619-452-0882
Fax 619-452-0891

Energy & Environmental Research Corp.
18 Mason
Irvine, CA 92718

Founded 1973
Total employees 131
Industries Energy, Environmental
Growth Openings in past year 41; percentage growth 45%
Contact
Thomas Tyson, COB/CEO/ President
Tel 714-859-8851
Fax 714-859-3194

EnergyLine Systems, Inc.
2065 Kittredge St., Suite A
Berkeley, CA 94704

Founded 1985
Total employees 40
Annual sales $3 million
Industries Computer Hardware, Computer Software, Energy, Test and Measurement
Growth Openings in past year 20; percentage growth 100%
Contact
Ronald Hofmann, President
Tel 510-644-8182
Fax 510-644-2058

EPRO Corp.
3310 Victor Ct.
Santa Clara, CA 95054

Founded 1979
Total employees 27
Annual sales $9 million
Industries Computer Hardware, Factory Automation, Manufacturing Equipment
Growth Openings in past year 15; percentage growth 125%
Contact
David Peng, Chief Executive Officer
Tel 408-982-9707
Fax 408-982-9708

E-Tek Dynamics, Inc.
1885 Lundy Ave.
San Jose, CA 95131

Founded 1983
Total employees 72
Annual sales $7.8 million

Industries Factory Automation, Photonics
Growth Openings in past year 35; percentage growth 94%
Contact
Ms. Sherry Hsu Lee, Manager of General Administration
Tel 408-432-6300
Fax 408-432-8550

Everest Electronic Equipment, Inc.
2100 East Orangewood
Anaheim, CA 92806

Founded 1960
Total employees 300
Industries Computer Hardware, Manufacturing Equipment, Subassemblies and Components
Growth Openings in past year 50; percentage growth 20%
Contact
Wallace Twedt, President
Tel 714-634-2200
Fax 714-634-1369

Excalibur Extrusions, Inc.
110 East Crowther Ave.
Placentia, CA 92670

Founded 1970
Total employees 70
Annual sales $3 million
Industries Manufacturing Equipment, Subassemblies and Components
Growth Openings in past year 21; percentage growth 42%
Contact
Glenn Baldwin, President
Tel 714-528-8834
Fax 714-524-7453

Excalibur Technologies Corp.
9255 Towne Centre Dr.
San Diego, CA 92121

Founded 1980
Total employees 125
Annual sales $8 million
Industry Computer Software
Growth Openings in past year 50; percentage growth 66%

Contact
J.M. Kennedy, President
Tel 619-625-7900
Fax 619-625-7901

Exsil, Inc.
6541 Via Del Oro
San Jose, CA 95119

Founded 1980
Total employees 100
Annual sales $8.5 million
Industry Subassemblies and Components
Growth Openings in past year 40; percentage growth 66%
Contact
Ms. Sherry Bunnell, Human Resource Manager
Tel 408-629-3142
Fax 408-629-3168

Figgie International Inc., Interstate Engineering Division
522 East Vermont Ave.
Anaheim, CA 92805

Founded 1937
Total employees 120
Annual sales $11 million
Industries Advanced Materials, Subassemblies and Components, Test and Measurement
Growth Openings in past year 20; percentage growth 20%
Contact
Ms. Sherry Dowe, Director of Personnel
Tel 714-778-5700
Fax 714-758-4110

First International Computer of America, Inc.
5020 Brandin Ct.
Fremont, CA 94538

Founded 1991
Total employees 56
Annual sales $35 million
Industry Computer Hardware
Growth Openings in past year 40; percentage growth 250%
Contact
Peter Ow, President
Tel 510-252-7777
Fax 510-252-8888

Fora, Inc.
30 West Montague Expwy.
San Jose, CA 95134

Founded 1989
Total employees 160
Annual sales $26 million
Industry Computer
Hardware
Growth Openings in past
year 18; percentage
growth 12%
Contact
Victor Wu, President
Tel 408-944-0393
Fax 408-944-0392

Frame Technology Corp.
1010 Rincon Cir.
San Jose, CA 95131

Founded 1986
Total employees 443
Annual sales $76.6 million
Industries Computer
Software, Holding
Companies
Growth Openings in past
year 122; percentage
growth 38%
Contact
George Claus, President
Tel 408-433-3311
Fax 408-433-1928

Franklin Datacom, Inc.
733 Lakefield Rd.
Westlake Village, CA
91361

Founded 1981
Total employees 50
Annual sales $7 million
Industries Computer
Hardware, Computer
Software, Subassemblies
and Components,
Telecommunications
Growth Openings in past
year 25; percentage
growth 100%
Contact
Ms. Dianne Oliver,
Controller/Personnel
Manager
Tel 805-373-8688
Fax 805-373-7373

Furane Products Co.
5121 San Fernando Rd.
West
Los Angeles, CA 90039

Founded 1970
Total employees 120
Annual sales $17 million

Industries Advanced
Materials, Chemicals
Growth Openings in past
year 20; percentage
growth 20%
Contact
Dennis Farragher, General
Manager
Tel 818-247-6210
Fax 818-507-0167

Gaiser Tool Co.
4544 McGrath St.
Ventura, CA 93003

Founded 1962
Total employees 200
Annual sales $21 million
Industry Manufacturing
Equipment
Growth Openings in past
year 60; percentage
growth 42%
Contact
Dennis Gaiser, President
Tel 805-644-5583
Fax 805-644-2013

**GaSonics International,
Inc.**
2730 Junction Ave.
San Jose, CA 95134

Founded 1971
Total employees 278
Annual sales $45 million
Industries Manufacturing
Equipment, Test and
Measurement
Growth Openings in past
year 100; percentage
growth 56%
Contact
Ms. Donna Antosiak,
Human Resources
Manager
Tel 408-944-0212
Fax 408-473-9509

GEC-Marconi Materials
9630 Ridgehaven Ct.
San Diego, CA 92123

Founded 1973
Total employees 110
Industries Advanced
Materials,
Telecommunications,
Transportation
Growth Openings in past
year 40; percentage
growth 57%

Contact
Judson Greer, Human
Resources Manager
Tel 619-571-7715
Fax 619-278-0905

Genoa Systems Corp.
75 East Trimble Rd.
San Jose, CA 95131

Founded 1984
Total employees 65
Annual sales $10 million
Industry Computer
Hardware
Growth Openings in past
year 15; percentage
growth 30%
Contact
Su Huang, President
Tel 408-432-9090
Fax 408-434-0997

Gen-Probe, Inc.
9880 Campus Point Dr.
San Diego, CA 92121

Founded 1983
Total employees 280
Annual sales $30 million
Industry Medical
Growth Openings in past
year 30; percentage
growth 12%
Contact
Ms. Robin Vedova, VP of
Human Resources
Tel 619-546-8000
Fax 619-452-5848

**Gensia Pharmaceuticals,
Inc.**
11025 Roselle St.
San Diego, CA 92121

Founded 1986
Total employees 450
Annual sales $33.37
million
Industries Holding
Companies,
Pharmaceuticals
Growth Openings in past
year 150; percentage
growth 50%
Contact
David Hale, COB/
President/CEO
Tel 619-546-8300
Fax 619-453-0095

Genta, Inc.
3550 General Atomics Ct.
San Diego, CA 92121

Founded 1989
Total employees 80
Annual sales $2.3 million
Industries Biotechnology,
Holding Companies,
Pharmaceuticals
Growth Openings in past
year 35; percentage
growth 77%
Contact
Thomas H. Adams, Ph.D.,
COB/CEO
Tel 619-455-2700
Fax 619-455-2712

Gilead Sciences, Inc.
353 Lakeside Dr.
Foster City, CA 94404

Founded 1987
Total employees 175
Industry Pharmaceuticals
Growth Openings in past
year 75; percentage
growth 75%
Contact
Ms. Linda A. Fitzpatrick,
VP of Human Resources
and Corporate Comm
Tel 415-574-3000
Fax 415-578-9264

**Global Village
Communication, Inc.**
685 B East Middlefield Rd.
Mountain View, CA 94043

Founded 1989
Total employees 125
Industry
Telecommunications
Growth Openings in past
year 25; percentage
growth 25%
Contact
Len Lehmann, COB/VP of
Advanced Products
Tel 415-390-8200
Fax 415-390-8282

**Granite Computer
Products, Inc.**
1350 South Loop Rd.
Alameda, CA 94501

Founded 1986
Total employees 65
Annual sales $24.6 million
Industries Computer
Hardware,
Telecommunications

Growth Openings in past
year 25; percentage
growth 62%
Contact
Peter Jackson, President
Tel 510-769-2800
Fax 510-769-2899

Gupta Corp.
1060 Marsh Rd.
Menlo Park, CA 94025

Founded 1984
Total employees 300
Annual sales $56.13
million
Industry Computer
Software
Growth Openings in past
year 140; percentage
growth 87%
Contact
Umang P. Gupta,
President/CEO
Tel 415-321-9500
Fax 415-321-5471

Gyration, Inc.
12930 Saratoga Ave.,
Bldg. C
Saratoga, CA 95070

Founded 1989
Total employees 50
Annual sales $10 million
Industries Test and
Measurement,
Transportation
Growth Openings in past
year 36; percentage
growth 257%
Contact
Thomas Quinn, COB/CEO
Tel 408-255-3016
Fax 408-255-9075

**Haig Precision
Manufacturing Corp.**
186 Gilman Ave.
Campbell, CA 95008

Founded 1960
Total employees 75
Industry Manufacturing
Equipment
Growth Openings in past
year 25; percentage
growth 50%
Contact
Daniel Sarkisian, President
Tel 408-378-4920
Fax 408-378-5995

**Harris Corp., Digital
Telephone Systems
Division**
300 Bel Marin Keys Blvd.
Novato, CA 94949

Founded 1968
Total employees 350
Annual sales $60 million
Industry
Telecommunications
Growth Openings in past
year 49; percentage
growth 16%
Contact
Harry Roberts, Director of
Human Resources
Tel 415-382-5000
Fax 415-883-1626

Hash-Tech, Inc.
3140 Alfred St.
Santa Clara, CA 95054

Founded 1983
Total employees 65
Industry Subassemblies
and Components
Growth Openings in past
year 20; percentage
growth 44%
Contact
Hal Neuenswander,
President
Tel 408-988-2646
Fax 408-492-1140

HM Electronics, Inc.
6675 Mesa Ridge Rd.
San Diego, CA 92121

Founded 1971
Total employees 170
Annual sales $23 million
Industry
Telecommunications
Growth Openings in past
year 20; percentage
growth 13%
Contact
Ms. Pauline Mraz,
Personnel Manager
Tel 619-535-6000
Fax 619-452-7207

HNC, Inc.
5501 Oberlin Dr.
San Diego, CA 92121

Founded 1986
Total employees 90
Annual sales $10 million
Industry Computer
Software

Growth Openings in past
year 30; percentage
growth 50%
Contact
Robert L. North, President/
CEO
Tel 619-546-8877
Fax 619-452-6524

**Hollingsead
International, Inc.**
13701 Excelsior Dr.
Santa Fe Springs, CA
90670

Founded 1959
Total employees 125
Annual sales $20 million
Industry Transportation
Growth Openings in past
year 55; percentage
growth 78%
Contact
Raymond Pease,
President
Tel 310-921-3438
Fax 310-921-6313

Holz Precision, Inc.
2099 Fortune Dr., PO Box
32058
San Jose, CA 95152

Founded 1970
Total employees 111
Annual sales $8.4 million
Industry Manufacturing
Equipment
Growth Openings in past
year 36; percentage
growth 48%
Contact
Ms. Ardythe Storing,
Controller
Tel 408-943-9204
Fax 408-943-0978

Horizon Technology, Inc.
3990 Ruffin Rd.
San Diego, CA 92123

Founded 1977
Total employees 480
Annual sales $40 million
Industries Computer
Hardware, Computer
Software, Manufacturing
Equipment
Growth Openings in past
year 44; percentage
growth 10%
Contact
Dr. James T. Palmer, Chief
Executive Officer
Tel 619-292-8331
Fax 619-292-7321

IA Corporation
1301 Harbor Bay Pkwy.,
PO Box 4004
Alameda, CA 94501

Founded 1979
Total employees 200
Annual sales $35 million
Industries Computer
Software,
Telecommunications
Growth Openings in past
year 50; percentage
growth 33%
Contact
Dr. C.V. Ravi, Ph.D.,
President
Tel 510-769-5400
Fax 510-521-5499

**ICN Biomedicals, Inc.,
Diagnostics Division**
3300 Hyland Ave.
Costa Mesa, CA 92626

Founded 1969
Total employees 100
Annual sales $15 million
Industry Medical
Growth Openings in past
year 15; percentage
growth 17%
Contact
Milan Panic, Chief
Executive Officer
Tel 714-545-0113

**IDB Communications
Group, Inc.**
10525 West Washington
Blvd.
Culver City, CA 90232

Founded 1983
Total employees 558
Annual sales $310.7
million
Industries Holding
Companies,
Telecommunications
Growth Openings in past
year 133; percentage
growth 31%
Contact
Ms. Carrie Armenta,
Director of Personnel
Tel 213-870-9000
Fax 213-240-3902

ILC Technology, Inc.
399 Java Dr.
Sunnyvale, CA 94089

Founded 1967
Total employees 270
Annual sales $52 million

Industries Holding
Companies, Photonics,
Telecommunications
Growth Openings in past
year 20; percentage
growth 8%
Contact
Henry Baumgartner,
President/CEO
Tel 408-745-7900
Fax 408-744-0829

Indus Group
60 Spear St.
San Francisco, CA 94133

Founded 1987
Total employees 250
Annual sales $23.9 million
Industry Computer
Software
Growth Openings in past
year 69; percentage
growth 38%
Contact
Bob Felton, President
Tel 415-904-5000
Fax 415-904-4949

**Industrial Dynamics Co.,
Ltd.**
2927 Lomita Blvd.
Torrance, CA 90505

Founded 1960
Total employees 350
Annual sales $44 million
Industry Factory
Automation
Growth Openings in past
year 29; percentage
growth 9%
Contact
Ms. Kris Booz, Personnel
Manager
Tel 310-325-5633
Fax 310-530-1000

Inference Corp.
550 North Continental
Blvd.
El Segundo, CA 90245

Founded 1979
Total employees 200
Annual sales $21 million
Industry Computer
Software
Growth Openings in past
year 55; percentage
growth 37%
Contact
Peter R. Tierney, President
Tel 310-322-0200
Fax 310-322-3242

Inforite Corp.
1670 South Amphlett
Blvd., Suite 100
San Mateo, CA 94402

Founded 1983
Total employees 100
Annual sales $20 million
Industry Computer
Hardware
Growth Openings in past
year 30; percentage
growth 42%
Contact
K. Kato, President
Tel 415-571-8766
Fax 415-571-7547

**Information Management
Associates, Inc.**
17550 New Hope St.,
Suite A
Fountain Valley, CA 92708

Founded 1983
Total employees 107
Annual sales $12 million
Industry Computer
Software
Growth Openings in past
year 27; percentage
growth 33%
Contact
Al Subbloie, President
Tel 714-549-3068
Fax 714-641-0689

Infrasonics, Inc.
3911 Sorrento Valley Blvd.
San Diego, CA 92121

Founded 1982
Total employees 215
Annual sales $18.69
million
Industry Medical
Growth Openings in past
year 95; percentage
growth 79%
Contact
Jim Hitchen, President
Tel 619-450-9898
Fax 619-450-4372

**Innovative Data
Technology**
5340 Eastgate Mall
San Diego, CA 92121

Founded 1976
Total employees 60
Annual sales $12 million
Industries Computer
Hardware, Computer
Software

Growth Openings in past
year 15; percentage
growth 33%
Contact
Ms. Geri Westberg,
Human Resources
Director
Tel 619-587-0555
Fax 619-587-0160

**Innovative Interfaces,
Inc.**
2344 Sixth St.
Berkeley, CA 94710

Founded 1978
Total employees 100
Industry Computer
Software
Growth Openings in past
year 40; percentage
growth 66%
Contact
Gerald Kline, President
Tel 510-644-3600
Fax 510-644-3650

**Integrated Decision
Systems, Inc.**
1950 Sawtelle, Suite 255
Los Angeles, CA 90025

Founded 1981
Total employees 54
Industry Computer
Software
Growth Openings in past
year 19; percentage
growth 54%
Contact
Gerald Jackrel, President
Tel 310-478-4015
Fax 310-473-4352

Integrated Systems, Inc.
3260 Jay St.
Santa Clara, CA 95054

Founded 1980
Total employees 252
Annual sales $32.3 million
Industry Computer
Software
Growth Openings in past
year 56; percentage
growth 28%
Contact
Narendra K. Gupta,
COB/CEO
Tel 408-980-1500
Fax 408-980-0400

IntelliCorp, Inc.
1975 El Camino Real
West
Mountain View, CA 94040

Founded 1980
Total employees 120
Annual sales $9 million
Industry Computer
Software
Growth Openings in past
year 20; percentage
growth 20%
Contact
Kenneth H. Haas,
President
Tel 415-965-5500
Fax 415-965-5647

Interactive Network, Inc.
1991 Landings Dr.
Mountain View, CA 94043

Founded 1988
Total employees 100
Annual sales $5.3 million
Industry
Telecommunications
Growth Openings in past
year 20; percentage
growth 25%
Contact
David B. Lockton, Chief
Executive Officer
Tel 415-960-1000
Fax 415-960-3331

**Interconnect Solutions,
Inc.**
7968 Arjons Dr., Suite D
San Diego, CA 92126

Founded 1981
Total employees 45
Annual sales $4 million
Industries Subassemblies
and Components,
Telecommunications
Growth Openings in past
year 15; percentage
growth 50%
Contact
David Ginsburg, President/
CEO
Tel 619-536-8888

**Interlink Electronics
Corp.**
546 Flynn Rd.
Camarillo, CA 93012

Founded 1985
Total employees 56
Annual sales $3.03 million
Industry Subassemblies
and Components

Growth Openings in past year 21; percentage growth 60%
Contact
E. Michael Thoben, III, President/COO
Tel 805-484-8855
Fax 805-484-8989

International Antex, Inc.
30580 Whipple Rd.
Union City, CA 94587

Founded 1974
Total employees 40
Annual sales $5 million
Industry Holding Companies
Growth Openings in past year 27; percentage growth 207%
Contact
Ken Chow, President
Tel 510-487-0200

International Circuits and Components, Inc.
3701 East Miraloma Ave.
Anaheim, CA 92806

Founded 1981
Total employees 30
Annual sales $8 million
Industries Manufacturing Equipment, Subassemblies and Components
Growth Openings in past year 18; percentage growth 150%
Contact
Richard Cheng, President
Tel 714-572-1900
Fax 714-527-2900

International Management Systems, Inc.
4676 Admiralty Way, Suite 217
Marina Del Rey, CA 90292

Founded 1973
Total employees 105
Annual sales $8 million
Industry Computer Hardware
Growth Openings in past year 35; percentage growth 50%
Contact
Gerald Plier, President
Tel 310-822-2022
Fax 310-305-8683

International Microcomputer Software, Inc.
1938 Fourth St.
San Rafael, CA 94901

Founded 1982
Total employees 102
Annual sales $13 million
Industries Computer Hardware, Computer Software
Growth Openings in past year 67; percentage growth 191%
Contact
Geoff Koblick, Chief Executive Officer
Tel 415-454-7101
Fax 415-454-8901

ISE Labs, Inc.
2095 Ringwood Ave.
San Jose, CA 95131

Founded 1980
Total employees 93
Annual sales $14 million
Industries Computer Software, Factory Automation, Subassemblies and Components
Growth Openings in past year 28; percentage growth 43%
Contact
Saeed Malik, President
Tel 408-954-8378
Fax 408-954-1676

Isis Pharmaceuticals, Inc.
2280 Faraday Ave.
Carlsbad, CA 92008

Founded 1989
Total employees 180
Annual sales $12.14 million
Industries Biotechnology, Pharmaceuticals
Growth Openings in past year 50; percentage growth 38%
Contact
Ms. Pat Lowenstam, Director of Human Resources
Tel 619-931-9200
Fax 619-931-0265

IWI
1648 Mabury Rd.
San Jose, CA 95133

Founded 1986
Total employees 30
Annual sales $4.1 million
Industry Telecommunications
Growth Openings in past year 15; percentage growth 100%
Contact
Arty Chang, President
Tel 408-923-0301
Fax 408-923-0427

J & R Films Co., Inc.
1135 North Mansfield Ave.
Los Angeles, CA 90038

Founded 1962
Total employees 170
Annual sales $8.9 million
Industries Holding Companies, Telecommunications
Growth Openings in past year 40; percentage growth 30%
Contact
Joe Paskal, President
Tel 213-467-3107
Fax 213-962-8601

J&L Information Systems, Inc.
9600 Topanga Canyon Blvd.
Chatsworth, CA 91311

Founded 1988
Total employees 65
Annual sales $15 million
Industry Telecommunications
Growth Openings in past year 15; percentage growth 30%
Contact
Chuck Lubash, President
Tel 818-709-1778
Fax 818-882-9134

Jandel Scientific
2591 Kerner Blvd.
San Rafael, CA 94901

Founded 1982
Total employees 65
Annual sales $6 million
Industry Computer Software
Growth Openings in past year 15; percentage growth 30%

Contact
Dr. John Osborn, Chief
Executive Officer
Tel 415-453-6700
Fax 415-453-7769

Johanson Dielectrics, Inc.
15191 Bledsoe St.
Sylmar, CA 91342

Founded 1956
Total employees 450
Annual sales $43 million
Industry Subassemblies
and Components
Growth Openings in past
year 22; percentage
growth 5%
Contact
Robert Belter, President
Tel 818-364-9800
Fax 818-364-6100

Jones Futurex, Inc.
3715 Atherton Rd.
Rocklin, CA 95675

Founded 1981
Total employees 75
Annual sales $7.3 million
Industries Computer
Hardware,
Subassemblies and
Components,
Telecommunications
Growth Openings in past
year 15; percentage
growth 25%
Contact
James J. Krejci, President
Tel 916-632-3456
Fax 916-632-3445

Joystick Technologies, Inc.
970 Park Center Dr.
Vista, CA 92083

Founded 1985
Total employees 95
Industry Holding
Companies
Growth Openings in past
year 45; percentage
growth 90%
Contact
Charles Hayes, President
Tel 619-598-2518
Fax 619-598-2524

Kalpana, Inc.
1154 East Arques Ave.
Sunnyvale, CA 94086

Founded 1987
Total employees 120
Industry
Telecommunications
Growth Openings in past
year 70; percentage
growth 140%
Contact
Jim Jordan, President/
CEO
Tel 408-749-1600
Fax 408-749-1690

Kavlico Corp.
14501 Los Angeles Ave.
Moorpark, CA 93021

Founded 1959
Total employees 840
Annual sales $70 million
Industry Subassemblies
and Components
Growth Openings in past
year 140; percentage
growth 20%
Contact
Michael Gibson, President
Tel 805-523-2000
Fax 805-523-7125

Kinetics Technology International Corp.
650 Cienega Ave.
San Dimas, CA 91773

Founded 1963
Total employees 260
Annual sales $120 million
Industries Chemicals,
Manufacturing Equipment
Growth Openings in past
year 34; percentage
growth 15%
Contact
David Baker, President
Tel 909-592-4455
Fax 909-592-3399

Kingston Technology Corp.
17600 Newhope
Fountain Valley, CA 92708

Founded 1987
Total employees 280
Annual sales $456 million
Industry Computer
Hardware
Growth Openings in past
year 135; percentage
growth 93%

Contact
John Tu, President/Co-
owner
Tel 714-435-2600
Fax 714-435-2699

Kiss International, Inc.
965 Park Center Dr.
Vista, CA 92083

Founded 1985
Total employees 45
Annual sales $5 million
Industry Environmental
Growth Openings in past
year 15; percentage
growth 50%
Contact
Joel C. Edison, President
Tel 619-599-0200
Fax 619-599-0207

Knowledge Data Systems, Inc.
80 East Sir Francis Drake
Blvd.
Larkspur, CA 94939

Founded 1964
Total employees 130
Annual sales $15 million
Industry Computer
Software
Growth Openings in past
year 32; percentage
growth 32%
Contact
Joe Sullivan, Chief
Executive Officer
Tel 415-461-5374
Fax 415-461-0616

Kobe Precision, Inc.
31031 Huntwood Ave.
Hayward, CA 94544

Founded 1988
Total employees 380
Annual sales $37 million
Industry Subassemblies
and Components
Growth Openings in past
year 79; percentage
growth 26%
Contact
Ms. Toni Hampton,
Director of Human
Resources
Tel 510-487-3200
Fax 510-487-9550

Kubota Pacific Computer, Inc.
2630 Walsh Ave.
Santa Clara, CA 95051

Founded 1990
Total employees 300
Annual sales $49 million
Industries Computer Hardware, Factory Automation
Growth Openings in past year 50; percentage growth 20%
Contact
Ben Wegbreit, COB/CEO
Tel 408-727-8100

Label-Aire, Inc.
550 Burning Tree Rd.
Fullerton, CA 92633

Founded 1968
Total employees 150
Annual sales $18 million
Industry Factory Automation
Growth Openings in past year 50; percentage growth 50%
Contact
Ms. Stella Rodriguez, Personnel Manager
Tel 714-441-0700
Fax 714-526-0300

Lantronix Corp.
15353 Barranca Pkwy.
Irvine, CA 92718

Founded 1989
Total employees 40
Annual sales $18 million
Industry Telecommunications
Growth Openings in past year 26; percentage growth 185%
Contact
Brad Freeburg, President
Tel 714-453-3990
Fax 714-453-3995

LaserByte Corporation
1330 Bordeaux Dr.
Sunnyvale, CA 94089

Founded 1990
Total employees 40
Annual sales $6.5 million
Industry Computer Hardware
Growth Openings in past year 20; percentage growth 100%

Contact
Robert Toda, President
Tel 408-734-9200
Fax 408-734-2974

Learning Co.
6493 Kaiser Dr.
Fremont, CA 94555

Founded 1979
Total employees 130
Annual sales $19.59 million
Industry Computer Software
Growth Openings in past year 19; percentage growth 17%
Contact
Les Schmidt, Chief Financial Officer
Tel 510-792-2101
Fax 510-792-9628

Legato Systems, Inc.
260 Sheridan Ave.
Palo Alto, CA 94306

Founded 1988
Total employees 85
Annual sales $9.8 million
Industries Computer Hardware, Computer Software
Growth Openings in past year 35; percentage growth 70%
Contact
Louis Cole, President/CEO
Tel 415-329-7880
Fax 415-329-8898

Level One Communications, Inc.
105 Lake Forrest Way
Folsom, CA 95630

Founded 1985
Total employees 110
Annual sales $25.9 million
Industry Telecommunications
Growth Openings in past year 60; percentage growth 120%
Contact
Dr. Robert S. Pepper, President/CEO
Tel 916-985-3670
Fax 916-985-3512

Linear Technology Corp.
1630 McCarthy Blvd.
Milpitas, CA 95035

Founded 1981
Total employees 825
Annual sales $119.44 million
Industries Subassemblies and Components, Test and Measurement, Telecommunications
Growth Openings in past year 25; percentage growth 3%
Contact
Paul Coghlan, VP of Finance/CFO
Tel 408-432-1900
Fax 408-434-0507

Ling Electronics, Inc.
4890 East LaPalma Ave.
Anaheim, CA 92806

Founded 1956
Total employees 90
Annual sales $13 million
Industry Factory Automation
Growth Openings in past year 15; percentage growth 20%
Contact
Steve Sullivan, President
Tel 714-779-1900
Fax 714-779-7714

Liposome Technology, Inc.
1050 Hamilton Ct.
Menlo Park, CA 94025

Founded 1981
Total employees 145
Annual sales $3.15 million
Industry Biotechnology
Growth Openings in past year 60; percentage growth 70%
Contact
Ms. Jeannine Niacaris, Director of Human Resources
Tel 415-323-9011
Fax 415-323-9106

Logistix
48021 Warm Springs Blvd.
Fremont, CA 94539

Founded 1974
Total employees 500
Annual sales $58 million

Industries Computer
Hardware, Computer
Software,
Telecommunications
Growth Openings in past
year 300; percentage
growth 150%
Contact
Stephen Weinstein,
President
Tel 510-656-8000
Fax 510-438-9486

**Loral/Rolm Computer
Systems**
3151 Zanker Rd.
San Jose, CA 95134

Founded 1969
Total employees 140
Annual sales $16 million
Industries Computer
Hardware, Computer
Software
Growth Openings in past
year 15; percentage
growth 12%
Contact
Ms. Janice Ramsey, HR
and Administration
Services Manager
Tel 408-432-8000
Fax 408-432-7961

**Lotus Development
Corp., cc:Mail Division**
800 El Camino Real West
Mountain View, CA 94040

Founded 1983
Total employees 200
Industry Computer
Software
Growth Openings in past
year 50; percentage
growth 33%
Contact
Larry Crume, Vice
President/General
Manager
Tel 415-335-6400

**MacNeal-Schwendler
Corp.**
815 Colorado Blvd.
Los Angeles, CA 90041

Founded 1963
Total employees 300
Annual sales $65.47
million
Industries Computer
Software, Holding
Companies

Growth Openings in past
year 20; percentage
growth 7%
Contact
Louis A. Greco, CFO/
Secretary
Tel 213-258-9111
Fax 213-259-3838

Magellan Systems Corp.
960 Overland Ct.
San Dimas, CA 91773

Founded 1986
Total employees 160
Annual sales $30 million
Industries Test and
Measurement,
Transportation
Growth Openings in past
year 50; percentage
growth 45%
Contact
Randy Hoffman, President
Tel 909-394-5000
Fax 909-394-7050

**Magnetek Power
Technologies Systems,
Inc.**
711 West Knox St.
Gardena, CA 90248

Founded 1923
Total employees 85
Annual sales $8.3 million
Industry Subassemblies
and Components
Growth Openings in past
year 19; percentage
growth 28%
Contact
James C. Cole, Vice
President
Tel 213-321-4355
Fax 310-323-8846

**Manzanita Software
Systems**
2130 Professional Dr.,
Suite 150
Roseville, CA 95661

Founded 1984
Total employees 50
Annual sales $5.05 million
Industry Computer
Software
Growth Openings in past
year 18; percentage
growth 56%
Contact
Ms. Lynn Marks, Human
Resources Manager
Tel 916-781-3880
Fax 916-781-3814

**MAST Immunosystems,
Inc.**
630 Clyde Ct.
Mountain View, CA 94043

Founded 1979
Total employees 190
Industries Holding
Companies,
Pharmaceuticals
Growth Openings in past
year 29; percentage
growth 18%
Contact
Clint Severson, President/
CEO
Tel 415-961-5501
Fax 415-969-2745

**Matrix Pharmaceutical,
Inc.**
1430 O'Brien Dr.
Menlo Park, CA 94025

Founded 1985
Total employees 85
Industries Biotechnology,
Pharmaceuticals
Growth Openings in past
year 35; percentage
growth 70%
Contact
Craig R. McMullen,
President/CEO
Tel 415-326-6100
Fax 415-326-1407

**Maxwell Laboratories,
Inc.**
8888 Balboa Ave.
San Diego, CA 92123

Founded 1965
Total employees 750
Annual sales $90.1 million
Industries Factory
Automation, Holding
Companies,
Manufacturing
Equipment,
Subassemblies and
Components
Growth Openings in past
year 62; percentage
growth 9%
Contact
Dr. Alan C. Kolb, Ph.D.,
COB/CEO/President
Tel 619-279-5100
Fax 619-277-6754

McLaren, Hart Environmental Engineering Corp.
11101 White Rock Rd.
Rancho Cordova, CA 95670

Founded 1968
Total employees 700
Annual sales $74 million
Industry Environmental
Growth Openings in past year 46; percentage growth 7%
Contact
Gary M Carlton, President/CEO
Tel 916-638-3696
Fax 916-638-2842

MDL Information Systems, Inc.
14600 Catalina St.
San Leandro, CA 94577

Founded 1978
Total employees 350
Annual sales $50.58 million
Industry Computer Software
Growth Openings in past year 49; percentage growth 16%
Contact
Dan E. Kingman, VP of Human Resources
Tel 510-895-1313
Fax 510-352-2870

Media Vision, Inc.
47300 Bayside Pkwy.
Fremont, CA 94538

Founded 1991
Total employees 378
Annual sales $241 million
Industries Computer Hardware, Telecommunications
Growth Openings in past year 178; percentage growth 89%
Contact
Paul Jain, President/CEO
Tel 510-770-8600
Fax 510-770-9592

Mediashare, Inc.
2035 Corte Del Nogale, Suite 200
Carlsbad, CA 92009

Founded 1990
Total employees 90

Industry Computer Software
Growth Openings in past year 15; percentage growth 20%
Contact
Greg Bestick, President
Tel 619-931-7171
Fax 619-931-5752

Megatest Corp.
880 Fox Ln.
San Jose, CA 95131

Founded 1975
Total employees 450
Annual sales $90 million
Industry Factory Automation
Growth Openings in past year 49; percentage growth 12%
Contact
Jack Halter, President
Tel 408-437-9700
Fax 408-453-8729

Megatool, Inc.
6955 Aragon Cir.
Buena Park, CA 90620

Founded 1982
Total employees 275
Annual sales $23 million
Industry Manufacturing Equipment
Growth Openings in past year 55; percentage growth 25%
Contact
Dave Hemmings, President
Tel 714-521-6242
Fax 714-521-8642

Mentor Corp.
5425 Hollister Ave.
Santa Barbara, CA 93111

Founded 1969
Total employees 900
Annual sales $115 million
Industries Holding Companies, Medical
Growth Openings in past year 35; percentage growth 4%
Contact
Christopher J. Conway, COB/CEO
Tel 805-681-6000
Fax 805-964-2712

Meta-Software, Inc.
1300 White Oaks Rd.
Campbell, CA 95008

Founded 1977
Total employees 67
Annual sales $7.7 million
Industries Computer Software, Factory Automation
Growth Openings in past year 15; percentage growth 28%
Contact
Shawn Hailey, President
Tel 408-396-5400
Fax 408-371-5638

MetroLaser
18006 Skypark Cir., Suite 108
Irvine, CA 92714

Founded 1988
Total employees 27
Industry Photonics
Growth Openings in past year 17; percentage growth 170%
Contact
Dr. James Trollinger, Ph.D., Partner
Tel 714-553-0688
Fax 714-553-0495

MICOM Communications Corp.
4100 Los Angeles Ave.
Simi Valley, CA 93063

Founded 1973
Total employees 378
Annual sales $67 million
Industry Telecommunications
Growth Openings in past year 22; percentage growth 6%
Contact
Gil Cabral, President
Tel 805-583-8600
Fax 805-583-1997

Micrel Semiconductor, Inc.
1849 Fortune Dr.
San Jose, CA 95131

Founded 1979
Total employees 160
Annual sales $15 million
Industries Subassemblies and Components, Test and Measurement

Growth Openings in past year 25; percentage growth 18%
Contact
Ray Zinn, President
Tel 408-944-0800
Fax 408-944-0970

Micro Express, Inc.
1801 Carnegie Ave.
Santa Ana, CA 92705

Founded 1985
Total employees 100
Annual sales $16 million
Industry Computer Hardware
Growth Openings in past year 50; percentage growth 100%
Contact
Art Afshar, President/CEO
Tel 714-852-1400
Fax 714-852-1225

Micro Focus, Inc.
2465 East Bayshore Rd., Suite 400
Palo Alto, CA 94303

Founded 1976
Total employees 625
Annual sales $117 million
Industry Computer Software
Growth Openings in past year 47; percentage growth 8%
Contact
Richard Butts, Human Resources Manager
Tel 415-856-4161
Fax 415-856-6134

Micro-Frame Technologies, Inc.
430 North Vinyard Ave., Suite 120
Ontario, CA 91764

Founded 1985
Total employees 102
Annual sales $11 million
Industry Computer Software
Growth Openings in past year 22; percentage growth 27%
Contact
John O'Neil, Jr., President
Tel 909-983-2711
Fax 909-984-5382

Microgenics Corp.
2380A Bisso Ln.
Concord, CA 94520

Founded 1981
Total employees 250
Industry Medical
Growth Openings in past year 69; percentage growth 38%
Contact
Ms. Terry Hanson, Personnel Manager
Tel 510-674-0667
Fax 510-674-1130

Micro-MRP, Inc.
1065 East Hillsdale Blvd., Suite 301
Foster City, CA 94404

Founded 1982
Total employees 70
Annual sales $8.1 million
Industry Computer Software
Growth Openings in past year 25; percentage growth 55%
Contact
Philip Shore, Controller
Tel 415-345-6000
Fax 415-345-3079

MicroNet Technology, Inc.
80 Technology
Irvine, CA 92718

Founded 1987
Total employees 150
Industry Computer Hardware
Growth Openings in past year 50; percentage growth 50%
Contact
Charles McConathy, President
Tel 714-453-6000
Fax 714-453-6001

Micropublication Systems, Inc.
20430 South Tillman Ave.
Carson, CA 90746

Founded 1986
Total employees 85
Industry Computer Hardware
Growth Openings in past year 20; percentage growth 30%

Contact
Richard Ross, President
Tel 310-763-7575
Fax 310-763-7211

Microtec Research, Inc.
2350 Mission College Blvd., Suite 500
Santa Clara, CA 95054

Founded 1975
Total employees 250
Industry Computer Software
Growth Openings in past year 19; percentage growth 8%
Contact
Ms. Mary Heeney, Human Resources Manager
Tel 408-980-1300
Fax 408-982-8266

Microtek Lab, Inc.
680 Knox St.
Torrance, CA 90502

Founded 1980
Total employees 90
Industry Photonics
Growth Openings in past year 20; percentage growth 28%
Contact
Dr. S.C. Lee, President
Tel 310-297-5000
Fax 310-538-1193

MiLAN Technology, Inc.
894 Ross Dr., Suite 101
Sunnyvale, CA 94089

Founded 1990
Total employees 54
Annual sales $13 million
Industries Computer Hardware, Photonics, Telecommunications
Growth Openings in past year 29; percentage growth 116%
Contact
Michael Conrad, President
Tel 408-752-2770
Fax 408-752-2790

Molecular Biosystems, Inc.
10030 Barnes Canyon Rd.
San Diego, CA 92121

Founded 1980
Total employees 205
Annual sales $3.7 million
Industry Pharmaceuticals

Growth Openings in past year 35; percentage growth 20%
Contact
Ms. Cynthia Mendez, Director of Human Resources
Tel 619-452-0681
Fax 619-452-6187

Molecular Devices Corp.
4700 Bohannon Dr., Menlo Oaks Corporate Ctr.
Menlo Park, CA 94025

Founded 1983
Total employees 135
Industry Biotechnology
Growth Openings in past year 35; percentage growth 35%
Contact
Jim Iuliano, President
Tel 415-322-4700
Fax 415-322-2069

Molecular Dynamics, Inc.
880 East Arques Ave.
Sunnyvale, CA 94086

Founded 1987
Total employees 152
Annual sales $47 million
Industries Medical, Test and Measurement, Telecommunications
Growth Openings in past year 17; percentage growth 12%
Contact
John Gordon, VP of Human Relations
Tel 408-773-1222
Fax 408-773-8343

Moller International, Inc.
1222 Research Park Dr.
Davis, CA 95616

Founded 1971
Total employees 40
Industries Defense, Transportation
Growth Openings in past year 18; percentage growth 81%
Contact
Dr. Paul Moller, Ph.D., President
Tel 916-756-5086
Fax 916-756-5179

Moore Industries International, Inc.
16650 Schoenborn St.
Sepulveda, CA 91343

Founded 1968
Total employees 350
Annual sales $44 million
Industry Factory Automation
Growth Openings in past year 100; percentage growth 40%
Contact
Ms. Susan Shrader, Director of Personnel
Tel 818-894-7111
Fax 818-891-2816

Mozart Systems Corp.
1350 Bayshore Hwy., Suite 630
Burlingame, CA 94010

Founded 1985
Total employees 50
Annual sales $7 million
Industry Computer Software
Growth Openings in past year 15; percentage growth 42%
Contact
Alan P. Parnass, President
Tel 415-340-1588
Fax 415-340-1648

Multi-Pure Corp.
21339 Nordhoff St.
Chatsworth, CA 91311

Founded 1970
Total employees 170
Annual sales $30 million
Industry Environmental
Growth Openings in past year 20; percentage growth 13%
Contact
H. Allen Rice, Chief Executive Officer
Tel 818-341-7577
Fax 818-341-5275

Nano Pulse Industries, Inc.
440 Nibus St., PO Box 9398
Brea, CA 92621

Founded 1972
Total employees 800
Annual sales $9 million
Industries Subassemblies and Components, Telecommunications

Growth Openings in past year 199; percentage growth 33%
Contact
Jay A. Harman, President
Tel 714-529-2600
Fax 714-671-7919

Natel Engineering Co., Inc.
4450 Runway St.
Simi Valley, CA 93063

Founded 1975
Total employees 175
Annual sales $16 million
Industry Subassemblies and Components
Growth Openings in past year 25; percentage growth 16%
Contact
Sudesh Arora, President
Tel 805-581-3950
Fax 805-584-4357

National Magnetics Corp.
17030 Muskrat Ave.
Adelanto, CA 92301

Founded 1971
Total employees 165
Annual sales $16 million
Industry Subassemblies and Components
Growth Openings in past year 70; percentage growth 73%
Contact
Ms. Sherri Girardin, Benefits Manager
Tel 619-246-3020
Fax 619-246-3870

Navigation Technologies
740 East Arques Ave.
Sunnyvale, CA 94086

Founded 1985
Total employees 170
Annual sales $19 million
Industry Computer Software
Growth Openings in past year 24; percentage growth 16%
Contact
Ms. Linda Duff, Support Services Administrator
Tel 408-737-3200
Fax 408-736-3734

nCHIP, Inc.
1971 North Capital Ave.
San Jose, CA 95132

Founded 1989
Total employees 70
Industry Subassemblies
and Components
Growth Openings in past
year 30; percentage
growth 75%
Contact
Bruce McWilliams,
President/CEO
Tel 408-945-9991
Fax 408-945-0151

**NDE Environmental
Corp.**
20000 Mariner Ave., Suite
500
Torrance, CA 90503

Founded 1981
Total employees 85
Annual sales $6.1 million
Industries Energy,
Environmental,
Transportation
Growth Openings in past
year 40; percentage
growth 88%
Contact
J. Chaffee, President/CEO
Tel 310-542-4342
Fax 310-542-6657

Nelco Products, Inc.
1411 East Orangethorpe
Ave.
Fullerton, CA 92631

Founded 1965
Total employees 300
Annual sales $44 million
Industry Advanced
Materials
Growth Openings in past
year 35; percentage
growth 13%
Contact
Ron Hart, President
Tel 714-879-4293
Fax 714-879-2983

NetFRAME Systems, Inc.
1545 Barber Ln.
Milpitas, CA 95035

Founded 1987
Total employees 225
Annual sales $39 million
Industries Computer
Software,
Telecommunications

Growth Openings in past
year 100; percentage
growth 80%
Contact
Ms. Vivian M. Golub, VP
of Human Resources
Tel 408-944-0600
Fax 408-434-4190

NetManage Inc.
20823 Stevens Creek
Blvd.
Cupertino, CA 95014

Founded 1990
Total employees 85
Annual sales $5.0 million
Industry Computer
Software
Growth Openings in past
year 25; percentage
growth 41%
Contact
Zvi Alon, COB/President/
CEO
Tel 408-973-7171
Fax 408-257-6405

Netra Corp.
185 East Dana St.
Mountain View, CA 94041

Founded 1967
Total employees 40
Industries Advanced
Materials, Photonics,
Subassemblies and
Components
Growth Openings in past
year 15; percentage
growth 60%
Contact
William Harry, President
Tel 415-964-1230
Fax 415-968-3115

NetSoft
39 Argonaut
Laguna Hills, CA 92656

Founded 1980
Total employees 150
Annual sales $17 million
Industries Computer
Hardware, Computer
Software,
Telecommunications
Growth Openings in past
year 50; percentage
growth 50%
Contact
Ms. Carol Carson,
Personnel Manager
Tel 714-768-4013
Fax 714-768-5049

**Network Computing
Devices, Inc.**
350 North Bernardo Ave.
Mountain View, CA 94043

Founded 1988
Total employees 340
Annual sales $120.34
million
Industries Computer
Hardware, Computer
Software
Growth Openings in past
year 133; percentage
growth 64%
Contact
Ms. JoAnn Rogers,
Director of Human
Resources
Tel 415-694-0650
Fax 415-961-7711

Network General Corp.
4200 Bohannon Dr.
Menlo Park, CA 94025

Founded 1986
Total employees 412
Annual sales $95.0 million
Industries Computer
Software, Test and
Measurement
Growth Openings in past
year 60; percentage
growth 17%
Contact
Leslie G. Denend,
President/CEO
Tel 415-473-2000
Fax 415-321-0855

**Network Security
Systems, Inc.**
9401 Waples St.
San Diego, CA 92121

Founded 1991
Total employees 60
Annual sales $6.9 million
Industries Computer
Software, Energy
Growth Openings in past
year 20; percentage
growth 50%
Contact
Bill Humphreys, CEO/
President
Tel 619-587-7950
Fax 619-552-9162

Neuron Data, Inc.
156 University Ave.
Palo Alto, CA 94301

Founded 1985
Total employees 100

Annual sales $11 million
Industry Computer
Software
Growth Openings in past
year 30; percentage
growth 42%
Contact
Patrick F. Perez, CEO/
COB
Tel 415-321-4488
Fax 415-321-9648

**New Horizons Computer
Learning Center**
1231 East Dyer Rd., Suite
140
Santa Ana, CA 92705

Founded 1982
Total employees 120
Annual sales $19 million
Industry Computer
Hardware
Growth Openings in past
year 45; percentage
growth 60%
Contact
Mike Brinda, Owner
Tel 714-556-1220
Fax 714-556-4612

New Technologies, Inc.
11861 East Telegraph Rd.
Santa Fe Springs, CA
90670

Founded 1984
Total employees 50
Annual sales $8.2 million
Industries Computer
Hardware,
Telecommunications
Growth Openings in past
year 30; percentage
growth 150%
Contact
David Chang, President
Tel 310-948-2060
Fax 310-942-0440

Norris Communications
12725 Stowe Dr.
Poway, CA 92064

Founded 1983
Total employees 135
Annual sales $8.2 million
Industries Holding
Companies,
Telecommunications
Growth Openings in past
year 44; percentage
growth 48%

Contact
Elwood Norris, President
Tel 619-679-1504
Fax 619-748-2129

Novabiochem
10394 Pacific Center Ct.
San Diego, CA 92121

Founded 1952
Total employees 140
Annual sales $25 million
Industries Biotechnology,
Chemicals
Growth Openings in past
year 20; percentage
growth 16%
Contact
Ms. Lee Hart, Manager of
Human Resources
Tel 619-450-9600
Fax 619-453-3552

NovaStor Corp.
30961 Agoura Rd., Suite
109
Westlake Village, CA
91361

Founded 1987
Total employees 24
Industry Computer
Software
Growth Openings in past
year 16; percentage
growth 200%
Contact
Peter Means, President
Tel 818-707-9900
Fax 818-707-9902

Novellus Systems, Inc.
81 Vista Montana
San Jose, CA 95134

Founded 1984
Total employees 350
Annual sales $70 million
Industry Manufacturing
Equipment
Growth Openings in past
year 100; percentage
growth 40%
Contact
Richard Hill, President/
COO
Tel 408-943-9700
Fax 408-943-0202

**Oclassen
Pharmaceuticals, Inc.**
100 Pelican Way
San Rafael, CA 94901

Founded 1985
Total employees 85

Annual sales $25 million
Industry Pharmaceuticals
Growth Openings in past
year 20; percentage
growth 30%
Contact
Terry L. Johnson,
President/CEO
Tel 415-258-4500
Fax 415-258-4550

**OHM Corporation,
Northern California
Division**
3018-B Alvarado Blvd.
San Leandro, CA 94577

Founded 1984
Total employees 50
Industries Biotechnology,
Environmental
Growth Openings in past
year 30; percentage
growth 150%
Contact
Thomas Warren, Division
Manager
Tel 510-357-9026
Fax 510-357-8205

**OKI America, Inc., OKI
Semiconductor Group**
785 North Mary Ave.
Sunnyvale, CA 94086

Founded 1978
Total employees 280
Annual sales $375 million
Industry Subassemblies
and Components
Growth Openings in past
year 19; percentage
growth 7%
Contact
Kazuhiko Shimizu,
President/CEO
Tel 408-720-1900
Fax 408-720-1918

On Command Video, Inc.
3301 Olcott St.
Santa Clara, CA 95054

Founded 1986
Total employees 152
Annual sales $20 million
Industry
Telecommunications
Growth Openings in past
year 107; percentage
growth 237%
Contact
Dr. Bob Fenwick, Chief
Executive Officer
Tel 408-496-1800
Fax 408-496-0668

Optical Engineering, Inc.
3310 Coffey Ln.
Santa Rosa, CA 95403

Founded 1969
Total employees 50
Annual sales $5.7 million
Industries Factory
Automation, Photonics,
Test and Measurement
Growth Openings in past
year 20; percentage
growth 66%
Contact
John Macken, President
Tel 707-528-1080
Fax 707-527-8514

Orchid Technology
45365 Northport Loop
West
Fremont, CA 94538

Founded 1982
Total employees 145
Industry Computer
Hardware
Growth Openings in past
year 25; percentage
growth 20%
Contact
Saiid Shahabi, VP of
Finance and
Administration
Tel 510-683-0300
Fax 510-490-9312

Oryx Corp.
47341 Bayside Pkwy.
Fremont, CA 94538

Founded 1990
Total employees 35
Annual sales $3.4 million
Industry Holding
Companies
Growth Openings in past
year 20; percentage
growth 133%
Contact
Arvind Patel, Chief
Executive Officer
Tel 510-249-1155
Fax 510-249-1150

Owl Software Corp.
7633 Fulton Ave.
North Hollywood, CA
91605

Founded 1981
Total employees 30
Annual sales $1 million
Industry Computer
Software

Growth Openings in past
year 20; percentage
growth 200%
Contact
John Campbell, President
Tel 818-765-5585
Fax 818-765-5877

**Pacific Communication
Sciences, Inc.**
10075 Barnes Canyon Rd.
San Diego, CA 92121

Founded 1987
Total employees 310
Annual sales $42 million
Industries Computer
Software,
Telecommunications
Growth Openings in past
year 110; percentage
growth 55%
Contact
Dr. David L. Lyon,
President/CEO
Tel 619-535-9500
Fax 619-535-9235

Pacific Device, Inc.
8572 Spectrum Ln.
San Diego, CA 92121

Founded 1983
Total employees 150
Industry Medical
Growth Openings in past
year 72; percentage
growth 92%
Contact
Mike Shannon, President
Tel 619-457-1988
Fax 619-558-7264

**Paradigm Technology,
Inc.**
71 Vista Montana
San Jose, CA 95134

Founded 1987
Total employees 200
Annual sales $40 million
Industry Subassemblies
and Components
Growth Openings in past
year 50; percentage
growth 33%
Contact
Michael Gulett, President
Tel 408-954-0500
Fax 408-954-8913

Paragon, Inc.
2318 Calle de Luna
Santa Clara, CA 95054

Founded 1981
Total employees 190
Annual sales $18 million
Industries Computer
Hardware,
Subassemblies and
Components
Growth Openings in past
year 60; percentage
growth 46%
Contact
Stanley Nelson, President
Tel 408-727-8824
Fax 408-727-8932

Parallan Computers, Inc.
1310 Villa St.
Mountain View, CA 94041

Founded 1988
Total employees 90
Annual sales $4.5 million
Industry Computer
Software
Growth Openings in past
year 45; percentage
growth 100%
Contact
Gianluca Rattazzi,
President/CEO
Tel 415-960-0288
Fax 415-962-8141

ParcPlace Systems, Inc.
999 East Arques Ave.
Sunnyvale, CA 94086

Founded 1988
Total employees 160
Annual sales $18 million
Industry Computer
Software
Growth Openings in past
year 50; percentage
growth 45%
Contact
William Lyons, President/
CEO
Tel 408-481-9090
Fax 408-481-9095

**Parker Hannifin Corp.,
Racor Division**
3400 Finch Rd., PO Box
3208
Modesto, CA 95353

Founded 1969
Total employees 250
Industries Subassemblies
and Components, Test
and Measurement

Growth Openings in past
year 50; percentage
growth 25%
Contact
Ms. Cathy Medeiros,
Personnel Manager
Tel 209-521-7860
Fax 209-529-3278

**Paul-Munroe Engineering
International, Inc.**
1701 West Sequoia Ave.
Orange, CA 92668

Founded 1952
Total employees 120
Annual sales $20 million
Industries Energy, Factory
Automation,
Subassemblies and
Components
Growth Openings in past
year 20; percentage
growth 20%
Contact
Ms. Margie Hales, Director
of Personnel
Tel 714-978-9600
Fax 714-978-0840

PDA Engineering
2975 Redhill Ave.
Costa Mesa, CA 92626

Founded 1972
Total employees 273
Annual sales $43 million
Industry Holding
Companies
Growth Openings in past
year 23; percentage
growth 9%
Contact
Ms. Linda Baker Sherman,
Personnel Director
Tel 714-540-8900
Fax 714-979-2990

PeopleSoft, Inc.
1331 North California
Blvd., Suite 400
Walnut Creek, CA 94596

Founded 1987
Total employees 173
Annual sales $31.5 million
Industry Computer
Software
Growth Openings in past
year 43; percentage
growth 33%
Contact
David Duffield, President/
CEO
Tel 510-946-9460
Fax 510-946-9461

Peregrine Systems, Inc.
1959 Palomar Oaks Way
Carlsbad, CA 92009

Founded 1979
Total employees 100
Annual sales $20 million
Industry Computer
Software
Growth Openings in past
year 20; percentage
growth 25%
Contact
James Butler, President
Tel 619-431-2400
Fax 619-431-0696

Pharmingen, Inc.
11555 Sorrento Valley Rd.
San Diego, CA 92121

Founded 1987
Total employees 105
Industry Biotechnology
Growth Openings in past
year 51; percentage
growth 94%
Contact
Dr. Ernest Huang, Ph.D.,
President
Tel 619-792-5730
Fax 619-792-5238

Pinnacle Micro, Inc.
19 Technology
Irvine, CA 92718

Founded 1987
Total employees 70
Annual sales $37 million
Industry Computer
Hardware
Growth Openings in past
year 20; percentage
growth 40%
Contact
Ms. Nancy Rosen,
Manager of Human
Resources
Tel 714-727-3300
Fax 714-727-1913

Pioneer Magnetics, Inc.
1745 Berkeley St.
Santa Monica, CA 90404

Founded 1957
Total employees 350
Annual sales $44 million
Industry Holding
Companies
Growth Openings in past
year 79; percentage
growth 29%

Contact
S. Gindoff, President
Tel 310-829-3305
Fax 310-453-3929

Pixar
1001 West Cutting Blvd.
Richmond, CA 94804

Founded 1986
Total employees 100
Industry Computer
Software
Growth Openings in past
year 50; percentage
growth 100%
Contact
Dr. Edwin E. Catmull,
Ph.D., President/CEO
Tel 510-236-4000
Fax 510-236-0388

Plant Equipment, Inc.
28075 Diaz Rd.
Temecula, CA 92590

Founded 1967
Total employees 275
Industry
Telecommunications
Growth Openings in past
year 25; percentage
growth 10%
Contact
Tim Fuller, President
Tel 909-676-4802
Fax 909-676-9651

Platinum Software Corp.
15615 Alton Pkwy., Suite
300
Irvine, CA 92718

Founded 1987
Total employees 500
Annual sales $38.6 million
Industry Computer
Software
Growth Openings in past
year 199; percentage
growth 66%
Contact
Gerald Blackie, President/
CEO
Tel 714-727-1250
Fax 714-727-1255

Plexcom, Inc.
2255 Agate Ct.
Simi Valley, CA 93065

Founded 1980
Total employees 85
Annual sales $20 million

Industries Photonics, Subassemblies and Components, Test and Measurement, Telecommunications
Growth Openings in past year 30; percentage growth 54%
Contact
Alan Pocrass, President
Tel 805-522-3333
Fax 805-583-4764

Primary Access Corp.
10080 Carroll Canyon Rd.
San Diego, CA 92131

Founded 1988
Total employees 100
Annual sales $24 million
Industries Computer Software, Telecommunications
Growth Openings in past year 30; percentage growth 42%
Contact
William R. Stensrud, President/CEO
Tel 619-536-3000
Fax 619-693-8829

Printrak International, Inc.
1250 North Tustin Ave.
Anaheim, CA 92807

Founded 1981
Total employees 225
Annual sales $37 million
Industry Computer Hardware
Growth Openings in past year 25; percentage growth 12%
Contact
Ms. Karen Hunter, Director of Personnel
Tel 714-666-2700
Fax 714-666-1055

Prism Solutions, Inc.
480 Oakmead Pkwy.
Sunnyvale, CA 94086

Founded 1991
Total employees 60
Annual sales $6.9 million
Industry Computer Software
Growth Openings in past year 30; percentage growth 100%

Contact
Jim Ashbrook, President
Tel 408-481-0240
Fax 408-481-0260

Pro-Log Corp.
2555 Garden Rd.
Monterey, CA 93940

Founded 1972
Total employees 140
Annual sales $20 million
Industries Computer Hardware, Computer Software, Factory Automation
Growth Openings in past year 15; percentage growth 12%
Contact
Dr. Richard McClellan, Ph.D., President/CEO
Tel 408-372-4593
Fax 408-646-3517

Pyxis Corp.
9380 Carroll Park Dr.
San Diego, CA 92121

Founded 1985
Total employees 212
Annual sales $46.3 million
Industries Computer Hardware, Medical
Growth Openings in past year 92; percentage growth 76%
Contact
Ronald Taylor, COB/CEO
Tel 619-625-3300
Fax 619-625-3310

qad.inc
6450 Via Real
Carpinteria, CA 93013

Founded 1979
Total employees 320
Annual sales $37 million
Industry Computer Software
Growth Openings in past year 110; percentage growth 52%
Contact
Ms. Pamela Lopker, President
Tel 805-684-6614
Fax 805-684-1890

Quadrex Corp., Engineering and Operations Division
1700 Dell Ave.
Campbell, CA 95008

Founded 1969
Total employees 40
Annual sales $12 million
Industries Energy, Manufacturing Equipment
Growth Openings in past year 15; percentage growth 60%
Contact
Scott Darling, VP of Western Region
Tel 408-866-4510
Fax 408-370-4391

Qualimetrics, Inc.
1165 National Dr.
Sacramento, CA 95834

Founded 1977
Total employees 85
Annual sales $9.1 million
Industry Energy
Growth Openings in past year 17; percentage growth 25%
Contact
Dick Beck, President
Tel 916-928-1000
Fax 916-928-1165

Quantum Group, Inc.
11211 Sorrento Valley Rd., Suite D
San Diego, CA 92121

Founded 1982
Total employees 35
Annual sales $2.2 million
Industries Advanced Materials, Test and Measurement
Growth Openings in past year 16; percentage growth 84%
Contact
Mark K. Goldstein, President
Tel 619-457-3048
Fax 619-457-3229

Quarterdeck Office Systems, Inc.
150 Pico Blvd.
Santa Monica, CA 90405

Founded 1982
Total employees 238
Annual sales $44.94 million

Industry Computer
Software
Growth Openings in past
year 48; percentage
growth 25%
Contact
Ms. Therese E. Myers,
President/CEO/CFO
Tel 310-392-9851
Fax 310-314-4218

Quidel Corp.
10165 McKellar Ct.
San Diego, CA 92121

Founded 1982
Total employees 300
Annual sales $27.7 million
Industry Medical
Growth Openings in past
year 50; percentage
growth 20%
Contact
Darryll Getzlaff, VP of
Human Resources
Tel 619-552-1100
Fax 619-546-8955

**R. Howard Strasbaugh,
Inc.**
825 Buckley Rd.
San Luis Obispo, CA
93401

Founded 1948
Total employees 90
Annual sales $15 million
Industries Factory
Automation, Test and
Measurement
Growth Openings in past
year 20; percentage
growth 28%
Contact
Larry H. Strasbaugh,
President
Tel 805-541-6424
Fax 805-541-6425

**RAD Network Devices,
Inc.**
3505 Cadillac Ave.
Costa Mesa, CA 92626

Founded 1986
Total employees 160
Annual sales $22 million
Industry
Telecommunications
Growth Openings in past
year 60; percentage
growth 60%

Contact
Thomas B. Martin,
President
Tel 714-436-9700
Fax 714-436-1941

Radio Mail Corp.
2600 Campus Dr.
San Mateo, CA 94403

Founded 1992
Total employees 40
Annual sales $5.5 million
Industry
Telecommunications
Growth Openings in past
year 25; percentage
growth 166%
Contact
Alan Beringsmith, Chief
Operating Officer
Tel 415-286-7800
Fax 415-286-7801

**Rainbow Technologies,
Inc.**
9292 Jeronimo Rd.
Irvine, CA 92718

Founded 1983
Total employees 130
Annual sales $28 million
Industries Computer
Hardware, Computer
Software
Growth Openings in past
year 35; percentage
growth 36%
Contact
Walter Straub, President
Tel 714-454-2100
Fax 714-454-8557

Ramtek Corp.
810 West Maude Ave.
Sunnyvale, CA 94086

Founded 1971
Total employees 80
Annual sales $16 million
Industry Holding
Companies
Growth Openings in past
year 15; percentage
growth 23%
Contact
Billy Finley, President/
CEO/CFO
Tel 408-522-1310
Fax 408-733-5987

Rasna Corp.
2590 North 1st St., Suite
200
San Jose, CA 95131

Founded 1987
Total employees 110
Annual sales $12 million
Industry Computer
Software
Growth Openings in past
year 50; percentage
growth 83%
Contact
Steven J. Wong, VP of
Finance/CFO
Tel 408-922-6833
Fax 408-922-7256

Raster Graphics, Inc.
285 North Wolfe Rd.
Sunnyvale, CA 94086

Founded 1987
Total employees 75
Annual sales $12 million
Industry Computer
Hardware
Growth Openings in past
year 25; percentage
growth 50%
Contact
Rak Kumar, President/
CEO
Tel 408-738-7800
Fax 408-749-0544

RasterOps Corp.
2500 Walsh Ave.
Santa Clara, CA 95051

Founded 1987
Total employees 321
Annual sales $100.02
million
Industries Computer
Hardware, Holding
Companies, Photonics
Growth Openings in past
year 42; percentage
growth 15%
Contact
Kieth E. Sorenson,
COB/CEO
Tel 408-562-4200
Fax 408-562-4066

Rational
3320 Scott Blvd.
Santa Clara, CA 95054

Founded 1981
Total employees 340
Annual sales $39 million
Industry Computer
Software

Growth Openings in past
year 20; percentage
growth 6%
Contact
Burr Gibbons, Director of
Human Resources
Tel 408-496-3600
Fax 408-496-3636

Raytek, Inc.
1201 Shaffer Rd.
Santa Cruz, CA 95060

Founded 1963
Total employees 90
Annual sales $10 million
Industry Test and
Measurement
Growth Openings in past
year 25; percentage
growth 38%
Contact
Steve Mangelsen, VP of
Finance
Tel 408-458-1110
Fax 408-458-1239

Real Time Solutions, Inc.
831 D Latour Ct.
Napa, CA 94559

Founded 1987
Total employees 55
Industries Computer
Hardware, Computer
Software
Growth Openings in past
year 20; percentage
growth 57%
Contact
William Dixon, President
Tel 707-252-5300
Fax 707-224-0585

**Recognition
International, Inc.,
Software Division**
1310 Chesapeake Terr.
Sunnyvale, CA 94089

Founded 1980
Total employees 150
Annual sales $17 million
Industry Computer
Software
Growth Openings in past
year 50; percentage
growth 50%
Contact
Ms. Joanne Anderson,
Human Resources
Manager
Tel 408-747-1210
Fax 408-747-1245

**Recom Technologies,
Inc.**
1245 South Winchester
Blvd., Suite 201
San Jose, CA 95128

Founded 1980
Total employees 300
Industry Computer
Software
Growth Openings in past
year 89; percentage
growth 42%
Contact
Jack G. Lee, President
Tel 408-261-7688
Fax 408-261-7699

Red Brick Systems
485 Alberto Way
Los Gatos, CA 95032

Founded 1986
Total employees 52
Annual sales $6.0 million
Industry Computer
Software
Growth Openings in past
year 19; percentage
growth 57%
Contact
Robert Hausmann, Vice
President/CFO
Tel 408-399-3200
Fax 408-399-3277

Resumix, Inc.
2953 Bunker Hill Ln., 3rd
Floor
Santa Clara, CA 95054

Founded 1988
Total employees 100
Annual sales $11 million
Industry Computer
Software
Growth Openings in past
year 30; percentage
growth 42%
Contact
Stephen Ciesinski,
President
Tel 408-988-0444
Fax 408-727-9893

RFI Enterprises, Inc.
360 Turtle Creek Ct.
San Jose, CA 95125

Founded 1979
Total employees 206
Industry Holding
Companies
Growth Openings in past
year 16; percentage
growth 8%

Contact
Lawrence L. Reece,
President
Tel 408-298-5400
Fax 408-275-0156

RGB Systems, Inc.
13554 Larwin Cir.
Santa Fe Springs, CA
90670

Founded 1983
Total employees 98
Annual sales $13 million
Industry
Telecommunications
Growth Openings in past
year 48; percentage
growth 96%
Contact
Ms. Betty Werbung,
Personnel Manager
Tel 310-802-8804
Fax 310-802-2741

Rhetorex, Inc.
200 East Hacienda Ave.
Campbell, CA 95008

Founded 1988
Total employees 55
Annual sales $9.0 million
Industry Computer
Hardware
Growth Openings in past
year 20; percentage
growth 57%
Contact
Allan Wokas, President
Tel 408-370-0881
Fax 408-370-1171

Ross Systems, Inc.
555 Twin Dolphin Dr.
Redwood City, CA 94065

Founded 1972
Total employees 685
Annual sales $87.1 million
Industries Computer
Hardware, Computer
Software, Holding
Companies
Growth Openings in past
year 45; percentage
growth 7%
Contact
Selby Little, CFO/
Secretary/VP of Finance
and Administ
Tel 415-593-2500
Fax 415-592-9364

SafetyTek Corporation
49050 Milmont Dr.
Fremont, CA 94538

Founded 1987
Total employees 175
Annual sales $19 million
Industry Holding
Companies
Growth Openings in past
year 45; percentage
growth 34%
Contact
James B. Hawkins,
President
Tel 510-226-9600
Fax 510-226-1112

Sanmina Corp.
2121 O'Toole Ave.
San Jose, CA 95131

Founded 1980
Total employees 640
Annual sales $88.5 million
Industries Computer
Hardware, Holding
Companies,
Subassemblies and
Components
Growth Openings in past
year 112; percentage
growth 21%
Contact
Jure Sola, President
Tel 408-435-8444
Fax 408-435-1401

**SANYO Video
Components.] Corp.**
2001 Sanyo Ave.
San Diego, CA 92173

Founded 1981
Total employees 590
Annual sales $57 million
Industry Subassemblies
and Components
Growth Openings in past
year 68; percentage
growth 13%
Contact
M. Konno, President
Tel 619-661-6322
Fax 619-661-1055

**Satellite Technology
Management, Inc.**
3530 Highland Ave.
Costa Mesa, CA 92626

Founded 1982
Total employees 96
Annual sales $19 million
Industry
Telecommunications

Growth Openings in past
year 26; percentage
growth 37%
Contact
Emil Youssefzadeh,
President/CEO
Tel 714-557-2400
Fax 714-557-4239

**Scantibodies
Laboratories, Inc.**
9336 Abraham Way
Santee, CA 92071

Founded 1977
Total employees 102
Annual sales $9.8 million
Industry Biotechnology
Growth Openings in past
year 32; percentage
growth 45%
Contact
Tom Cantor, President
Tel 619-258-9300
Fax 619-258-9366

**Science Applications
International Corp., S.A.I
Technology Division**
10240 Sorrento Valley Rd.,
Suite 100
San Diego, CA 92121

Founded 1975
Total employees 500
Annual sales $120 million
Industries Computer
Hardware, Defense
Growth Openings in past
year 50; percentage
growth 11%
Contact
Roger Garrett, President
Tel 619-452-9150
Fax 619-450-3800

**Scientific Technologies
Inc.**
31069 Genstar Rd.
Hayward, CA 94544

Founded 1971
Total employees 145
Annual sales $12.68
million
Industries Factory
Automation, Photonics,
Subassemblies and
Components, Test and
Measurement,
Transportation
Growth Openings in past
year 30; percentage
growth 26%

Contact
Ms. Brooke Lazzara,
Human Resources
Manager
Tel 510-471-9717
Fax 510-471-9752

**Sequana Therapeutics,
Inc.**
11099 North Torrey Pines
Rd.
La Jolla, CA 92037

Founded 1993
Total employees 30
Industry Medical
Growth Openings in past
year 28; percentage
growth 1400%
Contact
Ken Kinsella, COB/CEO/
President
Tel 619-452-6550
Fax 619-452-6653

Serra Corp.
4841 Davenport Pl.
Fremont, CA 94538

Founded 1979
Total employees 300
Industries Holding
Companies,
Manufacturing Equipment
Growth Openings in past
year 20; percentage
growth 7%
Contact
Gary Izad, General
Manager
Tel 510-651-7333
Fax 510-657-5860

Sherpa Corp.
611 River Oaks Pkwy.
San Jose, CA 95134

Founded 1984
Total employees 145
Annual sales $16 million
Industry Computer
Software
Growth Openings in past
year 25; percentage
growth 20%
Contact
Tom Shanahan, VP of
Finance/CFO
Tel 408-433-0455
Fax 408-943-9507

SHURflo Pump Manufacturing Co.
12650 Westminster Ave.
Santa Ana, CA 92706

Founded 1970
Total employees 380
Annual sales $37 million
Industry Subassemblies and Components
Growth Openings in past year 53; percentage growth 16%
Contact
John Casey, President
Tel 714-554-7709
Fax 714-554-4721

Siemens Medical Systems, Inc., Oncology Care Systems
4040 Nelson Ave.
Concord, CA 94520

Founded 1974
Total employees 450
Annual sales $49 million
Industries Computer Software, Medical, Test and Measurement
Growth Openings in past year 110; percentage growth 32%
Contact
Karl Haug, VP of Business and Administration
Tel 510-246-8200
Fax 510-246-8284

Sierra Semiconductor Corp.
2075 North Capital Ave.
San Jose, CA 95132

Founded 1984
Total employees 350
Annual sales $95 million
Industry Subassemblies and Components
Growth Openings in past year 20; percentage growth 6%
Contact
James V. Diller, President
Tel 408-263-9300
Fax 408-263-3337

Smartflex Systems, Inc.
14312 Franklin Ave.
Tustin, CA 92680

Founded 1985
Total employees 560
Annual sales $67 million
Industry Subassemblies and Components

Growth Openings in past year 259; percentage growth 86%
Contact
Ms. Sherrie Suskie, Director of Human Resources
Tel 714-838-8737
Fax 714-573-6918

Smith Micro Software, Inc.
51 Columbia
Aliso Viejo, CA 92656

Founded 1983
Total employees 75
Annual sales $20 million
Industry Computer Software
Growth Openings in past year 23; percentage growth 44%
Contact
William W. Smith, Jr., President
Tel 714-362-5800
Fax 714-362-2300

Solectek Corp.
6370 Nancy Ridge Dr., Suite 109
San Diego, CA 92121

Founded 1990
Total employees 50
Annual sales $6.9 million
Industry Telecommunications
Growth Openings in past year 20; percentage growth 66%
Contact
James DeBello, President/CEO
Tel 619-450-1220
Fax 619-457-2681

Solitec, Inc.
3901 Burton Dr.
Santa Clara, CA 95054

Founded 1970
Total employees 75
Annual sales $25 million
Industry Holding Companies
Growth Openings in past year 25; percentage growth 50%
Contact
Ms. Marcella Wells, Director of Human Resources
Tel 408-980-1355
Fax 408-980-9230

South Bay Circuits, Inc.
3620 Charter Park Dr.
San Jose, CA 95136

Founded 1981
Total employees 480
Annual sales $46 million
Industries Computer Hardware, Subassemblies and Components
Growth Openings in past year 40; percentage growth 9%
Contact
Roland Satterlee, President
Tel 408-978-8992
Fax 408-723-0916

Sparta, Inc.
23041 Ave. de la Carlota, Suite 400
Laguna Hills, CA 92653

Founded 1979
Total employees 600
Annual sales $79 million
Industries Defense, Holding Companies
Growth Openings in past year 100; percentage growth 20%
Contact
Wayne Winton, President/CEO
Tel 714-768-8161
Fax 714-583-9113

Specialty Laboratories, Inc.
2211 Michigan Ave.
Santa Monica, CA 90404

Founded 1977
Total employees 300
Annual sales $33 million
Industry Medical
Growth Openings in past year 50; percentage growth 20%
Contact
Dr. James B. Peter, MD, Ph.D, President
Tel 310-828-6543
Fax 310-828-6634

SSE Telecom, Inc.
47823 Westinghouse Dr.
Fremont, CA 94539

Founded 1986
Total employees 200
Annual sales $23.4 million
Industry Holding Companies

Growth Openings in past year 20; percentage growth 11%
Contact
Frank Trumbower, President
Tel 510-657-7552
Fax 510-490-8501

ST Microwave (California) Corp.
955 Benicia Ave.
Sunnyvale, CA 94086

Founded 1967
Total employees 228
Industries Subassemblies and Components, Telecommunications
Growth Openings in past year 19; percentage growth 9%
Contact
Gene Joles, President
Tel 408-730-6300
Fax 408-733-0254

Stanford Telecommunications, Inc.
1221 Crossman Ave.
Sunnyvale, CA 94089

Founded 1973
Total employees 925
Annual sales $92 million
Industries Defense, Holding Companies, Subassemblies and Components, Telecommunications, Transportation
Growth Openings in past year 45; percentage growth 5%
Contact
Ms. Cher Forman, Personnel Director
Tel 408-745-0818
Fax 408-745-7756

State Of The Art, Inc.
56 Technology Dr.
Irvine, CA 92718

Founded 1981
Total employees 215
Annual sales $21.6 million
Industry Computer Software
Growth Openings in past year 65; percentage growth 43%

Contact
David S. Samuels, President/CEO
Tel 714-753-1222
Fax 714-753-0374

Statek Corp.
512 North Main St.
Orange, CA 92668

Founded 1970
Total employees 170
Industries Advanced Materials, Test and Measurement
Growth Openings in past year 20; percentage growth 13%
Contact
Brian McCarthy, Executive VP of Finance
Tel 714-639-7810
Fax 714-997-1256

Strategic Mapping, Inc.
3135 Kifer Rd.
Santa Clara, CA 95051

Founded 1983
Total employees 200
Annual sales $25 million
Industry Computer Software
Growth Openings in past year 100; percentage growth 100%
Contact
Stephen Poizner, President
Tel 408-970-9600
Fax 408-970-9999

Structural Integrity Associates, Inc.
3150 Almaden Expwy., Suite 145
San Jose, CA 95118

Founded 1983
Total employees 78
Industries Computer Software, Energy
Growth Openings in past year 28; percentage growth 56%
Contact
Peter Riccardella, President
Tel 408-978-8200

SunDisk Corp.
3270 Jay St.
Santa Clara, CA 95054

Founded 1988
Total employees 120

Annual sales $19 million
Industry Computer Hardware
Growth Openings in past year 20; percentage growth 20%
Contact
Dr. Eli Harari, CEO/ President
Tel 408-562-0500
Fax 408-980-8607

Sunrise Medical Inc., Quickie Designs
2842 Business Park Ave.
Fresno, CA 93727

Founded 1983
Total employees 500
Annual sales $55 million
Industry Medical
Growth Openings in past year 91; percentage growth 22%
Contact
Dave Lauger, Director of Human Resources
Tel 209-292-2171
Fax 209-292-7412

Supercom, Inc.
410 South Abbott Ave.
Milpitas, CA 95035

Founded 1983
Total employees 135
Annual sales $120 million
Industries Computer Hardware, Holding Companies
Growth Openings in past year 35; percentage growth 35%
Contact
Ms. Beverly Sato, Personnel Manager
Tel 408-456-8888
Fax 408-263-1234

SuperMac Technology, Inc.
215 Moffett Park Dr.
Sunnyvale, CA 94089

Founded 1985
Total employees 400
Annual sales $125.02 million
Industries Computer Hardware, Computer Software
Growth Openings in past year 59; percentage growth 17%

Contact
Lawrence W. Finch,
  COB/CEO
Tel 408-541-6106
Fax 408-541-6150

Sutter Corporation
9425 Chesapeake Dr.
San Diego, CA 92123
Founded 1980
Total employees 300
Industry Medical
Growth Openings in past
  year 50; percentage
  growth 20%
Contact
Timothy Wollaeger,
  President/CEO
Tel 619-569-8148
Fax 619-279-8249

Sync Research, Inc.
7 Studebaker
Irvine, CA 92718
Founded 1978
Total employees 88
Annual sales $20 million
Industries Computer
  Hardware, Computer
  Software
Growth Openings in past
  year 38; percentage
  growth 76%
Contact
John Rademaker, COB/
  President/CEO
Tel 714-588-2070
Fax 714-588-2080

Synopsys, Inc.
700 East Middlefield Rd.
Mountain View, CA 94043
Founded 1986
Total employees 550
Annual sales $63 million
Industry Computer
  Software
Growth Openings in past
  year 149; percentage
  growth 37%
Contact
Ms. Tricia Tomlinson,
  Director of Human
  Resources
Tel 415-962-5000
Fax 415-965-8637

SyStemix, Inc.
3155 Porter Dr.
Palo Alto, CA 94304
Founded 1988
Total employees 210

Annual sales $5.2 million
Industries Biotechnology,
  Pharmaceuticals
Growth Openings in past
  year 62; percentage
  growth 41%
Contact
Ms. Linda Sonntag, Ph.D.,
  President/CEO
Tel 415-856-4901
Fax 415-856-4919

**T&R Communications,
Inc.**
1411 South Milpitas Blvd.
Milpitas, CA 95035
Founded 1982
Total employees 80
Industries Computer
  Hardware, Holding
  Companies,
  Telecommunications
Growth Openings in past
  year 30; percentage
  growth 60%
Contact
Russell Hayslip, President
Tel 408-945-5700
Fax 408-945-2910

**Tanon Manufacturing,
Inc.**
46360 Fremont Blvd.
Fremont, CA 94538
Founded 1982
Total employees 335
Annual sales $40 million
Industries Computer
  Hardware, Manufacturing
  Equipment,
  Subassemblies and
  Components
Growth Openings in past
  year 34; percentage
  growth 11%
Contact
Ms. Sherry Inselman,
  Personnel Manager
Tel 510-249-5100
Fax 510-249-5197

Tekelec
26580 West Agoura Rd.
Calabasas, CA 91302
Founded 1979
Total employees 360
Annual sales $58.1 million
Industry Factory
  Automation
Growth Openings in past
  year 30; percentage
  growth 9%

Contact
Peter N. Vicars, President/
  CEO
Tel 818-880-5656
Fax 818-880-6993

Telebit Corp.
1315 Chesapeake Terr.
Sunnyvale, CA 94089
Founded 1984
Total employees 225
Annual sales $64 million
Industry
  Telecommunications
Growth Openings in past
  year 30; percentage
  growth 15%
Contact
Jamed D. Narrod,
  Chairman of the Board
Tel 408-734-4333
Fax 408-734-3333

Tencor Instruments
2400 Charleston Rd.
Mountain View, CA 94043
Founded 1976
Total employees 400
Annual sales $72.14
  million
Industries Factory
  Automation, Holding
  Companies
Growth Openings in past
  year 23; percentage
  growth 6%
Contact
Ms. Cynthia Dooley,
  Manager of Human
  Resources
Tel 415-969-6767
Fax 415-969-6371

**Teradyne, Inc.,
Semiconductor Test
Division**
30801 Agoura Rd.
Agoura Hills, CA 91301
Founded 1970
Total employees 650
Annual sales $82 million
Industry Factory
  Automation
Growth Openings in past
  year 19; percentage
  growth 3%
Contact
Jerry Cellner, Personnel
  Manager
Tel 818-991-2900

Terrapin Technologies, Inc.
750-H Gateway Blvd.
South San Francisco, CA 94080

Founded 1986
Total employees 28
Industries Biotechnology, Medical
Growth Openings in past year 16; percentage growth 133%
Contact
Renaldo Gomez, President/CEO
Tel 415-244-9303
Fax 415-244-9388

Tetra Tech, Inc.
670 North Rosemead Blvd.
Pasadena, CA 91107

Founded 1966
Total employees 570
Annual sales $65 million
Industries Environmental, Manufacturing Equipment
Growth Openings in past year 38; percentage growth 7%
Contact
Rich Lemmon, Personnel Manager
Tel 818-449-6400
Fax 818-351-8126

Thermoscan, Inc.
10309 Pacific Center Ct.
San Diego, CA 92121

Founded 1984
Total employees 110
Industry Medical
Growth Openings in past year 50; percentage growth 83%
Contact
John Trenary, President
Tel 619-556-2100
Fax 619-535-9784

TIW Systems, Inc.
1284 Geneva Dr.
Sunnyvale, CA 94089

Founded 1976
Total employees 125
Annual sales $25 million
Industries Computer Hardware, Telecommunications
Growth Openings in past year 19; percentage growth 17%

Contact
Dr. Rein Luik, President
Tel 408-734-3900
Fax 408-734-9012

TopoMetrix Corp.
5403 Betsy Ross Dr.
Santa Clara, CA 95054

Founded 1990
Total employees 65
Industries Factory Automation, Photonics
Growth Openings in past year 20; percentage growth 44%
Contact
Dr. Gary Aden, President/CEO
Tel 408-982-9700
Fax 408-982-9751

Toshiba America Electronic Components, Inc., Microelectronics Center
1220 Midas Way
Sunnyvale, CA 94086

Founded 1980
Total employees 325
Annual sales $75 million
Industry Subassemblies and Components
Growth Openings in past year 35; percentage growth 12%
Contact
Katsuhiro Kawabuchi, Senior Vice President/General Manager
Tel 408-739-0560
Fax 408-746-0577

Triconex Corp.
15091 Bake Pkwy.
Irvine, CA 92718

Founded 1983
Total employees 200
Annual sales $29 million
Industries Factory Automation, Holding Companies
Growth Openings in past year 75; percentage growth 60%
Contact
William Barkovitz, President/COB
Tel 714-768-3709
Fax 714-768-6601

Trident Data Systems, Inc.
5933 West Century Blvd., Suite 700
Los Angeles, CA 90045

Founded 1975
Total employees 640
Industries Computer Hardware, Computer Software
Growth Openings in past year 159; percentage growth 33%
Contact
Ms. Scherri Pearson, Personnel Manager
Tel 310-645-6483
Fax 310-670-5121

Trident Microsystems
205 Ravendale Dr.
Mountain View, CA 94043

Founded 1987
Total employees 114
Annual sales $67 million
Industries Computer Hardware, Computer Software
Growth Openings in past year 20; percentage growth 21%
Contact
Frank C. Lin, COB/President/CEO
Tel 415-691-9211
Fax 415-691-9260

Twinhead Corp.
1537 Centre Point Dr.
Milpitas, CA 95035

Founded 1986
Total employees 60
Annual sales $40 million
Industry Computer Hardware
Growth Openings in past year 15; percentage growth 33%
Contact
Clark Fan, President
Tel 408-945-0808
Fax 408-945-1080

Tylan General
9577 Chesapeake Dr.
San Diego, CA 92123

Founded 1977
Total employees 250
Annual sales $29 million
Industry Test and Measurement

Growth Openings in past year 25; percentage growth 11%
Contact
Michael Chick, Director of Administration
Tel 619-571-1222
Fax 619-576-1703

UDT Sensors, Inc.
12525 Chadron Ave.
Hawthorne, CA 90250

Founded 1956
Total employees 300
Industries Factory Automation, Photonics, Subassemblies and Components, Test and Measurement
Growth Openings in past year 86; percentage growth 40%
Contact
Mrs. Verna Jacobs, Personnel Manager
Tel 310-978-0516
Fax 310-644-1727

Ultra Clean Technology
150 Independence Dr.
Menlo Park, CA 94025

Founded 1991
Total employees 20
Industry Manufacturing Equipment
Growth Openings in past year 16; percentage growth 400%
Contact
H. Kobayashi, President
Tel 415-323-4100
Fax 415-323-7159

Ultratech Stepper
3050 Zanker Rd.
San Jose, CA 95134

Founded 1981
Total employees 400
Annual sales $43 million
Industry Manufacturing Equipment
Growth Openings in past year 50; percentage growth 14%
Contact
Robert Weston, VP of Human Resources
Tel 408-321-8835
Fax 408-577-3376

Uniphase Corporation
163 Baypointe Pkwy.
San Jose, CA 95134

Founded 1979
Total employees 220
Annual sales $28 million
Industry Holding Companies
Growth Openings in past year 20; percentage growth 10%
Contact
Charles D. Rider, Human Resources Director
Tel 408-434-1800
Fax 408-433-3838

Unisyn Technologies, Inc.
14272 Franklin Ave.
Tustin, CA 92680

Founded 1990
Total employees 60
Industries Biotechnology, Test and Measurement
Growth Openings in past year 20; percentage growth 50%
Contact
Peter Savas, CEO/President
Tel 714-544-4035
Fax 714-544-0322

Ventritex, Inc.
701 East Evelyn Ave.
Sunnyvale, CA 94086

Founded 1985
Total employees 474
Annual sales $25 million
Industries Computer Hardware, Medical
Growth Openings in past year 73; percentage growth 18%
Contact
Frank Fischer, CEO/President
Tel 408-738-4883
Fax 408-735-8750

Verity, Inc.
1550 Plymouth St.
Mountain View, CA 94043

Founded 1988
Total employees 150
Annual sales $17 million
Industry Computer Software
Growth Openings in past year 40; percentage growth 36%

Contact
Ms. Loraine Sanford, Manager of Human Resources
Tel 415-960-7600
Fax 415-960-7698

Vertex Semiconductor Corp.
1060 Rincon Cir.
San Jose, CA 95131

Founded 1984
Total employees 133
Industry Subassemblies and Components
Growth Openings in past year 33; percentage growth 33%
Contact
Bruce Bourbon, President/CEO
Tel 408-456-8900
Fax 408-456-8910

Vestar, Inc.
650 Cliffside Dr.
San Dimas, CA 91773

Founded 1981
Total employees 150
Annual sales $30.28 million
Industries Biotechnology, Pharmaceuticals
Growth Openings in past year 50; percentage growth 50%
Contact
Dr. Roger J. Crossley, COB/President/CEO
Tel 909-394-4000
Fax 909-592-8530

ViaSat, Inc.
2290 Cosmos Ct.
Carlsbad, CA 92009

Founded 1986
Total employees 90
Annual sales $5 million
Industries Computer Software, Factory Automation, Telecommunications
Growth Openings in past year 45; percentage growth 100%
Contact
Mark Dankberg, President
Tel 619-438-8099
Fax 619-438-8499

ViewStar Corp.
5820 Shellmound St.
Emeryville, CA 94608

Founded 1986
Total employees 230
Annual sales $26 million
Industry Computer
 Software
Growth Openings in past
 year 100; percentage
 growth 76%
Contact
Phil Johnston, VP of
 Personnel
Tel 510-652-7827
Fax 510-653-9926

**Virgin Interactive
Entertainment**
18061 Fitch Ave.
Irvine, CA 92714

Founded 1983
Total employees 200
Industry Computer
 Software
Growth Openings in past
 year 100; percentage
 growth 100%
Contact
Martin Alper, President
Tel 714-833-8710
Fax 714-833-8717

VISX, Inc.
3400 Centeral Expwy.
Santa Clara, CA 95051

Founded 1987
Total employees 120
Annual sales $13 million
Industry Medical
Growth Openings in past
 year 50; percentage
 growth 71%
Contact
Dr. Charles R. Munnerlyn,
 COB/CEO
Tel 408-733-2020
Fax 408-733-0227

VMX, Inc.
2115 O'Nel Dr.
San Jose, CA 95131

Founded 1978
Total employees 575
Annual sales $91 million
Industries Holding
 Companies,
 Telecommunications
Growth Openings in past
 year 92; percentage
 growth 19%

Contact
Patrick S. Howard,
 President/CEO
Tel 408-441-1144
Fax 408-451-2000

Voysys, Inc.
2540 Junction Ave.
San Jose, CA 95134

Founded 1987
Total employees 70
Annual sales $17 million
Industries Computer
 Hardware, Computer
 Software,
 Telecommunications
Growth Openings in past
 year 15; percentage
 growth 27%
Contact
Donald Heitt, President
Tel 408-954-9500
Fax 408-954-9501

Western Multiplex Corp.
300 Harbor Blvd.
Belmont, CA 94002

Founded 1980
Total employees 75
Industry
 Telecommunications
Growth Openings in past
 year 30; percentage
 growth 66%
Contact
John Woods, President/
 CEO
Tel 415-592-8832
Fax 415-592-4249

Wind River Systems
1010 Atlantic Ave.
Alameda, CA 94501

Founded 1981
Total employees 160
Annual sales $25 million
Industry Computer
 Software
Growth Openings in past
 year 30; percentage
 growth 23%
Contact
Wally Breitman, Director of
 Personnel
Tel 510-748-4100
Fax 510-814-2010

Wireless Access, Inc.
125 Nicholson Ln.
San Jose, CA 95134

Founded 1992
Total employees 40

Annual sales $5.5 million
Industry
 Telecommunications
Growth Openings in past
 year 20; percentage
 growth 100%
Contact
Ms. Judy Owen, President
Tel 408-383-1900
Fax 408-383-0503

Wollongong Group, Inc.
1129 San Antonio Rd., PO
 Box 51860
Palo Alto, CA 94303

Founded 1980
Total employees 250
Annual sales $29 million
Industry Computer
 Software
Growth Openings in past
 year 60; percentage
 growth 31%
Contact
Noel O. Kile, COB/CEO
Tel 415-962-7100
Fax 415-969-5547

Wonderware Corp.
100 Technology Dr.
Irvine, CA 92718

Founded 1987
Total employees 100
Annual sales $11.3 million
Industry Computer
 Software
Growth Openings in past
 year 54; percentage
 growth 117%
Contact
Dennis Morin, COB/CEO/
 President
Tel 714-727-3200
Fax 714-727-3270

Xircom, Inc.
26025 Mureau Rd.
Calabasas, CA 91302

Founded 1988
Total employees 200
Annual sales $48 million
Industry
 Telecommunications
Growth Openings in past
 year 75; percentage
 growth 60%
Contact
Dirk Gates, President
Tel 818-878-7100
Fax 818-878-7630

Xontech, Inc.
6862 Hayvenhurst Ave.
Van Nuys, CA 91406

Founded 1970
Total employees 300
Annual sales $38 million
Industries Defense,
Environmental
Growth Openings in past
year 25; percentage
growth 9%
Contact
Kenneth Schultz,
President
Tel 818-787-7380
Fax 818-786-4275

Yardi Systems, Inc.
819 Reddick St.
Santa Barbara, CA 93103

Founded 1982
Total employees 62
Annual sales $7.1 million
Industry Computer
Software
Growth Openings in past
year 22; percentage
growth 55%
Contact
Anant Yardi, President
Tel 805-966-3666
Fax 805-963-3155

Young Minds, Inc.
1910 Orange Tree Ln.,
Suite 300
Redlands, CA 92374

Founded 1989
Total employees 68
Annual sales $7.8 million
Industry Computer
Software
Growth Openings in past
year 43; percentage
growth 172%
Contact
Dave Cote, Chief
Executive Officer
Tel 909-335-1350
Fax 909-798-0488

Zycad Corp.
47100 Bayside Pkwy.
Fremont, CA 94538

Founded 1979
Total employees 275
Annual sales $41.45
million
Industries Computer
Software, Factory
Automation, Holding
Companies

Growth Openings in past
year 34; percentage
growth 14%
Contact
Phillips W. Smith,
President/CEO
Tel 510-623-4400
Fax 510-623-4550

ZyXEL USA
4920 East La Palma Ave.
Anaheim, CA 92807

Founded 1989
Total employees 40
Annual sales $55 million
Industry
Telecommunications
Growth Openings in past
year 16; percentage
growth 66%
Contact
Gordon Yang, President
Tel 714-693-0804
Fax 714-693-8811

Colorado

Aguirre Engineers, Inc.
13276 East Fremont Pl.
Englewood, CO 80112

Founded 1977
Total employees 154
Industries Advanced
Materials, Environmental
Growth Openings in past
year 54; percentage
growth 54%
Contact
Ms. Jeanne Blackwell,
Director of Human
Resources
Tel 303-799-8378
Fax 303-799-8392

Baxa Corp.
13760 East Arapahoe Rd.
Englewood, CO 80112

Founded 1975
Total employees 125
Industries Manufacturing
Equipment, Medical,
Pharmaceuticals
Growth Openings in past
year 50; percentage
growth 66%

Contact
Ms. Heather Dackrow,
Director of Human
Resources
Tel 303-690-4204
Fax 303-690-4804

BI, Inc.
6400 Lookout Rd.
Boulder, CO 80301

Founded 1978
Total employees 200
Annual sales $24.6 million
Industry Test and
Measurement
Growth Openings in past
year 50; percentage
growth 33%
Contact
David J. Hunter, President/
CEO
Tel 303-530-2911
Fax 303-530-5349

Ciber, Inc.
1200 17th St., Suite 2700
Denver, CO 80202

Founded 1980
Total employees 600
Industry Computer
Hardware
Growth Openings in past
year 100; percentage
growth 20%
Contact
Bob Stevenson, President
Tel 303-572-6400
Fax 303-572-6405

CliniCom, Inc.
4720 Walnut St.
Boulder, CO 80301

Founded 1985
Total employees 106
Annual sales $20.15
million
Industries Computer
Hardware, Computer
Software, Medical
Growth Openings in past
year 21; percentage
growth 24%
Contact
Ms. Marcie Levine,
Director of Human
Resources
Tel 303-443-9660
Fax 303-442-4916

ConferTech International, Inc.
12110 North Pecos St.
Westminster, CO 80234

Founded 1976
Total employees 470
Annual sales $35.8 million
Industry
Telecommunications
Growth Openings in past
year 194; percentage
growth 70%
Contact
H. Robert Gill, President/
CEO
Tel 303-633-3000
Fax 303-633-3001

Cortech, Inc.
6850 North Broadway
Denver, CO 80221

Founded 1982
Total employees 125
Annual sales $4.72 million
Industry Pharmaceuticals
Growth Openings in past
year 53; percentage
growth 73%
Contact
Paul Jerde, CEO/Vice
President
Tel 303-650-1200
Fax 303-650-5023

**CTB, Columbia
Computing Services, Inc.**
8101 East Prentice Ave.
Englewood, CO 80111

Founded 1968
Total employees 72
Annual sales $8.3 million
Industry Computer
Software
Growth Openings in past
year 37; percentage
growth 105%
Contact
David Deffley, President
Tel 303-773-6440
Fax 303-773-9630

Data Storage Marketing, Inc.
5718 Central Ave.
Boulder, CO 80301

Founded 1987
Total employees 152
Annual sales $71 million
Industry Computer
Hardware

Growth Openings in past
year 39; percentage
growth 34%
Contact
Ms. Lynn Cyprian,
Personnel Manager
Tel 303-442-4747
Fax 303-442-7985

Denver Instrument Co.
6542 Fig St.
Arvada, CO 80004

Founded 1869
Total employees 180
Annual sales $21 million
Industry Test and
Measurement
Growth Openings in past
year 20; percentage
growth 12%
Contact
Scott Schuler, President
Tel 303-431-7255
Fax 303-423-4831

Electromedics, Inc.
18501 East Plaza Dr.
Parker, CO 80134

Founded 1972
Total employees 320
Annual sales $37.47
million
Industry Medical
Growth Openings in past
year 40; percentage
growth 14%
Contact
Ms. Susie Perlman,
Director of Personnel
Tel 303-840-4000

Golden Ribbon, Inc.
3075 North 75th St.
Boulder, CO 80301

Founded 1981
Total employees 90
Industry Computer
Hardware
Growth Openings in past
year 20; percentage
growth 28%
Contact
William Patterson,
President
Tel 303-443-6866

Hathaway Corp.
8700 Turnpike Dr., Suite
300
Westminster, CO 80030

Founded 1961
Total employees 658

Annual sales $45.74
million
Industry Holding
Companies
Growth Openings in past
year 13; percentage
growth 2%
Contact
Eugene E. Prince,
President/COB/CEO
Tel 303-426-1600
Fax 303-426-0932

**Hauser Chemical
Research, Inc.**
5555 Airport Blvd.
Boulder, CO 80301

Founded 1983
Total employees 375
Annual sales $59.2 million
Industry Chemicals
Growth Openings in past
year 25; percentage
growth 7%
Contact
Thomas A. Scales,
President
Tel 303-443-4662
Fax 303-441-5800

Integral Peripherals, Inc.
5775 Flatiron Pkwy., Suite
100
Boulder, CO 80301

Founded 1990
Total employees 136
Annual sales $22 million
Industry Computer
Hardware
Growth Openings in past
year 36; percentage
growth 36%
Contact
Steven B. Volk, President/
CEO
Tel 303-449-8009
Fax 303-449-8089

**Integrated Medical
Systems, Inc.**
15000 West 6th Ave.
Golden, CO 80401

Founded 1985
Total employees 125
Annual sales $14 million
Industry Computer
Software
Growth Openings in past
year 55; percentage
growth 78%

Contact
John A. McChesney,
  President
Tel 303-279-6116
Fax 303-279-0079

Jetstream Systems, Inc.
4690 Joliet St.
Denver, CO 80239

Founded 1967
Total employees 120
Annual sales $15 million
Industry Factory
  Automation
Growth Openings in past
  year 20; percentage
  growth 20%
Contact
Jeff Kipp, President
Tel 303-371-9002
Fax 303-371-9012

**Johnson Engineering
Corp.**
3055 Center Green Dr.
Boulder, CO 80301

Founded 1973
Total employees 250
Industries Computer
  Software, Defense,
  Factory Automation,
  Manufacturing
  Equipment,
  Subassemblies and
  Components,
  Transportation
Growth Openings in past
  year 50; percentage
  growth 25%
Contact
Dale R. Johnson,
  President
Tel 303-449-8152
Fax 303-444-8254

Micro Decisionware, Inc.
3335 Center Green Dr.
Boulder, CO 80301

Founded 1980
Total employees 105
Annual sales $12 million
Industry Computer
  Software
Growth Openings in past
  year 40; percentage
  growth 61%
Contact
Michael Forster, President
Tel 303-443-2706
Fax 303-443-2797

M-Mash, Inc.
6402 South Troy Cir.
Englewood, CO 80111

Founded 1984
Total employees 51
Industry Computer
  Software
Growth Openings in past
  year 16; percentage
  growth 45%
Contact
Ms. Janis Monroe,
  President
Tel 303-799-0099
Fax 303-799-1425

NBI, Inc.
1900 Pike Rd., Suite A
Longmont, CO 80501

Founded 1973
Total employees 65
Annual sales $5.88 million
Industry Computer
  Hardware
Growth Openings in past
  year 35; percentage
  growth 116%
Contact
Jay Lustig, COB/CEO
Tel 303-684-2700
Fax 303-684-2704

NSR Information, Inc.
5475 Mark Dabling Blvd.,
  Suite 200
Colorado Springs, CO
  80918

Founded 1990
Total employees 80
Annual sales $3 million
Industries Computer
  Hardware, Computer
  Software
Growth Openings in past
  year 30; percentage
  growth 60%
Contact
Tom Harman, President
Tel 719-590-8880
Fax 719-590-8983

NTI
980 Technology Ct.
Colorado Springs, CO
  80915

Founded 1973
Total employees 200
Industry Subassemblies
  and Components
Growth Openings in past
  year 50; percentage
  growth 33%

Contact
David St. Andre, Human
  Resource Manager
Tel 719-574-4900
Fax 719-574-4905

Omnipoint Corp.
7150 Campus Dr., Suite
  155
Colorado Springs, CO
  80920

Founded 1987
Total employees 50
Industry
  Telecommunications
Growth Openings in past
  year 15; percentage
  growth 42%
Contact
Doug Smith, President
Tel 719-548-1200
Fax 719-548-1393

**Otsuka Electronics USA,
Inc.**
2555 Midpoint Dr.
Fort Collins, CO 80525

Founded 1978
Total employees 182
Annual sales $21 million
Industry Test and
  Measurement
Growth Openings in past
  year 57; percentage
  growth 45%
Contact
Kenji Nakayama, COB/
  President
Tel 303-484-0428
Fax 303-484-0487

Philips LMS
4425 Arrowswest Dr.
Colorado Springs, CO
  80907

Founded 1984
Total employees 475
Industry Computer
  Hardware
Growth Openings in past
  year 110; percentage
  growth 30%
Contact
Charles D. Johnston,
  President
Tel 719-593-7900
Fax 719-599-8713

Polydyne International, Inc.
1115 Elkton Dr., Suite 100
Colorado Springs, CO 80907

Founded 1992
Total employees 28
Annual sales $6.2 million
Industry Holding Companies
Growth Openings in past year 24; percentage growth 600%
Contact
Kurt Kissmann, Chief Executive Officer
Tel 719-522-0900
Fax 719-599-0815

RUST Geotech Inc.
PO Box 14000
Grand Junction, CO 81502

Founded 1986
Total employees 825
Annual sales $88 million
Industry Environmental
Growth Openings in past year 75; percentage growth 10%
Contact
David Van Leuven, President/General Manager
Tel 303-248-6000
Fax 303-248-6040

Simon Hydro-Search
350 Indiana St., Suite 300
Golden, CO 80401

Founded 1970
Total employees 134
Annual sales $8.5 million
Industry Environmental
Growth Openings in past year 54; percentage growth 67%
Contact
Ms. Lee Wagner, Human Resource Manager
Tel 303-279-7982
Fax 303-279-7988

S.M. Stoller Corp.
5700 Flatiron Pkwy.
Boulder, CO 80301

Founded 1959
Total employees 170
Annual sales $19 million
Industries Computer Software, Energy

Growth Openings in past year 45; percentage growth 36%
Contact
Michael Raudenbush, President
Tel 303-449-7220
Fax 303-443-1408

Somatogen, Inc.
2545 Central Ave.
Boulder, CO 80301

Founded 1986
Total employees 225
Industries Medical, Pharmaceuticals
Growth Openings in past year 105; percentage growth 87%
Contact
Charles Scoggin, President
Tel 303-440-9988
Fax 303-443-7343

Soricon Corp.
5621 Arapahoe Ave.
Boulder, CO 80303

Founded 1984
Total employees 50
Annual sales $7 million
Industry Computer Hardware
Growth Openings in past year 15; percentage growth 42%
Contact
David Kempf, Chief Financial Officer
Tel 303-440-2800
Fax 303-442-2438

Spectrum Human Resources Systems Corp.
1625 Broadway, Suite 2700
Denver, CO 80202

Founded 1984
Total employees 125
Annual sales $7 million
Industry Computer Software
Growth Openings in past year 25; percentage growth 25%
Contact
James Spoor, President
Tel 303-534-8813
Fax 303-595-9970

Staodyn, Inc.
1225 Florida Ave., PO Box 1379
Longmont, CO 80502

Founded 1975
Total employees 160
Annual sales $8 million
Industry Medical
Growth Openings in past year 100; percentage growth 166%
Contact
W. Bayne Gibson, COB/ President/CEO
Tel 303-772-3631
Fax 303-651-0266

Synergen, Inc.
1885 33rd St.
Boulder, CO 80301

Founded 1981
Total employees 600
Annual sales $82 million
Industry Pharmaceuticals
Growth Openings in past year 208; percentage growth 53%
Contact
Ms. Karen Hildebrand, Director of Human Resources
Tel 303-938-6200
Fax 303-938-6268

Tomtec Imaging Systems, Inc.
100 Technology Dr., Suite 225
Broomfield, CO 80021

Founded 1993
Total employees 100
Annual sales $11 million
Industries Computer Software, Medical
Growth Openings in past year 25; percentage growth 33%
Contact
Robert Zieseri, Chief Executive Officer
Tel 303-466-9300

Vari-L Co., Inc.
11101 East 51st Ave.
Denver, CO 80239

Founded 1953
Total employees 100
Industries Subassemblies and Components, Telecommunications

Growth Openings in past year 15; percentage growth 17%
Contact
David Sherman, President/CFO
Tel 303-371-1560
Fax 303-371-0845

Wedding & Associates, Inc.
PO Box 1756
Fort Collins, CO 80522

Founded 1982
Total employees 36
Annual sales $3.8 million
Industry Environmental
Growth Openings in past year 16; percentage growth 80%
Contact
Dr. James Wedding, Ph.D., President
Tel 303-221-0678
Fax 303-221-0400

Xenometrix, Inc.
2860 Wilderness Pl., Suite 150
Boulder, CO 80301

Founded 1992
Total employees 24
Industries Biotechnology, Medical
Growth Openings in past year 19; percentage growth 380%
Contact
Spencer Farr, Ph.D., President/CEO
Tel 303-447-1773
Fax 303-447-1758

XVT Software, Inc.
4900 Pearl East Circle, PO Box 18750
Boulder, CO 80308

Founded 1988
Total employees 130
Annual sales $15 million
Industry Computer Software
Growth Openings in past year 65; percentage growth 100%
Contact
Marc Rochkind, Chief Executive Officer
Tel 303-443-4223
Fax 303-443-0969

Connecticut

ABB Power Plant Controls, Inc.
2 Waterside Crossing
Windsor, CT 06095

Founded 1984
Total employees 180
Annual sales $24 million
Industries Energy, Test and Measurement
Growth Openings in past year 30; percentage growth 20%
Contact
Ms. Nancy Waniewski, Manager of Human Resources
Tel 203-683-8781
Fax 203-285-6999

Accutron, Inc.
6 Northwood Dr.
Bloomfield, CT 06002

Founded 1989
Total employees 50
Industry Subassemblies and Components
Growth Openings in past year 20; percentage growth 66%
Contact
Vijay Faldu, President
Tel 203-243-1200
Fax 203-243-1149

Advanced Technology Materials, Inc.
7 Commerce Dr.
Danbury, CT 06810

Founded 1986
Total employees 77
Annual sales $10.3 million
Industries Advanced Materials, Holding Companies, Subassemblies and Components
Growth Openings in past year 24; percentage growth 45%
Contact
Dr. E.G. Banucci, President/CEO
Tel 203-794-1100
Fax 203-830-4116

Alexion Pharmaceuticals, Inc.
25 Science Park
New Haven, CT 06511

Founded 1992
Total employees 47
Industries Biotechnology, Medical, Pharmaceuticals
Growth Openings in past year 19; percentage growth 67%
Contact
Dr. Leonard Bell, MD, President
Tel 203-776-1790
Fax 203-772-3655

Alinabal Holdings, Corp.
28 Woodmont Rd.
Milford, CT 06460

Founded 1974
Total employees 320
Annual sales $30 million
Industries Advanced Materials, Computer Hardware, Holding Companies, Subassemblies and Components, Transportation
Growth Openings in past year 19; percentage growth 6%
Contact
Bruce M. Bickley, Director of Human Resources
Tel 203-877-3241
Fax 203-874-5063

American Lightwave Systems, Inc.
999 Research Pkwy.
Meriden, CT 06450

Founded 1977
Total employees 125
Annual sales $30 million
Industries Photonics, Telecommunications
Growth Openings in past year 55; percentage growth 78%
Contact
Dr. M. Farooque Mesiya, President/CEO
Tel 203-630-5700
Fax 203-630-5701

APEX Machine Tool Co., Inc.
21 Spring Ln.
Farmington, CT 06032

Founded 1944
Total employees 175

Annual sales $13 million
Industry Factory
Automation
Growth Openings in past
year 25; percentage
growth 16%
Contact
James G. Biondi,
President
Tel 203-677-2884
Fax 203-678-7629

**Applied Information for
Marketing, Inc.**
15 Katchum St.
Westport, CT 06880

Founded 1988
Total employees 27
Annual sales $3.1 million
Industry Computer
Software
Growth Openings in past
year 19; percentage
growth 237%
Contact
Joseph Anstey, President
Tel 203-226-0316
Fax 203-227-8969

Bio-Plexus, Inc.
PO Box 826
Tolland, CT 06084

Founded 1987
Total employees 50
Annual sales $5.5 million
Industry Medical
Growth Openings in past
year 24; percentage
growth 92%
Contact
Carl Sahi, President
Tel 203-871-8601
Fax 203-872-9108

Biosystems, Inc.
PO Box 158
Rockfall, CT 06481

Founded 1982
Total employees 80
Annual sales $6 million
Industries Environmental,
Test and Measurement
Growth Openings in past
year 15; percentage
growth 23%
Contact
John F. Burt, Jr., President
Tel 203-344-1079
Fax 203-344-1068

C&M Corp.
51 South Walnut St., PO
Box 348
Wauregan, CT 06387

Founded 1965
Total employees 500
Annual sales $48 million
Industry Subassemblies
and Components
Growth Openings in past
year 100; percentage
growth 25%
Contact
Vinnie Carminati, Director
of Human Resources
Tel 203-774-4812
Fax 203-774-7330

Centrix, Inc.
770 River Rd.
Shelton, CT 06484

Founded 1970
Total employees 60
Industry Medical
Growth Openings in past
year 20; percentage
growth 50%
Contact
Mel Drumm, President
Tel 203-878-7875
Fax 203-929-6804

CMX Systems, Inc.
135 North Plains Industrial
Rd.
Wallingford, CT 06492

Founded 1982
Total employees 38
Industries Manufacturing
Equipment, Photonics
Growth Openings in past
year 19; percentage
growth 100%
Contact
Bob Gilbertson, President
Tel 203-269-3700
Fax 203-949-1898

CNC Software, Inc.
344 Merrow Rd.
Tolland, CT 06084

Founded 1985
Total employees 50
Annual sales $5.8 million
Industry Computer
Software
Growth Openings in past
year 20; percentage
growth 66%

Contact
John D. Summers,
President
Tel 203-875-5006
Fax 203-872-1565

**Colonial Data
Technologies Corp.**
80 Pickett District Rd.
New Milford, CT 06776

Founded 1980
Total employees 80
Annual sales $9.7 million
Industry
Telecommunications
Growth Openings in past
year 20; percentage
growth 33%
Contact
Robert J. Schock,
President/CEO
Tel 203-355-3178
Fax 203-354-2392

Command Systems, Inc.
One Corporate Ctr., 15th
Floor
Hartford, CT 06103

Founded 1985
Total employees 100
Annual sales $10 million
Industry Computer
Hardware
Growth Openings in past
year 40; percentage
growth 66%
Contact
Ed Caputo, President/
Owner
Tel 203-548-0222
Fax 203-549-5039

**Coopers & Lybrand,
Solution Thru
Technology**
41 North Main St.
West Hartford, CT 06107

Founded 1967
Total employees 975
Industry Computer
Software
Growth Openings in past
year 350; percentage
growth 56%
Contact
Carl Sellberg, Managing
Partner
Tel 203-521-3284
Fax 203-561-5075

DDL OMNI Engineering Corp.
156 Cross Rd.
Waterford, CT 06385

Founded 1966
Total employees 160
Annual sales $17 million
Industries Computer
Hardware, Computer
Software, Defense,
Environmental
Growth Openings in past
year 28; percentage
growth 21%
Contact
James Schaeffer,
President/CEO
Tel 203-447-1762
Fax 203-447-3073

Diversified Technologies Corporation
556 Washington Ave.
North Haven, CT 06473

Founded 1979
Total employees 45
Industry Environmental
Growth Openings in past
year 17; percentage
growth 60%
Contact
Dr. Murali Atluru, PE,
President
Tel 203-239-4200
Fax 203-234-7376

Eyelematic Manufacturing Co., Inc.
1 Seemar Rd.
Watertown, CT 06795

Founded 1953
Total employees 250
Annual sales $27 million
Industry Manufacturing
Equipment
Growth Openings in past
year 90; percentage
growth 56%
Contact
Pete Allvin, Director of
Personnel
Tel 203-274-6791
Fax 203-274-8464

EZ Form Cable Corp.
315 Peck St., Bldg. 24
New Haven, CT 06513

Founded 1984
Total employees 50
Annual sales $3 million
Industry Subassemblies
and Components

Growth Openings in past
year 25; percentage
growth 100%
Contact
Ed Parker, President
Tel 203-785-8215
Fax 203-785-0466

Fire-Lite Alarms, Inc.
12 Clintonville Rd.
Northford, CT 06472

Founded 1952
Total employees 290
Annual sales $34 million
Industry Test and
Measurement
Growth Openings in past
year 40; percentage
growth 16%
Contact
Ms. Joan Nichols, Human
Resource Manager
Tel 203-484-7161
Fax 203-484-7118

Fluidyne Ansonia, LP
1 Riverside Dr.
Ansonia, CT 06401

Founded 1896
Total employees 45
Annual sales $5 million
Industries Factory
Automation,
Manufacturing Equipment
Growth Openings in past
year 15; percentage
growth 50%
Contact
Trum Cary, Controller
Tel 203-735-9311
Fax 203-735-3489

Food Automation Service Techniques, Inc.
905 Honeyspot Rd.
Stratford, CT 06497

Founded 1969
Total employees 200
Industries Computer
Hardware, Energy,
Holding Companies
Growth Openings in past
year 45; percentage
growth 29%
Contact
S.H. Chandler, Personnel
Administrator
Tel 203-377-4414
Fax 203-377-8187

GMN, Whitnon Spindle Division
Rte. 6 & New Britain Ave.
Farmington, CT 06032

Founded 1982
Total employees 92
Annual sales $8.75 million
Industry Factory
Automation
Growth Openings in past
year 27; percentage
growth 41%
Contact
Mrs. Donna Reale,
Personnel Manager
Tel 203-677-2607
Fax 203-674-0176

IMRS Inc.
777 Long Ridge Rd.
Stamford, CT 06902

Founded 1981
Total employees 419
Annual sales $61.03
million
Industry Computer
Software
Growth Openings in past
year 84; percentage
growth 25%
Contact
James A. Perakis, COB/
CEO/President
Tel 203-321-3500
Fax 203-322-3904

Kip, Inc.
72 Spring Ln.
Farmington, CT 06032

Founded 1964
Total employees 110
Annual sales $15 million
Industries Subassemblies
and Components, Test
and Measurement
Growth Openings in past
year 33; percentage
growth 42%
Contact
Nicholas Testanero,
President
Tel 203-677-0272
Fax 203-677-4999

Lorad Corp.
36 Apple Ridge Rd.
Danbury, CT 06810

Founded 1983
Total employees 180
Industry Medical

Growth Openings in past year 30; percentage growth 20%
Contact
Raymond B. Calvo, VP/Controller
Tel 203-790-1188
Fax 203-743-3370

Lydall, Inc.
One Colonial Rd., PO Box 151
Manchester, CT 06045

Founded 1879
Total employees 917
Annual sales $151 million
Industry Holding Companies
Growth Openings in past year 91; percentage growth 11%
Contact
Leonard R. Jaskol, President/CEO/COB
Tel 203-646-1233
Fax 203-646-4917

Magnetec Corp.
61 West Dudley Town Rd.
Bloomfield, CT 06002

Founded 1974
Total employees 180
Annual sales $22 million
Industries Computer Hardware, Subassemblies and Components
Growth Openings in past year 30; percentage growth 20%
Contact
Ronald Pueschel, President
Tel 203-243-8941
Fax 203-243-5152

Micrognosis, Inc.
100 Sawmill Rd.
Danbury, CT 06810

Founded 1978
Total employees 250
Annual sales $41 million
Industries Computer Hardware, Computer Software
Growth Openings in past year 50; percentage growth 25%
Contact
Greg O'Brien, VP of Human Resources
Tel 203-730-5300
Fax 203-730-5365

National Medical Research Corp.
25 Main St.
Hartford, CT 06106

Founded 1983
Total employees 90
Annual sales $12 million
Industries Medical, Pharmaceuticals
Growth Openings in past year 20; percentage growth 28%
Contact
David Hallee, Director of Personnel
Tel 203-724-0091
Fax 203-278-4717

Noise Cancellation Technologies, Inc.
800 Summer St.
Stamford, CT 06901

Founded 1986
Total employees 162
Annual sales $5 million
Industries Environmental, Holding Companies, Medical
Growth Openings in past year 100; percentage growth 161%
Contact
John J. McCloy, COB/CEO
Tel 203-961-0500
Fax 203-348-4106

Notifier
12 Clintonville Rd.
Northford, CT 06472

Founded 1950
Total employees 325
Annual sales $50 million
Industries Test and Measurement, Telecommunications
Growth Openings in past year 125; percentage growth 62%
Contact
Mark Levy, President
Tel 203-484-7161
Fax 203-484-7118

Numetrix, Inc.
401 Merrit 7
Norwalk, CT 06851

Founded 1977
Total employees 35
Annual sales $4.0 million
Industry Computer Software

Growth Openings in past year 15; percentage growth 75%
Contact
Josef Schengili, President
Tel 203-847-3452
Fax 203-846-3537

Ortronics, Inc.
595 Green Haven Rd.
Pawcatuck, CT 06379

Founded 1966
Total employees 260
Annual sales $36 million
Industries Subassemblies and Components, Telecommunications
Growth Openings in past year 60; percentage growth 30%
Contact
Ms. Lisa Stapleton, Personnel Manager
Tel 203-599-1760
Fax 203-599-1774

Peak Electronics, Inc.
51 Carlson Rd.
Orange, CT 06477

Founded 1989
Total employees 127
Annual sales $12 million
Industry Subassemblies and Components
Growth Openings in past year 27; percentage growth 27%
Contact
Paul Carozza, Personnel Administrator
Tel 203-795-0241
Fax 203-795-5804

Photronics, Inc.
15 Secor Rd., PO Box 5226
Brookfield, CT 06804

Founded 1969
Total employees 475
Annual sales $33.6 million
Industry Manufacturing Equipment
Growth Openings in past year 139; percentage growth 41%
Contact
Constantine Macricostas, COB/CEO
Tel 203-775-9000
Fax 203-775-5944

Programming Resources Co.
875 Asylum Ave.
Hartford, CT 06105

Founded 1971
Total employees 120
Annual sales $13 million
Industries Computer
Hardware, Computer
Software
Growth Openings in past
year 45; percentage
growth 60%
Contact
Steven Weber, President/
Owner
Tel 203-728-1428
Fax 203-541-6077

Revelation Technologies, Inc.
181 Harbor Dr.
Stamford, CT 06902

Founded 1983
Total employees 150
Annual sales $17 million
Industry Computer
Software
Growth Openings in past
year 50; percentage
growth 50%
Contact
Ms. Jean Brady, Personnel
Manager
Tel 203-973-1000
Fax 203-975-8744

Siemon Co.
76 Westbury Park Rd.
Watertown, CT 06795

Founded 1903
Total employees 275
Annual sales $26 million
Industries Computer
Hardware, Factory
Automation,
Subassemblies and
Components
Growth Openings in past
year 55; percentage
growth 25%
Contact
Carl N. Siemon, President
Tel 203-274-2523
Fax 203-945-4225

SNET Cellular, Inc.
555 Long Wharf Dr.
New Haven, CT 06510

Founded 1986
Total employees 275
Annual sales $37 million

Industry
Telecommunications
Growth Openings in past
year 75; percentage
growth 37%
Contact
Peter P. Basserman,
President
Tel 203-553-7600
Fax 203-624-8514

Systems Group, Inc.
155 Sycamore St.
Glastonbury, CT 06033

Founded 1985
Total employees 150
Annual sales $17 million
Industry Computer
Software
Growth Openings in past
year 20; percentage
growth 15%
Contact
Carl Foster, President
Tel 203-633-0359
Fax 203-657-4503

TranSwitch Corp.
8 Progress Dr.
Shelton, CT 06484

Founded 1988
Total employees 63
Annual sales $6.1 million
Industry Subassemblies
and Components
Growth Openings in past
year 18; percentage
growth 40%
Contact
Michael McCoy, Director of
Finance and
Administration
Tel 203-929-8810
Fax 203-926-9453

TRC Companies, Inc.
5 Waterside Crossing
Windsor, CT 06095

Founded 1969
Total employees 700
Annual sales $55 million
Industry Holding
Companies
Growth Openings in past
year 97; percentage
growth 16%
Contact
Bruce Cowen, President
Tel 203-289-8631
Fax 203-298-6399

Tri-Tech, Inc.
1500 Meriden Rd.
Waterbury, CT 06705

Founded 1951
Total employees 120
Annual sales $10 million
Industry Holding
Companies
Growth Openings in past
year 20; percentage
growth 20%
Contact
Ms. Jane Angelone,
Personnel Manager
Tel 203-756-7441
Fax 203-756-8724

Voltarc Technologies, Inc.
186 Linwood Ave.
Fairfield, CT 06430

Founded 1927
Total employees 354
Annual sales $31 million
Industries Energy,
Photonics
Growth Openings in past
year 103; percentage
growth 41%
Contact
Vinnie Mehta, President
Tel 203-255-2633
Fax 203-259-1194

Zeitech, Inc.
1029 East Main St.
Stamford, CT 06902

Founded 1987
Total employees 140
Annual sales $23 million
Industry Computer
Hardware
Growth Openings in past
year 50; percentage
growth 55%
Contact
Mike Ornstein, President
Tel 203-359-9807
Fax 203-325-9308

Delaware

Ciba-Geigy Corp., Pigments Division
315 Water St.
Newport, DE 19804

Founded 1970
Total employees 300

Annual sales $65 million
Industry Chemicals
Growth Openings in past
year 75; percentage
growth 33%
Contact
Jean Schaefle, President
Tel 302-992-5600

**Dentsply International
Inc., LD Caulk Division**
Lakeview and Clarke Aves.
Milford, DE 19963

Founded 1878
Total employees 500
Annual sales $55 million
Industries Advanced
Materials, Medical
Growth Openings in past
year 50; percentage
growth 11%
Contact
Thomas L. Whiting,
General Manager
Tel 302-422-4511
Fax 302-422-3480

Intervet, Inc.
405 State St.
Millsboro, DE 19966

Founded 1980
Total employees 250
Industry Pharmaceuticals
Growth Openings in past
year 29; percentage
growth 13%
Contact
Klaus Olbers, President
Tel 302-934-8051
Fax 302-934-8591

Lanxide Corp.
1300 Marrows Rd., PO
Box 6077
Newark, DE 19714

Founded 1983
Total employees 370
Annual sales $12 million
Industries Advanced
Materials, Subassemblies
and Components
Growth Openings in past
year 18; percentage
growth 5%
Contact
Marc Newkirk, President
Tel 302-456-6200
Fax 302-454-1712

District of Columbia

**Chemonics Industries,
Inc., Chemonics
International Consulting
Division**
2000 M St. Northwest,
Suite 200
Washington, DC 20036
Founded 1975
Total employees 210
Annual sales $37.19
million
Industry Environmental
Growth Openings in past
year 25; percentage
growth 13%
Contact
Ms. Nancy Jaffie, Manager
of Personnel
Tel 202-466-5340
Fax 202-331-8202

**Engineering Design
Group, Inc.**
1825 K St. Northwest
Washington, DC 20006
Founded 1986
Total employees 37
Industry Manufacturing
Equipment
Growth Openings in past
year 22; percentage
growth 146%
Contact
Peter Gruemberg,
President
Tel 202-862-9600
Fax 202-862-8590

Florida

**Abra Cadabra Software,
Inc.**
888 Executive Center Dr.
West, #300
Saint Petersburg, FL
33702
Founded 1985
Total employees 75
Annual sales $8.7 million
Industry Computer
Software
Growth Openings in past
year 20; percentage
growth 36%

Contact
Jim Foster, President
Tel 813-579-1111
Fax 813-578-2178

Addison Product Co.
7050 Overland Rd.
Orlando, FL 32810

Founded 1949
Total employees 140
Annual sales $18 million
Industries Energy,
Holding Companies
Growth Openings in past
year 20; percentage
growth 16%
Contact
V.C. Knight, President
Tel 407-292-4400
Fax 407-290-1329

Aero Corp.
5530 East Hwy. 90, PO
Box 1909
Lake City, FL 32056

Founded 1951
Total employees 400
Annual sales $46 million
Industry Transportation
Growth Openings in past
year 23; percentage
growth 6%
Contact
Ms. Ruth Corb, Personnel
Supervisor
Tel 904-758-3000
Fax 904-752-0807

**Applied Measurement
Systems, Inc.**
1 Oakwood Blvd., Suite
180
Hollywood, FL 33020

Founded 1978
Total employees 110
Industries Defense,
Manufacturing
Equipment, Test and
Measurement
Growth Openings in past
year 30; percentage
growth 37%
Contact
Barry Douglas, President
Tel 305-925-0200
Fax 305-925-0205

A.W. Industries, Inc.
6788 Northwest 17th Ave.
Fort Lauderdale, FL 33309

Founded 1973
Total employees 75

Industries Computer
Hardware,
Subassemblies and
Components
Growth Openings in past
year 25; percentage
growth 50%
Contact
Arthur B. Weaver,
President
Tel 305-979-5696
Fax 305-979-5764

Boca Research, Inc.
6413 Congress Ave.
Boca Raton, FL 33487

Founded 1985
Total employees 250
Annual sales $44.5 million
Industries Computer
Hardware,
Telecommunications
Growth Openings in past
year 150; percentage
growth 150%
Contact
Howard Yenke, President/
CEO
Tel 407-997-6227
Fax 407-997-0918

C-MAC of America, Inc.
1601 Hill Ave.
West Palm Beach, FL
33407

Founded 1974
Total employees 425
Annual sales $41 million
Industries Computer
Hardware,
Subassemblies and
Components
Growth Openings in past
year 25; percentage
growth 6%
Contact
David Holmes, Vice
President/General
Manager of Hybrid
Tel 407-845-8455
Fax 407-881-2342

CMS/Data Corp.
124 Marriott Dr., Suite 200
Tallahassee, FL 32301

Founded 1978
Total employees 250
Annual sales $12.83
million
Industries Computer
Software, Holding
Companies

Growth Openings in past
year 19; percentage
growth 8%
Contact
P. Scott Kadlec, Executive
Vice President
Tel 904-878-5155
Fax 904-656-4093

Coleman Research Corp.
5950 Lakehurst Dr.
Orlando, FL 32819

Founded 1980
Total employees 750
Annual sales $50 million
Industries Defense,
Environmental, Holding
Companies,
Manufacturing
Equipment,
Telecommunications
Growth Openings in past
year 324; percentage
growth 76%
Contact
Ms. Vicki Goldenson,
Director of Human
Resources
Tel 407-352-3700
Fax 407-345-8616

Computer Power, Inc.
661 Riverside Ave., Suite
110E
Jacksonville, FL 32204

Founded 1969
Total employees 950
Annual sales $110 million
Industry Computer
Software
Growth Openings in past
year 247; percentage
growth 35%
Contact
Joseph Eberly, VP of
Human Resources
Tel 904-359-5000
Fax 904-359-5298

Conelec of Florida, Inc.
2675 South Design Ct.
Sanford, FL 32773

Founded 1983
Total employees 70
Annual sales $6.8 million
Industry Subassemblies
and Components
Growth Openings in past
year 15; percentage
growth 27%

Contact
Roger Thomson, President
Tel 407-321-9000
Fax 407-322-6165

Corvita Corp.
8210 Northwest 27th St.
Miami, FL 33122

Founded 1987
Total employees 52
Annual sales $1 million
Industries Advanced
Materials, Biotechnology,
Medical
Growth Openings in past
year 23; percentage
growth 79%
Contact
Dr. Norman Weldon,
President
Tel 305-599-3100
Fax 305-599-9301

**Crestview Aerospace
Corp.**
5486 Fairchild Rd.
Crestview, FL 32536

Founded 1991
Total employees 70
Annual sales $3 million
Industry Transportation
Growth Openings in past
year 20; percentage
growth 40%
Contact
Jack Owen, President
Tel 904-682-2753
Fax 904-682-0489

**Crystal Software
International-U.S., Inc.**
1110 Pinellas Bayway
Saint Petersburg, FL
33715

Founded 1991
Total employees 65
Annual sales $7.5 million
Industry Computer
Software
Growth Openings in past
year 25; percentage
growth 62%
Contact
John Christman, President
Tel 813-864-2990
Fax 813-864-1736

Custom Cable Industries, Inc.
3221 Cherry Palm Dr.
Tampa, FL 33619

Founded 1980
Total employees 207
Annual sales $10 million
Industries Computer
Hardware,
Subassemblies and
Components,
Telecommunications
Growth Openings in past
year 39; percentage
growth 23%
Contact
Richard Watson, President
Tel 813-623-2232
Fax 813-626-9630

DATAMAX Corp.
4501 Parkway Commerce
Blvd.
Orlando, FL 32808

Founded 1980
Total employees 150
Annual sales $24 million
Industries Computer
Hardware, Computer
Software, Subassemblies
and Components
Growth Openings in past
year 25; percentage
growth 20%
Contact
Robert Strandberg,
President
Tel 407-578-8007
Fax 407-578-8377

DME Corp.
111 South West 33rd
Fort Lauderdale, FL 33315

Founded 1977
Total employees 205
Annual sales $24.5 million
Industries Defense,
Subassemblies and
Components,
Transportation
Growth Openings in past
year 45; percentage
growth 28%
Contact
Ms. Shawna McDowell,
Director of Personnel
Tel 305-463-5066
Fax 305-462-5503

Equitrac Corp.
836 Ponce De Leon Blvd.
Coral Gables, FL 33134

Founded 1977
Total employees 310
Annual sales $29 million
Industry Computer
Software
Growth Openings in past
year 29; percentage
growth 10%
Contact
George P. Wilson,
President/CEO
Tel 305-442-2060
Fax 305-442-0687

Fiserv, Inc., CBS Division
2601 Technology Dr.
Orlando, FL 32804

Founded 1983
Total employees 220
Annual sales $25 million
Industry Computer
Software
Growth Openings in past
year 42; percentage
growth 23%
Contact
Ms. Jane Greggory, VP of
Human Resources
Tel 407-299-5400
Fax 800-723-3675

GeoSyntec Consultants
621 Northwest 53rd St.,
#650
Boca Raton, FL 33487

Founded 1983
Total employees 180
Annual sales $19 million
Industries Environmental,
Holding Companies
Growth Openings in past
year 20; percentage
growth 12%
Contact
Neil D. Williams, Ph.D.,
Chief Executive Officer
Tel 407-995-0900
Fax 407-995-0995

Gerardo International, Inc.
112 Water Turkey Ct.
Daytona Beach, FL 32119

Founded 1976
Total employees 523
Annual sales $257 million
Industries Chemicals,
Environmental, Medical

Growth Openings in past
year 69; percentage
growth 15%
Contact
Neil Gerardo, President
Tel 904-756-1916
Fax 904-756-4300

Harris Corp., Air Traffic Control Systems Division
PO Box 5100
Melbourne, FL 32902

Founded 1986
Total employees 750
Annual sales $125 million
Industries
Telecommunications,
Transportation
Growth Openings in past
year 250; percentage
growth 50%
Contact
Ms. Brenda Moye, Director
of Human Resources
Tel 407-727-4000
Fax 407-727-6816

Hobart Brothers Co., Diversified Products Group
6950 Northwest 77th Ct.
Miami, FL 33166

Founded 1917
Total employees 125
Industries Factory
Automation,
Transportation
Growth Openings in past
year 50; percentage
growth 66%
Contact
Brooks Price, Quality
Control Manager
Tel 305-592-5450
Fax 305-477-4105

L.E.A. Dynatech, Inc.
6520 Harney Rd.
Tampa, FL 33610

Founded 1971
Total employees 45
Annual sales $5 million
Industry Subassemblies
and Components
Growth Openings in past
year 15; percentage
growth 50%
Contact
Robert J. Stanger,
President
Tel 813-621-1324
Fax 813-621-8980

Logicon Eagle Technology, Inc.
950 North Orlando Ave.
Winter Park, FL 32789

Founded 1900
Total employees 529
Industry Defense
Growth Openings in past year 57; percentage growth 12%
Contact
Dr. James F. Harvey, President
Tel 407-629-6010
Fax 407-629-5636

M & W Pump Corp.
33 Northwest St.
Deerfield Beach, FL 33441

Founded 1926
Total employees 200
Industry Subassemblies and Components
Growth Openings in past year 15; percentage growth 8%
Contact
Ms. Carol Stefanizzi, Personnel Director
Tel 305-426-1500

Mathematica, Inc.
402 South Kentucky Ave.
Lakeland, FL 33801

Founded 1986
Total employees 45
Industry Computer Software
Growth Openings in past year 22; percentage growth 95%
Contact
Derek Hodges, CEO/President
Tel 813-682-1130
Fax 813-686-5969

Medical Technology Systems, Inc.
12920 Automobile Blvd.
Clearwater, FL 34622

Founded 1984
Total employees 235
Annual sales $15.98 million
Industries Computer Software, Factory Automation, Manufacturing Equipment, Medical, Pharmaceuticals

Growth Openings in past year 35; percentage growth 17%
Contact
Todd E. Siegel, President/CEO
Tel 813-576-6311
Fax 813-579-8067

MediTek Health Corp.
8875 Hidden River Pkwy., Suite 110
Tampa, FL 33637

Founded 1957
Total employees 115
Annual sales $12 million
Industry Medical
Growth Openings in past year 35; percentage growth 43%
Contact
Paul M. Stanley, President
Tel 813-971-5574
Fax 813-977-8950

Micro Design International, Inc.
6985 University Blvd.
Winter Park, FL 32792

Founded 1976
Total employees 100
Annual sales $19 million
Industries Computer Hardware, Computer Software
Growth Openings in past year 50; percentage growth 100%
Contact
Geoffrey Legat, President
Tel 407-677-8333
Fax 407-677-8365

National Water Purifiers Corp.
1065 East 14th St.
Hialeah, FL 33010

Founded 1970
Total employees 40
Annual sales $1.0 million
Industry Environmental
Growth Openings in past year 30; percentage growth 300%
Contact
Ms. Judy Garcia, President
Tel 305-887-0703
Fax 305-887-6209

OHM Corporation, Florida Division
13400 Mohawk Rd., PO Box 121190
Clermont, FL 34712

Founded 1980
Total employees 100
Annual sales $3 million
Industry Environmental
Growth Openings in past year 30; percentage growth 42%
Contact
Bob Mangham, Division Manager
Tel 904-394-8601
Fax 904-394-7722

Openware Technology Corp.
8000 Arlington Expwy., Suite #600
Jacksonville, FL 32211

Founded 1979
Total employees 60
Annual sales $14 million
Industry Computer Software
Growth Openings in past year 30; percentage growth 100%
Contact
Jamie W. Ellertson, President/CEO
Tel 904-725-7187
Fax 904-723-3370

Opto Mechanik, Inc.
PO Box 361907
Melbourne, FL 32936

Founded 1969
Total employees 320
Annual sales $35 million
Industries Defense, Holding Companies, Photonics
Growth Openings in past year 19; percentage growth 6%
Contact
Ms. Cece Cloonan, Personnel Director
Tel 407-254-1212
Fax 407-253-4494

PC DOCS, Inc.
124 Marriott Dr.
Tallahassee, FL 32301

Founded 1990
Total employees 120
Industry Computer Software

Growth Openings in past year 74; percentage growth 160%
Contact
Scott Kadlec, President
Tel 904-942-3627
Fax 904-942-1517

Precisionaire, Inc.
2399 26th Ave. North, PO Box 7568
Saint Petersburg, FL 33713

Founded 1951
Total employees 700
Annual sales $35 million
Industry Environmental
Growth Openings in past year 200; percentage growth 40%
Contact
Gustavo Hernandez, Chief Executive Officer
Tel 813-822-4411
Fax 813-823-5510

Protel, Inc.
4150 Kidron Rd.
Lakeland, FL 33811

Founded 1983
Total employees 160
Annual sales $22 million
Industries Factory Automation, Subassemblies and Components, Telecommunications
Growth Openings in past year 80; percentage growth 100%
Contact
Ms. Lunitta Thomas, Human Resources Manager
Tel 813-644-5558
Fax 813-646-5855

Quality Contract Manufacturing, Inc.
3900 Dow Rd., Suite E
Melbourne, FL 32934

Founded 1992
Total employees 35
Annual sales $1.5 million
Industries Computer Hardware, Defense, Medical, Subassemblies and Components, Transportation
Growth Openings in past year 18; percentage growth 105%

Contact
Ms. Joyce Wade, Treasurer
Tel 407-259-3658
Fax 407-253-9240

Reflectone, Inc.
4908 Tampa West Blvd.
Tampa, FL 33634

Founded 1985
Total employees 625
Annual sales $80 million
Industries Defense, Transportation
Growth Openings in past year 62; percentage growth 11%
Contact
Ms. Kelley Rexroad, VP of Human Resources
Tel 813-885-7481
Fax 813-885-1177

Reptron Electronics, Inc.
14401 McCormick Dr.
Tampa, FL 33626

Founded 1974
Total employees 650
Annual sales $120 million
Industry Holding Companies
Growth Openings in past year 249; percentage growth 62%
Contact
Michael L. Musto, President
Tel 813-854-2351
Fax 813-855-0942

Reptron Electronics, Inc., K-Byte Division
14201 McCormick Dr.
Tampa, FL 33626

Founded 1982
Total employees 500
Annual sales $70 million
Industry Subassemblies and Components
Growth Openings in past year 180; percentage growth 56%
Contact
William J. Carlin, Human Resources Manager
Tel 813-854-2000
Fax 813-855-5346

Ryan Electronics Products, Inc.
8353 Northwest 36th St.
Miami, FL 33166

Founded 1964
Total employees 72
Annual sales $4.5 million
Industry Subassemblies and Components
Growth Openings in past year 27; percentage growth 60%
Contact
Jack Ryan, President
Tel 305-594-9424
Fax 305-594-9949

Scientific-Atlanta, Inc., Private Networks Business Division
420 North Wickham Rd.
Melbourne, FL 32935

Founded 1951
Total employees 175
Annual sales $24 million
Industry Telecommunications
Growth Openings in past year 35; percentage growth 25%
Contact
Bob Walters, Director of Personnel
Tel 407-255-3000
Fax 407-253-3701

Siemens Nixdorf Printing Systems
5500 Broken Sound Blvd.
Boca Raton, FL 33487

Founded 1980
Total employees 600
Annual sales $173 million
Industry Computer Hardware
Growth Openings in past year 50; percentage growth 9%
Contact
H. Werner Krause, President/CEO
Tel 407-997-3100
Fax 407-998-9160

Solar Plastics, Inc.
4510 West Alva St.
Tampa, FL 33614

Founded 1969
Total employees 100
Annual sales $8 million
Industry Manufacturing Equipment

Growth Openings in past
year 30; percentage
growth 42%
Contact
Alan Thomas, President
Tel 813-872-7959
Fax 813-878-0199

**Startech Innovations,
Inc.**
50 2nd St.
Shalimar, FL 32579

Founded 1987
Total employees 30
Industry Subassemblies
and Components
Growth Openings in past
year 25; percentage
growth 500%
Contact
Clint McCowen, President
Tel 904-651-4890
Fax 904-651-5037

Symbiosis Corporation
8600 Northwest 41st St.
Miami, FL 33166

Founded 1985
Total employees 700
Annual sales $77 million
Industry Medical
Growth Openings in past
year 97; percentage
growth 16%
Contact
Kevin W. Smith, President/
CEO
Tel 305-597-4000
Fax 305-597-4001

**Syquest Technology,
Sydos Division**
6501 Park of Commerce
Blvd., Suite 110
Boca Raton, FL 33487

Founded 1991
Total employees 70
Annual sales $11 million
Industry Computer
Hardware
Growth Openings in past
year 20; percentage
growth 40%
Contact
Don Mattson, President
Tel 407-998-5400
Fax 407-998-5414

Targ-It-Tronics, Inc.
7100 Technology Dr.
West Melbourne, FL 32904

Founded 1986
Total employees 150
Annual sales $14 million
Industry Subassemblies
and Components
Growth Openings in past
year 50; percentage
growth 50%
Contact
Larry Groves, President/
CEO
Tel 407-725-6993
Fax 407-724-6682

**Technology Research
Corp.**
5250 140th Ave. North
Clearwater, FL 34620

Founded 1981
Total employees 300
Annual sales $12.87
million
Industry Subassemblies
and Components
Growth Openings in past
year 145; percentage
growth 93%
Contact
Ms. Carol Diehl, Director
of Personnel
Tel 813-353-0572
Fax 813-535-4828

Tensolite Company
100 Tensolite Dr.
Saint Augustine, FL 32092

Founded 1940
Total employees 250
Industry Subassemblies
and Components
Growth Openings in past
year 74; percentage
growth 42%
Contact
Tim Neville, President
Tel 904-829-5600
Fax 904-829-3447

Trak Microwave Corp.
4726 Eisenhower Blvd.
Tampa, FL 33634

Founded 1960
Total employees 500
Annual sales $69 million
Industries Test and
Measurement,
Telecommunications

Growth Openings in past
year 50; percentage
growth 11%
Contact
Mrs. Linda Reynolds,
Personnel Manager
Tel 813-884-1411
Fax 813-886-2794

**TransTechnology Corp.,
Lundy Technical Center**
3901 Northeast 12th Ave.
Pompano Beach, FL
33064

Founded 1934
Total employees 120
Annual sales $15 million
Industries Advanced
Materials, Defense,
Factory Automation
Growth Openings in past
year 20; percentage
growth 20%
Contact
Richard Evans, Director of
Human Resources
Tel 305-943-1500
Fax 305-782-8835

TYBRIN Corp.
1283 North Eglin Pkwy.
Shalimar, FL 32579

Founded 1972
Total employees 230
Annual sales $7 million
Industries Computer
Hardware, Computer
Software
Growth Openings in past
year 80; percentage
growth 53%
Contact
Ms. Ellen C. Taylor,
Personnel Manager
Tel 904-651-1150
Fax 904-651-6335

Unipower Corporation
3900 Coral Ridge Dr.
Coral Springs, FL 33065

Founded 1988
Total employees 260
Annual sales $16 million
Industry Subassemblies
and Components
Growth Openings in past
year 105; percentage
growth 67%
Contact
Ms. Renee Bobula, Human
Resource Manager
Tel 305-346-2442
Fax 305-340-7901

VAC-CON, Inc.
969 Hall Park Dr.
Green Cove Springs, FL
 32043

Founded 1986
Total employees 127
Annual sales $16 million
Industries Environmental,
 Factory Automation,
 Subassemblies and
 Components
Growth Openings in past
 year 17; percentage
 growth 15%
Contact
Ms. Julie Walker,
 Purchasing/Personnel
 Manager
Tel 904-284-4200
Fax 904-284-3305

**Williams Earth Sciences,
Inc.**
12290 U.S. Hwy. #19
 North
Clearwater, FL 34624

Founded 1972
Total employees 70
Annual sales $3 million
Industries Advanced
 Materials, Environmental
Growth Openings in past
 year 20; percentage
 growth 40%
Contact
Ms. Marcia H. Stern,
 President
Tel 813-535-9802
Fax 813-535-5954

Wire Tech, Inc.
3800 Progress Blvd.
Mount Dora, FL 32757

Founded 1983
Total employees 37
Annual sales $2 million
Industries Manufacturing
 Equipment,
 Subassemblies and
 Components
Growth Openings in past
 year 22; percentage
 growth 146%
Contact
Lou Arasi, President
Tel 904-589-6611
Fax 904-357-3021

**Zytek Quality Computer
Services, Inc.**
100 Technology Pk.
Lake Mary, FL 32746

Founded 1984
Total employees 45
Annual sales $3.5 million
Industry Computer
 Hardware
Growth Openings in past
 year 20; percentage
 growth 80%
Contact
Michael James, Chief
 Executive Officer
Tel 407-333-9363
Fax 407-333-9367

Georgia

**AEL Industries, Inc.,
Cross Systems Division**
1355 Bluegrass Lakes
 Pkwy.
Alpharetta, GA 30201

Founded 1980
Total employees 180
Annual sales $28 million
Industries Defense,
 Transportation
Growth Openings in past
 year 30; percentage
 growth 20%
Contact
Ms. Karen Brown, Human
 Resource Administrator
Tel 404-475-3633
Fax 404-475-0176

**AER Energy Resources,
Inc.**
1500 Wilson Way, Suite
 250
Smyrna, GA 30082

Founded 1989
Total employees 75
Industry Energy
Growth Openings in past
 year 25; percentage
 growth 50%
Contact
David Dorheim, President/
 CEO
Tel 404-433-2127
Fax 404-433-2286

**Atlanta Group Systems,
Inc.**
3700 Cresswood Pkwy.,
 Suite 290
Duluth, GA 30136

Founded 1980
Total employees 120
Annual sales $13 million
Industries Computer
 Hardware, Computer
 Software
Growth Openings in past
 year 20; percentage
 growth 20%
Contact
Ms. Terri Jones, Owner/
 CEO
Tel 404-806-8080
Fax 404-806-8090

AVL Scientific Corp.
33 Mansell Ct., PO Box
 337
Roswell, GA 30077

Founded 1973
Total employees 115
Annual sales $16 million
Industry Medical
Growth Openings in past
 year 24; percentage
 growth 26%
Contact
Alfred Marek, President
Tel 404-587-4040
Fax 404-587-4163

Ayres Corp.
PO Box 3090
Albany, GA 31708

Founded 1968
Total employees 208
Annual sales $24 million
Industry Transportation
Growth Openings in past
 year 38; percentage
 growth 22%
Contact
Fred P. Ayres, President
Tel 912-883-1440
Fax 912-439-9790

**BellSouth Information
Systems**
1967 Lakeside Pkwy.,
 Suite 412
Tucker, GA 30084

Founded 1983
Total employees 367
Industry Computer
 Hardware

Growth Openings in past year 67; percentage growth 22%
Contact
Ms. Llurah Hardin, Director of Human Resources
Tel 404-621-3419
Fax 404-414-6860

Brock Control Systems, Inc.
2859 Paces Ferry Rd., Suite 1000
Atlanta, GA 30339

Founded 1984
Total employees 180
Annual sales $25.47 million
Industry Computer Software
Growth Openings in past year 21; percentage growth 13%
Contact
Ms. Robin Haight, Personnel Coordinator
Tel 404-431-1200
Fax 404-431-1201

Chemical Products Corp.
PO Box 2470
Cartersville, GA 30120

Founded 1934
Total employees 275
Annual sales $40 million
Industry Chemicals
Growth Openings in past year 75; percentage growth 37%
Contact
Charles Adams, Jr., President
Tel 404-382-2144
Fax 404-386-6053

Comprehensive Computer Consulting, Inc.
7000 Central Pkwy., Suite 940
Atlanta, GA 30328

Founded 1978
Total employees 110
Annual sales $6.2 million
Industry Computer Software
Growth Openings in past year 18; percentage growth 19%

Contact
Pat McBrayer, President/ CEO
Tel 404-512-0100
Fax 404-512-0101

Crispaire Corp.
Hwy. 41 North, PO Box 400
Cordele, GA 31015

Founded 1972
Total employees 200
Industries Energy, Subassemblies and Components
Growth Openings in past year 70; percentage growth 53%
Contact
Bub Denhan, Director of Purchasing and Personnel
Tel 912-273-3636
Fax 912-273-5154

CytRx Corp.
150 Technology Pkwy.
Norcross, GA 30092

Founded 1985
Total employees 33
Industries Biotechnology, Pharmaceuticals
Growth Openings in past year 16; percentage growth 94%
Contact
William V. Fleck, VP of Human Resources
Tel 404-368-9500
Fax 404-368-0622

DayStar Digital, Inc.
5556 Atlanta Hwy.
Flowery Branch, GA 30542

Founded 1984
Total employees 150
Industries Computer Hardware, Telecommunications
Growth Openings in past year 85; percentage growth 130%
Contact
Andrew Lewis, President
Tel 404-967-2077
Fax 404-967-3018

DISC ACCESS Products Group, Inc.
3340 Peachtree Rd., Suite 2635
Atlanta, GA 30326

Founded 1980
Total employees 50
Annual sales $5.8 million
Industry Computer Software
Growth Openings in past year 20; percentage growth 66%
Contact
Dan Myers, President
Tel 404-261-1264
Fax 404-261-7289

Dolphin Networks, Inc.
4405 International Blvd., Suite B108
Norcross, GA 30092

Founded 1989
Total employees 80
Annual sales $9.2 million
Industry Computer Software
Growth Openings in past year 20; percentage growth 33%
Contact
Bob Palmer, President
Tel 404-279-7050
Fax 404-279-1615

Dynamic Resources, Inc.
1866 Independence Square
Atlanta, GA 30338

Founded 1978
Total employees 70
Annual sales $4 million
Industry Computer Software
Growth Openings in past year 50; percentage growth 250%
Contact
Russ Maclin, Vice President
Tel 404-391-9330
Fax 404-393-4317

EcoTek Laboratory Services, Inc.
3342 International Park Dr., Southeast
Atlanta, GA 30316

Founded 1988
Total employees 90
Annual sales $9.6 million
Industry Environmental

Growth Openings in past year 20; percentage growth 28%
Contact
Jack R. Tuschall, President
Tel 404-244-0827
Fax 404-243-5355

Electronic Systems Products, Inc.
1000 Holcomb Woods Pkwy., Suite 342
Roswell, GA 30076

Founded 1989
Total employees 50
Industry Subassemblies and Components
Growth Openings in past year 30; percentage growth 150%
Contact
John Lippington, President
Tel 404-552-9355
Fax 404-552-9442

ENCORE Systems, Inc.
900 Cir. 75 Pkwy., Suite 1700
Atlanta, GA 30339

Founded 1979
Total employees 128
Annual sales $14 million
Industry Computer Software
Growth Openings in past year 68; percentage growth 113%
Contact
Ms. Penny Sellers, President
Tel 404-612-3500
Fax 404-951-6875

General Engineering Services, Inc.
PO Box 1303
Forest Park, GA 30050

Founded 1962
Total employees 100
Industry Transportation
Growth Openings in past year 60; percentage growth 150%
Contact
Clay Womack, President
Tel 404-366-0651
Fax 404-366-0657

Harbinger*EDI Services, Inc.
1055 Lenox Park Blvd.
Atlanta, GA 30319

Founded 1983
Total employees 125
Annual sales $14 million
Industry Computer Software
Growth Openings in past year 45; percentage growth 56%
Contact
David L. Leach, President
Tel 404-841-4334
Fax 404-841-4399

IMNET, Inc.
8601 Dun Woody Pl., Suite 420
Atlanta, GA 30350

Founded 1986
Total employees 64
Annual sales $10 million
Industries Computer Hardware, Computer Software
Growth Openings in past year 32; percentage growth 100%
Contact
Kenneth Rardin, President/CEO
Tel 404-998-2200
Fax 404-992-6357

Industrial Computer Corp.
5871 Glenridge Dr., Suite 300
Atlanta, GA 30328

Founded 1980
Total employees 65
Annual sales $4.9 million
Industry Computer Software
Growth Openings in past year 20; percentage growth 44%
Contact
Frank Wingate, President
Tel 404-255-8336
Fax 404-250-0602

IQ Software Corporation
3295 River Exchange Dr., Suite 550
Norcross, GA 30092

Founded 1984
Total employees 151
Annual sales $19.12 million

Industry Computer Software
Growth Openings in past year 38; percentage growth 33%
Contact
Rick Chitty, President
Tel 404-446-8880
Fax 404-448-4088

KASEWORKS, Inc.
3295 River Exchange Dr., Suite 430
Norcross, GA 30092

Founded 1987
Total employees 62
Annual sales $5 million
Industry Computer Software
Growth Openings in past year 17; percentage growth 37%
Contact
Joseph Richburg, COB/CEO
Tel 404-448-4240
Fax 404-448-4163

KnowledgeWare, Inc.
3340 Peachtree Rd. Northeast
Atlanta, GA 30326

Founded 1979
Total employees 845
Annual sales $129 million
Industry Computer Software
Growth Openings in past year 48; percentage growth 6%
Contact
Francis A. Tarkenton, COB/CEO
Tel 404-231-8575

Mayo Chemical Co., Inc.
5544 Oakdale Rd. Southeast
Smyrna, GA 30082

Founded 1952
Total employees 130
Industries Chemicals, Holding Companies
Growth Openings in past year 30; percentage growth 30%
Contact
Dr. Atif Dabdoub, Ph.D., President
Tel 404-696-6711
Fax 404-696-7463

Melita International Corporation
6630 Bay Circle
Norcross, GA 30071

Founded 1979
Total employees 160
Industry Computer Hardware
Growth Openings in past year 30; percentage growth 23%
Contact
Aleksander Szlam, President
Tel 404-446-7800
Fax 404-409-4444

Norton Construction Products
4600 Cantrell Rd., PO Box 2898
Gainesville, GA 30503

Founded 1978
Total employees 250
Annual sales $26 million
Industries Energy, Factory Automation
Growth Openings in past year 50; percentage growth 25%
Contact
Trevor Callender, Personnel Manager
Tel 404-967-3954
Fax 404-967-4287

Patterson Pump Co.
PO Box 790
Toccoa, GA 30577

Founded 1874
Total employees 360
Annual sales $35 million
Industries Factory Automation, Subassemblies and Components, Test and Measurement
Growth Openings in past year 110; percentage growth 44%
Contact
Charles Craig, Human Resources Manager
Tel 706-886-2101
Fax 706-886-0023

PCC Airfoils, Inc.
1400 Pope Dr.
Douglas, GA 31533

Founded 1985
Total employees 350
Annual sales $40 million

Industry Transportation
Growth Openings in past year 23; percentage growth 7%
Contact
Ron Swymer, Human Resources Manager
Tel 912-384-6633
Fax 912-384-0100

Phillips & Brooks/ Gladwin, Inc.
PO Box 267
Cumming, GA 30130

Founded 1958
Total employees 230
Annual sales $43 million
Industry Telecommunications
Growth Openings in past year 30; percentage growth 15%
Contact
Frank Jarman, President
Tel 404-887-9901
Fax 404-887-9511

RealCom Office Communications, Inc.
2030 Powers Ferry Rd., Suite 580
Atlanta, GA 30339

Founded 1989
Total employees 265
Annual sales $49 million
Industries Computer Software, Telecommunications
Growth Openings in past year 45; percentage growth 20%
Contact
Thomas Thorsen, Director of Human Resources
Tel 404-859-1100
Fax 404-859-9277

Rhone Merieux, Inc.
115 Transtech Dr.
Athens, GA 30601

Founded 1983
Total employees 220
Industry Pharmaceuticals
Growth Openings in past year 140; percentage growth 175%
Contact
Donald Hildebrand, President
Tel 706-548-9292
Fax 706-548-0608

Royal Oak Enterprises, Inc.
900 Ashwood Pkwy., Suite 800
Atlanta, GA 30338

Founded 1970
Total employees 700
Annual sales $100 million
Industry Holding Companies
Growth Openings in past year 200; percentage growth 40%
Contact
James P. Keeter, President/CEO
Tel 404-393-1430
Fax 404-394-9208

SofNet, Inc.
380 Interstate North Pkwy., Suite 150
Atlanta, GA 30339

Founded 1990
Total employees 45
Industry Computer Software
Growth Openings in past year 27; percentage growth 150%
Contact
Patrick Dane, President
Tel 404-984-8088
Fax 404-984-9956

Softlab, Inc.
1000 Abernathy Rd., Suite 1000
Atlanta, GA 30328

Founded 1979
Total employees 32
Industry Computer Software
Growth Openings in past year 17; percentage growth 113%
Contact
Dan Jenkins, President/ CEO
Tel 404-668-8811
Fax 404-668-8812

Solvay Pharmaceuticals
901 Sawyer Rd.
Marietta, GA 30062

Founded 1962
Total employees 971
Annual sales $110 million
Industry Pharmaceuticals
Growth Openings in past year 120; percentage growth 14%

Contact
Dr. James Warren,
President/CEO
Tel 404-578-9000
Fax 404-565-3311

**Stockholder Systems,
Inc.**
4411 East Jones Bridge
Rd.
Norcross, GA 30092

Founded 1971
Total employees 350
Annual sales $40 million
Industry Computer
Software
Growth Openings in past
year 38; percentage
growth 12%
Contact
Robert L. Campbell,
President
Tel 404-441-3387
Fax 404-242-7935

System Builder Corp.
5901A Peachtree
Dunwoody Rd., Suite 550
Atlanta, GA 30328

Founded 1982
Total employees 120
Annual sales $13 million
Industry Computer
Software
Growth Openings in past
year 20; percentage
growth 20%
Contact
Giora Friede, President
Tel 404-392-8370
Fax 404-640-9441

System Works, Inc.
1640 Powers Ferry Rd.,
Bldg. 11
Marietta, GA 30067

Founded 1976
Total employees 190
Annual sales $20 million
Industry Computer
Software
Growth Openings in past
year 65; percentage
growth 52%
Contact
David P. Welden,
President
Tel 404-952-8444
Fax 404-955-2977

Walker Equipment Corp.
Hwy. 151 South, PO Box
829
Ringgold, GA 30736

Founded 1971
Total employees 85
Industry
Telecommunications
Growth Openings in past
year 35; percentage
growth 70%
Contact
Marv Tseu, President
Tel 706-935-2600
Fax 706-935-4603

**Waste Abatement
Technology**
1300 Williams Dr.
Marietta, GA 30066

Founded 1986
Total employees 50
Annual sales $12.2 million
Industry Environmental
Growth Openings in past
year 25; percentage
growth 100%
Contact
Gerald Mann, President
Tel 404-427-1947
Fax 404-427-1907

**Westinghouse
Remediation Services,
Inc.**
675 Park North Blvd.,
Suite F-100
Clarkston, GA 30021

Founded 1983
Total employees 278
Annual sales $29 million
Industry Environmental
Growth Openings in past
year 128; percentage
growth 85%
Contact
Ralph Fernandez,
Manager
Tel 404-299-4650
Fax 404-296-9752

World Travel Partners
1055 Lenox Park Blvd.,
Suite 420
Atlanta, GA 30319

Founded 1987
Total employees 650
Industry Holding
Companies
Growth Openings in past
year 249; percentage
growth 62%

Contact
Jack Alexander, Chief
Executive Officer
Tel 404-841-6600
Fax 404-841-2983

**Yokogawa Corp. of
America**
2 Dart Rd.
Newnan, GA 30265

Founded 1957
Total employees 260
Annual sales $36.5 million
Industries Factory
Automation,
Subassemblies and
Components, Test and
Measurement
Growth Openings in past
year 34; percentage
growth 15%
Contact
Tadanori Fukuda,
President
Tel 404-253-7000
Fax 404-251-2088

Idaho

**Advanced Hardware
Architecture Corp.**
PO Box 9669
Moscow, ID 83843

Founded 1988
Total employees 50
Annual sales $4.8 million
Industry Subassemblies
and Components
Growth Openings in past
year 20; percentage
growth 66%
Contact
John Overby, President/
CEO
Tel 208-883-8000
Fax 208-883-8001

Advanced Input Devices
West 250 Aid Dr.
Coeur D'Alene, ID 83814

Founded 1978
Total employees 240
Annual sales $21 million
Industry Computer
Hardware
Growth Openings in past
year 40; percentage
growth 20%

Contact
Les Larsen, President
Tel 208-765-8000
Fax 208-772-7613

Electronic Controls Co.
PO Box 7246
Boise, ID 83707

Founded 1972
Total employees 110
Annual sales $13 million
Industries Photonics, Test
and Measurement
Growth Openings in past
year 20; percentage
growth 22%
Contact
Ed Zimmer, President/
COO
Tel 208-376-0707
Fax 208-376-3410

**Micron Custom
Manufacturing Services,
Inc.**
8455 West Park St.
Boise, ID 83704

Founded 1978
Total employees 400
Annual sales $39 million
Industries Computer
Hardware,
Subassemblies and
Components
Growth Openings in past
year 50; percentage
growth 14%
Contact
Joseph M. Daltoso,
COB/President
Tel 208-368-2661
Fax 208-368-2789

Scientech, Inc.
1690 International Way
Idaho Falls, ID 83402

Founded 1983
Total employees 275
Industries Energy,
Environmental,
Manufacturing Equipment
Growth Openings in past
year 75; percentage
growth 37%
Contact
L.J. Ybarrondo, Ph.D.,
President
Tel 208-523-2077
Fax 208-529-4721

Illinois

Alfred Benesch & Co.
205 North Michigan, 24th
Floor
Chicago, IL 60601

Founded 1946
Total employees 165
Annual sales $20 million
Industries Manufacturing
Equipment,
Telecommunications
Growth Openings in past
year 19; percentage
growth 13%
Contact
Michael Goodkind,
President
Tel 312-565-0450
Fax 312-565-2497

**Allied Products Corp.,
Verson Corp.**
1355 East 93rd St.
Chicago, IL 60619

Founded 1920
Total employees 600
Industries Factory
Automation,
Manufacturing Equipment
Growth Openings in past
year 50; percentage
growth 9%
Contact
John Perish, VP of Human
Resources
Tel 312-933-8200
Fax 312-933-8225

**AlliedSignal Inc.,
AlliedSignal Research
and Technology**
50 East Algonquin Rd., PO
Box 5016
Des Plaines, IL 60017

Founded 1955
Total employees 445
Industries Advanced
Materials, Biotechnology,
Chemicals
Growth Openings in past
year 95; percentage
growth 27%
Contact
Dr. Mary Good, Executive
Vice President
Tel 708-391-3500
Fax 708-391-3291

Alltech Associates, Inc.
2051 Waukegan Rd.
Deerfield, IL 60015

Founded 1971
Total employees 170
Annual sales $20 million
Industries Subassemblies
and Components, Test
and Measurement
Growth Openings in past
year 30; percentage
growth 21%
Contact
Ms. Joanne Topcik,
Personnel Manager
Tel 708-948-8600
Fax 708-948-1078

**American Colloid Co.,
Inc.**
1500 West Shure Dr.
Arlington Heights, IL
60004

Founded 1924
Total employees 975
Annual sales $183 million
Industry Advanced
Materials
Growth Openings in past
year 89; percentage
growth 10%
Contact
John Hughes, President/
CEO
Tel 708-392-4600
Fax 708-506-6199

Anatol Automation, Inc.
1060 High St.
Mundelein, IL 60060

Founded 1982
Total employees 100
Annual sales $10 million
Industry Factory
Automation
Growth Openings in past
year 25; percentage
growth 33%
Contact
Anatol Topolewski,
President
Tel 708-949-0330
Fax 708-949-2901

ANGUS Chemical Co.
1500 East Lake Cook Rd.
Buffalo Grove, IL 60089

Founded 1983
Total employees 358
Annual sales $77 million

Industries Advanced
Materials, Biotechnology,
Chemicals,
Pharmaceuticals
Growth Openings in past
year 30; percentage
growth 9%
Contact
Gary W. Granzow,
President/CEO
Tel 708-215-8600
Fax 708-215-8626

**Application Engineering
Corp.**
801 AEC Dr.
Wood Dale, IL 60191

Founded 1980
Total employees 330
Annual sales $41 million
Industry Factory
Automation
Growth Openings in past
year 80; percentage
growth 32%
Contact
Robert Zega, VP of
Human Resources
Tel 708-595-1060
Fax 708-595-6641

Applied Systems, Inc.
2500 Bond St.
University Park, IL 60466

Founded 1980
Total employees 650
Annual sales $52 million
Industry Computer
Software
Growth Openings in past
year 150; percentage
growth 30%
Contact
Bob Eustace, COB/CEO
Tel 708-534-5575
Fax 708-534-1216

BACG, Inc.
1301 West 22nd St., Suite
914
Oak Brook, IL 60521

Founded 1988
Total employees 200
Annual sales $25 million
Industry Computer
Software
Growth Openings in past
year 50; percentage
growth 33%

Contact
Steve Jarrett, General
Manager/North America
Tel 708-571-1616
Fax 708-571-2193

**Barrett Industrial Trucks,
Inc.**
240 North Prospect St.
Marengo, IL 60152

Founded 1914
Total employees 400
Industry Factory
Automation
Growth Openings in past
year 100; percentage
growth 33%
Contact
Ms. Shirley Kennedy,
Personnel Manager
Tel 815-568-6525
Fax 815-568-8340

**Blackstone
Manufacturing Co., Inc.**
4630 West Harrison St.
Chicago, IL 60644

Founded 1924
Total employees 300
Industries Subassemblies
and Components,
Transportation
Growth Openings in past
year 70; percentage
growth 30%
Contact
1ichard Youmans, Division
Manager
Tel 312-378-7800
Fax 312-378-8194

**Boots Pharmaceutical,
Inc.**
300 Tri State International
Ctr., Suite 200
Lincolnshire, IL 60069

Founded 1986
Total employees 850
Industry Pharmaceuticals
Growth Openings in past
year 148; percentage
growth 21%
Contact
Carter H. Eckert, President
Tel 708-405-7400
Fax 708-405-7505

Brake Parts, Inc.
4400 Prime Pkwy.
Mc Henry, IL 60050

Founded 1988
Total employees 200

Annual sales $19 million
Industry Subassemblies
and Components
Growth Openings in past
year 40; percentage
growth 25%
Contact
Larry Pavey, President
Tel 815-363-9000
Fax 815-363-9303

**Brunswick Corp.,
Intellitec Division**
131 Eisenhower Ln.
Lombard, IL 60148

Founded 1976
Total employees 65
Annual sales $4.5 million
Industries Manufacturing
Equipment,
Subassemblies and
Components,
Transportation
Growth Openings in past
year 25; percentage
growth 62%
Contact
William H. Slavik, General
Manager
Tel 708-268-0010
Fax 708-916-7890

**Burgess-Norton
Manufacturing Co.**
737 Peyton St.
Geneva, IL 60134

Founded 1903
Total employees 850
Annual sales $83 million
Industries Advanced
Materials, Subassemblies
and Components
Growth Openings in past
year 49; percentage
growth 6%
Contact
Steve Kelm, Director of
Industrial Relations
Tel 708-232-4100
Fax 708-232-3634

Cara Corp.
1900 Spring Rd., Suite
450
Oak Brook, IL 60521

Founded 1975
Total employees 270
Industries Computer
Software, Manufacturing
Equipment
Growth Openings in past
year 120; percentage
growth 80%

Contact
Anthony F. Durkin,
President
Tel 708-990-2272
Fax 708-368-2800

Chemtool, Inc., Metalcote
PO Box 538
Crystal Lake, IL 60039

Founded 1955
Total employees 90
Annual sales $10 million
Industries Advanced
Materials, Chemicals
Growth Openings in past
year 30; percentage
growth 50%
Contact
James Athans, President
Tel 815-459-1250
Fax 815-459-1955

**Chicago Miniature Lamp,
Inc.**
1080 Johnson Dr.
Buffalo Grove, IL 60089

Founded 1987
Total employees 225
Industry Photonics
Growth Openings in past
year 25; percentage
growth 12%
Contact
Don MacCrindle, Executive
Vice President
Tel 708-459-3400
Fax 708-459-2708

Circuit Systems, Inc.
2350 East Lunt Ave.
Elk Grove Village, IL
60007

Founded 1967
Total employees 520
Annual sales $51.42
million
Industry Subassemblies
and Components
Growth Openings in past
year 20; percentage
growth 4%
Contact
D.S. Patel, COB/President/
CEO
Tel 708-439-1999
Fax 708-437-5910

Clean Air Engineering
500 West Wood St.
Palatine, IL 60067

Founded 1973
Total employees 240

Industry Environmental
Growth Openings in past
year 20; percentage
growth 9%
Contact
William Walker, President
Tel 708-991-3300
Fax 708-991-3385

**Commercial Testing &
Engineering Co.**
1919 South Highland Ave.,
Suite 210B
Lombard, IL 60148

Founded 1908
Total employees 750
Annual sales $89 million
Industries Manufacturing
Equipment, Test and
Measurement
Growth Openings in past
year 50; percentage
growth 7%
Contact
Dr. M.A. Hildon, President
Tel 708-953-9300
Fax 708-953-9306

Compaction America
2000 Kentville Rd.
Kewanee, IL 61443

Founded 1880
Total employees 240
Annual sales $50 million
Industry Environmental
Growth Openings in past
year 40; percentage
growth 20%
Contact
John Blake, Human
Resources Manager
Tel 309-853-1002
Fax 309-853-1319

**Construction
Engineering Research
Laboratories**
2902 Newmark Dr., PO
Box 9005
Champaign, IL 61826

Founded 1969
Total employees 959
Industries Defense,
Energy, Environmental
Growth Openings in past
year 103; percentage
growth 12%
Contact
Dr. L.R. Shaffer, Director
Tel 217-352-6511
Fax 217-373-7222

C.P. Hall Co.
311 South Wacker Dr.,
#4700
Chicago, IL 60606

Founded 1919
Total employees 225
Industry Advanced
Materials
Growth Openings in past
year 25; percentage
growth 12%
Contact
George Vincent, President
Tel 312-767-4600
Fax 708-458-0428

**Daily & Associates
Engineers, Inc.**
1610 Broadmoor Dr.
Champaign, IL 61821

Founded 1964
Total employees 120
Annual sales $10 million
Industries Holding
Companies,
Manufacturing Equipment
Growth Openings in past
year 20; percentage
growth 20%
Contact
Woodrow Chenault,
President
Tel 217-352-4169
Fax 217-352-0085

**Daily Analytical
Laboratories**
1621 West Candletree Dr.
Peoria, IL 61614

Founded 1965
Total employees 60
Industry Environmental
Growth Openings in past
year 17; percentage
growth 39%
Contact
Doug Bischoff, Operations
Director
Tel 309-692-5252
Fax 309-692-0488

**Darome
Teleconferencing, Inc.**
8750 West Bryn Mawr
Ave., Suite 850
Chicago, IL 60631

Founded 1969
Total employees 250
Industry
Telecommunications

Growth Openings in past year 50; percentage growth 25%
Contact
Ms. Rebecca Watkins, Personnel Manager
Tel 312-399-1610
Fax 312-380-4314

Dauphin Technology, Inc.
377 East Butterfield Rd., Suite 900
Lombard, IL 60148

Founded 1988
Total employees 70
Annual sales $24 million
Industry Computer Hardware
Growth Openings in past year 25; percentage growth 55%
Contact
Alan Yong, President
Tel 708-971-3400
Fax 708-971-8443

Dearborn Wire & Cable L.P.
250 West Carpenter Ave.
Wheeling, IL 60090

Founded 1962
Total employees 250
Annual sales $50 million
Industry Subassemblies and Components
Growth Openings in past year 15; percentage growth 6%
Contact
Bud Greene, President
Tel 708-459-1000
Fax 708-459-0170

Delphi Information Systems, Inc.
3501 Algonquin Rd., Suite #500
Rolling Meadows, IL 60008

Founded 1976
Total employees 400
Annual sales $50 million
Industries Computer Software, Holding Companies
Growth Openings in past year 50; percentage growth 14%
Contact
David J. Torrence, President
Tel 708-506-3100
Fax 708-590-8280

Desktop Sales, Inc.
3210 Doolittle Dr.
Northbrook, IL 60062

Founded 1988
Total employees 140
Annual sales $23 million
Industry Computer Hardware
Growth Openings in past year 40; percentage growth 40%
Contact
Mark Polinsky, Chief Executive Officer
Tel 708-272-9695
Fax 708-272-8244

Educational Resources
1550 Executive Dr.
Elgin, IL 60123

Founded 1984
Total employees 120
Annual sales $19 million
Industry Computer Hardware
Growth Openings in past year 30; percentage growth 33%
Contact
Forest Barbieri, President
Tel 708-888-8300
Fax 708-888-8689

Enterprise Systems, Inc.
1400 South Wolf Rd., Suite 500
Wheeling, IL 60090

Founded 1981
Total employees 220
Annual sales $21 million
Industry Computer Software
Growth Openings in past year 28; percentage growth 14%
Contact
Thomas Pirelli, Chief Executive Officer
Tel 708-537-4800
Fax 708-537-4866

Envirodyne Engineers, Inc.
168 North Clinton St.
Chicago, IL 60661

Founded 1977
Total employees 300
Annual sales $23 million
Industries Environmental, Manufacturing Equipment

Growth Openings in past year 37; percentage growth 14%
Contact
James J. Powers, President
Tel 312-648-1700
Fax 312-648-4544

Fansteel, Inc., Escast Division
21 North Church St.
Addison, IL 60101

Founded 1943
Total employees 120
Annual sales $15 million
Industries Factory Automation, Manufacturing Equipment
Growth Openings in past year 40; percentage growth 50%
Contact
P.J. Manning, General Manager
Tel 708-543-6800
Fax 708-543-2095

FCS Computing Services, Inc.
601 West Randolph St.
Chicago, IL 60606

Founded 1979
Total employees 50
Industry Computer Hardware
Growth Openings in past year 29; percentage growth 138%
Contact
John R. Finch, President
Tel 312-993-3434
Fax 312-993-3433

Fotel, Inc.
41 West Home Ave.
Villa Park, IL 60181

Founded 1964
Total employees 48
Annual sales $4.6 million
Industries Computer Hardware, Photonics, Subassemblies and Components
Growth Openings in past year 17; percentage growth 54%
Contact
John Nachtrieb, COB/CEO
Tel 708-834-4920
Fax 708-834-5250

Frasca International, Inc.
906 East Airport Rd.
Urbana, IL 61801

Founded 1958
Total employees 165
Annual sales $19 million
Industry Transportation
Growth Openings in past
year 15; percentage
growth 10%
Contact
Ms. Karen Crewell,
Director of Personnel
Tel 217-344-9200
Fax 217-344-9207

Greenbrier & Russel, Inc.
1450 East American Ln.
Schaumburg, IL 60173

Founded 1984
Total employees 210
Annual sales $15 million
Industry Computer
Software
Growth Openings in past
year 65; percentage
growth 44%
Contact
Nick Blake, VP of
Operations
Tel 708-706-4000
Fax 708-706-4020

Hanson Engineers, Inc.
1525 South 6th St.
Springfield, IL 62703

Founded 1954
Total employees 193
Annual sales $15 million
Industries Advanced
Materials, Environmental,
Manufacturing Equipment
Growth Openings in past
year 31; percentage
growth 19%
Contact
Leo J. Dondanville, Jr.,
COB/CEO
Tel 217-788-2450
Fax 217-788-2503

Homaco, Inc.
1875 West Fullerton Ave.
Chicago, IL 60614

Founded 1968
Total employees 140
Annual sales $11 million
Industry Subassemblies
and Components
Growth Openings in past
year 20; percentage
growth 16%

Contact
Bruce D. Holcomb,
President
Tel 312-384-5575
Fax 312-384-6080

**Indeck Energy Services,
Inc.**
1130 Lake Cook Rd., Suite
300
Buffalo Grove, IL 60089

Founded 1985
Total employees 180
Annual sales $24 million
Industry Energy
Growth Openings in past
year 50; percentage
growth 38%
Contact
Russell F. Lindsay,
President
Tel 708-520-3212
Fax 708-520-9883

Internet Systems Corp.
180 North Stetson, 42nd
Floor
Chicago, IL 60601

Founded 1981
Total employees 400
Annual sales $46 million
Industry Computer
Software
Growth Openings in past
year 50; percentage
growth 14%
Contact
W. Ron Mahoney,
President/CEO
Tel 312-540-0100
Fax 312-540-0118

**Kalmus and Associates,
Inc.**
2424 South 25th Ave.
Broadview, IL 60153

Founded 1937
Total employees 300
Annual sales $29 million
Industry Subassemblies
and Components
Growth Openings in past
year 25; percentage
growth 9%
Contact
Henry J. Kalmus, Jr.,
President/CEO
Tel 708-343-7004
Fax 708-343-7016

**Levi, Ray and Shoup,
Inc.**
2401 West Monroe St.
Springfield, IL 62704

Founded 1979
Total employees 140
Annual sales $16 million
Industries Computer
Hardware, Computer
Software
Growth Openings in past
year 15; percentage
growth 12%
Contact
Roger Ray, Executive Vice
President
Tel 217-793-3800
Fax 217-787-3286

LoDan Electronics, Inc.
220 West Campus Dr.,
Suite A
Arlington Heights, IL
60004

Founded 1967
Total employees 190
Annual sales $18 million
Industry Subassemblies
and Components
Growth Openings in past
year 40; percentage
growth 26%
Contact
Ms. Danielle Rossini,
Human Resources
Manager
Tel 708-398-5311
Fax 708-398-5340

**Macrotech Fluid Sealing,
Inc., Selastomer Division**
345 East Green St.
Bensenville, IL 60106

Founded 1974
Total employees 160
Annual sales $15 million
Industry Subassemblies
and Components
Growth Openings in past
year 40; percentage
growth 33%
Contact
Brian Rericha, General
Manager
Tel 708-860-4600
Fax 708-860-5256

**Marketing Information
Systems, Inc.**
1840 Oak Ave.
Evanston, IL 60201

Founded 1981
Total employees 65

Industry Computer
Software
Growth Openings in past
year 15; percentage
growth 30%
Contact
John B. Kennedy,
President
Tel 708-491-3885
Fax 708-491-0682

**Medicus Systems
Corporation**
One Rotary Ctr., Suite 400
Evanston, IL 60201

Founded 1984
Total employees 250
Annual sales $24.99
million
Industries Computer
Hardware, Computer
Software
Growth Openings in past
year 50; percentage
growth 25%
Contact
Richard C. Jelinek,
COB/CEO/President
Tel 708-570-7500
Fax 708-570-7518

Metform, Inc.
2551 Wacker Rd.
Savanna, IL 61074

Founded 1976
Total employees 230
Annual sales $25 million
Industries Manufacturing
Equipment,
Subassemblies and
Components
Growth Openings in past
year 32; percentage
growth 16%
Contact
Barry MacLean, President
Tel 815-273-2201
Fax 815-273-7837

**Micro Solutions
Computer Products, Inc.**
132 West Lincoln Hwy.
De Kalb, IL 60115

Founded 1980
Total employees 50
Annual sales $8.2 million
Industry Computer
Hardware
Growth Openings in past
year 15; percentage
growth 42%

Contact
Ms. Debby Armstrong,
Marketing Manager
Tel 815-756-3421
Fax 815-756-2928

**Mid-West Automation
Systems, Inc.**
1400 Busch Pkwy.
Buffalo Grove, IL 60089

Founded 1965
Total employees 375
Annual sales $36 million
Industry Factory
Automation
Growth Openings in past
year 100; percentage
growth 36%
Contact
Richard Deron, Personnel
Manager
Tel 708-541-3570
Fax 708-541-8562

**Mostardi-Platt
Associates, Inc.**
945 Oaklawn Ave.
Elmhurst, IL 60126

Founded 1976
Total employees 94
Industry Environmental
Growth Openings in past
year 16; percentage
growth 20%
Contact
Robert J. Platt, PE,
President
Tel 708-993-9000
Fax 708-993-9017

**MultiMedia
Communication Systems**
8707 Skokie Blvd.
Skokie, IL 60076

Founded 1987
Total employees 35
Annual sales $10 million
Industries Computer
Hardware, Computer
Software,
Telecommunications
Growth Openings in past
year 25; percentage
growth 250%
Contact
Stanley M. Abramson,
Chief Executive Officer
Tel 708-673-8488
Fax 708-673-9244

**Nashua Precision
Technologies**
1401 Interstate Dr.
Champaign, IL 61821

Founded 1982
Total employees 234
Annual sales $38 million
Industry Computer
Hardware
Growth Openings in past
year 27; percentage
growth 13%
Contact
Kirk Bales, Purchasing and
Human Resources
Manager
Tel 217-359-3700
Fax 217-359-3702

Nissan Forklift Corp.
240 North Prospect St.
Marengo, IL 60152

Founded 1965
Total employees 450
Annual sales $170 million
Industries Factory
Automation, Holding
Companies
Growth Openings in past
year 49; percentage
growth 12%
Contact
John Hoyce, VP of
Personnel
Tel 815-568-0061
Fax 815-568-0179

Nunc, Inc.
2000 North Aurora Rd.
Naperville, IL 60563

Founded 1987
Total employees 169
Annual sales $16 million
Industries Biotechnology,
Test and Measurement
Growth Openings in past
year 29; percentage
growth 20%
Contact
Verner B. Andersen,
President
Tel 708-983-5700
Fax 708-416-2519

**Platinum Technology,
Inc.**
1815 South Meyers Rd.
Oak Brook Terrace, IL
60181

Founded 1987
Total employees 285
Annual sales $49 million

Industry Computer
Software
Growth Openings in past
year 97; percentage
growth 51%
Contact
Ms. Jennifer Werneke,
Director of Human
Resources
Tel 708-620-5000
Fax 708-691-0710

Polyfoam Packers Corp.
2320 Foster Ave.
Wheeling, IL 60090

Founded 1946
Total employees 250
Annual sales $25 million
Industry Factory
Automation
Growth Openings in past
year 50; percentage
growth 25%
Contact
Tevy Osterman, Personnel
Manager
Tel 708-398-0110
Fax 708-398-0653

**Pre Finish Metals
Incorporated**
2300 East Pratt Blvd.
Elk Grove Village, IL
60007

Founded 1971
Total employees 675
Annual sales $120 million
Industry Advanced
Materials
Growth Openings in past
year 14; percentage
growth 2%
Contact
Gerald G. Nadig, President
Tel 708-439-2210
Fax 708-439-0737

Rauland-Borg Corp.
3450 West Oakton St.
Skokie, IL 60076

Founded 1978
Total employees 240
Annual sales $50 million
Industry
Telecommunications
Growth Openings in past
year 14; percentage
growth 6%
Contact
William Krucks, President/
CEO
Tel 708-679-0900
Fax 708-679-0950

**Resource Information
Management Systems,
Inc.**
500 Technology Dr., PO
Box 3094
Naperville, IL 60566

Founded 1981
Total employees 160
Annual sales $19 million
Industry Computer
Software
Growth Openings in past
year 30; percentage
growth 23%
Contact
Thomas Heimsoth, Chief
Executive Officer
Tel 708-369-5300
Fax 708-369-5168

Seaquist Dispensing
1160 North Silver Lake Rd.
Cary, IL 60013

Founded 1947
Total employees 350
Annual sales $44 million
Industry Factory
Automation
Growth Openings in past
year 49; percentage
growth 16%
Contact
James Reed, President
Tel 708-639-2124
Fax 708-639-2142

**Siemens Medical
Systems, Inc., Nuclear
Medicine Group**
2501 North Barrington Rd.
Hoffman Estates, IL 60195

Founded 1947
Total employees 924
Annual sales $100 million
Industries Computer
Software, Medical,
Photonics
Growth Openings in past
year 19; percentage
growth 2%
Contact
Allen Jakes, Director of
Personnel
Tel 708-304-7700
Fax 708-304-7701

Sierra, Inc.
1 Sierra Place
Litchfield, IL 62056

Founded 1924
Total employees 95
Annual sales $26 million

Industry Subassemblies
and Components
Growth Openings in past
year 20; percentage
growth 26%
Contact
Peter Venter, General
Manager
Tel 217-324-9400
Fax 217-324-2461

**SoloPak
Pharmaceuticals, Inc.**
1845 Tonne Rd.
Elk Grove Village, IL
60007

Founded 1970
Total employees 400
Industries Medical,
Pharmaceuticals
Growth Openings in past
year 100; percentage
growth 33%
Contact
Dave Dvorak, Director of
Human Resources
Tel 708-806-0080
Fax 708-806-0087

**Speedfam Corp.,
Machine Tool Group**
509 North Third Ave.
Des Plaines, IL 60016

Founded 1970
Total employees 65
Annual sales $10 million
Industry Factory
Automation
Growth Openings in past
year 15; percentage
growth 30%
Contact
Byron Sheets, General
Manager
Tel 708-803-3200
Fax 708-803-9875

Stericycle, Inc.
1419 Lake Cook Rd.
Deerfield, IL 60015

Founded 1989
Total employees 130
Annual sales $13 million
Industry Environmental
Growth Openings in past
year 30; percentage
growth 30%
Contact
Mark Miller, President/CEO
Tel 708-945-6550
Fax 708-945-6583

SunGard Investment Systems, Inc.
11 Salt Creek Ln.
Hinsdale, IL 60521

Founded 1967
Total employees 100
Annual sales $6.9 million
Industry Computer Software
Growth Openings in past year 40; percentage growth 66%
Contact
Phillip Dowd, President
Tel 708-920-3100
Fax 708-920-8038

Superior Graphite Co.
120 South Riverside Plaza
Chicago, IL 60606

Founded 1917
Total employees 275
Annual sales $40 million
Industry Advanced Materials
Growth Openings in past year 44; percentage growth 19%
Contact
Peter Carney, President
Tel 312-559-2999
Fax 312-559-9064

Surya Electronics, Inc.
600 Windy Point Dr.
Glendale Heights, IL 60139

Founded 1983
Total employees 90
Industries Computer Software, Manufacturing Equipment, Subassemblies and Components
Growth Openings in past year 25; percentage growth 38%
Contact
Bob Patel, President
Tel 708-858-8000
Fax 708-858-0103

Systems and Programming Resources, Inc.
635 Executive Dr.
Willowbrook, IL 60521

Founded 1973
Total employees 125
Annual sales $14 million
Industry Computer Software

Growth Openings in past year 25; percentage growth 25%
Contact
Robert Figliulo, President
Tel 708-323-1652
Fax 708-323-1732

Telular Group L.P.
1215 Washington Ave.
Wilmette, IL 60091

Founded 1986
Total employees 57
Industry Telecommunications
Growth Openings in past year 20; percentage growth 54%
Contact
Steven P. Wolfe, President
Tel 708-256-8000
Fax 708-256-3555

THK America, Inc.
200 East Commerce Dr.
Schaumburg, IL 60173

Founded 1971
Total employees 50
Annual sales $4.8 million
Industries Factory Automation, Subassemblies and Components
Growth Openings in past year 21; percentage growth 72%
Contact
H. Teremachi, President
Tel 708-310-1111
Fax 708-310-1182

Total Control Products, Inc.
2001 North Janice Ave.
Melrose Park, IL 60160

Founded 1982
Total employees 90
Annual sales $13 million
Industry Computer Hardware
Growth Openings in past year 15; percentage growth 20%
Contact
Julius Sparacino, COB/ President
Tel 708-345-5500
Fax 708-345-5670

TransTechnology Corp., Electronics Division
8800 North Allen Rd.
Peoria, IL 61615

Founded 1962
Total employees 272
Annual sales $20 million
Industry Subassemblies and Components
Growth Openings in past year 166; percentage growth 156%
Contact
Randy Skender, Director of Human Resources
Tel 309-693-3322
Fax 309-693-3308

U.S. Robotics, Inc.
8100 North McCormick Blvd.
Skokie, IL 60076

Founded 1976
Total employees 479
Annual sales $189.16 million
Industries Computer Software, Telecommunications
Growth Openings in past year 77; percentage growth 19%
Contact
Ms. Elizabeth Ryan, VP of Human Resources
Tel 708-982-5010
Fax 708-982-5203

Vapor Mark IV, Transportation Products Group
6420 West Howard St.
Niles, IL 60714

Founded 1904
Total employees 500
Annual sales $58 million
Industry Holding Companies
Growth Openings in past year 50; percentage growth 11%
Contact
Dennis Hubner, Director of Human Resources
Tel 708-967-8300
Fax 708-470-7824

Velsicol Chemical Corp.
10400 West Higgins Rd., Suite 600
Rosemont, IL 60018

Founded 1975
Total employees 475

Annual sales $100 million
Industries Advanced
Materials, Chemicals
Growth Openings in past
year 23; percentage
growth 5%
Contact
Ms. Donna Jennings,
Director of Human
Resources and
Communic
Tel 708-298-9000
Fax 708-298-9014

**Viktron Technologies,
Inc., Electronics Support
Systems Division**
475 Industrial Dr.
West Chicago, IL 60185

Founded 1972
Total employees 120
Annual sales $11 million
Industry Subassemblies
and Components
Growth Openings in past
year 40; percentage
growth 50%
Contact
Robert Duke, Vice
President/General
Manager
Tel 708-293-7300
Fax 708-293-7176

**Wes-Tech Automation
Systems, Inc.**
720 Dartmouth Dr.
Buffalo Grove, IL 60089

Founded 1976
Total employees 85
Annual sales $10 million
Industries Factory
Automation,
Manufacturing Equipment
Growth Openings in past
year 25; percentage
growth 41%
Contact
Robert Weskamp,
President
Tel 708-541-5070
Fax 708-541-0096

Wizdom Systems, Inc.
1300 Iroquois Dr.
Naperville, IL 60563

Founded 1986
Total employees 67
Annual sales $5 million
Industry Holding
Companies

Growth Openings in past
year 33; percentage
growth 97%
Contact
Dennis Wisnosky,
President
Tel 708-357-3000
Fax 708-357-3059

Wolfram Research, Inc.
100 Trade Center Dr.
Champaign, IL 61820

Founded 1987
Total employees 150
Annual sales $17 million
Industry Computer
Software
Growth Openings in past
year 30; percentage
growth 25%
Contact
Stephen Wolfram,
President
Tel 217-398-0700
Fax 217-398-0747

**Zebra Technologies
Corp.**
333 Corporate Woods
Pkwy.
Vernon Hills, IL 60061

Founded 1969
Total employees 300
Annual sales $45 million
Industry Computer
Hardware
Growth Openings in past
year 85; percentage
growth 39%
Contact
Walter Newborn,
Personnel Manager
Tel 708-634-6700
Fax 708-913-8766

Zenith Controls, Inc.
830 West 40th St.
Chicago, IL 60609

Founded 1923
Total employees 250
Annual sales $33 million
Industries Energy,
Subassemblies and
Components
Growth Openings in past
year 50; percentage
growth 25%
Contact
Arthur Coren, President
Tel 312-247-6400
Fax 312-247-7805

Indiana

Allomatic Products Co.
609 East Cheney St., PO
Box 267
Sullivan, IN 47882

Founded 1954
Total employees 126
Annual sales $14.5 million
Industry Subassemblies
and Components
Growth Openings in past
year 16; percentage
growth 14%
Contact
Bob Fink, Personnel
Manager
Tel 812-268-0322
Fax 812-268-0417

**Arrowhead Plastic
Engineering, Inc.**
2909 Hoyt Ave.
Muncie, IN 47302

Founded 1972
Total employees 92
Industries Factory
Automation,
Manufacturing Equipment
Growth Openings in past
year 32; percentage
growth 53%
Contact
Tom Kishel, President
Tel 317-286-0533
Fax 317-286-1681

Auburn Foundry, Inc.
635 West 11th St.
Auburn, IN 46706

Founded 1911
Total employees 450
Annual sales $66 million
Industry Advanced
Materials
Growth Openings in past
year 69; percentage
growth 18%
Contact
Walt Bienz, VP of Benefits
Tel 219-925-0900
Fax 219-925-5137

BRC Rubber Group, Inc.
PO Box 227
Churubusco, IN 46723

Founded 1971
Total employees 870
Annual sales $94 million

Industries Advanced
 Materials, Manufacturing
 Equipment
Growth Openings in past
 year 26; percentage
 growth 3%
Contact
Charles V. Chaffee,
 President
Tel 219-693-2171
Fax 219-693-6511

Corson Research, Inc.
3134 Mallard Cove Ln.
Fort Wayne, IN 46804

Founded 1975
Total employees 220
Annual sales $15 million
Industry Holding
 Companies
Growth Openings in past
 year 55; percentage
 growth 33%
Contact
Charles A. Wilson, VP of
 Human Resources
Tel 219-432-3600
Fax 219-436-2364

Crowe Chizek and Co.
330 East Jefferson Blvd.,
 PO Box 7
South Bend, IN 46624

Founded 1942
Total employees 750
Annual sales $58 million
Industry Computer
 Software
Growth Openings in past
 year 150; percentage
 growth 25%
Contact
Ron Cohen, Managing
 Partner
Tel 219-232-3992
Fax 219-236-8692

Crown International, Inc.
1718 West Mishawaka Rd.
Elkhart, IN 46517

Founded 1947
Total employees 600
Annual sales $82 million
Industry Holding
 Companies
Growth Openings in past
 year 50; percentage
 growth 9%
Contact
Richard Pede, Human
 Resource Director
Tel 219-294-8000
Fax 219-294-8329

**Crown Unlimited
Machine, Inc.**
1336 West Wiley Ave.
Bluffton, IN 46714

Founded 1978
Total employees 45
Industry Factory
 Automation
Growth Openings in past
 year 15; percentage
 growth 50%
Contact
Steve Stroup, Sr., Chief
 Executive Officer
Tel 219-824-2630
Fax 219-824-0129

Dome Software Corp.
655 West Carmel Dr.,
 Suite 151
Carmel, IN 46032

Founded 1981
Total employees 50
Industries Computer
 Hardware, Computer
 Software
Growth Openings in past
 year 32; percentage
 growth 177%
Contact
Dr. Robert D. Hogan, Jr.,
 President
Tel 317-573-8100
Fax 317-573-8109

Dwyer Instruments, Inc.
PO Box 373
Michigan City, IN 46360

Founded 1932
Total employees 850
Annual sales $64 million
Industries Holding
 Companies,
 Subassemblies and
 Components, Test and
 Measurement
Growth Openings in past
 year 49; percentage
 growth 6%
Contact
Gregg Miller, Director of
 Industrial Relations
Tel 219-879-8000
Fax 219-872-9057

E/M Corp.
2801 Kent Ave., PO Box
 2400
West Lafayette, IN 47906

Founded 1970
Total employees 380
Annual sales $26 million

Industries Advanced
 Materials, Manufacturing
 Equipment, Photonics
Growth Openings in past
 year 79; percentage
 growth 26%
Contact
Lowell C. Horwedel,
 President
Tel 317-497-6346
Fax 317-497-6348

Ensolite, Inc.
312 North Hill St.
Mishawaka, IN 46544

Founded 1980
Total employees 300
Annual sales $50 million
Industry Advanced
 Materials
Growth Openings in past
 year 50; percentage
 growth 20%
Contact
Joe Bell, Manager of
 Personnel
Tel 219-255-2181

Galbreath, Inc.
PO Box 220
Winamac, IN 46996

Founded 1956
Total employees 275
Annual sales $29 million
Industry Environmental
Growth Openings in past
 year 14; percentage
 growth 5%
Contact
James Herrman, President
Tel 219-946-6631
Fax 219-946-4579

Grote Industries, Inc.
PO Box 1550
Madison, IN 47250

Founded 1901
Total employees 800
Annual sales $93 million
Industry Transportation
Growth Openings in past
 year 99; percentage
 growth 14%
Contact
Bruce Gruemmer, VP of
 Human Resources
Tel 812-273-2121
Fax 812-265-8440

Hammond Lead Products, Inc.
5231 Hohman Ave., PO Box 6408
Hammond, IN 46325

Founded 1933
Total employees 200
Industries Advanced Materials, Chemicals
Growth Openings in past year 50; percentage growth 33%
Contact
William P. Wilke, IV, President
Tel 219-931-9360
Fax 219-931-2140

Integrated Technologies, Inc.
9855 Crospoint Blvd., Suite 126
Indianapolis, IN 46256

Founded 1987
Total employees 43
Annual sales $4.9 million
Industry Computer Software
Growth Openings in past year 15; percentage growth 53%
Contact
W. Herbert Senft, II, President
Tel 317-577-8100
Fax 317-577-0450

JFW Industries, Inc.
5134 Commerce Square Dr.
Indianapolis, IN 46237

Founded 1979
Total employees 170
Annual sales $5 million
Industry Subassemblies and Components
Growth Openings in past year 67; percentage growth 65%
Contact
Ms. Joetta Walker, President
Tel 317-887-1340
Fax 317-881-6790

PHD, Inc.
PO Box 9070
Fort Wayne, IN 46899

Founded 1957
Total employees 303
Annual sales $38 million

Industries Factory Automation, Subassemblies and Components, Test and Measurement
Growth Openings in past year 87; percentage growth 40%
Contact
Jerry Hannah, Organizational Development Director
Tel 219-747-6151
Fax 219-747-6754

Polygon Co.
103 Industrial Park, PO Box 176
Walkerton, IN 46574

Founded 1950
Total employees 300
Annual sales $12 million
Industries Advanced Materials, Subassemblies and Components
Growth Openings in past year 20; percentage growth 7%
Contact
James Shobert, Chief Executive Officer
Tel 219-586-3122
Fax 219-586-7336

Reilly Industries, Inc., Chemical Division
1500 South Tibbs Ave.
Indianapolis, IN 46242

Founded 1896
Total employees 500
Annual sales $100 million
Industries Advanced Materials, Chemicals, Pharmaceuticals
Growth Openings in past year 24; percentage growth 5%
Contact
John Rogers, Plant Manager
Tel 317-247-8141
Fax 317-248-6413

Simpson Industries, Inc., Bluffton Operations
131 West Harvest St., PO Box 477
Bluffton, IN 46714

Founded 1945
Total employees 162
Annual sales $40 million

Industries Environmental, Subassemblies and Components
Growth Openings in past year 87; percentage growth 116%
Contact
Robert Flynn, Plant Manager
Tel 219-824-2360
Fax 219-824-5032

Software Artistry, Inc.
3500 Depauw Blvd., Suite 1100
Indianapolis, IN 46268

Founded 1988
Total employees 100
Annual sales $11 million
Industry Computer Software
Growth Openings in past year 50; percentage growth 100%
Contact
Don Brown, Chief Executive Officer
Tel 317-876-3042
Fax 317-876-3258

Thermwood Corp.
Old Buffaloville Rd.
Dale, IN 47523

Founded 1975
Total employees 150
Annual sales $12.0 million
Industry Factory Automation
Growth Openings in past year 45; percentage growth 42%
Contact
Ken Susnajara, President
Tel 812-937-4476
Fax 812-937-2956

Iowa

Alexander Batteries
PO Box 1508
Mason City, IA 50402

Founded 1967
Total employees 350
Annual sales $30 million
Industries Energy, Manufacturing Equipment
Growth Openings in past year 38; percentage growth 12%

Contact
Steve Alexandres,
  President/COO
Tel 515-423-8955
Fax 515-423-1644

Ambico, Inc.
902 Sugar Grove Ave.
Dallas Center, IA 50063

Founded 1974
Total employees 80
Industry Pharmaceuticals
Growth Openings in past
  year 30; percentage
  growth 60%
Contact
Mrs. Doris Welter,
  Executive Vice President
Tel 515-992-3842
Fax 515-992-3831

**Compressor Controls
Corp.**
11359 Aurora Ave.
Des Moines, IA 50322

Founded 1975
Total employees 182
Industries Subassemblies
  and Components, Test
  and Measurement
Growth Openings in past
  year 52; percentage
  growth 40%
Contact
Naum Staroselsky,
  President/CEO
Tel 515-270-0857
Fax 515-270-1331

Eagle Iron Works, Inc.
129 East Holcomb Ave.,
  PO Box 934
Des Moines, IA 50304

Founded 1872
Total employees 250
Industries Environmental,
  Manufacturing Equipment
Growth Openings in past
  year 29; percentage
  growth 13%
Contact
Ms. Norma Fousek,
  Personnel Manager
Tel 515-243-1123
Fax 515-243-8214

Norand Corp.
550 Second St. Southeast
Cedar Rapids, IA 52401

Founded 1968
Total employees 790

Annual sales $157.21
  million
Industries Computer
  Hardware, Computer
  Software
Growth Openings in past
  year 38; percentage
  growth 5%
Contact
Mike Wakefield, Personnel
  Director
Tel 319-369-3100
Fax 319-369-3453

Parsons Technology
One Parsons Dr., PO Box
  100
Hiawatha, IA 52233

Founded 1984
Total employees 300
Annual sales $37.3 million
Industry Computer
  Software
Growth Openings in past
  year 50; percentage
  growth 20%
Contact
Bob Parsons, President
Tel 319-395-9626
Fax 319-395-0217

**Source Data Systems,
Inc.**
950 Ridgemont Dr.
  Northeast
Cedar Rapids, IA 52402

Founded 1978
Total employees 140
Annual sales $16 million
Industries Computer
  Hardware, Computer
  Software
Growth Openings in past
  year 20; percentage
  growth 16%
Contact
Gary Ford, President
Tel 319-393-3343
Fax 319-393-5173

Uticor Technology, Inc.
3140 Utica Ridge Rd., PO
  Box 1327
Bettendorf, IA 52722

Founded 1987
Total employees 135
Annual sales $10 million
Industries Factory
  Automation, Photonics
Growth Openings in past
  year 35; percentage
  growth 35%

Contact
Donald Henry, President
Tel 319-359-7501
Fax 319-359-9094

Kansas

Brite Voice Systems, Inc.
7309 East 21st St. North
Wichita, KS 67206

Founded 1984
Total employees 300
Annual sales $46.8 million
Industries Computer
  Hardware, Holding
  Companies,
  Telecommunications
Growth Openings in past
  year 100; percentage
  growth 50%
Contact
Stanley G. Brannan,
  President/CEO
Tel 316-652-6500

**Computer Concepts
Corp.**
8375 Melrose Dr.
Lenexa, KS 66214

Founded 1974
Total employees 60
Annual sales $6.9 million
Industry Computer
  Software
Growth Openings in past
  year 20; percentage
  growth 50%
Contact
Mark Bailey, President
Tel 913-541-0900
Fax 913-541-0169

**Continental Healthcare
Systems, Inc.**
7300 West 110th St., Suite
  700
Overland Park, KS 66210

Founded 1963
Total employees 153
Annual sales $17 million
Industry Computer
  Software
Growth Openings in past
  year 25; percentage
  growth 19%

Contact
Ms. Donna Holloway,
 Human Resources/
 Payroll Supervisor
Tel 913-451-6161
Fax 913-661-8893

Great Bend Industries
Rte. 1, Box 106
Great Bend, KS 67530

Founded 1967
Total employees 265
Industry Subassemblies
 and Components
Growth Openings in past
 year 39; percentage
 growth 17%
Contact
Marion F. Lightfoot,
 President
Tel 316-792-4368
Fax 316-792-3935

JRH Biosciences
13804 West 107th St., PO
 Box 14848
Lenexa, KS 66215

Founded 1979
Total employees 170
Annual sales $16 million
Industries Biotechnology,
 Chemicals,
 Pharmaceuticals
Growth Openings in past
 year 20; percentage
 growth 13%
Contact
Dennis Wain, President
Tel 913-469-5580
Fax 913-469-5584

Kustom Signals, Inc.
9325 Pflumm St.
Lenexa, KS 66215

Founded 1965
Total employees 134
Annual sales $12 million
Industries
 Telecommunications,
 Transportation
Growth Openings in past
 year 19; percentage
 growth 16%
Contact
Ms. Beverly Gordon,
 Human Resources
 Manager
Tel 913-492-1400
Fax 913-492-1703

NewTek, Inc.
215 Southeast 8th St.
Topeka, KS 66603

Founded 1986
Total employees 75
Annual sales $8.7 million
Industries Computer
 Hardware, Computer
 Software
Growth Openings in past
 year 25; percentage
 growth 50%
Contact
Tim Jenison, President
Tel 913-231-0100
Fax 913-231-0101

**Sprint OEM Products
Group**
600 Industrial Pkwy.
Industrial Airport, KS
 66031

Founded 1983
Total employees 78
Industries Subassemblies
 and Components,
 Telecommunications
Growth Openings in past
 year 18; percentage
 growth 30%
Contact
Steve McMahon, President
Tel 913-791-7700
Fax 913-791-7022

**Terracon Companies,
Inc.**
16000 College Blvd.
Lenexa, KS 66219

Founded 1962
Total employees 470
Annual sales $48 million
Industry Holding
 Companies
Growth Openings in past
 year 100; percentage
 growth 27%
Contact
Jerry Henson, Director of
 Human Resources
Tel 913-599-6886
Fax 913-599-0574

Kentucky

A&S Fabricating Co.
Hwy. 431 North
Livermore, KY 42352

Founded 1969
Total employees 45

Annual sales $3.0 million
Industry Manufacturing
 Equipment
Growth Openings in past
 year 15; percentage
 growth 50%
Contact
Henry Sonner, President
Tel 502-278-2371
Fax 502-278-2374

Alltech, Inc.
3031 Catnip Hill Pike
Nicholasville, KY 40356

Founded 1980
Total employees 165
Annual sales $30 million
Industry Biotechnology
Growth Openings in past
 year 24; percentage
 growth 17%
Contact
Dana Cheeks, General
 Manager
Tel 606-885-9613
Fax 606-885-6736

B&H Tool Works, Inc.
1785 Lancaster Rd.
Richmond, KY 40475

Founded 1984
Total employees 80
Annual sales $5.0 million
Industries Factory
 Automation,
 Manufacturing Equipment
Growth Openings in past
 year 20; percentage
 growth 33%
Contact
Tom Brown, President
Tel 606-624-2458
Fax 606-624-2511 X19

Blue Grass Plating, Inc.
451 North Estill Ave.
Richmond, KY 40475

Founded 1969
Total employees 57
Annual sales $6.2 million
Industry Manufacturing
 Equipment
Growth Openings in past
 year 23; percentage
 growth 67%
Contact
Robert A. Cornelison,
 Chairman of the Board
Tel 606-623-7903
Fax 606-623-7028

BP Chemicals Inc., Filon Products
7310 Turfway Rd.
Florence, KY 41042

Founded 1951
Total employees 285
Annual sales $42 million
Industry Advanced
  Materials
Growth Openings in past
  year 74; percentage
  growth 35%
Contact
Phil Vancil, Director of
  Employee Relations
Tel 606-282-3640
Fax 606-282-3667

CDR Manufacturing, Inc.
744 West Hwy. 80
Somerset, KY 42501

Founded 1987
Total employees 100
Industry Subassemblies
  and Components
Growth Openings in past
  year 50; percentage
  growth 100%
Contact
Donald R. Curtis,
  President
Tel 606-679-5703
Fax 606-678-0473

CDR Pigments and Dispersions
305 Ring Rd.
Elizabethtown, KY 42701

Founded 1948
Total employees 360
Industry Chemicals
Growth Openings in past
  year 39; percentage
  growth 12%
Contact
W. Rucker Wickline,
  President
Tel 502-737-1700
Fax 502-737-0318

Ceramichrome, Inc.
PO Box 327
Stanford, KY 40484

Founded 1970
Total employees 100
Annual sales $12.5 million
Industry Advanced
  Materials
Growth Openings in past
  year 20; percentage
  growth 25%

Contact
Stan Clifford, President
Tel 606-365-3193
Fax 606-365-9739

Corpane Industries, Inc.
10100 Bluegrass Pkwy.
Louisville, KY 40299

Founded 1972
Total employees 55
Annual sales $6.9 million
Industries Energy, Factory
  Automation,
  Manufacturing
  Equipment, Test and
  Measurement
Growth Openings in past
  year 15; percentage
  growth 37%
Contact
Bill Haines, President
Tel 502-491-4433
Fax 502-491-9944

Custom Products, Inc.
1100 Industrial Blvd.
Louisville, KY 40219

Founded 1953
Total employees 50
Industries Energy,
  Holding Companies,
  Manufacturing
  Equipment, Test and
  Measurement
Growth Openings in past
  year 15; percentage
  growth 42%
Contact
Robert McAdams,
  Chairman of the Board
Tel 502-969-3163
Fax 502-969-9028

Fuller, Mossbarger, Scott and May Engineers, Inc.
1409 North Forbes Rd.
Lexington, KY 40511

Founded 1966
Total employees 130
Industries Environmental,
  Manufacturing Equipment
Growth Openings in past
  year 20; percentage
  growth 18%
Contact
W.A. Mossbarger, Jr.,
  President
Tel 606-233-0574
Fax 606-254-4800

GCA Group, Inc.
PO Box 476
Georgetown, KY 40324

Founded 1963
Total employees 700
Annual sales $68 million
Industry Subassemblies
  and Components
Growth Openings in past
  year 400; percentage
  growth 133%
Contact
Greg Martin, President
Tel 502-863-0936
Fax 502-863-5393

Hazelet & Erdal, Inc.
Waterfront Plaza, Tower 1,
  325 W Main St., #1200
Louisville, KY 40202

Founded 1897
Total employees 95
Annual sales $6 million
Industry Computer
  Hardware
Growth Openings in past
  year 17; percentage
  growth 21%
Contact
Stanley J. Sylwestrak,
  President
Tel 502-583-2723
Fax 502-583-2723

Hitachi Automotive Products USA, Inc.
955 Warwick Rd., PO Box
  510
Harrodsburg, KY 40330

Founded 1985
Total employees 538
Annual sales $220 million
Industries Subassemblies
  and Components, Test
  and Measurement,
  Transportation
Growth Openings in past
  year 36; percentage
  growth 7%
Contact
Mamoru Okumura,
  President
Tel 606-734-9451
Fax 606-734-5309

IDC Engineering
4630 Melton Ave.
Louisville, KY 40213

Founded 1976
Total employees 50

Industries Factory
Automation, Test and
Measurement
Growth Openings in past
year 25; percentage
growth 100%
Contact
John Kircher, President
Tel 502-363-4113
Fax 502-363-4666

**Jideco of Bardstown,
Inc.**
901 Withrow Ct., PO Box
816
Bardstown, KY 40004

Founded 1986
Total employees 200
Industry Subassemblies
and Components
Growth Openings in past
year 50; percentage
growth 33%
Contact
Shozo Uchio, President
Tel 502-348-3100
Fax 502-348-3204

Mineral Labs, Inc.
PO Box 549
Salyersville, KY 41465

Founded 1974
Total employees 100
Industries Advanced
Materials, Environmental
Growth Openings in past
year 15; percentage
growth 17%
Contact
Paul Lyon, President
Tel 606-349-6145
Fax 606-349-6106

National Magnetics Co.
222 John Rowan Blvd.
Bardstown, KY 40004

Founded 1988
Total employees 68
Annual sales $2.5 million
Industry Subassemblies
and Components
Growth Openings in past
year 16; percentage
growth 30%
Contact
Keith Hays, Manager of
Human Resources
Tel 502-348-3765
Fax 502-348-6202

**Olicon Imaging Systems,
Inc.**
602 North English Station
Rd.
Louisville, KY 40223

Founded 1981
Total employees 120
Annual sales $7 million
Industries Environmental,
Medical
Growth Openings in past
year 30; percentage
growth 33%
Contact
Dick Paulsen, Chief
Executive Officer
Tel 502-244-0035
Fax 502-244-9284

**Quality Manufacturing
Co., Inc.**
5855 Rockwell Rd., PO
Box 616
Winchester, KY 40392

Founded 1965
Total employees 350
Annual sales $38 million
Industries Energy,
Subassemblies and
Components
Growth Openings in past
year 150; percentage
growth 75%
Contact
James Barker, President
Tel 606-744-0420
Fax 606-254-2442

Service Tool & Die, Inc.
2323 Green St.
Henderson, KY 42420

Founded 1969
Total employees 140
Annual sales $9 million
Industries Factory
Automation, Holding
Companies
Growth Openings in past
year 15; percentage
growth 12%
Contact
Richard E. Fruit, President
Tel 502-827-9582
Fax 502-826-4067

**Stauble Machine and
Tool, Inc.**
1427 Hugh Ave.
Louisville, KY 40213

Founded 1952
Total employees 140
Annual sales $12 million

Industries Factory
Automation,
Manufacturing Equipment
Growth Openings in past
year 20; percentage
growth 16%
Contact
Thomas Yates, President
Tel 502-451-7060
Fax 502-451-6694

Stiglitz Corp.
1747 Mellwood Ave.
Louisville, KY 40206

Founded 1818
Total employees 90
Annual sales $9.8 million
Industry Manufacturing
Equipment
Growth Openings in past
year 55; percentage
growth 157%
Contact
Doug Stiglitz, President
Tel 502-897-1543
Fax 502-893-1669

Tekno, Inc.
PO Box 426
Cave City, KY 42127

Founded 1988
Total employees 30
Annual sales $10 million
Industry Factory
Automation
Growth Openings in past
year 16; percentage
growth 114%
Contact
Tom Clopton, President
Tel 502-773-4181
Fax 502-773-4180

**Tri County Manufacture
and Assembly, Inc.**
PO Box 539
Williamsburg, KY 40769

Founded 1978
Total employees 320
Annual sales $14.5 million
Industries Computer
Hardware,
Subassemblies and
Components
Growth Openings in past
year 140; percentage
growth 77%
Contact
Steven Hart, President
Tel 606-549-2613
Fax 606-549-2651

Vincent Industrial Plastic, Inc.
1225 Pringle St., PO Box 47
Henderson, KY 42420

Founded 1981
Total employees 180
Annual sales $19 million
Industry Manufacturing Equipment
Growth Openings in past year 50; percentage growth 38%
Contact
James F. Vincent, Sr., President
Tel 502-827-8881
Fax 502-827-8889

White Hydraulics, Inc.
110 Bill Bryan Blvd., PO Box 1127
Hopkinsville, KY 42240

Founded 1983
Total employees 170
Annual sales $17 million
Industry Subassemblies and Components
Growth Openings in past year 20; percentage growth 13%
Contact
Jim Mossey, President
Tel 502-885-1110
Fax 502-886-8462

Zoeller Co.
3280 Old Millers Ln.
Louisville, KY 40216

Founded 1939
Total employees 205
Annual sales $32.8 million
Industries Environmental, Subassemblies and Components
Growth Openings in past year 35; percentage growth 20%
Contact
Joe Shoemaker, Personnel Manager
Tel 502-778-2731
Fax 502-774-3624

Louisiana

Digicourse, Inc.
5200 Toler St.
Harahan, LA 70123

Founded 1970
Total employees 80
Annual sales $6.9 million
Industry Transportation
Growth Openings in past year 20; percentage growth 33%
Contact
Roy Kelm, General Manager
Tel 504-733-6061
Fax 504-734-8627

Environmental Remediation, Inc.
10201 Mayfair Dr.
Baton Rouge, LA 70809

Founded 1986
Total employees 150
Annual sales $15 million
Industries Environmental, Holding Companies
Growth Openings in past year 58; percentage growth 63%
Contact
Ms. Cheryl Chiquet, Human Resources Manager
Tel 504-293-2033
Fax 504-292-6665

Global Industries, Ltd.
107 Teledyne Dr.
Lafayette, LA 70593

Founded 1992
Total employees 600
Annual sales $66.0 million
Industry Holding Companies
Growth Openings in past year 50; percentage growth 9%
Contact
W.J. Dore, Owner/ President
Tel 318-989-0000
Fax 318-989-5752

Global Movible Offshore, Inc.
PO Box 67
Amelia, LA 70340

Founded 1992
Total employees 150

Annual sales $23.85 million
Industry Energy
Growth Openings in past year 18; percentage growth 13%
Contact
Jim Kiesler, General Manager
Tel 504-631-2124
Fax 504-631-2135

Laitram Corp.
PO Box 50699
New Orleans, LA 70150

Founded 1949
Total employees 700
Annual sales $88 million
Industry Holding Companies
Growth Openings in past year 149; percentage growth 27%
Contact
J.M. Lapeyre, Jr., President
Tel 504-733-6000
Fax 504-733-2143

RPM Engineering, Inc.
9969 Professional Blvd.
Baton Rouge, LA 70809

Founded 1980
Total employees 157
Annual sales $10 million
Industries Environmental, Manufacturing Equipment
Growth Openings in past year 27; percentage growth 20%
Contact
Robert A. Marks, President
Tel 504-292-9901
Fax 504-292-0905

Weatherford International, Inc., Gemoco Division
PO Box 7036
Houma, LA 70361

Founded 1953
Total employees 260
Industry Energy
Growth Openings in past year 34; percentage growth 15%
Contact
Frank Streva, Human Resources Manager
Tel 504-872-3266
Fax 504-872-9310

Maine

DownEast Technology, Inc.
15 Lower Main St.
Belfast, ME 04915

Founded 1989
Total employees 35
Annual sales $3 million
Industries Computer
Software, Holding
Companies
Growth Openings in past
year 20; percentage
growth 133%
Contact
Edward Regan, President
Tel 207-338-6906
Fax 207-338-6904

Gates Formed-Fibre Products, Inc.
Washington St.
Auburn, ME 04210

Founded 1984
Total employees 400
Annual sales $59 million
Industry Advanced
Materials
Growth Openings in past
year 50; percentage
growth 14%
Contact
David MacMahon,
President
Tel 207-784-1118
Fax 207-784-1123

Jackson Laboratory
600 Main St.
Bar Harbor, ME 04609

Founded 1929
Total employees 600
Annual sales $12.9 million
Industries Biotechnology,
Computer Hardware
Growth Openings in past
year 40; percentage
growth 7%
Contact
Ms. Joanne Harris,
Personnel Manager
Tel 207-288-3371
Fax 207-288-4152

James W. Sewall Co.
PO Box 433
Old Town, ME 04468

Founded 1890
Total employees 130

Industries Computer
Software, Energy,
Environmental,
Manufacturing
Equipment, Photonics
Growth Openings in past
year 20; percentage
growth 18%
Contact
David Sewall, President
Tel 207-827-4456
Fax 207-827-3641

Maine Poly, Inc.
Rte. 202, PO Box 8
Greene, ME 04236

Founded 1971
Total employees 163
Annual sales $24 million
Industry Advanced
Materials
Growth Openings in past
year 33; percentage
growth 25%
Contact
Robert Ray, President
Tel 207-946-7440
Fax 207-946-5492

Nutrite Corp.
825 Main St.
Presque Isle, ME 04769

Founded 1980
Total employees 50
Annual sales $40 million
Industry Chemicals
Growth Openings in past
year 25; percentage
growth 100%
Contact
Paul LeBlanc, General
Manager
Tel 207-768-5791
Fax 207-764-7550

Springfield Press and Machine Co., Inc.
59 Washington St., PO
Box 65
Sanford, ME 04073

Founded 1975
Total employees 60
Annual sales $5 million
Industry Subassemblies
and Components
Growth Openings in past
year 25; percentage
growth 71%
Contact
William Trotter, President
Tel 207-324-0790
Fax 207-490-2510

Maryland

A&T Systems, Inc.
12520 Prosperity Dr., Suite
300
Silver Spring, MD 20904

Founded 1984
Total employees 50
Annual sales $5.8 million
Industry Computer
Software
Growth Openings in past
year 20; percentage
growth 66%
Contact
Mrs. Cynthia Oliver,
Personnel and Facilities
Manager
Tel 301-384-1425
Fax 301-384-1405

American Computer and Electronics Corp.
209 Perry Pkwy.
Gaithersburg, MD 20877

Founded 1983
Total employees 100
Annual sales $10 million
Industries Computer
Hardware, Computer
Software, Test and
Measurement
Growth Openings in past
year 40; percentage
growth 66%
Contact
George T. Jimenez,
President
Tel 301-258-9850
Fax 301-921-0434

American Red Cross, Jerome H. Holland Laboratory for the Biomedical Sciences
15601 Crabbs Branch Way
Rockville, MD 20855

Founded 1970
Total employees 375
Industry Biotechnology
Growth Openings in past
year 44; percentage
growth 13%
Contact
Jerry Roberts, Human
Resources Associate
Tel 301-738-0633
Fax 301-738-0553

American Urethane, Inc.
1320 Defense Hwy.
Gambrills, MD 21054

Founded 1977
Total employees 65
Industry Manufacturing
Equipment
Growth Openings in past
year 15; percentage
growth 30%
Contact
Jude Masters, President
Tel 301-261-6550
Fax 301-261-6119

Andrulis Research Corp.
4600 East-West Hwy.,
Suite 900
Bethesda, MD 20814

Founded 1971
Total employees 235
Industries Computer
Software, Defense, Test
and Measurement
Growth Openings in past
year 35; percentage
growth 17%
Contact
Dr. Marilyn W. Andrulis,
President/CEO
Tel 301-657-1700
Fax 301-657-3555

**Applied Ordnance
Technology, Inc.**
103 Paul Mellon Ct., Suite
A
Waldorf, MD 20602

Founded 1984
Total employees 100
Annual sales $5 million
Industry Defense
Growth Openings in past
year 45; percentage
growth 81%
Contact
Ms. Jenny Domatto,
Personnel Director
Tel 301-843-4045
Fax 301-843-5499

Applied Research Corp.
8201 Corporate Dr., Suite
1120
Landover, MD 20785

Founded 1979
Total employees 115
Annual sales $7.2 million
Industries Computer
Software, Defense,
Environmental, Holding
Companies,

Manufacturing
Equipment,
Transportation
Growth Openings in past
year 26; percentage
growth 29%
Contact
Dr. S.P.S. Anand, COB/
CEO/President
Tel 301-459-8442
Fax 301-731-0765

**Automated Information
Management, Inc.**
4403 Forbes Blvd.
Lanham, MD 20706

Founded 1983
Total employees 350
Industries Computer
Hardware, Manufacturing
Equipment
Growth Openings in past
year 75; percentage
growth 27%
Contact
Ms. Cynthia Hardy,
President
Tel 301-794-8200
Fax 301-794-7268

Bay Resins, Inc.
3011 Millington Rd.
Millington, MD 21651

Founded 1983
Total employees 64
Annual sales $8.6 million
Industry Advanced
Materials
Growth Openings in past
year 22; percentage
growth 52%
Contact
John Bunting, President
Tel 410-928-3083
Fax 410-928-5412

**Becton Dickinson
Diagnostic Instrument
Systems**
PO Box 999
Sparks, MD 21152

Founded 1974
Total employees 725
Annual sales $79 million
Industries Biotechnology,
Factory Automation,
Medical
Growth Openings in past
year 22; percentage
growth 3%

Contact
Nancy Lake, Human
Resources Coordinator
Tel 410-316-4000
Fax 410-316-4066

**Becton Dickinson
Microbiology Systems**
250 Schilling Cir., PO Box
243
Cockeysville, MD 21030

Founded 1935
Total employees 940
Annual sales $100 million
Industries Biotechnology,
Medical, Test and
Measurement
Growth Openings in past
year 19; percentage
growth 2%
Contact
Lou Childress, Director of
Human Resources
Tel 410-771-0100
Fax 410-584-7121

BioWhittaker, Inc.
8830 Biggs Ford Rd.
Walkersville, MD 21793

Founded 1947
Total employees 450
Annual sales $51.6 million
Industry Holding
Companies
Growth Openings in past
year 49; percentage
growth 12%
Contact
William White, Director of
Human Resources
Tel 301-898-7025
Fax 301-845-8338

**Boehringer Mannheim
Pharmaceuticals**
15204 Omega Dr.
Rockville, MD 20850

Founded 1985
Total employees 325
Industry Pharmaceuticals
Growth Openings in past
year 125; percentage
growth 62%
Contact
Ted Wood, President
Tel 301-216-3900
Fax 301-330-7260

Bohdan Associates, Inc.
220 Girard St.
Gaithersburg, MD 20877

Founded 1983
Total employees 300
Annual sales $205 million
Industry Computer
 Hardware
Growth Openings in past
 year 100; percentage
 growth 50%
Contact
Charles Mathews,
 President/CEO
Tel 301-258-2965
Fax 301-258-9122

Bowles Fluidics Corp.
6625 Dobbins Rd.
Columbia, MD 21045

Founded 1961
Total employees 150
Annual sales $10 million
Industries Manufacturing
 Equipment,
 Subassemblies and
 Components
Growth Openings in past
 year 20; percentage
 growth 15%
Contact
Julian M. Lazrus,
 President
Tel 410-381-0400
Fax 410-381-2718

**CDA Investment
Technologies, Inc.**
1355 Piccard Dr.
Rockville, MD 20850

Founded 1962
Total employees 140
Annual sales $23 million
Industries Computer
 Hardware, Computer
 Software
Growth Openings in past
 year 57; percentage
 growth 68%
Contact
Al Girod, Chief Executive
 Officer
Tel 301-975-9600
Fax 301-590-1350

**Century Technologies,
Inc.**
8405 Colesville Rd., Suite
 400
Silver Spring, MD 20910

Founded 1977
Total employees 330

Annual sales $38 million
Industries Computer
 Software, Holding
 Companies
Growth Openings in past
 year 19; percentage
 growth 6%
Contact
Donald Campbell,
 President/CEO
Tel 301-426-9220

COMNET Corporation
4200 Parliament Pl., Suite
 600
Lanham, MD 20706

Founded 1967
Total employees 231
Annual sales $33 million
Industry Holding
 Companies
Growth Openings in past
 year 39; percentage
 growth 20%
Contact
Robert S. Bowen,
 President/CEO
Tel 301-918-0400
Fax 301-918-0430

Compliance Corp.
34 Essex South
Lexington Park, MD 20653

Founded 1980
Total employees 240
Annual sales $12 million
Industries Defense, Test
 and Measurement
Growth Openings in past
 year 35; percentage
 growth 17%
Contact
Michael Herndon, Director
Tel 301-863-8070
Fax 301-863-8290

**COMSYS Technical
Services, Inc.**
4 Research Pl.
Rockville, MD 20850

Founded 1979
Total employees 550
Industries Computer
 Hardware, Computer
 Software
Growth Openings in past
 year 169; percentage
 growth 44%
Contact
Fred Shulman, COB/
 President
Tel 301-921-3600
Fax 301-921-3670

**Cryomedical Sciences,
Inc.**
1300 Piccard Dr., Suite
 102
Rockville, MD 20850

Founded 1989
Total employees 100
Annual sales $6 million
Industry Medical
Growth Openings in past
 year 25; percentage
 growth 33%
Contact
J.J. Finkelstein, COB/CEO/
 President
Tel 301-417-7070
Fax 301-417-7077

CSC Intelicom, Inc.
6707 Democracy Blvd.
Bethesda, MD 20817

Founded 1977
Total employees 500
Annual sales $58 million
Industry Computer
 Software
Growth Openings in past
 year 148; percentage
 growth 42%
Contact
Ms. Lynn Aminzadeh,
 Director of Human
 Resources
Tel 301-564-6600
Fax 301-571-8399

CSCI Association Group
4715 Sellman Rd.
Beltsville, MD 20705

Founded 1978
Total employees 65
Industries Computer
 Hardware, Computer
 Software
Growth Openings in past
 year 25; percentage
 growth 62%
Contact
Carson A. Soule, President
Tel 301-937-9500
Fax 301-937-5348

**Davis Instrument
Manufacturing Co., Inc.**
4701 Mount Hope Dr.,
 Suite J
Baltimore, MD 21215

Founded 1912
Total employees 74
Annual sales $39 million
Industries Energy,
 Manufacturing Equipment

Growth Openings in past year 37; percentage growth 100%
Contact
Maurice Rudow, President
Tel 410-358-3900
Fax 410-358-0252

DIGICON Corp.
6903 Rockledge Dr., Suite 600
Bethesda, MD 20817

Founded 1985
Total employees 325
Annual sales $20 million
Industries Computer Hardware, Computer Software
Growth Openings in past year 95; percentage growth 41%
Contact
John Wu, President
Tel 301-564-6400
Fax 301-564-6076

Eagan, McAllister Associates, Inc.
300 Three Notch Rd. South, Suite 200
Lexington Park, MD 20653

Founded 1984
Total employees 150
Annual sales $12 million
Industries Computer Software, Defense
Growth Openings in past year 50; percentage growth 50%
Contact
Rex Eagan, President
Tel 301-863-2192
Fax 301-863-8140

Environmental Technologies Group, Inc.
1400 Taylor Ave., PO Box 9840
Baltimore, MD 21284

Founded 1988
Total employees 352
Annual sales $35 million
Industries Biotechnology, Defense, Energy, Environmental, Test and Measurement
Growth Openings in past year 125; percentage growth 55%

Contact
Richard Beery, Director of Personnel
Tel 410-321-5200
Fax 410-321-5255

Federal Data Corp.
4800 Hampden Ln.
Bethesda, MD 20814

Founded 1969
Total employees 138
Annual sales $105 million
Industry Computer Hardware
Growth Openings in past year 28; percentage growth 25%
Contact
Robert Hanley, COB/CEO
Tel 301-986-0800
Fax 301-961-3892

FileTek, Inc.
9400 Key West Ave.
Rockville, MD 20850

Founded 1984
Total employees 86
Annual sales $14 million
Industry Computer Hardware
Growth Openings in past year 36; percentage growth 72%
Contact
William C. Thompson, COB/CEO
Tel 301-251-0600
Fax 301-251-1990

Fil-Tec, Inc.
PO Box B
Hagerstown, MD 21741

Founded 1978
Total employees 80
Annual sales $11 million
Industry Advanced Materials
Growth Openings in past year 20; percentage growth 33%
Contact
Vincent Schoeck, President
Tel 301-824-6166
Fax 301-824-6938

Futron Corp.
7315 Wisconsin Ave., Suite 900 West
Bethesda, MD 20814

Founded 1986
Total employees 126

Annual sales $8 million
Industries Computer Hardware, Manufacturing Equipment
Growth Openings in past year 41; percentage growth 48%
Contact
Kevin Fuller, Director of Personnel and Human Resource
Tel 301-907-7100
Fax 301-907-7125

General Sciences Corp.
6100 Chevy Chase Dr.
Laurel, MD 20707

Founded 1977
Total employees 225
Annual sales $15.4 million
Industries Computer Software, Manufacturing Equipment, Transportation
Growth Openings in past year 19; percentage growth 9%
Contact
Ms. Patricia Robinson, Personnel Manager
Tel 301-953-2700
Fax 301-953-1213

Genetic Therapy, Inc.
19 Firstfield Rd.
Gaithersburg, MD 20878

Founded 1986
Total employees 117
Annual sales $2.04 million
Industry Biotechnology
Growth Openings in past year 30; percentage growth 34%
Contact
Michael Casey, President/COO
Tel 301-590-2626
Fax 301-948-3774

HCIA, Inc.
300 East Lombard St., Suite 1700
Baltimore, MD 21202

Founded 1985
Total employees 300
Annual sales $49 million
Industries Computer Hardware, Computer Software
Growth Openings in past year 130; percentage growth 76%

Contact
George Pillari, COB/
President/CEO
Tel 410-576-9600
Fax 410-783-0575

Hi-Tech Plastics, Inc.
822 Chesapeake Dr., PO
Box 838
Cambridge, MD 21613

Founded 1983
Total employees 55
Industry Manufacturing
Equipment
Growth Openings in past
year 30; percentage
growth 120%
Contact
Douglas Bennett,
President
Tel 410-228-0080
Fax 410-228-0093

**Information Systems and
Services, Inc.**
8403 Colesville Rd., Suite
750
Silver Spring, MD 20910

Founded 1979
Total employees 60
Annual sales $4.8 million
Industries Computer
Hardware, Computer
Software
Growth Openings in past
year 18; percentage
growth 42%
Contact
Bhasker Agarwal,
President
Tel 301-588-3800
Fax 301-588-3986

**International Computers
& Telecommunications,
Inc.**
18310 Montgomery Village
Ave., Suite 610
Gaithersburg, MD 20879

Founded 1981
Total employees 250
Annual sales $16.5 million
Industries Computer
Hardware, Manufacturing
Equipment,
Telecommunications
Growth Openings in past
year 19; percentage
growth 8%

Contact
David Y. Sohn, COB/
President/CEO
Tel 301-948-0200
Fax 301-948-9851

INTRAFED, Inc.
6903 Rockledge Dr., 11th
Floor
Bethesda, MD 20817

Founded 1985
Total employees 40
Annual sales $8 million
Industries Computer
Hardware, Computer
Software
Growth Openings in past
year 20; percentage
growth 100%
Contact
Ms. Michele Engel,
Personnel Manager
Tel 301-564-5600
Fax 301-564-5606

**Jackson & Tull, Inc.,
Aerospace Division**
7375 Executive Pl., Suite
200
Seabrook, MD 20706

Founded 1987
Total employees 275
Annual sales $31 million
Industry Transportation
Growth Openings in past
year 75; percentage
growth 37%
Contact
Knox W. Tull, President/
Owner
Tel 301-805-4545
Fax 301-805-4538

J.F. Taylor, Inc.
Rte. 235 & Maple Rd.
Lexington Park, MD 20653

Founded 1984
Total employees 80
Annual sales $8.6 million
Industries Defense,
Manufacturing Equipment
Growth Openings in past
year 20; percentage
growth 33%
Contact
John F. Taylor, Sr.,
President
Tel 301-862-3939
Fax 301-862-4069

**Martek Biosciences
Corp.**
6480 Dobbin Rd.
Columbia, MD 21045

Founded 1985
Total employees 56
Annual sales $4.52 million
Industries Advanced
Materials, Biotechnology,
Chemicals,
Pharmaceuticals
Growth Openings in past
year 16; percentage
growth 40%
Contact
Henry Linsert, COB/CEO
Tel 410-740-0081
Fax 410-740-2985

**Merkle Computer
Systems, Inc.**
5200-E Philadelphia Way
Lanham, MD 20706

Founded 1953
Total employees 50
Annual sales $8.2 million
Industries Computer
Hardware, Computer
Software
Growth Openings in past
year 20; percentage
growth 66%
Contact
David Williams, President
Tel 301-459-9700
Fax 301-459-8431

Microlog Corporation
20270 Goldenrod Ln.
Germantown, MD 20876

Founded 1969
Total employees 250
Annual sales $19.6 million
Industries Defense,
Telecommunications
Growth Openings in past
year 19; percentage
growth 8%
Contact
Ms. Linda Cononie,
Director of Personnel
Tel 301-428-9100
Fax 301-916-2474

Micronetics Design Corp.
1375 Piccard Dr., Suite
300
Rockville, MD 20850

Founded 1980
Total employees 52
Annual sales $6.0 million

Industry Computer
Software
Growth Openings in past
year 17; percentage
growth 48%
Contact
David Marcus, Vice
President
Tel 301-258-2605
Fax 301-840-8943

MicroProse, Inc.
180 Lake Front Dr.
Hunt Valley, MD 21030

Founded 1982
Total employees 267
Annual sales $46.5 million
Industries Computer
Software, Holding
Companies
Growth Openings in past
year 67; percentage
growth 33%
Contact
Patrick Feeley, Chief
Executive Officer
Tel 410-771-0440
Fax 410-771-1174

MICROS Systems, Inc.
12000 Baltimore Ave.
Beltsville, MD 20705

Founded 1977
Total employees 350
Annual sales $44.3 million
Industries Computer
Hardware, Computer
Software
Growth Openings in past
year 29; percentage
growth 9%
Contact
Ronald J. Kolson, VP of
Finance and
Administration/CFO
Tel 301-210-6000
Fax 301-210-6699

Mobile Telesystems, Inc.
300 Professional Dr.
Gaithersburg, MD 20879

Founded 1988
Total employees 85
Annual sales $30 million
Industries
Telecommunications,
Transportation
Growth Openings in past
year 30; percentage
growth 54%

Contact
Kenneth Homon, President
Tel 301-590-8500
Fax 301-590-8588

North American Vaccine, Inc.
12103 Indian Creek Ct.
Beltsville, MD 20705

Founded 1987
Total employees 80
Annual sales $1.53 million
Industries Biotechnology,
Defense,
Pharmaceuticals
Growth Openings in past
year 44; percentage
growth 122%
Contact
Dr. Sharon Mates,
President
Tel 301-470-6100
Fax 301-470-6198

One Call Concepts, Inc.
14504 Greenview Dr.,
Suite 300
Laurel, MD 20708

Founded 1982
Total employees 350
Industry Computer
Software
Growth Openings in past
year 49; percentage
growth 16%
Contact
Ms. Susan Volkman, Vice
President
Tel 301-776-0202
Fax 410-792-7032

Orion Network Systems, Inc.
2440 Research Blvd.,
Suite 400
Rockville, MD 20850

Founded 1982
Total employees 61
Industry Holding
Companies
Growth Openings in past
year 41; percentage
growth 205%
Contact
John G. Puente, COB/
CEO
Tel 301-258-8101
Fax 301-258-8119

**Otsuka America
Pharmaceutical Inc.,
Maryland Research
Laboratories**
2440 Research Blvd.
Rockville, MD 20850

Founded 1985
Total employees 200
Annual sales $5.5 million
Industries Biotechnology,
Pharmaceuticals
Growth Openings in past
year 80; percentage
growth 66%
Contact
Norman D. Mattson, VP of
Human Resources/
Administration
Tel 301-990-0030
Fax 301-990-0035

Patapsco Designs, Inc.
5350 Partners Ct.
Frederick, MD 21701

Founded 1977
Total employees 100
Annual sales $9.7 million
Industry Subassemblies
and Components
Growth Openings in past
year 20; percentage
growth 25%
Contact
Miles Circo, General
Manager
Tel 301-694-8744
Fax 301-694-5152

Pathology Associates, Inc.
15 Worman's Mill Ct.,
Suite I
Frederick, MD 21701

Founded 1981
Total employees 150
Annual sales $8.5 million
Industry Biotechnology
Growth Openings in past
year 25; percentage
growth 20%
Contact
Dr. Gary L. Knutsen,
COB/CEO
Tel 301-663-1644
Fax 301-663-8994

Patton Electronics Co.
7958 Cessna Ave.
Gaithersburg, MD 20879

Founded 1984
Total employees 74
Annual sales $5 million

Industries Computer
Hardware, Energy,
Factory Automation,
Telecommunications
Growth Openings in past
year 24; percentage
growth 48%
Contact
Bruce E. Patton, VP of
Operations
Tel 301-975-1000
Fax 301-869-9293

**Peak Technologies
Group, Inc.**
8990 Old Annapolis Rd.
Columbia, MD 21045

Founded 1969
Total employees 425
Annual sales $82.09
million
Industries Computer
Hardware, Computer
Software
Growth Openings in past
year 49; percentage
growth 13%
Contact
Nick Toms, President/CEO
Tel 410-992-9922
Fax 410-992-0520

**PharmaKinetics
Laboratories, Inc.**
302 West Fayette St.
Baltimore, MD 21201

Founded 1975
Total employees 140
Annual sales $13 million
Industry Pharmaceuticals
Growth Openings in past
year 40; percentage
growth 40%
Contact
V. Brewster Jones,
President/CEO
Tel 410-385-4500
Fax 410-385-1957

PRB Associates, Inc.
47 Airport View Dr.
Hollywood, MD 20636

Founded 1977
Total employees 188
Annual sales $21 million
Industries Computer
Software, Defense
Growth Openings in past
year 22; percentage
growth 13%

Contact
Lawrence Schadegg,
President
Tel 301-373-2360
Fax 301-373-3421

**Racal Communications,
Inc.**
5 Research Pl.
Rockville, MD 20850

Founded 1955
Total employees 300
Industry
Telecommunications
Growth Openings in past
year 80; percentage
growth 36%
Contact
Joe Guilfoyle, Personnel
Director
Tel 301-948-4420
Fax 301-948-6015

Rockleigh Technologies
2909 Valley Brook Ct.
Kingsville, MD 21087

Founded 1991
Total employees 30
Annual sales $3.4 million
Industries Computer
Hardware, Computer
Software
Growth Openings in past
year 15; percentage
growth 100%
Contact
J. Scott Silen, President
Tel 410-877-0347
Fax 410-877-3072

R.O.W. Sciences, Inc.
1700 Research Blvd.
Rockville, MD 20850

Founded 1983
Total employees 450
Annual sales $28.3 million
Industries Biotechnology,
Computer Hardware,
Computer Software
Growth Openings in past
year 124; percentage
growth 38%
Contact
James Lenoir, Director of
Human Resources
Tel 301-294-5400
Fax 301-294-5401

SFA, Inc.
1401 McCormick Dr.
Landover, MD 20785

Founded 1969
Total employees 450
Annual sales $50 million
Industries Defense,
Factory Automation,
Holding Companies,
Manufacturing Equipment
Growth Openings in past
year 99; percentage
growth 28%
Contact
Dr. William C. Moyer,
President/CEO/COB
Tel 301-925-9400
Fax 301-925-8612

**Swales and Associates,
Inc.**
5050 Powder Mill Rd.
Beltsville, MD 20705

Founded 1978
Total employees 350
Annual sales $36 million
Industries Defense,
Manufacturing Equipment
Growth Openings in past
year 123; percentage
growth 54%
Contact
Thomas G. Swales,
President
Tel 301-595-5500
Fax 301-595-2871

Trans-Tech, Inc.
5520 Adamstown Rd.
Adamstown, MD 21710

Founded 1956
Total employees 242
Annual sales $18.7 million
Industries Advanced
Materials, Subassemblies
and Components
Growth Openings in past
year 42; percentage
growth 21%
Contact
Ms. Judy Eaton,
Supervisor of Human
Resources
Tel 301-695-9400
Fax 301-695-7065

**United Container
Machinery Group**
5200 Glen Arm Rd.
Glen Arm, MD 21057

Founded 1986
Total employees 300

Annual sales $43 million
Industry Factory
Automation
Growth Openings in past
year 20; percentage
growth 7%
Contact
Ronald D. Aulinin,
President/CEO
Tel 410-592-5400
Fax 410-592-5460

Univax Biologics, Inc.
12280 Wilkins Ave.
Rockville, MD 20852

Founded 1988
Total employees 130
Industries Biotechnology,
Pharmaceuticals
Growth Openings in past
year 42; percentage
growth 47%
Contact
Ms. Jane Barrett, Human
Resources Manager
Tel 301-770-3099
Fax 301-770-3097

Westat, Inc.
1650 Research Blvd.
Rockville, MD 20850

Founded 1963
Total employees 600
Annual sales $90 million
Industry Computer
Hardware
Growth Openings in past
year 50; percentage
growth 9%
Contact
Ms. Patricia Smith,
Personnel Director
Tel 301-251-1500
Fax 301-294-2040

XDB Systems, Inc.
14700 Sweitzer Ln.
Laurel, MD 20707

Founded 1982
Total employees 100
Annual sales $11 million
Industries Computer
Software,
Telecommunications
Growth Openings in past
year 20; percentage
growth 25%
Contact
Dr. S. Bing Yao, President
Tel 301-317-6800
Fax 301-317-7701

Massachusetts

ADRA Systems, Inc.
59 Technology Dr.
Lowell, MA 01851

Founded 1983
Total employees 150
Annual sales $17 million
Industry Computer
Software
Growth Openings in past
year 50; percentage
growth 50%
Contact
William L. Fiedler, Chief
Financial Officer
Tel 508-937-3700
Fax 508-453-2462

**Advanced Cable
Technologies, Inc.**
1 Robert Bonazzoli Ave.
Hudson, MA 01749

Founded 1983
Total employees 300
Annual sales $35 million
Industry Subassemblies
and Components
Growth Openings in past
year 100; percentage
growth 50%
Contact
John A. Pino, President/
CEO
Tel 508-562-1200
Fax 508-562-4502

**Advanced Electronics,
Inc.**
112 Beach St.
Boston, MA 02111

Founded 1976
Total employees 306
Industries Manufacturing
Equipment,
Subassemblies and
Components
Growth Openings in past
year 45; percentage
growth 17%
Contact
T.O. Young, Personnel
Manager
Tel 617-482-5266
Fax 617-542-6386

**Advanced NMR Systems,
Inc.**
46 Jonspin Rd.
Wilmington, MA 01887

Founded 1983
Total employees 68
Industry Medical
Growth Openings in past
year 21; percentage
growth 44%
Contact
Ms. Marion Waddington,
Human Resource
Manager
Tel 508-657-8876
Fax 508-658-3581

Aegis, Inc.
50 Welby Rd.
New Bedford, MA 02745

Founded 1984
Total employees 225
Annual sales $21 million
Industry Subassemblies
and Components
Growth Openings in past
year 25; percentage
growth 12%
Contact
John Manetti, President
Tel 508-998-3141
Fax 508-995-7315

**Agency Management
Services, Inc.**
700 Longwater Dr.
Norwell, MA 02061

Founded 1963
Total employees 850
Annual sales $98 million
Industry Computer
Software
Growth Openings in past
year 148; percentage
growth 21%
Contact
Bruce Norton, Director of
Human Resources
Tel 617-982-9400
Fax 617-982-9892

**Alpha-Beta Technology,
Inc.**
One Innovation Dr.
Worcester, MA 01605

Founded 1988
Total employees 97
Industries Biotechnology,
Pharmaceuticals
Growth Openings in past
year 57; percentage
growth 142%

Contact
Spiros Jamas, President/
  CEO
Tel 508-798-6900
Fax 508-754-2579

American Ink Jet Corp.
13 Alexander Rd.
Billerica, MA 01821

Founded 1984
Total employees 35
Industries Chemicals,
  Computer Hardware
Growth Openings in past
year 28; percentage
growth 400%
Contact
Michael Andreottola,
  President
Tel 508-667-0600
Fax 508-670-5637

**American
Superconductor Corp.**
2 Technology Dr.
Westborough, MA 01581

Founded 1987
Total employees 88
Annual sales $3.1 million
Industries Advanced
  Materials, Subassemblies
  and Components
Growth Openings in past
year 21; percentage
growth 31%
Contact
Dr. Gregory Yurek, Ph.D.,
  COB/President/CEO
Tel 508-836-4200
Fax 508-836-4248

**Analytical Systems
Engineering Corp.**
5 Burlington Woods Dr.
Burlington, MA 01803

Founded 1969
Total employees 400
Annual sales $43 million
Industry Manufacturing
  Equipment
Growth Openings in past
year 50; percentage
growth 14%
Contact
Ms. Dorothy Hayes,
  Human Resources
  Manager
Tel 617-272-7910
Fax 617-272-1341

**Application Systems
Group**
92 Montvale Ave.
Stoneham, MA 02180

Founded 1989
Total employees 95
Industries Computer
  Hardware, Holding
  Companies
Growth Openings in past
year 65; percentage
growth 216%
Contact
Gary Whear, President
Tel 617-279-2790
Fax 617-279-1009

**Applied Power, Inc.,
Barry Controls Division**
40 Guest St., PO Box
  9105
Brighton, MA 02135

Founded 1943
Total employees 650
Annual sales $84 million
Industry Test and
  Measurement
Growth Openings in past
year 49; percentage
growth 8%
Contact
Bruce Wright, VP of
  Human Resources
Tel 617-787-1555
Fax 617-782-4902

Applix, Inc.
112 Turnpike Rd.
Westborough, MA 01581

Founded 1983
Total employees 120
Annual sales $13 million
Industry Computer
  Software
Growth Openings in past
year 40; percentage
growth 50%
Contact
Jit Saxena, President
Tel 508-870-0300
Fax 508-366-9313

Ark-Les Corp.
51 Water St.
Watertown, MA 02172

Founded 1937
Total employees 900
Industries Subassemblies
  and Components,
  Telecommunications

Growth Openings in past
year 97; percentage
growth 12%
Contact
James Finch, Personnel
  Manager
Tel 617-924-2330
Fax 617-924-5460

ASA International Ltd.
10 Speen St.
Framingham, MA 01701

Founded 1969
Total employees 200
Annual sales $31.4 million
Industries Computer
  Software, Holding
  Companies
Growth Openings in past
year 20; percentage
growth 11%
Contact
Alfred Angelone, Chief
  Executive Officer
Tel 508-626-2727
Fax 508-626-0645

Astra USA, Inc.
50 Otis St.
Westborough, MA 01581

Founded 1948
Total employees 950
Annual sales $209 million
Industry Pharmaceuticals
Growth Openings in past
year 95; percentage
growth 11%
Contact
Stefan Solvell, Senior Vice
  President
Tel 508-366-1100
Fax 508-366-7406

ATI Orion Research
529 Main St.
Boston, MA 02129

Founded 1962
Total employees 350
Annual sales $41 million
Industry Test and
  Measurement
Growth Openings in past
year 20; percentage
growth 6%
Contact
Ms. Jennie Panico,
  Director of Human
  Resources
Tel 617-242-3900
Fax 617-242-7885

Atlantic Data Services, Inc.
One Batterymarch Park
Quincy, MA 02169

Founded 1980
Total employees 250
Annual sales $11 million
Industry Computer
Software
Growth Openings in past
year 150; percentage
growth 150%
Contact
Kenneth Grazioso,
Personnel Manager
Tel 617-770-3333
Fax 617-770-2307

AutoImmune, Inc.
128 Spring St.
Lexington, MA 02173

Founded 1988
Total employees 24
Industries Biotechnology,
Pharmaceuticals
Growth Openings in past
year 23; percentage
growth 2300%
Contact
Robert C. Bishop,
President/CEO
Tel 617-860-0710
Fax 617-860-0705

Avid Technology, Inc.
Metropolitan Technology
Park, 1 Park West, 2nd
Fl.
Tewksbury, MA 01876

Founded 1987
Total employees 320
Annual sales $51.9 million
Industries Computer
Software, Holding
Companies,
Telecommunications
Growth Openings in past
year 76; percentage
growth 31%
Contact
Ms. Judith Oppenheim, VP
of Human Resources
Tel 508-640-6789
Fax 508-640-1366

Barr Associates, Inc.
2 Lyberty Way, PO Box
557
Westford, MA 01886

Founded 1971
Total employees 100
Industry Photonics

Growth Openings in past
year 20; percentage
growth 25%
Contact
Jeff Maclaren, Controller
Tel 508-692-7513
Fax 508-692-7443

BASF Bioresearch Corp.
100 Research Dr.
Worcester, MA 01605

Founded 1989
Total employees 120
Industry Biotechnology
Growth Openings in past
year 42; percentage
growth 53%
Contact
Robert Kamen, President
Tel 508-849-2500
Fax 508-752-6506

Beyond Inc.
17 New England Executive
Pkwy.
Burlington, MA 01803

Founded 1988
Total employees 65
Annual sales $7.5 million
Industry Computer
Software
Growth Openings in past
year 30; percentage
growth 85%
Contact
Jeff Kalowski, VP of
Finance and Operations
Tel 617-229-0006
Fax 617-229-1114

BGS Systems, Inc.
128 Technology Ctr.
Waltham, MA 02254

Founded 1975
Total employees 165
Annual sales $30.3 million
Industry Computer
Software
Growth Openings in past
year 19; percentage
growth 13%
Contact
Dr. Harold S. Schwenk, Jr.,
President/CEO
Tel 617-891-0000
Fax 617-890-0000

Biogen, Inc.
14 Cambridge Ctr.
Cambridge, MA 02142

Founded 1978
Total employees 354

Annual sales $149.29
million
Industries Biotechnology,
Pharmaceuticals
Growth Openings in past
year 24; percentage
growth 7%
Contact
Frank A. Burke, VP of
Human Resources
Tel 617-252-9200
Fax 617-252-9617

Bird Environmental Technologies, Inc.
1 Dedham Pl.
Dedham, MA 02026

Founded 1986
Total employees 200
Annual sales $21 million
Industry Environmental
Growth Openings in past
year 70; percentage
growth 53%
Contact
Philip Giantris, President
Tel 617-461-1414

Boston Biomedica, Inc.
375 West St.
West Bridgewater, MA
02379

Founded 1986
Total employees 130
Annual sales $14 million
Industry Medical
Growth Openings in past
year 40; percentage
growth 44%
Contact
Richard Schumacher,
President
Tel 508-580-1900
Fax 508-580-2202

Boston Digital Corp.
Granite Park
Milford, MA 01757

Founded 1965
Total employees 150
Annual sales $15 million
Industry Factory
Automation
Growth Openings in past
year 15; percentage
growth 11%
Contact
Micheal Wicken, CEO/
President
Tel 508-473-4561
Fax 508-478-7224

Boston Technology, Inc.
100 Quannapowitt Pkwy.
Wakefield, MA 01880

Founded 1986
Total employees 270
Annual sales $70.3 million
Industry
Telecommunications
Growth Openings in past
year 29; percentage
growth 12%
Contact
Dr. John W. Taylor,
President/CEO
Tel 617-246-9000
Fax 617-246-4510

BR+A
1320 Soldiers Field Rd.
Boston, MA 02135

Founded 1975
Total employees 178
Annual sales $14 million
Industry Manufacturing
Equipment
Growth Openings in past
year 72; percentage
growth 67%
Contact
Eugene M. Bard, President
Tel 617-254-0016
Fax 617-254-9175

Briggs Associates, Inc.
400 Hingham St.
Rockland, MA 02370

Founded 1959
Total employees 150
Annual sales $10 million
Industries Environmental,
Holding Companies
Growth Openings in past
year 20; percentage
growth 15%
Contact
David S. Campbell,
President/Treasurer
Tel 617-871-6040
Fax 617-871-7982

Brooks Automation, Inc.
41 Wellman St
Lowell, MA 01851

Founded 1978
Total employees 110
Annual sales $14 million
Industry Manufacturing
Equipment
Growth Openings in past
year 20; percentage
growth 22%

Contact
Richard Sullivan,
Controller
Tel 508-453-1112
Fax 508-453-3455

Bruker Instruments, Inc.
19 Fortune Dr., Manning
Park
Billerica, MA 01821

Founded 1972
Total employees 150
Annual sales $17 million
Industries Medical,
Subassemblies and
Components, Test and
Measurement
Growth Openings in past
year 50; percentage
growth 50%
Contact
Guenther Laukien,
President
Tel 508-667-9580
Fax 508-667-3954

C. Centennial, Inc.
37 Manning Rd.
Billerica, MA 01821

Founded 1963
Total employees 37
Annual sales $4 million
Industry Computer
Hardware
Growth Openings in past
year 28; percentage
growth 311%
Contact
Ms. Carol Oulette, Chief
Financial Officer
Tel 508-670-0646
Fax 508-670-9025

**Cambridge
NeuroScience, Inc.**
1 Kendall Sq., Building
700
Cambridge, MA 02139

Founded 1986
Total employees 85
Industries Biotechnology,
Medical, Pharmaceuticals
Growth Openings in past
year 35; percentage
growth 70%
Contact
Elkan R. Gamzu,
President
Tel 617-225-0600
Fax 617-225-2741

**Cambridge Systematics,
Inc.**
222 Third St.
Cambridge, MA 02142

Founded 1972
Total employees 80
Annual sales $9.3 million
Industries Energy,
Environmental,
Transportation
Growth Openings in past
year 20; percentage
growth 33%
Contact
Lance Neumann,
President
Tel 617-354-0167
Fax 617-354-1542

CenterLine Software, Inc.
10 Fawcett St.
Cambridge, MA 02138

Founded 1987
Total employees 150
Annual sales $18 million
Industry Computer
Software
Growth Openings in past
year 15; percentage
growth 11%
Contact
Jim Meehan, President/
CEO
Tel 617-498-3000
Fax 617-868-5004

ChemDesign Corp.
99 Development Rd.
Fitchburg, MA 01420

Founded 1983
Total employees 350
Annual sales $43.6 million
Industries Biotechnology,
Chemicals
Growth Openings in past
year 38; percentage
growth 12%
Contact
Richard E.T. Brooks,
COB/CEO
Tel 508-345-9999
Fax 508-342-9769

Chipcom Corp.
118 Turnpike Rd.
Southborough, MA 01772

Founded 1983
Total employees 517
Annual sales $87.3 million
Industry
Telecommunications

Growth Openings in past year 117; percentage growth 29%
Contact
John C. Meyer, VP of Human Resources
Tel 508-460-8900
Fax 508-460-8950

CLAM Associates, Inc.
101 Main St.
Cambridge, MA 02142

Founded 1987
Total employees 75
Annual sales $8.7 million
Industries Computer Hardware, Computer Software
Growth Openings in past year 45; percentage growth 150%
Contact
Mike Munter, Business Manager
Tel 617-621-2542
Fax 617-252-0820

Coghlin Electric/ Electronics, Inc.
155 Summer St.
Worcester, MA 01615

Founded 1885
Total employees 150
Annual sales $14 million
Industry Holding Companies
Growth Openings in past year 20; percentage growth 15%
Contact
James W. Coghlin, President/Chief Quality Officer
Tel 508-791-7861
Fax 508-756-8312

Collaborative Research, Inc.
100 Beaver St.
Waltham, MA 02154

Founded 1961
Total employees 112
Annual sales $5.5 million
Industry Pharmaceuticals
Growth Openings in past year 28; percentage growth 33%
Contact
Ms. Sue Foster, Human Resources Manager
Tel 617-487-7979
Fax 617-487-7960

ColorAge, Inc.
900 Technology Park Dr.
Billerica, MA 01821

Founded 1980
Total employees 82
Industry Computer Software
Growth Openings in past year 32; percentage growth 64%
Contact
Frank Finneran, Controller
Tel 508-667-8585
Fax 508-667-8821

Columbia Technical Services
17 Bryden St.
Worcester, MA 01615

Founded 1992
Total employees 50
Annual sales $4.8 million
Industry Subassemblies and Components
Growth Openings in past year 20; percentage growth 66%
Contact
James Coghlin, President/ Chief Quality Officer
Tel 508-753-2354
Fax 508-756-8312

CommuniTech, Inc.
86 Morse St.
Norwood, MA 02062

Founded 1985
Total employees 50
Annual sales $6 million
Industry Telecommunications
Growth Openings in past year 20; percentage growth 66%
Contact
Stephen W. Bisson, President
Tel 617-769-7410
Fax 617-762-4508

Contract Assembly, Inc.
177 Ward Hill Ave.
Haverhill, MA 01835

Founded 1985
Total employees 60
Industry Subassemblies and Components
Growth Openings in past year 40; percentage growth 200%

Contact
Mario Forzese, President
Tel 508-373-2574
Fax 508-373-3681

Conversion Devices, Inc.
15 Jonathan Dr.
Brockton, MA 02401

Founded 1987
Total employees 89
Annual sales $8.6 million
Industry Subassemblies and Components
Growth Openings in past year 19; percentage growth 27%
Contact
James Zaros, President
Tel 508-559-0880
Fax 508-559-9288

Copley Pharmaceutical, Inc.
25 John Rd., Canton Commerce Ctr.
Canton, MA 02021

Founded 1972
Total employees 400
Annual sales $51.98 million
Industry Pharmaceuticals
Growth Openings in past year 250; percentage growth 166%
Contact
Ms. Jane C.I. Hirsh, COB/CEO
Tel 617-821-6111
Fax 617-821-4068

Corporate Software, Inc.
275 Dan Rd.
Canton, MA 02021

Founded 1983
Total employees 600
Annual sales $301 million
Industries Computer Hardware, Computer Software
Growth Openings in past year 181; percentage growth 43%
Contact
Stephen D.R. Moore, President
Tel 617-821-4500
Fax 617-821-5688

Course Technology, Inc.
One Main St.
Cambridge, MA 02142

Founded 1989
Total employees 45
Annual sales $5.2 million
Industry Computer
Software
Growth Openings in past
year 15; percentage
growth 50%
Contact
John M. Connolly,
President
Tel 617-225-2595
Fax 617-225-7976

**C.R. Bard, Inc.,
Electrophysiology
Division**
25 Computer Dr.
Haverhill, MA 01832

Founded 1986
Total employees 200
Annual sales $13 million
Industries Computer
Software, Medical
Growth Openings in past
year 80; percentage
growth 66%
Contact
Ms. Karen Uzar, Personnel
Director
Tel 508-373-3931
Fax 508-373-3931

**Creative Biomolecules,
Inc.**
45 South St.
Hopkinton, MA 01748

Founded 1981
Total employees 185
Annual sales $2.6 million
Industry Biotechnology
Growth Openings in past
year 50; percentage
growth 37%
Contact
Wayne Mayhew, III, VP of
Finance/CFO
Tel 508-435-9001
Fax 508-435-6951

CrossComm Corp.
450 Donald Lynch Blvd.
Marlborough, MA 01752

Founded 1986
Total employees 250
Annual sales $29 million
Industry
Telecommunications

Growth Openings in past
year 100; percentage
growth 66%
Contact
Tad Witkowicz, Founder/
President
Tel 508-481-4060
Fax 508-229-5535

**Dataware Technologies,
Inc.**
222 Third St., Suite 3300
Cambridge, MA 02142

Founded 1988
Total employees 120
Annual sales $19.3 million
Industries Computer
Hardware, Computer
Software
Growth Openings in past
year 35; percentage
growth 41%
Contact
Kurt Mueller, CEO/COB
Tel 617-621-0820
Fax 617-621-0307

Daymarc Corp.
301 Second Ave.
Waltham, MA 02154

Founded 1959
Total employees 90
Industry Factory
Automation
Growth Openings in past
year 20; percentage
growth 28%
Contact
Mel Bosch, President
Tel 617-890-2345
Fax 617-890-4229

Design Circuits, Inc.
374 Turnpike Rd.
Southborough, MA 01772

Founded 1984
Total employees 90
Industry Subassemblies
and Components
Growth Openings in past
year 30; percentage
growth 50%
Contact
Walter T. Burr, Chief
Executive Officer
Tel 508-485-0275
Fax 508-485-1810

Design Continuum, Inc.
648 Beacon St., 6th Floor
Boston, MA 02215

Founded 1983
Total employees 70
Annual sales $7.6 million
Industry Manufacturing
Equipment
Growth Openings in past
year 30; percentage
growth 75%
Contact
Gian Zaccai, President
Tel 617-267-5115
Fax 617-267-3923

Digital Consulting, Inc.
204 Andover St.
Andover, MA 01810

Founded 1981
Total employees 130
Annual sales $19 million
Industries Computer
Hardware, Computer
Software
Growth Openings in past
year 30; percentage
growth 30%
Contact
Ronald J. Gomes,
President
Tel 508-470-3870
Fax 508-470-0526

Distron Corp.
161 North St.
Newton, MA 02160

Founded 1970
Total employees 100
Annual sales $14 million
Industry Subassemblies
and Components
Growth Openings in past
year 20; percentage
growth 25%
Contact
Robert Donovan, President
Tel 617-969-6066
Fax 617-332-4671

**D.R.W. Computer
Services**
636 Washington St.
Canton, MA 02021

Founded 1982
Total employees 45
Annual sales $7.4 million
Industries Computer
Hardware,
Telecommunications

Growth Openings in past year 15; percentage growth 50%
Contact
Dom Rodriguez, President
Tel 617-821-2290

EcoScience Corp.
Three Biotech Park, One Innovation Dr.
Worcester, MA 01605

Founded 1982
Total employees 135
Annual sales $5.9 million
Industries Biotechnology, Chemicals
Growth Openings in past year 33; percentage growth 32%
Contact
James A. Wylie, Jr., President/CEO
Tel 508-754-0300
Fax 508-754-1134

EDS-Scicon, Inc.
8 New England Executive Park
Burlington, MA 01803

Founded 1984
Total employees 30
Annual sales $2.3 million
Industry Computer Software
Growth Openings in past year 20; percentage growth 200%
Contact
William Davison, General Manager
Tel 617-273-3030
Fax 617-273-3883

Education Development Center, Inc.
55 Chapel St.
Newton, MA 02160

Founded 1958
Total employees 300
Annual sales $29 million
Industry Computer Software
Growth Openings in past year 75; percentage growth 33%
Contact
Ms. Janet Whitla, President
Tel 617-969-7100
Fax 617-244-3436

Entwistle Co.
Bigelow St.
Hudson, MA 01749

Founded 1954
Total employees 310
Annual sales $40 million
Industries Defense, Manufacturing Equipment
Growth Openings in past year 60; percentage growth 24%
Contact
Paul Salek, Personnel Manager
Tel 508-481-4000
Fax 508-562-4808

Epoch Systems, Inc.
8 Technology Dr.
Westborough, MA 01581

Founded 1986
Total employees 170
Annual sales $30 million
Industry Computer Software
Growth Openings in past year 20; percentage growth 13%
Contact
Bob Divoli, Chief Executive Officer
Tel 508-836-4300
Fax 508-366-6853

Epsilon, Inc.
50 Cambridge St.
Burlington, MA 01803

Founded 1970
Total employees 873
Annual sales $71 million
Industries Computer Hardware, Holding Companies
Growth Openings in past year 73; percentage growth 9%
Contact
Stephen Cone, COB/CEO
Tel 617-273-0250
Fax 617-270-6760

FAX International, Inc.
60 Mall Rd.
Burlington, MA 01803

Founded 1991
Total employees 130
Annual sales $17 million
Industry Telecommunications
Growth Openings in past year 53; percentage growth 68%

Contact
Douglas J. Ranalli, President
Tel 617-221-0444
Fax 617-221-7210

Fiberspar, Inc.
2380 Cranberry Hwy.
West Wareham, MA 02576

Founded 1986
Total employees 82
Annual sales $12 million
Industries Advanced Materials, Subassemblies and Components
Growth Openings in past year 42; percentage growth 105%
Contact
Peter Quigley, President
Tel 508-291-2770
Fax 508-291-2772

Fibre Optic Communications Specialists, Inc.
50 D'Angelo Dr.
Marlborough, MA 01752

Founded 1982
Total employees 60
Annual sales $6.5 million
Industry Photonics
Growth Openings in past year 25; percentage growth 71%
Contact
Ms. Kelly Iverson, Personnel Manager
Tel 508-480-9600
Fax 508-480-9688

Flexcon Industries
300 Pond St., PO Box 782
Randolph, MA 02368

Founded 1980
Total employees 80
Annual sales $8.5 million
Industry Environmental
Growth Openings in past year 20; percentage growth 33%
Contact
Thomas J. Swan, Jr., President/CEO
Tel 617-986-2424
Fax 617-986-2029

Genetics Institute, Inc.
87 Cambridge Park Dr.
Cambridge, MA 02140

Founded 1981
Total employees 850

Annual sales $88 million
Industries Biotechnology,
  Pharmaceuticals
Growth Openings in past
  year 148; percentage
  growth 21%
Contact
Gabriel Schmergel,
  President/CEO
Tel 617-876-1170
Fax 617-868-1024

**Genica Pharmaceuticals
Corp.**
373 Plantation St., 2
  Biotech Park
Worcester, MA 01605

Founded 1987
Total employees 40
Annual sales $4.4 million
Industry Medical
Growth Openings in past
  year 25; percentage
  growth 166%
Contact
Bob Flaherty, President
Tel 508-756-2886

Gensym Corp.
125 Cambridge Park Dr.
Cambridge, MA 02140

Founded 1986
Total employees 140
Annual sales $18 million
Industry Computer
  Software
Growth Openings in past
  year 55; percentage
  growth 64%
Contact
Lowell B. Hawkinson,
  Chief Executive Officer
Tel 617-547-2500
Fax 617-547-1962

Geo-Centers, Inc.
7 Wells Ave.
Newton, MA 02159

Founded 1975
Total employees 600
Industries Chemicals,
  Environmental,
  Photonics, Test and
  Measurement
Growth Openings in past
  year 100; percentage
  growth 20%
Contact
James T. Kimble, Director
  of Human Resources
Tel 617-964-7070
Fax 617-527-7592

GIS, Trans, Ltd.
675 Massachusetts Ave.
Cambridge, MA 02139

Founded 1990
Total employees 25
Annual sales $2.9 million
Industry Computer
  Software
Growth Openings in past
  year 15; percentage
  growth 150%
Contact
Simon Lewis, President
Tel 617-354-2771
Fax 617-354-8964

Harlequin, Inc.
One Cambridge Ctr.
Cambridge, MA 02142

Founded 1986
Total employees 180
Annual sales $20 million
Industry Computer
  Software
Growth Openings in past
  year 50; percentage
  growth 38%
Contact
Jo Marks, President
Tel 617-252-0052
Fax 617-252-6505

**Harris Environmental
Systems, Inc.**
11 Connector Rd.
Andover, MA 01810

Founded 1939
Total employees 90
Annual sales $10 million
Industries Energy,
  Environmental,
  Manufacturing
  Equipment, Test and
  Measurement
Growth Openings in past
  year 20; percentage
  growth 28%
Contact
Phil Hunt, President
Tel 508-475-0104
Fax 508-475-7903

**Harte-Hanks Data
Technologies, Inc.**
25 Linnell Cir.
Billerica, MA 01821

Founded 1968
Total employees 210
Industries Computer
  Hardware, Computer
  Software

Growth Openings in past
  year 50; percentage
  growth 31%
Contact
Ms. Trish Clark, Director of
  Human Resources
Tel 508-663-9955
Fax 508-667-7297

HBM, Inc.
19 Bartlett St.
Marlborough, MA 01752

Founded 1973
Total employees 120
Annual sales $14 million
Industries Subassemblies
  and Components, Test
  and Measurement
Growth Openings in past
  year 15; percentage
  growth 14%
Contact
Mike Altwein, President
Tel 508-624-4500
Fax 508-485-7480

**Health Payment Review,
Inc.**
360 Newbury St.
Boston, MA 02115

Founded 1987
Total employees 65
Annual sales $15 million
Industry Computer
  Software
Growth Openings in past
  year 30; percentage
  growth 85%
Contact
Ms. Marcia Radosevich,
  Chief Executive Officer
Tel 617-266-2520
Fax 617-266-3170

Iconics, Inc.
100 Foxborough Blvd.
Foxboro, MA 02035

Founded 1986
Total employees 68
Annual sales $7.8 million
Industry Computer
  Software
Growth Openings in past
  year 18; percentage
  growth 36%
Contact
Russ Agrusa, President
Tel 508-543-8600
Fax 508-543-1503

ImmuLogic Pharmaceutical Corp.
610 Lincoln St.
Waltham, MA 02154

Founded 1987
Total employees 181
Annual sales $10 million
Industries Biotechnology, Pharmaceuticals
Growth Openings in past year 46; percentage growth 34%
Contact
Kevin Lawler, Director of Human Resources
Tel 617-466-6000
Fax 617-466-6010

ImmunoGen, Inc.
60 Hamilton St.
Cambridge, MA 02139

Founded 1981
Total employees 190
Annual sales $1.7 million
Industry Biotechnology
Growth Openings in past year 45; percentage growth 31%
Contact
Mitchel Sayare, Chief Executive Officer
Tel 617-661-9312
Fax 617-661-9334

Individual, Inc.
84 Sherman St.
Cambridge, MA 02140

Founded 1989
Total employees 55
Industry Telecommunications
Growth Openings in past year 33; percentage growth 150%
Contact
Joseph Amram, President
Tel 617-354-2230
Fax 617-864-4066

Ingold Electrodes, Inc.
261 Ballardvale St.
Wilmington, MA 01887

Founded 1948
Total employees 90
Annual sales $14 million
Industries Subassemblies and Components, Test and Measurement
Growth Openings in past year 15; percentage growth 20%

Contact
Maurice Knapp, President
Tel 508-658-7615
Fax 508-658-6973

Inspex, Inc.
47 Manning Park
Billerica, MA 01821

Founded 1973
Total employees 100
Industry Factory Automation
Growth Openings in past year 25; percentage growth 33%
Contact
Mario Maldari, President
Tel 508-667-5500
Fax 508-663-0011

Integrated Computer Solutions
201 Broadway
Cambridge, MA 02139

Founded 1987
Total employees 75
Annual sales $8.7 million
Industry Computer Software
Growth Openings in past year 15; percentage growth 25%
Contact
Ms. Sarah Lummus, Director of Human Resources
Tel 617-621-0060
Fax 617-547-0758

Intelligent Environments, Inc.
2 Highwood Dr.
Tewksbury, MA 01876

Founded 1985
Total employees 90
Annual sales $6 million
Industry Computer Software
Growth Openings in past year 25; percentage growth 38%
Contact
Dr. Terry Golesworthy, Ph.D., President/CEO
Tel 508-640-1080
Fax 508-640-1090

Interleaf, Inc.
9 Hillside Ave., Prospect Pl.
Waltham, MA 02154

Founded 1981
Total employees 950
Annual sales $117 million
Industry Computer Software
Growth Openings in past year 145; percentage growth 18%
Contact
Mark Ruport, President/ CEO
Tel 617-290-0710
Fax 617-290-4955

Interneuron Pharmaceuticals, Inc.
99 Hayden Ave., One Ledgemont Ctr., Suite 340
Lexington, MA 02173

Founded 1988
Total employees 68
Annual sales $11.5 million
Industries Biotechnology, Pharmaceuticals
Growth Openings in past year 32; percentage growth 88%
Contact
Glenn L. Cooper, M.D., President/CEO
Tel 617-861-8444

IntraNet, Inc.
255 Washington St.
Newton, MA 02158

Founded 1980
Total employees 70
Annual sales $6.5 million
Industry Computer Software
Growth Openings in past year 19; percentage growth 37%
Contact
Anthony Smith, President
Tel 617-527-7020
Fax 617-527-6779

Iris Associates, Inc.
1 Technology Park
Westford, MA 01886

Founded 1984
Total employees 42
Annual sales $4.8 million
Industry Computer Software

Growth Openings in past year 18; percentage growth 75%
Contact
Raymond Ozzie, President
Tel 508-692-2800
Fax 508-692-7365

IRIS Graphics, Inc.
6 Crosby Dr.
Bedford, MA 01730

Founded 1984
Total employees 250
Industry Computer Hardware
Growth Openings in past year 40; percentage growth 19%
Contact
Alphonse M. Lucchese, President/CEO
Tel 617-275-8777
Fax 617-275-8590

ISI Systems, Inc.
Two Tech Dr.
Andover, MA 01810

Founded 1969
Total employees 475
Annual sales $50 million
Industry Computer Software
Growth Openings in past year 32; percentage growth 7%
Contact
Ronald R. Musterait, VP of Operations and Human Resources
Tel 508-682-5500
Fax 508-686-0130

Jaco, Inc.
155 Farm St., PO Box 309
Bellingham, MA 02019

Founded 1973
Total employees 80
Annual sales $7.0 million
Industry Manufacturing Equipment
Growth Openings in past year 15; percentage growth 23%
Contact
Alfred P. Rossini, President
Tel 508-966-2141
Fax 508-966-0167

JetForm Corp.
800 South St., Suite 305
Waltham, MA 02154

Founded 1984
Total employees 78
Annual sales $6.7 million
Industry Computer Software
Growth Openings in past year 16; percentage growth 25%
Contact
Abe Ostrovsky, President
Tel 617-647-7700
Fax 617-647-4121

Keithley Instruments, Inc., Data Acquisition Division
440 Miles Standish Blvd.
Taunton, MA 02780

Founded 1983
Total employees 177
Industries Factory Automation, Test and Measurement
Growth Openings in past year 27; percentage growth 18%
Contact
Ms. Marcella Nelson, Director of Human Resources
Tel 508-880-3000
Fax 508-880-0179

Kendall Square Research Corp.
170 Tracer Ln.
Waltham, MA 02154

Founded 1986
Total employees 250
Annual sales $20.7 million
Industries Computer Hardware, Computer Software
Growth Openings in past year 98; percentage growth 64%
Contact
Dr. William I. Koch, Acting Chief Executive Officer
Tel 617-895-9400
Fax 617-890-0996

Koch Membrane Systems, Inc.
850 Main St.
Wilmington, MA 01887

Founded 1966
Total employees 320
Annual sales $34 million

Industries Biotechnology, Environmental
Growth Openings in past year 40; percentage growth 14%
Contact
Roger Dillon, Personnel Manager
Tel 508-657-4250
Fax 508-657-5208

Komatsu Cutting Technologies, Inc.
200 Boston Ave.
Medford, MA 02155

Founded 1991
Total employees 43
Industry Factory Automation
Growth Openings in past year 33; percentage growth 330%
Contact
Terry Mochizuki, President
Tel 617-396-1869
Fax 617-396-2280

Kopin Corp.
695 Myles Standish Blvd.
Taunton, MA 02780

Founded 1984
Total employees 75
Annual sales $12 million
Industries Photonics, Subassemblies and Components
Growth Openings in past year 15; percentage growth 25%
Contact
Paul Mitchell, Chief Financial Officer
Tel 508-824-6696
Fax 508-822-1381

Kronos, Inc.
400 Fifth Ave.
Waltham, MA 02154

Founded 1977
Total employees 670
Annual sales $58 million
Industry Computer Hardware
Growth Openings in past year 117; percentage growth 21%
Contact
Mark S. Ain, President
Tel 617-890-3232
Fax 617-890-8768

Marcam Corporation
95 Wells Ave.
Newton, MA 02159

Founded 1980
Total employees 950
Annual sales $126 million
Industry Computer
Software
Growth Openings in past
year 139; percentage
growth 17%
Contact
Paul Margolis, COB/
President
Tel 617-965-0220
Fax 617-965-7273

Mathsoft, Inc.
101 Main St.
Cambridge, MA 02139

Founded 1985
Total employees 100
Annual sales $6 million
Industries Computer
Software, Holding
Companies
Growth Openings in past
year 45; percentage
growth 81%
Contact
David Blohm, President
Tel 617-577-1017
Fax 617-577-8829

Medical Parameters, Inc.
30 G Commerce Way
Woburn, MA 01801

Founded 1973
Total employees 90
Annual sales $9.9 million
Industry Medical
Growth Openings in past
year 20; percentage
growth 28%
Contact
Ms. Mary Paiva, Personnel
Director
Tel 617-933-5558
Fax 617-935-5931

**MEDIQ Mobile X-Ray
Services, Inc.**
90 Glacier Dr.
Westwood, MA 02090

Founded 1977
Total employees 180
Annual sales $35 million
Industry Medical
Growth Openings in past
year 20; percentage
growth 12%

Contact
Lawrence Smith, President
Tel 617-329-4200
Fax 617-329-8484

Megapulse, Inc.
8 Preston Ct.
Bedford, MA 01730

Founded 1973
Total employees 120
Annual sales $20 million
Industries
Telecommunications,
Transportation
Growth Openings in past
year 40; percentage
growth 50%
Contact
Ms. Phyllis Hull, Human
Resources Director
Tel 617-275-2010
Fax 617-275-4149

Mentor O&O, Inc.
3000 Longwater Dr.
Norwell, MA 02061

Founded 1981
Total employees 200
Annual sales $20 million
Industry Medical
Growth Openings in past
year 75; percentage
growth 60%
Contact
Robert J. Mercier,
President
Tel 617-871-6950
Fax 617-871-7785

**Mercury Computer
Systems, Inc.**
199 Riverneck Rd.
Chelmsford, MA 01824

Founded 1982
Total employees 180
Annual sales $38.6 million
Industries Computer
Hardware, Computer
Software,
Telecommunications
Growth Openings in past
year 40; percentage
growth 28%
Contact
Jay Bertelli, President
Tel 508-256-1300
Fax 508-256-3599

Millitech Corp.
South Deerfield Research
Park, PO Box 109
South Deerfield, MA 01373

Founded 1982
Total employees 129
Annual sales $17 million
Industries
Telecommunications,
Transportation
Growth Openings in past
year 24; percentage
growth 22%
Contact
Ms. Gail Carroll, Director
of Human Resources
Tel 413-665-8551
Fax 413-665-4831

**Milton Roy Company,
Liquid Metronics
Division**
8 Post Office Sq.
Acton, MA 01720

Founded 1975
Total employees 140
Annual sales $20 million
Industries Environmental,
Subassemblies and
Components, Test and
Measurement
Growth Openings in past
year 20; percentage
growth 16%
Contact
Bryan Elliott, Human
Resource Manager
Tel 508-263-9800
Fax 508-264-9172

**Mitek Surgical Products,
Inc.**
27 Providence Hwy.
Norwood, MA 02062

Founded 1985
Total employees 60
Annual sales $13.8 million
Industry Medical
Growth Openings in past
year 20; percentage
growth 50%
Contact
Kenneth Anstey, CEO/
President
Tel 617-551-8500
Fax 617-551-8501

Mitotix, Inc.
One Kendall Square, Bldg.
600
Cambridge, MA 02139

Founded 1992
Total employees 31

Industry Biotechnology
Growth Openings in past
year 16; percentage
growth 106%
Contact
Ms. Alison Taunton-Rigby,
Ph, President/CEO
Tel 617-225-0001
Fax 617-225-0005

Mod-Tap Corp.
285 Ayer Rd., PO Box 706
Harvard, MA 01451

Founded 1977
Total employees 260
Annual sales $30 million
Industry Subassemblies
and Components
Growth Openings in past
year 100; percentage
growth 62%
Contact
David Bundy, President
Tel 508-772-5630
Fax 508-772-2011

**Mohawk, Cable Design
Technology**
9 Mohawk Dr.
Leominster, MA 01453

Founded 1952
Total employees 200
Industry Subassemblies
and Components
Growth Openings in past
year 15; percentage
growth 8%
Contact
Paul Olsen, President
Tel 508-537-9961
Fax 508-537-4358

**Molecular Simulations,
Inc.**
16 New England Executive
Park
Burlington, MA 01803

Founded 1984
Total employees 150
Annual sales $17 million
Industry Computer
Software
Growth Openings in past
year 50; percentage
growth 50%
Contact
Michael Savage,
President/CEO
Tel 617-229-9800
Fax 617-229-9899

MPM Corp.
10 Forge Park
Franklin, MA 02038

Founded 1968
Total employees 140
Industry Manufacturing
Equipment
Growth Openings in past
year 55; percentage
growth 64%
Contact
Thomas Bagley, President
Tel 508-520-6999
Fax 508-520-2288

MRS Technology, Inc.
10 Elizabeth Dr.
Chelmsford, MA 01824

Founded 1986
Total employees 70
Industry Photonics
Growth Openings in past
year 20; percentage
growth 40%
Contact
Ms. Joanne Carpenter,
Employment Manager
Tel 508-250-0450
Fax 508-256-3266

Music Factory
PO Box 1089
Saugus, MA 01906

Founded 1992
Total employees 20
Industries Computer
Hardware, Computer
Software
Growth Openings in past
year 19; percentage
growth 1900%
Contact
James Baker, President
Tel 617-595-0684
Fax 617-595-1854

Nelmor Co.
Rivulet St.
North Uxbridge, MA 01538

Founded 1956
Total employees 205
Annual sales $17 million
Industries Environmental,
Manufacturing Equipment
Growth Openings in past
year 75; percentage
growth 57%
Contact
Edward Ronca, VP of
Sales and Marketing
Tel 508-278-5584
Fax 508-278-6801

**New England Biolabs,
Inc.**
32 Tozer Rd.
Beverly, MA 01915

Founded 1975
Total employees 170
Annual sales $16 million
Industries Biotechnology,
Holding Companies
Growth Openings in past
year 20; percentage
growth 13%
Contact
Dr. Donald Comb,
President/CEO
Tel 508-927-5054
Fax 508-921-1350

Nidec-Power General
152 Will Dr.
Canton, MA 02021

Founded 1979
Total employees 253
Annual sales $24 million
Industry Subassemblies
and Components
Growth Openings in past
year 93; percentage
growth 58%
Contact
Charles Aubee, General
Manager
Tel 617-828-6216
Fax 617-828-3215

**Northern Technologies,
Ltd.**
680 Mechanic St., Suite
100
Leominster, MA 01453

Founded 1971
Total employees 100
Industries Computer
Hardware, Manufacturing
Equipment,
Subassemblies and
Components
Growth Openings in past
year 70; percentage
growth 233%
Contact
Michael Klar, President
Tel 508-534-0200
Fax 508-534-9387

**NOVASOFT Systems,
Inc.**
8 New England Executive
Pk.
Burlington, MA 01803

Founded 1987
Total employees 55

Industry Computer
Software
Growth Openings in past
year 27; percentage
growth 96%
Contact
Ray Ciliv, President
Tel 617-221-0300
Fax 617-221-0465

Novus, Inc.
8 New England Executive
Park
Burlington, MA 01803

Founded 1978
Total employees 45
Industry Computer
Software
Growth Openings in past
year 25; percentage
growth 125%
Contact
David Crowley, Manager of
Human Resources
Tel 617-221-7171
Fax 617-221-7175

Nutramax Products, Inc.
Blackburn Industrial Pk., 9
Blackburn Dr.
Gloucester, MA 01930

Founded 1971
Total employees 320
Annual sales $31.14
million
Industries Holding
Companies,
Pharmaceuticals, Test
and Measurement
Growth Openings in past
year 100; percentage
growth 45%
Contact
Donald Lepone, President/
CEO
Tel 508-283-1800
Fax 508-283-4067

Object Design, Inc.
1 New England Executive
Park
Burlington, MA 01803

Founded 1988
Total employees 140
Annual sales $16 million
Industry Computer
Software
Growth Openings in past
year 65; percentage
growth 86%

Contact
Kenneth Marshall, CEO/
President
Tel 617-270-9797
Fax 617-270-3509

**Open Software
Foundation, Inc.**
11 Cambridge Ctr.
Cambridge, MA 02142

Founded 1988
Total employees 320
Annual sales $30 million
Industry Computer
Software
Growth Openings in past
year 49; percentage
growth 18%
Contact
David Tory, President
Tel 617-621-8700
Fax 617-621-0631

PAGG Corp.
13 Airport Industrial Park
Hopedale, MA 01747

Founded 1981
Total employees 125
Annual sales $20 million
Industries Computer
Hardware,
Subassemblies and
Components
Growth Openings in past
year 20; percentage
growth 19%
Contact
Edward Price, President
Tel 508-478-8544
Fax 508-634-2409

Panametrics, Inc.
221 Crescent St.
Waltham, MA 02154

Founded 1960
Total employees 600
Annual sales $80 million
Industry Holding
Companies
Growth Openings in past
year 50; percentage
growth 9%
Contact
David Chleck, Chairman of
the Board
Tel 617-899-2719
Fax 617-899-1552

**Parametric Technology
Corp.**
128 Technology Dr.
Waltham, MA 02154

Founded 1985
Total employees 750
Annual sales $86.74
million
Industry Computer
Software
Growth Openings in past
year 400; percentage
growth 114%
Contact
Ms. Patricia White,
Director of Human
Resources
Tel 617-894-7111
Fax 617-891-1069

**PerSeptive Biosystems,
Inc.**
38 Sidney St.
Cambridge, MA 02139

Founded 1987
Total employees 165
Annual sales $14.22
million
Industries Holding
Companies, Test and
Measurement
Growth Openings in past
year 110; percentage
growth 200%
Contact
Dr. Noubar Afeyan,
President/CEO
Tel 617-621-1787
Fax 617-621-2575

Phoenix Controls Corp.
55 Chapel St.
Newton, MA 02158

Founded 1983
Total employees 113
Annual sales $13 million
Industry Test and
Measurement
Growth Openings in past
year 23; percentage
growth 25%
Contact
Gordon Sharp, President
Tel 617-964-6670
Fax 617-965-4503

Physical Sciences, Inc.
20 New England Business
Ctr.
Andover, MA 01810

Founded 1973
Total employees 160

Annual sales $12 million
Industries Energy,
 Holding Companies,
 Transportation
Growth Openings in past
 year 35; percentage
 growth 28%
Contact
George Caledonia,
 President
Tel 508-689-0003
Fax 508-689-3232

PictureTel Corp.
Northwood Towers, 222
 Rosewood Dr.
Danvers, MA 01923

Founded 1984
Total employees 741
Annual sales $176.25
 million
Industry
 Telecommunications
Growth Openings in past
 year 212; percentage
 growth 40%
Contact
Dr. Norman E. Gaut,
 COB/CEO/President
Tel 508-762-5000
Fax 508-762-5245

**PolyMedica Industries,
Inc.**
2 Constitution Way
Woburn, MA 01801

Founded 1988
Total employees 75
Annual sales $11 million
Industries Advanced
 Materials, Chemicals,
 Holding Companies,
 Medical, Pharmaceuticals
Growth Openings in past
 year 25; percentage
 growth 50%
Contact
Steven J. Lee, CEO/
 President
Tel 617-933-2020
Fax 617-933-7992

Powersoft Corp.
70 Blanchard Rd.
Burlington, MA 01803

Founded 1974
Total employees 180
Annual sales $50.97
 million
Industry Computer
 Software

Growth Openings in past
 year 74; percentage
 growth 69%
Contact
Mitchell E. Kertzman,
 COB/CEO
Tel 617-229-2200
Fax 617-272-2540

Precision Robots, Inc.
749 Middlesex Tpke.
Billerica, MA 01821

Founded 1982
Total employees 220
Annual sales $30 million
Industry Factory
 Automation
Growth Openings in past
 year 90; percentage
 growth 69%
Contact
Ms. Diane DeLucia,
 Director of Human
 Resources
Tel 508-663-8555
Fax 508-663-9755

Procept, Inc.
840 Memorial Dr.
Cambridge, MA 02139

Founded 1985
Total employees 70
Industry Biotechnology
Growth Openings in past
 year 20; percentage
 growth 40%
Contact
Jack Knox, Director of
 Human Resources
Tel 617-491-1100
Fax 617-491-9019

Progress Software Corp.
14 Oak Park
Bedford, MA 01730

Founded 1981
Total employees 650
Annual sales $111.64
 million
Industry Computer
 Software
Growth Openings in past
 year 199; percentage
 growth 44%
Contact
Joseph Alsop, President
Tel 617-280-4000
Fax 617-280-4095

Qualitronics, Inc.
50 Stedman St., Unit 9
Lowell, MA 01851

Founded 1984
Total employees 95
Annual sales $9.2 million
Industry Subassemblies
 and Components
Growth Openings in past
 year 24; percentage
 growth 33%
Contact
Louis Pedroso, President
Tel 508-453-4667
Fax 508-459-3810

Reed National Co.
260 North Elm St.
Westfield, MA 01085

Founded 1946
Total employees 250
Industry Energy
Growth Openings in past
 year 40; percentage
 growth 19%
Contact
John E. Reed, President
Tel 413-568-9571
Fax 413-568-2969

Ring Medical, Inc.
85 Rangeway Rd.
North Billerica, MA 01862

Founded 1986
Total employees 110
Industries Medical,
 Telecommunications
Growth Openings in past
 year 40; percentage
 growth 57%
Contact
David Forester, President
Tel 508-670-2100
Fax 508-663-3116

RISO, Inc.
300 Rosewood Dr., Suite
210
Danvers, MA 01923

Founded 1987
Total employees 130
Industries Computer
 Hardware,
 Telecommunications
Growth Openings in past
 year 30; percentage
 growth 30%
Contact
John Carillon, President
Tel 508-777-7377
Fax 508-777-2517

**Rohm Tech, Inc.,
Specialty Chemicals
Division**
195 Canal St.
Malden, MA 02148

Founded 1981
Total employees 136
Annual sales $50 million
Industries Advanced
Materials, Biotechnology,
Chemicals
Growth Openings in past
year 30; percentage
growth 28%
Contact
Ekkehard Grampp,
President
Tel 617-321-6984
Fax 617-322-0358

RWA, Inc.
37 Washington St.
Melrose, MA 02176

Founded 1984
Total employees 48
Industries Factory
Automation,
Manufacturing
Equipment,
Subassemblies and
Components
Growth Openings in past
year 18; percentage
growth 60%
Contact
Richard Aho, President
Tel 617-662-9322
Fax 617-662-6032

**Sager Electrical Supply
Co., Inc.**
60 Research Rd.
Hingham, MA 02043

Founded 1887
Total employees 240
Annual sales $80 million
Industry Holding
Companies
Growth Openings in past
year 40; percentage
growth 20%
Contact
Raymond Norton,
President
Tel 617-749-6700
Fax 617-749-3842

**Scientific Systems Co.,
Inc.**
500 West Cummings Park,
#3950
Woburn, MA 01801

Founded 1976
Total employees 20
Annual sales $2.3 million
Industries Computer
Hardware, Computer
Software, Factory
Automation
Growth Openings in past
year 15; percentage
growth 300%
Contact
Dr. Raman Mehra, Ph.D.,
President
Tel 617-933-5355
Fax 617-938-4752

Security Dynamics, Inc.
1 Alewife Ctr.
Cambridge, MA 02140

Founded 1984
Total employees 70
Annual sales $12 million
Industry Computer
Software
Growth Openings in past
year 20; percentage
growth 40%
Contact
Kenneth P. Weiss, CEO/
CTO
Tel 617-547-7820
Fax 617-354-8836

**Sencom Sensors and
Communications Corp.**
3 Preston Ct.
Bedford, MA 01730

Founded 1992
Total employees 110
Industries Computer
Hardware, Defense,
Manufacturing
Equipment,
Telecommunications
Growth Openings in past
year 61; percentage
growth 124%
Contact
Fredrick S. Yeatts, Ph.D.,
President
Tel 617-271-0258
Fax 617-275-3866

Serono Laboratories, Inc.
100 Longwater Cir.
Norwell, MA 02061

Founded 1970
Total employees 300

Industries Biotechnology,
Pharmaceuticals
Growth Openings in past
year 46; percentage
growth 18%
Contact
Ed Reiley, VP of
Personnel
Tel 617-982-9000
Fax 617-871-6754

Shiva Corp.
Northwest Park, 63 Third
Ave.
Burlington, MA 01803

Founded 1985
Total employees 160
Annual sales $35 million
Industries Computer
Software,
Telecommunications
Growth Openings in past
year 30; percentage
growth 23%
Contact
Frank Ingari, President/
CEO
Tel 617-270-8300
Fax 617-270-8852

**Signal Technology
Corporation**
60 Winter St.
Weymouth, MA 02188

Founded 1981
Total employees 850
Annual sales $80 million
Industry Holding
Companies
Growth Openings in past
year 92; percentage
growth 12%
Contact
Dale Peterson, President/
CEO
Tel 617-337-8823
Fax 617-337-8826

**SilverPlatter Information,
Inc.**
100 River Ridge Dr.
Norwood, MA 02062

Founded 1985
Total employees 140
Annual sales $16 million
Industries Computer
Software, Holding
Companies
Growth Openings in past
year 65; percentage
growth 86%

Contact
Bela Hatvany, President
Tel 617-769-2599
Fax 617-769-8763

SMT East Corp.
200 Foxborough Blvd.
Foxboro, MA 02035

Founded 1988
Total employees 70
Annual sales $5 million
Industries Manufacturing
Equipment,
Subassemblies and
Components
Growth Openings in past
year 20; percentage
growth 40%
Contact
John Baider, President
Tel 508-543-2600
Fax 508-543-3515

**Software Quality
Automation, Inc.**
10 State St.
Woburn, MA 01801

Founded 1990
Total employees 50
Industry Computer
Software
Growth Openings in past
year 25; percentage
growth 100%
Contact
Ron Nordin, President/
CEO
Tel 617-932-0110
Fax 617-932-3280

SpecTran Corp.
SpecTran Industrial Park,
50 Hall Rd.
Sturbridge, MA 01566

Founded 1982
Total employees 140
Annual sales $25.58
million
Industries Advanced
Materials, Photonics
Growth Openings in past
year 20; percentage
growth 16%
Contact
Raymond E. Jaeger,
President/CEO
Tel 508-347-2261
Fax 508-347-2747

**Spectrum Associates,
Inc.**
600 West Cummings Park
Woburn, MA 01801

Founded 1984
Total employees 150
Annual sales $14 million
Industry Computer
Software
Growth Openings in past
year 40; percentage
growth 36%
Contact
John Nugent, Principal
Tel 617-932-0932
Fax 617-932-3878

Steinbrecher Corp.
30 North Ave.
Burlington, MA 01803

Founded 1974
Total employees 90
Annual sales $10 million
Industries Subassemblies
and Components,
Telecommunications
Growth Openings in past
year 30; percentage
growth 50%
Contact
Ms. Patti Boyd, Manager
of Human Resources
Tel 617-935-8460
Fax 617-935-8848

Synernetics Inc.
85 Rangeway Rd.
North Billerica, MA 01862

Founded 1988
Total employees 100
Annual sales $17 million
Industries Computer
Software,
Telecommunications
Growth Openings in past
year 20; percentage
growth 25%
Contact
Allan L. Wallack,
President/CEO
Tel 508-670-9009
Fax 508-670-9015

Synetics Corp.
540 Edgewater Dr.
Wakefield, MA 01880

Founded 1985
Total employees 425
Annual sales $36 million

Industries Computer
Hardware, Computer
Software,
Telecommunications
Growth Openings in past
year 99; percentage
growth 30%
Contact
Bahar Uttam, President
Tel 617-245-9090
Fax 617-245-6311

System Resources Corp.
128 Wheeler Rd.
Burlington, MA 01803

Founded 1985
Total employees 285
Annual sales $18 million
Industries Computer
Hardware, Computer
Software, Manufacturing
Equipment
Growth Openings in past
year 85; percentage
growth 42%
Contact
Samir A. Desai, President
Tel 617-270-9228
Fax 617-272-2589

Systems Group, Inc.
92 Montvale Ave.
Stoneham, MA 02180

Founded 1980
Total employees 50
Industry Computer
Software
Growth Openings in past
year 20; percentage
growth 66%
Contact
Richard Merriam,
President
Tel 617-438-5900
Fax 617-438-4836

Tech Pak, Inc.
2 Fifth St.
Peabody, MA 01960

Founded 1965
Total employees 120
Annual sales $11 million
Industries Biotechnology,
Medical
Growth Openings in past
year 20; percentage
growth 20%
Contact
Ms. Kim Powers, Director
of Human Resources
Tel 508-532-3500
Fax 508-532-9135

Technology Integration, Inc.
54 Middlesex Tpke., 2nd Fl.
Bedford, MA 01730

Founded 1984
Total employees 50
Industry Computer Hardware
Growth Openings in past year 15; percentage growth 42%
Contact
Richard Hayden, President
Tel 617-275-4545
Fax 617-275-5035

Teledyne, Inc., Teledyne Rodney Metals
1357 East Rodney French Blvd., PO Box 6915
New Bedford, MA 02744

Founded 1952
Total employees 500
Industries Advanced Materials, Manufacturing Equipment
Growth Openings in past year 100; percentage growth 25%
Contact
George Wright, VP of Personnel Relations
Tel 508-996-5691
Fax 508-993-3176

Teleglobe Communications, Inc.
40 High St.
North Andover, MA 01845

Founded 1969
Total employees 350
Annual sales $48 million
Industry Telecommunications
Growth Openings in past year 49; percentage growth 16%
Contact
Constantino Topalidis, President/CEO
Tel 508-681-0600
Fax 508-681-0660

Telor Ophthalmic Pharmaceutical, Inc.
500 West Cummings Park, Suite 6950
Woburn, MA 01801

Founded 1988
Total employees 30
Industry Pharmaceuticals

Growth Openings in past year 15; percentage growth 100%
Contact
Dr. Stephen J. Riggi, Ph.D., President/CEO
Tel 617-937-0393
Fax 617-937-0292

TERC
2067 Massachusetts Ave.
Cambridge, MA 02140

Founded 1965
Total employees 130
Annual sales $7.5 million
Industries Computer Hardware, Computer Software
Growth Openings in past year 30; percentage growth 30%
Contact
Ms. Barbara Sampson, Chief Executive Officer
Tel 617-547-0430
Fax 617-349-3535

Thermedics, Inc.
470 Wildwood St., PO Box 2999
Woburn, MA 01888

Founded 1983
Total employees 200
Annual sales $80.22 million
Industries Advanced Materials, Biotechnology, Manufacturing Equipment, Medical, Test and Measurement
Growth Openings in past year 20; percentage growth 11%
Contact
John W. Wood, Jr., President/CEO
Tel 617-938-3786
Fax 617-933-4476

Thermo Environmental Instruments, Inc.
8 West Forge Pkwy.
Franklin, MA 02038

Founded 1970
Total employees 175
Industry Environmental
Growth Openings in past year 35; percentage growth 25%
Contact
Denis Holm, President
Tel 508-520-0430
Fax 508-520-1460

Tighe & Bond, Inc.
53 Southampton Rd.
Westfield, MA 01085

Founded 1911
Total employees 150
Annual sales $15 million
Industry Environmental
Growth Openings in past year 30; percentage growth 25%
Contact
John W. Powers, President
Tel 413-562-1600
Fax 413-562-5317

Tom Snyder Productions
80 Coolidge Hill Rd.
Watertown, MA 02172

Founded 1980
Total employees 40
Annual sales $3 million
Industries Computer Software, Telecommunications
Growth Openings in past year 15; percentage growth 60%
Contact
Thomas F. Snyder, Chief Executive Officer
Tel 617-926-6000
Fax 617-926-6222

TRC Environmental Corp.
Boot Mills South, Foot of John St.
Lowell, MA 01852

Founded 1960
Total employees 650
Annual sales $53 million
Industry Environmental
Growth Openings in past year 25; percentage growth 4%
Contact
Robert M. Bradway, President
Tel 508-970-5600
Fax 508-452-6033

TSI Mason Laboratories
57 Union St.
Worcester, MA 01608

Founded 1987
Total employees 204
Annual sales $28 million
Industry Pharmaceuticals
Growth Openings in past year 44; percentage growth 27%

Contact
Steve Niemi, President
Tel 508-791-0931
Fax 508-753-1834

Unex Corp.
27 Industrial Ave.
Chelmsford, MA 01824

Founded 1986
Total employees 105
Annual sales $14 million
Industry
Telecommunications
Growth Openings in past
year 55; percentage
growth 110%
Contact
George Taylor, Controller
Tel 508-256-8222
Fax 508-250-9055

Vanasse Hangen Bustlin, Inc.
101 Walnut St., PO Box 9151
Watertown, MA 02272

Founded 1979
Total employees 350
Annual sales $40 million
Industries Environmental,
Manufacturing
Equipment,
Transportation
Growth Openings in past
year 49; percentage
growth 16%
Contact
Richard E. Hangen,
President
Tel 617-924-1770
Fax 617-924-2286

Vertex Pharmaceuticals, Inc.
40 Allston St.
Cambridge, MA 02139

Founded 1989
Total employees 100
Annual sales $6 million
Industries Biotechnology,
Holding Companies,
Pharmaceuticals
Growth Openings in past
year 36; percentage
growth 56%
Contact
Dr. Joshua Boger,
President/Chief Executive
Officer
Tel 617-576-3111
Fax 617-576-2109

Vicor Corp.
23 Frontage Rd.
Andover, MA 01810

Founded 1981
Total employees 660
Annual sales $63.8 million
Industry Subassemblies
and Components
Growth Openings in past
year 132; percentage
growth 25%
Contact
Patrizio Vinciarelli, Ph.D.,
COB/President
Tel 508-470-2900
Fax 508-475-6715

VideoServer, Inc.
50 Forbes Rd.
Lexington, MA 02173

Founded 1990
Total employees 50
Annual sales $6.9 million
Industry
Telecommunications
Growth Openings in past
year 15; percentage
growth 42%
Contact
Robert Castle, President
Tel 617-863-2300
Fax 617-862-2833

Viewlogic Systems, Inc.
293 Boston Post Rd. West
Marlborough, MA 01752

Founded 1984
Total employees 430
Annual sales $65.78
million
Industries Computer
Software, Holding
Companies
Growth Openings in past
year 72; percentage
growth 20%
Contact
Eugene Connolly, VP of
Human Resources
Tel 508-480-0881
Fax 508-480-0882

Visibility Inc.
2 Main St.
Stoneham, MA 02180

Founded 1979
Total employees 120
Annual sales $18 million
Industry Computer
Software

Growth Openings in past
year 30; percentage
growth 33%
Contact
Michael Dunn, President
Tel 617-279-2100
Fax 617-279-2108

Vision-Sciences, Inc.
6 Strathmore Rd.
Natick, MA 01760

Founded 1990
Total employees 100
Annual sales $5.5 million
Industries Holding
Companies, Medical,
Photonics
Growth Openings in past
year 50; percentage
growth 100%
Contact
Alan West, Vice President/
Business Manager
Tel 508-650-9971
Fax 508-650-9976

VMARK Software, Inc.
30 Speen St.
Framingham, MA 01701

Founded 1984
Total employees 175
Annual sales $18.8 million
Industries Computer
Software, Holding
Companies
Growth Openings in past
year 35; percentage
growth 25%
Contact
James K. Walsh, VP of
Finance and
Administration
Tel 508-879-3311
Fax 508-879-3332

**Wellfleet
Communications, Inc.**
PO Box 7029
Billerica, MA 01821

Founded 1986
Total employees 767
Annual sales $85 million
Industries Computer
Software,
Telecommunications
Growth Openings in past
year 360; percentage
growth 88%

Contact
Steven Cheheyl, Senior
  VP of Finance and
  Administration
Tel 508-670-8888
Fax 508-436-3436

XLI Corp.
800 West Cummings Park,
  Suite 6650
Woburn, MA 01801

Founded 1979
Total employees 35
Annual sales $1.7 million
Industry Computer
  Hardware
Growth Openings in past
  year 17; percentage
  growth 94%
Contact
Vincent J. Spoto,
  President
Tel 617-932-9199
Fax 617-932-3449

Xylogics, Inc.
53 3rd Ave.
Burlington, MA 01803

Founded 1975
Total employees 205
Annual sales $41.5 million
Industries Computer
  Hardware,
  Telecommunications
Growth Openings in past
  year 35; percentage
  growth 20%
Contact
Bruce Sachs, President/
  CEO
Tel 617-272-8140
Fax 617-273-5392

Xyplex, Inc.
295 Foster St.
Littleton, MA 01460

Founded 1981
Total employees 350
Annual sales $68 million
Industries Subassemblies
  and Components,
  Telecommunications
Growth Openings in past
  year 49; percentage
  growth 16%
Contact
Peter Nesbeda, President
Tel 508-952-4700
Fax 508-952-4702

Zoll Medical Corporation
32 Second Ave.
Burlington, MA 01803

Founded 1980
Total employees 200
Annual sales $21.3 million
Industry Medical
Growth Openings in past
  year 40; percentage
  growth 25%
Contact
Ms. Patricia Hanson,
  Personnel Supervisor
Tel 617-229-0020

Zoom Telephonics, Inc.
207 South St.
Boston, MA 02111

Founded 1977
Total employees 130
Annual sales $55.23
  million
Industry
  Telecommunications
Growth Openings in past
  year 55; percentage
  growth 73%
Contact
Frank Manning, President
Tel 617-423-1072
Fax 617-423-9231

Zymark Corp.
Zymark Center
Hopkinton, MA 01748

Founded 1981
Total employees 270
Annual sales $13 million
Industries Computer
  Software, Factory
  Automation, Test and
  Measurement
Growth Openings in past
  year 36; percentage
  growth 15%
Contact
Ms. Pamela Duggan,
  Director of Human
  Resources
Tel 508-435-9500
Fax 508-435-3439

Michigan

**AAR Manufacturing
Corp., Cadillac
Manufacturing Division**
201 Haynes St., PO Box
  550
Cadillac, MI 49601

Founded 1962
Total employees 200
Annual sales $24 million
Industry Advanced
  Materials
Growth Openings in past
  year 50; percentage
  growth 33%
Contact
Don Larkins, Human
  Resources Manager
Tel 616-779-8808
Fax 616-779-8845

Arbor Technologies, Inc.
3728 Plaza Dr.
Ann Arbor, MI 48108

Founded 1985
Total employees 68
Annual sales $7.4 million
Industry Medical
Growth Openings in past
  year 20; percentage
  growth 41%
Contact
Monty Vincent, President
Tel 313-665-3300
Fax 313-665-3516

Autodesk, Inc.
26200 Town Center Dr.,
  Suite 340
Novi, MI 48375

Founded 1986
Total employees 75
Annual sales $8.7 million
Industry Computer
  Software
Growth Openings in past
  year 25; percentage
  growth 50%
Contact
Ronald S. Schlapitz,
  Controller
Tel 810-347-9650
Fax 810-347-1893

Automated Analysis Corp.
2805 South Industrial Hwy., Suite 100
Ann Arbor, MI 48104

Founded 1983
Total employees 160
Annual sales $7.2 million
Industries Computer Software, Manufacturing Equipment
Growth Openings in past year 40; percentage growth 33%
Contact
S.C. Wang, Chief Executive Officer
Tel 313-973-1000
Fax 313-973-1190

Baxter Diagnostics, Inc., Burdick & Jackson Division
1953 South Harvey St.
Muskegon, MI 49442

Founded 1983
Total employees 110
Industries Chemicals, Test and Measurement
Growth Openings in past year 20; percentage growth 22%
Contact
Russell Bromley, President
Tel 616-726-3171
Fax 616-728-8226

Bond Robotics, Inc.
6750 19 Mile Rd.
Sterling Heights, MI 48314

Founded 1978
Total employees 200
Industry Factory Automation
Growth Openings in past year 100; percentage growth 100%
Contact
Irvin D. Bond, President
Tel 810-254-7600
Fax 810-254-1860

BORIS Systems, Inc.
4660 South Hagadorn Blvd., Suite 420
East Lansing, MI 48823

Founded 1982
Total employees 135
Annual sales $22 million
Industry Computer Hardware

Growth Openings in past year 57; percentage growth 73%
Contact
Nicholas Alter, President
Tel 517-332-7702
Fax 517-332-4757

C.M. Smillie Group
1200 Woodward Heights
Ferndale, MI 48220

Founded 1889
Total employees 110
Annual sales $12 million
Industry Holding Companies
Growth Openings in past year 20; percentage growth 22%
Contact
Scott Smillie, Chief Executive Officer
Tel 810-544-3100
Fax 810-545-1076

Cold Heading Co.
4600 Bellevue Ave.
Detroit, MI 48207

Founded 1952
Total employees 270
Industries Holding Companies, Subassemblies and Components
Growth Openings in past year 13; percentage growth 5%
Contact
Ms. Elizabeth Stevens, Chief Executive Officer
Tel 313-923-7800
Fax 313-923-0812

Computer Methods Corp.
13740 Merriman Rd.
Livonia, MI 48150

Founded 1977
Total employees 400
Annual sales $29 million
Industries Computer Software, Holding Companies
Growth Openings in past year 40; percentage growth 11%
Contact
Andrew K. Stewart, President
Tel 313-522-5187
Fax 313-522-2705

CSC Healthcare Systems
34505 West Twelve Mile Rd., Suite 300
Farmington Hills, MI 48331

Founded 1974
Total employees 250
Annual sales $35 million
Industry Computer Software
Growth Openings in past year 25; percentage growth 11%
Contact
Ms. Sue Curtis, Manager of Human Resources
Tel 810-553-0900
Fax 810-553-7439

Detroit Edge Tool Co.
6570 East Nevada St.
Detroit, MI 48234

Founded 1872
Total employees 70
Annual sales $5 million
Industry Test and Measurement
Growth Openings in past year 20; percentage growth 40%
Contact
R.R. Ebbing, President
Tel 313-366-4120
Fax 313-366-1661

Durr Industries, Inc.
40600 Plymouth Rd.
Plymouth, MI 48170

Founded 1970
Total employees 550
Industries Environmental, Factory Automation
Growth Openings in past year 149; percentage growth 37%
Contact
Robert J. Mulholland, President
Tel 810-459-6800
Fax 810-459-5837

Eaton Corp., Torque Control Products
1101 West Hanover St.
Marshall, MI 49068

Founded 1911
Total employees 400
Annual sales $39 million
Industry Subassemblies and Components
Growth Openings in past year 30; percentage growth 8%

Contact
Ernest T. Thomas, General Manager
Tel 616-781-2811
Fax 616-789-3214

FANUC Robotics, Inc.
2000 South Adams Rd.
Auburn Hills, MI 48326

Founded 1982
Total employees 650
Industry Factory Automation
Growth Openings in past year 49; percentage growth 8%
Contact
Eric Mittelstadt, President/CEO
Tel 810-377-7000
Fax 810-377-7366

Ferndale Laboratories, Inc.
780 West Eight Mile Rd.
Ferndale, MI 48220

Founded 1897
Total employees 112
Annual sales $12 million
Industries Medical, Pharmaceuticals
Growth Openings in past year 16; percentage growth 16%
Contact
David Bens, President
Tel 810-548-0900
Fax 810-548-0279

Fishbeck, Thompson, Carr & Huber, Inc.
6090 East Fulton St.
Ada, MI 49301

Founded 1956
Total employees 175
Annual sales $18 million
Industries Environmental, Manufacturing Equipment
Growth Openings in past year 19; percentage growth 12%
Contact
Charles D. Carr, PE, President
Tel 616-676-2666
Fax 616-676-8173

Gentex Corp.
600 North Centennial St.
Zeeland, MI 49464

Founded 1974
Total employees 590

Annual sales $45 million
Industries Photonics, Test and Measurement
Growth Openings in past year 140; percentage growth 31%
Contact
John Van Haitsma, Director of Human Resources
Tel 616-772-1800
Fax 616-772-7348

Horiba Instruments, Automation Division
3901 Varsity Dr.
Ann Arbor, MI 48108

Founded 1977
Total employees 115
Annual sales $10 million
Industry Computer Software
Growth Openings in past year 30; percentage growth 35%
Contact
Ms. Doris Fatu, Personnel Director
Tel 313-973-2171
Fax 313-973-7868

Information Transfer Systems, Inc.
209 East Washington St., Suite 200
Ann Arbor, MI 48104

Founded 1984
Total employees 75
Industry Computer Software
Growth Openings in past year 58; percentage growth 341%
Contact
Dr. Bruce M. Brock, President
Tel 313-994-0003
Fax 313-994-1228

John Brown, Inc., Brown Machine Division
330 North Ross St., PO Box 434
Beaverton, MI 48612

Founded 1982
Total employees 200
Annual sales $25 million
Industries Energy, Factory Automation, Test and Measurement
Growth Openings in past year 25; percentage growth 14%

Contact
James Warheit, Director of Human Resources
Tel 517-435-7741
Fax 517-435-2821

Livernois Group
25315 Kean St.
Dearborn, MI 48124

Founded 1957
Total employees 600
Annual sales $42 million
Industry Holding Companies
Growth Openings in past year 250; percentage growth 71%
Contact
Ms. Norma Wallace, President
Tel 313-278-0200
Fax 313-278-1444

Macro Computer Products, Inc.
2523 Product Ct.
Rochester Hills, MI 48309

Founded 1981
Total employees 75
Annual sales $12 million
Industry Holding Companies
Growth Openings in past year 20; percentage growth 36%
Contact
Dave Shellenbarger, President
Tel 810-853-5353
Fax 810-853-7140

MACSTEEL
One Jackson Sq., Suite 500
Jackson, MI 49201

Founded 1974
Total employees 600
Annual sales $69 million
Industry Advanced Materials
Growth Openings in past year 135; percentage growth 29%
Contact
Robert V. Kelley, Jr., President
Tel 517-782-0415
Fax 517-782-8736

Mallinckrodt Sensor Systems, Inc.
1230 Eisenhower Pl.
Ann Arbor, MI 48108

Founded 1982
Total employees 200
Annual sales $22 million
Industry Medical
Growth Openings in past year 50; percentage growth 33%
Contact
Ms. Margaret Spurr, Manager of Human Resources
Tel 313-973-7000
Fax 313-973-3268

Medar, Inc.
38700 Grand River Ave.
Farmington Hills, MI 48335

Founded 1978
Total employees 160
Annual sales $24 million
Industries Factory Automation, Holding Companies
Growth Openings in past year 21; percentage growth 15%
Contact
Charles J. Drake, President/COB
Tel 810-477-3900
Fax 810-477-8877

Nartron Corp.
5000 North US 131
Reed City, MI 49677

Founded 1968
Total employees 200
Industries Energy, Factory Automation, Holding Companies, Photonics, Subassemblies and Components, Test and Measurement
Growth Openings in past year 30; percentage growth 17%
Contact
Ms. Heather Huber, Manager of Human Resources
Tel 616-832-5525
Fax 616-832-5513

National TechTeam, Inc.
22000 Garrison Ave.
Dearborn, MI 48124

Founded 1987
Total employees 365

Annual sales $20 million
Industries Computer Hardware, Computer Software
Growth Openings in past year 142; percentage growth 63%
Contact
William F. Coyro, Jr., COB/CEO
Tel 313-277-2277
Fax 313-277-6409

Newcor, Inc.
1825 South Woodward, Suite 240
Bloomfield Hills, MI 48302

Founded 1933
Total employees 750
Annual sales $89 million
Industry Holding Companies
Growth Openings in past year 150; percentage growth 25%
Contact
Thomas D. Parker, VP of Human Resources
Tel 810-253-2400
Fax 810-253-2413

NTH Consultants, Ltd.
38955 Hills Tech Dr.
Farmington Hills, MI 48331

Founded 1968
Total employees 190
Annual sales $25 million
Industries Advanced Materials, Environmental
Growth Openings in past year 15; percentage growth 8%
Contact
Jerome C. Neyer, Chief Executive Officer
Tel 810-553-6300
Fax 810-489-0727

Ovonic Battery Co.
1707 Northwood Dr.
Troy, MI 48084

Founded 1983
Total employees 80
Annual sales $10 million
Industry Energy
Growth Openings in past year 25; percentage growth 45%
Contact
Subhash K. Dhar, President
Tel 810-362-1750
Fax 810-362-0332

Peerless Metal Powders & Abrasive Co.
124 South Military Ave.
Detroit, MI 48209

Founded 1971
Total employees 58
Annual sales $4.0 million
Industries Advanced Materials, Holding Companies
Growth Openings in past year 23; percentage growth 65%
Contact
Paul Tousley, President
Tel 313-841-5400
Fax 313-841-0240

Petro-Chem Processing, Inc.
421 Lycaste St.
Detroit, MI 48214

Founded 1980
Total employees 238
Industry Environmental
Growth Openings in past year 38; percentage growth 19%
Contact
Norm Foster, President
Tel 313-824-5835
Fax 313-824-5842

Printek, Inc.
1517 Townline Rd.
Benton Harbor, MI 49022

Founded 1980
Total employees 100
Industry Computer Hardware
Growth Openings in past year 30; percentage growth 42%
Contact
Ms. Shirley Sommers, Personnel Manager
Tel 616-925-3200
Fax 616-925-8539

PVS Chemicals, Inc.
10900 Harper Ave.
Detroit, MI 48213

Founded 1946
Total employees 350
Industries Chemicals, Environmental, Holding Companies
Growth Openings in past year 49; percentage growth 16%

Contact
James B. Nicholson,
President
Tel 313-921-1200
Fax 313-921-1378

Randell Manufacturing, Inc.
0520 South Coldwater Rd.
Weidman, MI 48893

Founded 1975
Total employees 350
Industries Energy,
Manufacturing Equipment
Growth Openings in past
year 49; percentage
growth 16%
Contact
Lynn Bay, President
Tel 517-644-3331
Fax 800-634-5369

Recycling Systems, Inc.
PO Box 364
Winn, MI 48896

Founded 1988
Total employees 70
Annual sales $8 million
Industry Environmental
Growth Openings in past
year 26; percentage
growth 59%
Contact
Gary Bardos, President
Tel 517-866-2800
Fax 517-866-2280

Rocktron Corp.
2870 Technology Dr.
Rochester Hills, MI 48309

Founded 1988
Total employees 65
Annual sales $8.9 million
Industry Holding
Companies
Growth Openings in past
year 15; percentage
growth 30%
Contact
James K. Waller, President
Tel 810-853-3055
Fax 810-853-5937

Rockwell International Suspension Systems Co.
2135 West Maple Rd.
Troy, MI 48084

Founded 1986
Total employees 400
Annual sales $39 million

Industry Subassemblies
and Components
Growth Openings in past
year 75; percentage
growth 23%
Contact
Charles Weisbaum, Acting
CEO
Tel 810-435-1000
Fax 810-435-1224

Simpson Industries, Inc., Gladwin Division
650 Industrial Park Ave.
Gladwin, MI 48624

Founded 1969
Total employees 160
Annual sales $17 million
Industries Manufacturing
Equipment,
Subassemblies and
Components
Growth Openings in past
year 60; percentage
growth 60%
Contact
Michael J. Roan,
Operations Manager
Tel 517-426-9263
Fax 517-426-3131

Sirco Associates, Inc.
901 Wilshire Dr., Suite 540
Troy, MI 48084

Founded 1979
Total employees 75
Industry Computer
Hardware
Growth Openings in past
year 22; percentage
growth 41%
Contact
Hans W. Schweighoefer,
President
Tel 810-362-2200
Fax 810-362-0081

Techna Corp.
44808 Helm St.
Plymouth, MI 48170

Founded 1986
Total employees 48
Industries Environmental,
Holding Companies
Growth Openings in past
year 18; percentage
growth 60%
Contact
James Harless, President
Tel 313-454-1100
Fax 313-454-1233

Turchan Enterprises, Inc.
12825 Ford Rd.
Dearborn, MI 48126

Founded 1933
Total employees 50
Annual sales $6.3 million
Industries Factory
Automation,
Manufacturing Equipment
Growth Openings in past
year 30; percentage
growth 150%
Contact
Manuel Turchan, Chief
Executive Officer
Tel 313-581-0043
Fax 313-581-2480

Unitech Engineering, Inc.
32661 Edward Ave.
Madison Heights, MI
48071

Founded 1986
Total employees 75
Annual sales $5.9 million
Industry Manufacturing
Equipment
Growth Openings in past
year 20; percentage
growth 36%
Contact
Robert May, President
Tel 810-585-9790
Fax 810-585-0412

United Solar Systems, Corp.
1100C West Maple Rd.
Troy, MI 48084

Founded 1981
Total employees 120
Annual sales $4 million
Industry Energy
Growth Openings in past
year 60; percentage
growth 100%
Contact
Ms. Beth Swindell, Director
of Personnel
Tel 810-362-4170
Fax 810-362-4492

Universal Super Abrasive, Inc.
27588 Northline Rd.
Romulus, MI 48174

Founded 1888
Total employees 100
Industry Advanced
Materials

Growth Openings in past
year 25; percentage
growth 33%
Contact
Mike Tracy, Vice
President/General
Manager
Tel 313-941-1300
Fax 313-941-0940

**Variation Systems
Analysis, Inc.**
300 Maple Park Blvd.
Saint Clair Shores, MI
48081

Founded 1981
Total employees 125
Annual sales $6 million
Industries Computer
Hardware, Computer
Software
Growth Openings in past
year 25; percentage
growth 25%
Contact
Mrs. Shirley Kelly, Office
Sales Coordinator
Tel 810-774-2640
Fax 810-778-6470

Veratex Corp.
1304 East Maple Rd.
Troy, MI 48083

Founded 1960
Total employees 200
Annual sales $45 million
Industry Medical
Growth Openings in past
year 25; percentage
growth 14%
Contact
James H. Devlin, CEO/
President
Tel 810-588-2970

**X-Ray Industries, Inc.,
X-R-I Testing Division**
1961 Thunderbird Rd.
Troy, MI 48084

Founded 1941
Total employees 100
Annual sales $6 million
Industry Manufacturing
Equipment
Growth Openings in past
year 20; percentage
growth 25%
Contact
Scott Thams, President
Tel 810-362-5050
Fax 810-362-4422

X-Rite, Inc.
3100 44th St., Southwest
Grandville, MI 49418

Founded 1958
Total employees 290
Annual sales $36 million
Industries Factory
Automation, Medical,
Photonics, Test and
Measurement
Growth Openings in past
year 19; percentage
growth 7%
Contact
Ted Thompson, CEO/
President
Tel 616-534-7663
Fax 616-534-9212

Minnesota

Aetrium, Inc.
2350 Helen St.
North Saint Paul, MN
55109

Founded 1982
Total employees 130
Annual sales $20.9 million
Industry Manufacturing
Equipment
Growth Openings in past
year 30; percentage
growth 30%
Contact
Michael Jaeb, Director of
Corporate Administration
Tel 612-770-2000
Fax 612-770-7975

Americable, Inc.
7450 Flying Cloud Dr.
Eden Prairie, MN 55344

Founded 1981
Total employees 200
Annual sales $40 million
Industries Computer
Hardware,
Subassemblies and
Components,
Telecommunications
Growth Openings in past
year 50; percentage
growth 33%
Contact
Bill Dease, Manager of
Human Resources
Tel 612-942-3800
Fax 612-944-8021

AmeriData, Inc.
10200 51st Ave. North
Minneapolis, MN 55442

Founded 1969
Total employees 300
Annual sales $49 million
Industry Computer
Hardware
Growth Openings in past
year 25; percentage
growth 9%
Contact
Ms. Sharon Berglund,
Personnel Manager
Tel 612-557-2500
Fax 612-557-6946

Anderson Chemical Co.
PO Box 1041
Litchfield, MN 55355

Founded 1910
Total employees 68
Annual sales $9 million
Industry Chemicals
Growth Openings in past
year 16; percentage
growth 30%
Contact
J. Terry Anderson,
President
Tel 612-693-2477
Fax 612-693-8238

**Andreasen Engineering
and Manufacturing, Inc.**
1209 West County Rd. E
Arden Hills, MN 55112

Founded 1979
Total employees 62
Annual sales $3 million
Industry Manufacturing
Equipment
Growth Openings in past
year 22; percentage
growth 55%
Contact
Richard Bonn, President
Tel 612-483-4140
Fax 612-483-9221

Audiotone, Inc.
4120 Olson Memorial Hwy.
Golden Valley, MN 55422

Founded 1949
Total employees 100
Annual sales $29 million
Industry Medical
Growth Openings in past
year 20; percentage
growth 25%

Contact
Paul D'Amico, President
Tel 612-520-9723
Fax 612-520-9529

Ault, Inc.
7300 Boone Ave. North
Minneapolis, MN 55428

Founded 1961
Total employees 350
Annual sales $21 million
Industries Energy,
Subassemblies and
Components
Growth Openings in past
year 49; percentage
growth 16%
Contact
Ms. Linda Denson,
Director of Human
Resources
Tel 612-493-1900
Fax 612-493-1911

**B. Braun Medical, Inc.,
Cardiovascular Division**
13000 Hwy. 55
Plymouth, MN 55441,

Founded 1986
Total employees 162
Annual sales $17 million
Industry Medical
Growth Openings in past
year 35; percentage
growth 27%
Contact
Ms. Mary Sears, Director
of Personnel
Tel 612-559-3370
Fax 612-559-5909

**Baldor Motion Products
Group**
5205 U.S. 169 North
Plymouth, MN 55442

Founded 1983
Total employees 90
Annual sales $10 million
Industry Test and
Measurement
Growth Openings in past
year 20; percentage
growth 28%
Contact
Stan Heider, General
Manager
Tel 612-557-9250
Fax 612-557-9255

Barr Engineering Co.
8300 Norman Center Dr.
Minneapolis, MN 55437

Founded 1962
Total employees 250
Industry Environmental
Growth Openings in past
year 37; percentage
growth 17%
Contact
Allan M. Gebhard,
President
Tel 612-832-2600
Fax 612-835-0186

**Benchmark Computer
Systems, Inc.**
7625 Parklawn Ave.
Edina, MN 55435

Founded 1972
Total employees 100
Annual sales $11 million
Industries Computer
Hardware, Computer
Software
Growth Openings in past
year 15; percentage
growth 17%
Contact
Joe Mooney, President
Tel 612-831-2300
Fax 612-830-9952

B.H. Electronics, Inc.
12219 Wood Lake Dr.
Burnsville, MN 55337

Founded 1969
Total employees 300
Annual sales $6.8 million
Industry Subassemblies
and Components
Growth Openings in past
year 50; percentage
growth 20%
Contact
Eugene S. Lyman,
President
Tel 612-894-9590
Fax 612-894-9380

Colder Products Co.
1001 Westgate Dr.
Saint Paul, MN 55114

Founded 1979
Total employees 120
Annual sales $11 million
Industry Subassemblies
and Components
Growth Openings in past
year 20; percentage
growth 20%

Contact
Mike Lyon, President
Tel 612-645-0091
Fax 612-645-5404

**Computer Network
Technology Corp.**
6500 Wedgwood Rd.
Maple Grove, MN 55311

Founded 1983
Total employees 290
Annual sales $55.69
million
Industries Computer
Software, Holding
Companies,
Telecommunications
Growth Openings in past
year 98; percentage
growth 51%
Contact
Ms. Holly Kennedy,
Manager of Human
Resources
Tel 612-550-8000
Fax 612-550-8800

Connect Computer Co.
9855 West 78th St.
Eden Prairie, MN 55344

Founded 1985
Total employees 75
Annual sales $12 million
Industry Computer
Hardware
Growth Openings in past
year 25; percentage
growth 50%
Contact
Ms. Martha Kieffer, Vice
President
Tel 612-944-0181
Fax 612-944-9298

**David Mitchell &
Associates, Inc.**
2345 Rice St., Suite 205
Saint Paul, MN 55113

Founded 1986
Total employees 130
Annual sales $10 million
Industry Computer
Software
Growth Openings in past
year 20; percentage
growth 18%
Contact
David Mitchell, President
Tel 612-482-0071
Fax 612-482-0976

Decision Systems, Inc.
60 South Sixth St..
Minneapolis, MN 55402

Founded 1974
Total employees 125
Annual sales $8 million
Industry Computer
Software
Growth Openings in past
year 15; percentage
growth 13%
Contact
Rich Borchers, President
Tel 612-338-2585
Fax 612-337-5967

Diametrics Medical Inc.
2658 Patton Rd.
Roseville, MN 55113

Founded 1989
Total employees 105
Annual sales $11 million
Industry Medical
Growth Openings in past
year 35; percentage
growth 50%
Contact
Mike Connoy, President
Tel 612-639-8035
Fax 612-639-8549

Digi International Inc.
6400 Flying Cloud Dr.
Eden Prairie, MN 55344

Founded 1985
Total employees 300
Annual sales $70.9 million
Industries Computer
Hardware, Holding
Companies
Growth Openings in past
year 40; percentage
growth 15%
Contact
Mike Moroz, President/
CEO
Tel 612-943-9020
Fax 612-943-5398

Empi, Inc.
1275 Grey Fox Rd.
Saint Paul, MN 55112

Founded 1977
Total employees 460
Annual sales $66.4 million
Industry Medical
Growth Openings in past
year 53; percentage
growth 13%

Contact
Donald D. Maurer,
COB/CEO
Tel 612-636-6600
Fax 612-639-2405

Fluoroware, Inc.
102 Jonathan Blvd. North
Chaska, MN 55318

Founded 1966
Total employees 535
Industries Manufacturing
Equipment,
Subassemblies and
Components
Growth Openings in past
year 35; percentage
growth 7%
Contact
Wayne Holtmeler,
Personnel Manager
Tel 612-448-3131
Fax 612-368-8087

Fourth Shift Corp.
7900 International Dr.,
Suite 450
Minneapolis, MN 55425

Founded 1984
Total employees 222
Annual sales $37.15
million
Industries Computer
Software, Holding
Companies
Growth Openings in past
year 72; percentage
growth 48%
Contact
Marion Melvin Stuckey,
COB/CEO/Secretary
Tel 612-851-1500
Fax 612-851-1560

**Health Systems
Integration, Inc.**
1 Appletree Sq., Suite 700,
8009 34th Ave. South
Bloomington, MN 55425

Founded 1977
Total employees 105
Annual sales $7 million
Industry Computer
Software
Growth Openings in past
year 35; percentage
growth 50%
Contact
Phillip Little, President
Tel 612-851-9696
Fax 612-851-9096

**Hibbing Electronics
Corp.**
3125 East 14th Ave.
Hibbing, MN 55746

Founded 1974
Total employees 405
Annual sales $39 million
Industry Subassemblies
and Components
Growth Openings in past
year 20; percentage
growth 5%
Contact
Ms. Lucy Coughlin,
Director of Personnel
Tel 218-263-8971
Fax 218-263-8970

Innovex, Inc.
1313 Fifth St. South
Hopkins, MN 55343

Founded 1972
Total employees 450
Annual sales $26.6 million
Industries Factory
Automation, Holding
Companies, Medical,
Subassemblies and
Components
Growth Openings in past
year 99; percentage
growth 28%
Contact
Jack Kilby, Director of
Human Resources
Tel 612-938-4155
Fax 612-938-7718

**Lake Region
Manufacturing Co., Inc.**
340 Lake Hazeltine Dr.
Chaska, MN 55318

Founded 1947
Total employees 680
Annual sales $32 million
Industries Holding
Companies, Medical
Growth Openings in past
year 68; percentage
growth 11%
Contact
Clayton Benish, Director of
Personnel
Tel 612-448-5111
Fax 612-448-3441

Mamac Systems, Inc.
7400 Flying Cloud Dr.
Eden Prairie, MN 55344

Founded 1980
Total employees 50
Annual sales $4.8 million

Industries Subassemblies
and Components, Test
and Measurement
Growth Openings in past
year 20; percentage
growth 66%
Contact
Asim Gul, President
Tel 612-835-1626
Fax 612-829-5331

Medical Devices, Inc.
833 3rd St. Southwest
Saint Paul, MN 55112

Founded 1972
Total employees 68
Annual sales $6 million
Industry Medical
Growth Openings in past
year 18; percentage
growth 36%
Contact
David B. Kaysen,
President/CEO
Tel 612-631-0590
Fax 612-631-8476

Medical Graphics Corp.
350 Oak Grove Pkwy.
Saint Paul, MN 55127

Founded 1977
Total employees 137
Annual sales $19.08
million
Industries Computer
Software, Medical, Test
and Measurement
Growth Openings in past
year 22; percentage
growth 19%
Contact
Ms. Catherine Anderson,
COB/President
Tel 612-484-4874
Fax 612-484-8941

**Milltronics
Manufacturing Co.**
7870 Park Dr.
Chanhassen, MN 55317

Founded 1982
Total employees 90
Annual sales $15 million
Industry Factory
Automation
Growth Openings in past
year 43; percentage
growth 91%
Contact
Tim Rashleger, VP of
Marketing/Owner
Tel 612-474-8100
Fax 612-474-7289

Multi-Tech Systems, Inc.
2205 Woodale Dr.
Mounds View, MN 55112

Founded 1970
Total employees 280
Annual sales $67 million
Industries Computer
Hardware,
Telecommunications
Growth Openings in past
year 49; percentage
growth 21%
Contact
Dr. Raghu Sharma,
President
Tel 612-785-3500
Fax 612-785-9874

Nortech Systems, Inc.
641 East Lake St.
Wayzata, MN 55391

Founded 1981
Total employees 220
Annual sales $10 million
Industries Manufacturing
Equipment,
Subassemblies and
Components
Growth Openings in past
year 110; percentage
growth 100%
Contact
Quent Finkelson,
President/CEO
Tel 612-473-4102
Fax 612-473-2514

Osmonics, Inc.
5951 Clearwater Dr.
Minnetonka, MN 55343

Founded 1969
Total employees 790
Annual sales $84 million
Industries Environmental,
Holding Companies,
Subassemblies and
Components, Test and
Measurement
Growth Openings in past
year 38; percentage
growth 5%
Contact
Howard W. Dicke, VP of
HR and Corp. Dev./
Treasurer
Tel 612-933-2277
Fax 612-933-0141

Pace, Inc.
1710 Douglas Dr.
Minneapolis, MN 55422

Founded 1978
Total employees 657

Annual sales $34 million
Industries Biotechnology,
Chemicals,
Environmental
Growth Openings in past
year 55; percentage
growth 9%
Contact
Ms. Susan V. Olsen,
Director of Personnel
Tel 612-544-5543
Fax 612-525-3366

Possis Medical, Inc.
2905 Northwest Blvd.
Minneapolis, MN 55441

Founded 1956
Total employees 120
Industry Medical
Growth Openings in past
year 35; percentage
growth 41%
Contact
Bob Dutcher, President
Tel 612-550-1010

QMC Technologies, Inc.
1500 North Front St.
New Ulm, MN 56073

Founded 1961
Total employees 110
Annual sales $8 million
Industry Subassemblies
and Components
Growth Openings in past
year 15; percentage
growth 15%
Contact
Brett Reese, President
Tel 507-354-3105
Fax 507-359-7827

**Reliance Motion Control,
Inc.**
6950 Washington Ave.
South
Eden Prairie, MN 55344

Founded 1960
Total employees 630
Annual sales $70 million
Industries Factory
Automation,
Subassemblies and
Components, Test and
Measurement
Growth Openings in past
year 53; percentage
growth 9%
Contact
William Gallagher, General
Manager
Tel 612-942-3600
Fax 612-942-3636

Remmele Engineering, Inc.
10 Old Highway 8 Southwest
New Brighton, MN 55112

Founded 1949
Total employees 470
Annual sales $72 million
Industry Factory Automation
Growth Openings in past year 23; percentage growth 5%
Contact
Michael Bates, Director of Personnel
Tel 612-635-4100
Fax 612-635-4168

Research Inc., Control Systems Division
6425 Flying Cloud Dr., PO Box 24064
Minneapolis, MN 55424

Founded 1963
Total employees 150
Annual sales $16 million
Industries Energy, Factory Automation
Growth Openings in past year 25; percentage growth 20%
Contact
Ms. Karen O'Rourke, VP Human Resources Manager
Tel 612-941-3300
Fax 612-941-3628

Riverside Electronics, Ltd.
One Riverside Ln.
Lewiston, MN 55952

Founded 1984
Total employees 325
Annual sales $22 million
Industries Holding Companies, Subassemblies and Components
Growth Openings in past year 50; percentage growth 18%
Contact
Ms. Sandy Creeley, Personnel Manager
Tel 507-523-3220
Fax 507-523-2831

RTP Company
580 East Front St., PO Box 439
Winona, MN 55987

Founded 1982
Total employees 300
Industry Advanced Materials
Growth Openings in past year 50; percentage growth 20%
Contact
Randy Andre, Office Manager
Tel 507-454-6900
Fax 507-454-8130

Schneider (USA) Inc
5905 Nathan Ln.
Minneapolis, MN 55442

Founded 1849
Total employees 550
Annual sales $60 million
Industry Medical
Growth Openings in past year 50; percentage growth 10%
Contact
Ms. Jan Dick, VP of Human Resources
Tel 612-550-5500
Fax 612-550-5880

Schott Corp.
1000 Parkers Lake Rd.
Wayzata, MN 55391

Founded 1951
Total employees 350
Annual sales $34 million
Industry Subassemblies and Components
Growth Openings in past year 23; percentage growth 7%
Contact
O.W. Schott, Chief Executive Officer
Tel 612-475-1173
Fax 612-475-1786

Serving Software Inc.
65 Main St., Suite 215
Minneapolis, MN 55414

Founded 1984
Total employees 180
Annual sales $12.8 million
Industry Computer Software
Growth Openings in past year 55; percentage growth 44%

Contact
John E. Haugo, President/ CEO
Tel 612-623-4038
Fax 612-623-4506

Shared Resource Management, Inc.
3550 Lexington Ave. North, Suite 300
Shoreview, MN 55126

Founded 1988
Total employees 120
Annual sales $8 million
Industries Computer Hardware, Computer Software
Growth Openings in past year 35; percentage growth 41%
Contact
Leon E. Kline, President
Tel 612-486-0417
Fax 612-486-0418

Slope Meter Co.
5947 Xerxes Ave. South
Minneapolis, MN 55410

Founded 1941
Total employees 50
Annual sales $5.9 million
Industry Test and Measurement
Growth Openings in past year 20; percentage growth 66%
Contact
A. Devlin Foster, President
Tel 612-929-3003
Fax 612-397-8200

St. Jude Medical, Inc.
1 Lillehei Plaza
Saint Paul, MN 55117

Founded 1976
Total employees 684
Annual sales $240 million
Industry Holding Companies
Growth Openings in past year 84; percentage growth 14%
Contact
Michael Kelly, VP of Human Resources
Tel 612-483-2000
Fax 612-490-4333

Tricord Systems, Inc.
3750 Annapolis Ln.
Plymouth, MN 55447

Founded 1987
Total employees 185
Annual sales $80.02
million
Industry
Telecommunications
Growth Openings in past
year 68; percentage
growth 58%
Contact
James D. Edwards,
President/CEO
Tel 612-557-9005
Fax 612-557-8403

Turck Inc.
3000 Campus Dr.
Minneapolis, MN 55441

Founded 1976
Total employees 130
Annual sales $16 million
Industries Factory
Automation,
Subassemblies and
Components, Test and
Measurement
Growth Openings in past
year 30; percentage
growth 30%
Contact
Lawrence G. Worth,
Director of Personnel/
Manager of Marketi
Tel 612-553-9224
Fax 612-553-0708

Turtle Mountain Corp.
380 Oak Grove Pkwy.,
Suite 116
Saint Paul, MN 55127

Founded 1974
Total employees 170
Annual sales $11 million
Industries Manufacturing
Equipment,
Subassemblies and
Components
Growth Openings in past
year 20; percentage
growth 13%
Contact
John E. Miller, President
Tel 612-481-1427
Fax 612-481-7253

Varitronic Systems, Inc.
300 Interchange North,
300 Hwy. 169 South
Minneapolis, MN 55426

Founded 1983
Total employees 233
Annual sales $39.4 million
Industry Computer
Hardware
Growth Openings in past
year 18; percentage
growth 8%
Contact
Scott Drill, COB/President/
CEO
Tel 612-542-1500
Fax 612-541-1503

VTC Inc.
2800 East Old Shakopee
Rd.
Bloomington, MN 55425

Founded 1984
Total employees 370
Industry Subassemblies
and Components
Growth Openings in past
year 100; percentage
growth 37%
Contact
Robert Rousseau, Director
of Human Resources
Tel 612-853-5100
Fax 612-853-3355

Zercom Corp.
PO Box 84
Merrifield, MN 56465

Founded 1978
Total employees 170
Annual sales $16 million
Industry Subassemblies
and Components
Growth Openings in past
year 20; percentage
growth 13%
Contact
Jeff Zernov, President
Tel 218-765-3151
Fax 218-765-3900

**3M, Verification and
Optical Systems Project**
3M Ctr., Bldg. 225-4N-14
Saint Paul, MN 55144

Founded 1986
Total employees 188
Industries Advanced
Materials,
Telecommunications,
Transportation

Growth Openings in past
year 18; percentage
growth 10%
Contact
James Rasnick, Project
Manager
Tel 612-736-3776
Fax 612-733-3294

**3M Superabrasive and
Microfinishing Systems
Department**
3M Ctr., Bldg. 251-2E-04
Saint Paul, MN 55144

Founded 1969
Total employees 100
Industry Advanced
Materials
Growth Openings in past
year 25; percentage
growth 33%
Contact
In Sun Hong, Department
Manager
Tel 612-737-1783
Fax 612-737-1790

Mississippi

**Mississippi Chemical
Corp.**
PO Box 388
Yazoo City, MS 39194

Founded 1948
Total employees 965
Annual sales $600 million
Industries Chemicals,
Holding Companies
Growth Openings in past
year 212; percentage
growth 28%
Contact
Charles O. Dunn,
President/CEO
Tel 601-746-4131
Fax 601-746-9158

**US Rubber Reclaiming,
Inc.**
PO Box 820165
Vicksburg, MS 39182

Founded 1893
Total employees 120
Industries Advanced
Materials, Environmental
Growth Openings in past
year 65; percentage
growth 118%

Contact
Bobby LaGrone, President
Tel 601-636-7071
Fax 601-638-0151

Missouri

**Access Industries, Inc.,
American Stair-Glide
Division**
4001 East 138th St.
Grandview, MO 64030

Founded 1947
Total employees 180
Annual sales $16 million
Industry Medical
Growth Openings in past
  year 40; percentage
  growth 28%
Contact
Michael Mahoney,
  President/CEO
Tel 816-763-3100
Fax 816-763-4467

**Allied Gear & Machine
Co.**
1101 Research Blvd.
Saint Louis, MO 63132

Founded 1944
Total employees 150
Annual sales $18 million
Industry Factory
  Automation
Growth Openings in past
  year 20; percentage
  growth 15%
Contact
Dave Bouchein, President
Tel 314-991-5900
Fax 314-991-5911

**Alucobond
Technologies, Inc.**
77 Westport Plaza, Suite
  421
Saint Louis, MO 63146

Founded 1977
Total employees 134
Industry Advanced
  Materials
Growth Openings in past
  year 19; percentage
  growth 16%
Contact
Randy Fox, Human
  Resources Manager
Tel 314-878-2303
Fax 314-878-7596

Atlas, Soundolier
1859 Intertech Dr.
Fenton, MO 63026

Founded 1935
Total employees 750
Annual sales $100 million
Industries Factory
  Automation,
  Subassemblies and
  Components,
  Telecommunications
Growth Openings in past
  year 50; percentage
  growth 7%
Contact
Ken Cation, President
Tel 314-349-3110
Fax 314-349-1251

**B&V Waste Science and
Technology Corp.**
4717 Grand Ave.
Kansas City, MO 64112

Founded 1988
Total employees 286
Annual sales $28 million
Industry Environmental
Growth Openings in past
  year 89; percentage
  growth 45%
Contact
Paul MacRoberts,
  President
Tel 913-339-2900
Fax 913-338-6645

bioMerieux Vitek, Inc.
595 Anglum Dr.
Hazelwood, MO 63042

Founded 1977
Total employees 775
Annual sales $140 million
Industry Medical
Growth Openings in past
  year 119; percentage
  growth 18%
Contact
Fred Pulson, Chief
  Executive Officer
Tel 314-731-8500
Fax 314-731-8800

Bock Pharmacal Co.
PO Box 419056
Saint Louis, MO 63141

Founded 1945
Total employees 350
Industry Pharmaceuticals
Growth Openings in past
  year 120; percentage
  growth 52%

Contact
Lawrence B. Moskoff,
  President
Tel 314-579-0770
Fax 314-579-0347

Cerner Corp.
2800 Rockcreek Pkwy.
Kansas City, MO 64117

Founded 1986
Total employees 910
Annual sales $120.57
  million
Industries Computer
  Software, Holding
  Companies
Growth Openings in past
  year 375; percentage
  growth 70%
Contact
Neal L. Patterson, COB/
  CEO
Tel 816-221-1024
Fax 816-474-1742

**CITATION Computer
Systems, Inc.**
2312 Millpark Dr.
Maryland Heights, MO
  63043

Founded 1979
Total employees 115
Annual sales $19.17
  million
Industries Computer
  Software, Holding
  Companies
Growth Openings in past
  year 25; percentage
  growth 27%
Contact
Kenneth R. Brown,
  COB/CEO
Tel 314-428-2900
Fax 314-428-7277

Continental Cement, Inc.
PO Box 71
Hannibal, MO 63401

Founded 1981
Total employees 230
Industry Holding
  Companies
Growth Openings in past
  year 19; percentage
  growth 9%
Contact
R.D. Powell, Vice
  President/General
  Manager
Tel 314-221-1740
Fax 314-221-1689

Data Research Associates, Inc.
1276 North Warson Rd.,
PO Box 8495
Saint Louis, MO 63132

Founded 1977
Total employees 110
Annual sales $23.72 million
Industries Computer Hardware, Computer Software, Telecommunications
Growth Openings in past year 20; percentage growth 22%
Contact
Michael J. Mellinger, President
Tel 314-432-1100
Fax 314-993-8927

Datastorm Technologies, Inc.
PO Box 1471
Columbia, MO 65205

Founded 1986
Total employees 146
Annual sales $16 million
Industry Computer Software
Growth Openings in past year 48; percentage growth 48%
Contact
Bruce Barkelew, President
Tel 314-443-3282
Fax 314-875-0595

Harmon Industries, Inc.
1300 Jefferson Ct.
Blue Springs, MO 64015

Founded 1946
Total employees 800
Annual sales $83 million
Industry Holding Companies
Growth Openings in past year 80; percentage growth 11%
Contact
Ronald G. Breshears, VP of Human Resources
Tel 816-229-3345
Fax 816-229-0556

Heatway Systems, Inc.
3131 West Chestnut Expwy.
Springfield, MO 65802

Founded 1981
Total employees 45

Annual sales $6.0 million
Industry Energy
Growth Openings in past year 16; percentage growth 55%
Contact
Mike Chiles, President
Tel 417-864-6108
Fax 417-864-8161

Hilco Technologies, Inc.
330 Rider Trail South, Suite 300
Earth City, MO 63045

Founded 1981
Total employees 90
Industries Computer Hardware, Computer Software, Holding Companies
Growth Openings in past year 25; percentage growth 38%
Contact
Ms. Shirley Hill, VP of Operations
Tel 314-298-9100
Fax 314-298-1729

Jack Henry & Associates, Inc.
West Hwy. 60, PO Box 807
Monett, MO 65708

Founded 1976
Total employees 150
Annual sales $24 million
Industry Computer Software
Growth Openings in past year 30; percentage growth 25%
Contact
Terry Thompson, Vice President/CFO
Tel 417-235-6652
Fax 417-235-8406

Jones Medical Industries, Inc.
PO Box 46903
Saint Louis, MO 63146

Founded 1981
Total employees 240
Annual sales $43.2 million
Industries Holding Companies, Pharmaceuticals
Growth Openings in past year 120; percentage growth 100%

Contact
Dennis M. Jones, President/CEO
Tel 314-432-7557
Fax 314-432-3785

K-V Pharmaceutical Co.
2503 South Hanley Rd.
Saint Louis, MO 63144

Founded 1942
Total employees 385
Annual sales $43.4 million
Industries Holding Companies, Pharmaceuticals
Growth Openings in past year 26; percentage growth 7%
Contact
Marc S. Hermelin, Vice Chairman/CEO
Tel 314-645-6600
Fax 314-645-6732

Milbank Manufacturing Co.
PO Box 419028
Kansas City, MO 64141

Founded 1927
Total employees 800
Annual sales $78 million
Industries Factory Automation, Holding Companies, Subassemblies and Components
Growth Openings in past year 99; percentage growth 14%
Contact
Ronald G. Owsley, President
Tel 816-483-5314
Fax 816-483-6357

Nooter/Eriksen Cogeneration Systems, Inc.
3630 South Geyer Rd., Suite 310
Saint Louis, MO 63127

Founded 1978
Total employees 115
Industries Energy, Subassemblies and Components
Growth Openings in past year 15; percentage growth 15%
Contact
Dr. Vern Eriksen, President
Tel 314-957-7800
Fax 314-966-6989

Nutra-Blend Corp.
Rte. 7, Box 192A
Neosho, MO 64850

Founded 1975
Total employees 75
Industry Pharmaceuticals
Growth Openings in past
 year 15; percentage
 growth 25%
Contact
Michael W. Osborne, Vice
 President/General
 Manager
Tel 417-451-6111
Fax 417-451-4515

OHM Corporation, Missouri Division
42 North Central Dr.
O'Fallon, MO 63366

Founded 1984
Total employees 80
Annual sales $8.5 million
Industry Environmental
Growth Openings in past
 year 60; percentage
 growth 300%
Contact
Tom Knueven, Division
 Manager
Tel 314-272-3303
Fax 314-272-9456

P.D. George & Co.
PO Box 66756
Saint Louis, MO 63166

Founded 1919
Total employees 235
Annual sales $55 million
Industry Advanced
 Materials
Growth Openings in past
 year 24; percentage
 growth 11%
Contact
J.E. George, Jr., President
Tel 314-621-5700
Fax 314-436-1030

Research Seeds, Inc.
PO Box 1393
Saint Joseph, MO 64502

Founded 1970
Total employees 100
Annual sales $21 million
Industry Holding
 Companies
Growth Openings in past
 year 50; percentage
 growth 100%

Contact
Robert Thedinger,
 President
Tel 816-238-7333
Fax 816-238-7849

Schreiber, Grana, Yonley, Inc.
271 Wolfner Dr.
Saint Louis, MO 63026

Founded 1992
Total employees 42
Annual sales $4 million
Industry Environmental
Growth Openings in past
 year 22; percentage
 growth 110%
Contact
Robert Schreiber, P.E.,
 President
Tel 314-349-8399
Fax 314-349-8384

Sverdrup Environmental, Inc.
13723 Riverport Dr.
Maryland Heights, MO
 63043

Founded 1988
Total employees 75
Industry Environmental
Growth Openings in past
 year 30; percentage
 growth 66%
Contact
H.G. Schwartz, Jr.,
 President
Tel 314-436-7600
Fax 314-298-1575

Montana

Mycotech Corporation
630 South Utah Ave., PO
 Box 4109
Butte, MT 59702

Founded 1982
Total employees 32
Annual sales $1.7 million
Industries Biotechnology,
 Chemicals,
 Environmental
Growth Openings in past
 year 16; percentage
 growth 100%
Contact
Robert Kearns, President
Tel 406-782-2386
Fax 406-782-9912

Nebraska

American Business Information, Inc.
5711 South 86th Cir.
Omaha, NE 68127

Founded 1972
Total employees 600
Annual sales $48.5 million
Industries Computer
 Hardware, Computer
 Software, Holding
 Companies
Growth Openings in past
 year 124; percentage
 growth 26%
Contact
Vinod Gupta, President
Tel 402-593-4500
Fax 402-331-1505

Applied Communications, Inc.
330 South 108th Ave.
Omaha, NE 68154

Founded 1975
Total employees 600
Annual sales $69 million
Industry Computer
 Software
Growth Openings in past
 year 100; percentage
 growth 20%
Contact
William F. Fisher,
 President/CEO
Tel 402-390-7600
Fax 402-330-1528

ASC
301 West O St.
Ogallala, NE 69153

Founded 1901
Total employees 330
Industry Subassemblies
 and Components
Growth Openings in past
 year 100; percentage
 growth 43%
Contact
David Jewell, Director of
 Personnel
Tel 308-284-3611
Fax 308-284-4905

George Risk Industries, Inc.
GRI Plaza, 802 South Elm St.
Kimball, NE 69145

Founded 1965
Total employees 175
Annual sales $7.02 million
Industry Computer Hardware
Growth Openings in past year 30; percentage growth 20%
Contact
Ms. Penney Stull, Personnel Director
Tel 308-235-4645
Fax 308-235-2609

Hydraulic Components Industries
PO Box 187
Hartington, NE 68739

Founded 1977
Total employees 105
Annual sales $10 million
Industry Subassemblies and Components
Growth Openings in past year 15; percentage growth 16%
Contact
Ms. Sharlene Guenther, Personnel Director
Tel 402-254-6805
Fax 402-254-7227

Isco, Inc., Environmental Division
PO Box 82531
Lincoln, NE 68501

Founded 1958
Total employees 248
Annual sales $20 million
Industries Environmental, Test and Measurement
Growth Openings in past year 27; percentage growth 12%
Contact
Dr. Robert Allington, President
Tel 402-474-2233
Fax 402-474-6685

Technical Management, Inc., Third-Party Administration Group
815 K St.
Lincoln, NE 68508

Founded 1964
Total employees 85

Annual sales $4 million
Industry Computer Software
Growth Openings in past year 17; percentage growth 25%
Contact
R.J. Lockard, COB/ President
Tel 402-434-2150
Fax 402-474-4607

Nevada

Cubix Corp.
2800 Lockheed Way
Carson City, NV 89706

Founded 1975
Total employees 140
Annual sales $16 million
Industry Computer Software
Growth Openings in past year 15; percentage growth 12%
Contact
Ms. Joanne Lanigir, Personnel Manager
Tel 702-883-7611
Fax 702-882-2407

Sigma Game, Inc.
1 Aerojet Way
North Las Vegas, NV 89030

Founded 1983
Total employees 160
Industry Computer Hardware
Growth Openings in past year 25; percentage growth 18%
Contact
T. Kurata, President
Tel 702-399-5000
Fax 702-399-5300

New Hampshire

AimTech Corp.
20 Trafalgar Sq., 3rd Fl.
Nashua, NH 03063

Founded 1984
Total employees 50

Industry Computer Software
Growth Openings in past year 20; percentage growth 66%
Contact
Usman Ismail, President
Tel 603-883-0220
Fax 603-883-5582

Assembly Solutions, Inc.
7 Perimeter Rd.
Manchester, NH 03103

Founded 1990
Total employees 90
Annual sales $6 million
Industry Subassemblies and Components
Growth Openings in past year 35; percentage growth 63%
Contact
James Pitts, COB/ President/Treasurer
Tel 603-623-5775
Fax 603-623-2874

Bottomline Technologies, Inc.
1 Court St.
Exeter, NH 03833

Founded 1989
Total employees 100
Annual sales $11 million
Industry Computer Software
Growth Openings in past year 60; percentage growth 150%
Contact
Dan McGurl, President
Tel 603-778-1924
Fax 603-778-3975

Cadec Systems, Inc.
8 East Perimeter Rd.
Londonderry, NH 03053

Founded 1976
Total employees 91
Annual sales $11 million
Industries Computer Hardware, Computer Software
Growth Openings in past year 21; percentage growth 30%
Contact
Roger Cimino, General Manager
Tel 603-668-1010
Fax 603-623-0604

Coda, Inc.
1155 Elm St.
Manchester, NH 03101

Founded 1979
Total employees 300
Annual sales $29 million
Industry Computer
Software
Growth Openings in past
year 50; percentage
growth 20%
Contact
James C. Wood, President
Tel 603-647-9600
Fax 603-647-2634

Computersmith, Inc.
141 Kimball Hill Rd.
Hudson, NH 03051

Founded 1982
Total employees 35
Industry Computer
Hardware
Growth Openings in past
year 15; percentage
growth 75%
Contact
Dustin Smith, President
Tel 603-889-2670
Fax 603-889-0476

Conceptronic, Inc.
6 Post Rd.
Portsmouth, NH 03801

Founded 1987
Total employees 140
Annual sales $14 million
Industry Manufacturing
Equipment
Growth Openings in past
year 70; percentage
growth 100%
Contact
Dr. Henry Gisler, President
Tel 603-431-6262
Fax 603-431-0717

Cyplex Corporation
472 Amherst St.
Nashua, NH 03063

Founded 1986
Total employees 25
Annual sales $2.5 million
Industry Factory
Automation
Growth Openings in past
year 16; percentage
growth 177%

Contact
Lawrence W. Hill,
President
Tel 603-882-8104
Fax 603-882-9539

Dexter Corp., Automotive Division
1 Dexter Dr.
Seabrook, NH 03874

Founded 1979
Total employees 125
Annual sales $18 million
Industry Advanced
Materials
Growth Openings in past
year 15; percentage
growth 13%
Contact
Charles Call, President
Tel 603-474-5541
Fax 603-474-5545

Granite Communications, Inc.
9 Townsend West, Suite 1
Nashua, NH 03063

Founded 1984
Total employees 35
Annual sales $1 million
Industry Computer
Hardware
Growth Openings in past
year 15; percentage
growth 75%
Contact
Pierre Dogan, President
Tel 603-881-8666
Fax 603-881-4042

Howtek, Inc.
21 Parke Ave.
Hudson, NH 03051

Founded 1984
Total employees 127
Annual sales $23.0 million
Industry Computer
Hardware
Growth Openings in past
year 34; percentage
growth 36%
Contact
David Bothwell, CEO/
Acting President
Tel 603-882-5200
Fax 603-880-3843

Johnson and Johnston Associates, Inc.
130 Rte. 111
Hampstead, NH 03841

Founded 1974
Total employees 100
Annual sales $8 million
Industry Advanced
Materials
Growth Openings in past
year 60; percentage
growth 150%
Contact
Ms. Anne Panniello,
Human Resources
Manager
Tel 603-329-5691
Fax 603-329-8307

Kenda Systems
1 Stiles Rd.
Salem, NH 03079

Founded 1984
Total employees 170
Annual sales $21 million
Industry Computer
Software
Growth Openings in past
year 30; percentage
growth 21%
Contact
Steve Kenda, President
Tel 603-898-7884
Fax 603-898-3703

Keyfile Corp.
22 Cotton Rd.
Nashua, NH 03063

Founded 1989
Total employees 75
Industry Computer
Software
Growth Openings in past
year 45; percentage
growth 150%
Contact
Chris Robert, President
Tel 603-883-3800
Fax 603-889-9259

Lilly Software Associates, Inc.
239 Drakeside Rd.
Hampton, NH 03842

Founded 1992
Total employees 35
Annual sales $2 million
Industry Computer
Software
Growth Openings in past
year 32; percentage
growth 1066%

Contact
Richard T. Lilly, President/
CEO
Tel 603-926-9696
Fax 603-926-4505

**Lockheed Sanders, Inc.,
Avionics Division**
95 Canal St., MS NCA1
6244
Nashua, NH 03061

Founded 1932
Total employees 310
Annual sales $36 million
Industries Computer
Hardware, Test and
Measurement,
Transportation
Growth Openings in past
year 50; percentage
growth 19%
Contact
Dr. Hugo Poza, Vice
President/General
Manager
Tel 603-885-5182
Fax 603-885-7264

**Newmarket Software
Systems, Inc.**
44 Newmarket Rd.
Durham, NH 03824

Founded 1981
Total employees 70
Industry Computer
Software
Growth Openings in past
year 35; percentage
growth 100%
Contact
Robert W. Horgan, Chief
Executive Officer
Tel 603-436-7500
Fax 603-436-1826

Palette Systems Corp.
6 Trafalgar Square
Nashua, NH 03063

Founded 1983
Total employees 57
Annual sales $6.6 million
Industry Computer
Software
Growth Openings in past
year 20; percentage
growth 54%
Contact
Ms. Carolyn Bernier, Office
Manager
Tel 603-886-1230
Fax 603-886-4799

Presstek, Inc.
8 Commercial St.
Hudson, NH 03051

Founded 1987
Total employees 70
Annual sales $12.5 million
Industry Photonics
Growth Openings in past
year 16; percentage
growth 29%
Contact
Ms. Jennifer Tardif,
Corporate Services
Manager
Tel 603-595-7000
Fax 603-595-2602

ProfitKey International
382 Main St.
Salem, NH 03079

Founded 1979
Total employees 100
Annual sales $11 million
Industry Computer
Software
Growth Openings in past
year 35; percentage
growth 53%
Contact
Michael Rapaport, COB/
CEO
Tel 603-898-9800
Fax 603-898-7554

QA Technology Co., Inc.
4 Merrill Industrial Dr.
Hampton, NH 03842

Founded 1980
Total employees 55
Industry Factory
Automation
Growth Openings in past
year 15; percentage
growth 37%
Contact
Michael Simonelli, General
Manager
Tel 603-926-1193
Fax 603-926-8071

Saphikon, Inc.
33 Powers St.
Milford, NH 03055

Founded 1965
Total employees 70
Annual sales $8.2 million
Industries Advanced
Materials, Photonics,
Subassemblies and
Components,
Telecommunications

Growth Openings in past
year 15; percentage
growth 27%
Contact
Ms. Susan Hume, Director
of Human Resources
Tel 603-673-5831
Fax 603-673-1256

**Simplex Technologies,
Inc.**
PO Box 479
Portsmouth, NH 03802

Founded 1962
Total employees 750
Annual sales $81 million
Industries Photonics,
Subassemblies and
Components,
Transportation
Growth Openings in past
year 150; percentage
growth 25%
Contact
Peter Bergeron, President
Tel 603-436-6100
Fax 603-427-0701

Softdesk, Inc.
7 Liberty Hill Rd.
Henniker, NH 03242

Founded 1985
Total employees 134
Annual sales $14.46
million
Industry Computer
Software
Growth Openings in past
year 34; percentage
growth 34%
Contact
David Arnold, President/
CEO
Tel 603-428-3199
Fax 603-428-7665

Source Electronics Corp.
26 Clinton Dr.
Hollis, NH 03049

Founded 1986
Total employees 60
Annual sales $9.8 million
Industries Computer
Hardware, Manufacturing
Equipment,
Subassemblies and
Components,
Telecommunications
Growth Openings in past
year 20; percentage
growth 50%

Contact
Richard Dellacanonica,
  President
Tel 603-595-2906

Summa Four, Inc.
25 Sundial Ave.
Manchester, NH 03103

Founded 1977
Total employees 120
Annual sales $15.13
  million
Industry
  Telecommunications
Growth Openings in past
  year 20; percentage
  growth 20%
Contact
James J. Fiedler,
  President
Tel 603-625-4050
Fax 603-668-4491

Tally Systems Corp.
PO Box 70
Hanover, NH 03755

Founded 1990
Total employees 56
Annual sales $6.5 million
Industry Computer
  Software
Growth Openings in past
  year 26; percentage
  growth 86%
Contact
Ted Jastrzembski,
  President
Tel 603-643-1300
Fax 603-643-9366

**Unitrode Integrated
Circuits Corp.**
7 Continental Blvd.
Merrimack, NH 03054

Founded 1981
Total employees 290
Annual sales $28 million
Industry Subassemblies
  and Components
Growth Openings in past
  year 69; percentage
  growth 31%
Contact
Ms. Sue Murphy,
  Personnel Director
Tel 603-424-2410
Fax 603-424-3460

New Jersey

A.L. Hyde Co.
1 Main St.
Grenloch, NJ 08032

Founded 1932
Total employees 140
Annual sales $15 million
Industry Manufacturing
  Equipment
Growth Openings in past
  year 20; percentage
  growth 16%
Contact
Richard Garthwaite,
  President
Tel 609-227-0500
Fax 609-232-1754

**A.L. Laboratories, Inc.,
Animal Health Division**
1 Executive Dr., PO Box
  1399
Fort Lee, NJ 07024

Founded 1975
Total employees 90
Industries Biotechnology,
  Pharmaceuticals
Growth Openings in past
  year 30; percentage
  growth 50%
Contact
David E. Cohen, President
Tel 201-947-7774
Fax 201-947-8262

**AMP Incorporated, Lytel
Division**
PO Box 1300
Somerville, NJ 08876

Founded 1983
Total employees 150
Annual sales $16 million
Industry Photonics
Growth Openings in past
  year 33; percentage
  growth 28%
Contact
Gerald Leehan, General
  Manager
Tel 908-685-2000
Fax 908-685-1282

Anadigics, Inc.
35 Technology Dr.
Warren, NJ 07059

Founded 1985
Total employees 200
Annual sales $20 million
Industry Subassemblies
  and Components

Growth Openings in past
  year 40; percentage
  growth 25%
Contact
Ronald Rosenzweig,
  President/CEO
Tel 908-668-5000
Fax 908-668-5068

**Bergen Cable
Technologies, Inc.**
170 Gregg St., PO Box
  1300
Lodi, NJ 07644

Founded 1987
Total employees 180
Annual sales $10 million
Industry Subassemblies
  and Components
Growth Openings in past
  year 20; percentage
  growth 12%
Contact
Tom Carr, President
Tel 201-487-3521
Fax 201-368-0532

Biomatrix, Inc.
65 Railroad Ave.
Ridgefield, NJ 07657

Founded 1981
Total employees 97
Annual sales $1.8 million
Industry Biotechnology
Growth Openings in past
  year 27; percentage
  growth 38%
Contact
Dr. Endre Balazs, CEO/
  Chief Scientific Officer
Tel 201-945-9550
Fax 201-945-0363

**Blonder-Tongue
Laboratories, Inc.**
1 Jake Brown Rd.
Old Bridge, NJ 08857

Founded 1950
Total employees 305
Annual sales $42 million
Industries Subassemblies
  and Components,
  Telecommunications
Growth Openings in past
  year 80; percentage
  growth 35%
Contact
James A. Luksch,
  President
Tel 908-679-4000
Fax 908-679-4353

Bluestone Consulting, Inc.
1200 Church St., Suite 7
Mount Laurel, NJ 08054

Founded 1989
Total employees 65
Annual sales $7.5 million
Industries Computer
Hardware, Computer
Software
Growth Openings in past
year 20; percentage
growth 44%
Contact
Mel Baiada, President
Tel 609-727-4600
Fax 609-778-8125

Bogen Communications, Inc.
50 Spring St.
Ramsey, NJ 07446

Founded 1932
Total employees 125
Annual sales $18 million
Industry
Telecommunications
Growth Openings in past
year 38; percentage
growth 43%
Contact
Gerardo Sarmiento,
President
Tel 201-934-8500
Fax 201-934-9832

Brightwork Development, Inc.
766 Shrewsbury Ave.,
Jerral Ctr. West
Tinton Falls, NJ 07724

Founded 1986
Total employees 60
Annual sales $6.9 million
Industry Computer
Software
Growth Openings in past
year 15; percentage
growth 33%
Contact
Greg Gianforte, President
Tel 908-530-0440
Fax 908-530-0622

Card Technology Corporation
70 Eisenhower Dr.
Paramus, NJ 07652
Founded 1975
Total employees 150
Annual sales $12 million

Industry Factory
Automation
Growth Openings in past
year 30; percentage
growth 25%
Contact
Paul Smith, President
Tel 201-845-7373
Fax 201-845-3337

Celwave RF
2 Ryan Rd.
Marlboro, NJ 07746

Founded 1983
Total employees 600
Annual sales $82 million
Industries Subassemblies
and Components,
Telecommunications
Growth Openings in past
year 100; percentage
growth 20%
Contact
Ms. Rosa DeJesus,
Personnel Manager
Tel 908-462-1880
Fax 908-462-6919

Computer Systems Development, Inc.
242 Old New Brunswick
Rd.
Piscataway, NJ 08854

Founded 1970
Total employees 200
Annual sales $23 million
Industries Computer
Hardware, Computer
Software
Growth Openings in past
year 125; percentage
growth 166%
Contact
Ms. Rosemary Sarafian,
President
Tel 908-562-0100
Fax 908-562-0102

Crestek, Inc.
Scotch Rd., Mercer County
Airport, PO Box 7266
Trenton, NJ 08628

Founded 1980
Total employees 230
Annual sales $25 million
Industry Holding
Companies
Growth Openings in past
year 80; percentage
growth 53%

Contact
J. Michael Goodson,
COB/CEO
Tel 609-883-4000
Fax 609-883-6452

Datapro Information Services Group
600 Delran Pkwy.
Delran, NJ 08075

Founded 1970
Total employees 600
Annual sales $82 million
Industry Computer
Hardware
Growth Openings in past
year 100; percentage
growth 20%
Contact
Ms. Renie Crowder,
Manager of Human
Resources
Tel 609-764-0100
Fax 609-764-2812

Denon America, Inc.
222 New Rd.
Parsippany, NJ 07054

Founded 1980
Total employees 400
Industry Computer
Hardware
Growth Openings in past
year 34; percentage
growth 9%
Contact
John Langen, VP of
Administration
Tel 201-575-7810
Fax 201-575-2532

Dialight Corp.
1913 Atlantic Ave.
Manasquan, NJ 08736

Founded 1938
Total employees 320
Annual sales $37 million
Industries Energy,
Photonics,
Subassemblies and
Components, Test and
Measurement
Growth Openings in past
year 19; percentage
growth 6%
Contact
Tony Cortina, Director of
Human Resources
Tel 908-223-9400
Fax 908-223-8788

Dialogic Corp.
300 Littleton Rd.
Parsippany, NJ 07054

Founded 1983
Total employees 350
Annual sales $57 million
Industry Computer
Hardware
Growth Openings in past
year 49; percentage
growth 16%
Contact
Steven Wentzel, Director
of Human Resources
Tel 201-334-8450
Fax 201-334-1257

ECCS, Inc.
1 Shelia Dr., Bldg. 6A
Tinton Falls, NJ 07724

Founded 1980
Total employees 140
Annual sales $36 million
Industry Computer
Hardware
Growth Openings in past
year 40; percentage
growth 40%
Contact
Ms. Marbeth Shay,
Chairman of the Board
Tel 908-747-6995
Fax 908-747-6542

Edwards and Kelcey, Inc.
70 South Orange Ave.
Livingston, NJ 07039

Founded 1946
Total employees 385
Annual sales $41 million
Industries Manufacturing
Equipment,
Telecommunications
Growth Openings in past
year 80; percentage
growth 26%
Contact
John S. Urban, CEO/
President
Tel 201-994-4520
Fax 201-994-7176

EG&G Instruments, Inc.
375 Phillips Blvd.
Trenton, NJ 08618

Founded 1962
Total employees 400
Industries Biotechnology,
Test and Measurement,
Telecommunications

Growth Openings in past
year 12; percentage
growth 3%
Contact
Warren Davis, Human
Resources Manager
Tel 609-530-1000
Fax 609-883-7259

Enviroplan, Inc.
3 Becker Farm Rd.
Roseland, NJ 07068

Founded 1972
Total employees 110
Annual sales $17 million
Industries Environmental,
Test and Measurement
Growth Openings in past
year 60; percentage
growth 120%
Contact
Dr. Howard M. Ellis,
President
Tel 201-994-2300
Fax 201-994-5100

Epitaxx, Inc.
7 Graphic Dr.
West Trenton, NJ 08628

Founded 1984
Total employees 90
Industry Photonics
Growth Openings in past
year 15; percentage
growth 20%
Contact
Ken Fujiwara, President
Tel 609-538-1800
Fax 609-538-1684

Esselte Meto
1200 The American Rd.,
PO Box 595
Morris Plains, NJ 07950

Founded 1975
Total employees 300
Annual sales $38 million
Industry Computer
Hardware
Growth Openings in past
year 50; percentage
growth 20%
Contact
Carl Cramer, President
Tel 201-455-8100
Fax 201-455-8866

Geotek Industries, Inc.
20 Craig Rd.
Montvale, NJ 07645

Founded 1989
Total employees 425

Annual sales $27.18
million
Industry Holding
Companies
Growth Openings in past
year 25; percentage
growth 6%
Contact
Yaron Eitan, President/
CEO
Tel 201-930-9305
Fax 201-930-9614

**Glasgal
Communications, Inc.**
151 Veterans Dr.
Northvale, NJ 07647

Founded 1974
Total employees 150
Annual sales $32 million
Industry
Telecommunications
Growth Openings in past
year 18; percentage
growth 13%
Contact
Isaac Gaon, Chief
Executive Officer
Tel 201-768-8082
Fax 201-768-2947

IGI, Inc.
2285 East Landis Ave.
Vineland, NJ 08360

Founded 1977
Total employees 203
Annual sales $25 million
Industry Holding
Companies
Growth Openings in past
year 17; percentage
growth 9%
Contact
Edward B. Hagar, COB/
CEO
Tel 609-697-1441
Fax 609-697-1001

Immunomedics, Inc.
300 American Rd.
Morris Plains, NJ 07950

Founded 1982
Total employees 100
Annual sales $5.1 million
Industries Biotechnology,
Medical
Growth Openings in past
year 15; percentage
growth 17%

Contact
Ms. Ellen Eisenhandler,
Director of Human
Resources
Tel 201-605-8200
Fax 201-605-8282

Integra Life Science, Inc.
105 Morgan Ln.
Plainsboro, NJ 08536

Founded 1988
Total employees 60
Annual sales $6 million
Industry Holding
Companies
Growth Openings in past
year 30; percentage
growth 100%
Contact
Bob Towarnicki, President/
CEO
Tel 609-683-0900
Fax 609-799-3297

Isomedix Inc.
11 Apollo Dr.
Whippany, NJ 07981

Founded 1973
Total employees 363
Annual sales $43.23
million
Industries Holding
Companies, Medical
Growth Openings in past
year 51; percentage
growth 16%
Contact
John Masefield, COB/
CEO/President
Tel 201-887-4700
Fax 201-887-1476

JBA International, Inc.
161 Gaither Dr., Suite 200
Mount Laurel, NJ 08054

Founded 1981
Total employees 225
Industries Computer
Hardware, Computer
Software
Growth Openings in past
year 25; percentage
growth 12%
Contact
Alistair Clague, President/
CEO
Tel 609-231-9400
Fax 609-231-9874

Joyce Molding Corp.
52 Green Pond Rd.
Rockaway, NJ 07866

Founded 1957
Total employees 335
Annual sales $42 million
Industry Manufacturing
Equipment
Growth Openings in past
year 13; percentage
growth 4%
Contact
Edward F. Joyce, Sr.,
Chief Executive Officer
Tel 201-586-2900
Fax 201-627-5730

**KDI Triangle Electronics,
Inc.**
60 South Jefferson Rd.
Whippany, NJ 07981

Founded 1977
Total employees 450
Annual sales $49 million
Industries Subassemblies
and Components, Test
and Measurement,
Telecommunications
Growth Openings in past
year 30; percentage
growth 7%
Contact
Mike Pirozek, VP of
Human Resources
Tel 201-887-5700

KTI Holdings, Inc.
7000 Blvd. East
Guttenberg, NJ 07093

Founded 1982
Total employees 250
Annual sales $85 million
Industry Holding
Companies
Growth Openings in past
year 50; percentage
growth 25%
Contact
Nicholas Menonna, Jr.,
President
Tel 201-854-7777
Fax 201-854-1771

K-Tron International, Inc.
Commerce Center 1810
Chappel Ave. West, Suite
130
Cherry Hill, NJ 08002

Founded 1964
Total employees 800
Annual sales $119 million

Industries Factory
Automation, Test and
Measurement
Growth Openings in past
year 180; percentage
growth 29%
Contact
Ms. Patricia Daniels,
Director of Human
Resources
Tel 609-661-6240
Fax 609-661-6241

Liposome Co., Inc.
One Research Way,
Princeton Forrestal
Center
Princeton, NJ 08540

Founded 1981
Total employees 170
Annual sales $13.04
million
Industry Biotechnology
Growth Openings in past
year 70; percentage
growth 70%
Contact
Leon M. Rosenson, Ph.D.,
VP of Administration
Tel 609-452-7060
Fax 609-452-1890

Logos Corp.
200 Valley Rd., Suite 400
Mount Arlington, NJ 07856

Founded 1969
Total employees 40
Annual sales $4.6 million
Industry Computer
Software
Growth Openings in past
year 15; percentage
growth 60%
Contact
Jens Thomas Luck,
CEO/President
Tel 201-398-8710
Fax 201-398-6102

Lynx Technologies, Inc.
PO Box 368
Little Falls, NJ 07424

Founded 1976
Total employees 90
Annual sales $10 million
Industry
Telecommunications
Growth Openings in past
year 15; percentage
growth 20%

Contact
Leonard Elfenbein,
President
Tel 201-256-7200
Fax 201-882-3583

Magnetic Metals Corp.
21st and Hayes Ave.
Camden, NJ 08101

Founded 1944
Total employees 620
Industries Advanced
Materials, Subassemblies
and Components
Growth Openings in past
year 120; percentage
growth 24%
Contact
John Eisennagel, Director
of Personnel
Tel 609-964-7842
Fax 609-963-8569

**MICRO HealthSystems,
Inc.**
414 Eagle Rock Ave.
West Orange, NJ 07052

Founded 1971
Total employees 180
Industries Computer
Software, Holding
Companies
Growth Openings in past
year 40; percentage
growth 28%
Contact
Salvador Carravetta,
COB/CEO
Tel 201-731-9252
Fax 201-731-9810

**Mosler, Inc., Electronic
Systems Division**
415 Hamburg Tpke.
Wayne, NJ 07470

Founded 1965
Total employees 175
Industry Test and
Measurement
Growth Openings in past
year 45; percentage
growth 34%
Contact
Alfred R. Rabasca,
General Manager
Tel 201-595-4000
Fax 201-595-4198

**Ortho Pharmaceutical
Corp., Advanced Care
Products Division**
1001 US Hwy. 202, PO
Box 610
Raritan, NJ 08869

Founded 1887
Total employees 195
Annual sales $26 million
Industries Medical,
Pharmaceuticals
Growth Openings in past
year 85; percentage
growth 77%
Contact
R.B. Miller, President
Tel 908-218-6000
Fax 908-218-8649

Osteotech, Inc.
1151 Shrewsbury Ave.
Shrewsbury, NJ 07702

Founded 1986
Total employees 145
Annual sales $19.12
million
Industries Biotechnology,
Medical, Pharmaceuticals
Growth Openings in past
year 45; percentage
growth 45%
Contact
Vincent Rizzo, Director of
Human Resources
Tel 908-542-2800
Fax 908-542-2906

Penta Manufacturing Co.
PO Box 1448
Fairfield, NJ 07007

Founded 1977
Total employees 515
Annual sales $19 million
Industry Chemicals
Growth Openings in past
year 25; percentage
growth 5%
Contact
Ms. Grace Calamito,
President
Tel 201-740-2300
Fax 201-575-8907

**TeleSciences C O
Systems, Inc.**
351 New Albany Rd.
Moorestown, NJ 08057

Founded 1966
Total employees 230
Annual sales $31 million

Industries Computer
Software, Test and
Measurement,
Telecommunications
Growth Openings in past
year 30; percentage
growth 15%
Contact
Howard Oringer, Chief
Executive Officer
Tel 609-866-1000
Fax 609-866-0185

Teleware, Inc.
300 Roundhill Dr.
Rockaway, NJ 07866

Founded 1982
Total employees 50
Annual sales $5.8 million
Industry Computer
Software
Growth Openings in past
year 33; percentage
growth 194%
Contact
Ms. Kendra Snyder,
Director of Administration
Tel 201-586-2200
Fax 201-586-8885

Troy Corp.
72 Eagle Rock Ave.
East Hanover, NJ 07936

Founded 1952
Total employees 175
Annual sales $50 million
Industry Chemicals
Growth Openings in past
year 25; percentage
growth 16%
Contact
Daryl Smith, President
Tel 201-884-4300
Fax 201-884-4317

**Unified Systems
Solutions**
49 Old Bloomfield Ave.
Mountain Lakes, NJ 07046

Founded 1969
Total employees 75
Annual sales $4.5 million
Industries Computer
Hardware, Computer
Software
Growth Openings in past
year 55; percentage
growth 275%
Contact
Mike Fitton, President
Tel 201-402-2333
Fax 201-402-5151

Vital Signs, Inc.
20 Campus Rd.
Totowa, NJ 07512

Founded 1972
Total employees 600
Annual sales $56 million
Industries Holding
Companies, Medical
Growth Openings in past
year 100; percentage
growth 20%
Contact
Terence Wall, President/
CEO
Tel 201-790-1330
Fax 201-790-3307

**Warner Insurance
Services, Inc.**
17-01 Pollitt Dr.
Fair Lawn, NJ 07410

Founded 1971
Total employees 550
Annual sales $69.75
million
Industry Holding
Companies
Growth Openings in past
year 50; percentage
growth 10%
Contact
Harvey Krieger, COB/
President
Tel 201-794-4800
Fax 201-791-9113

Wesgo, Duramic
26 Maddison Rd.
Fairfield, NJ 07004

Founded 1955
Total employees 50
Industry Advanced
Materials
Growth Openings in past
year 20; percentage
growth 66%
Contact
Ray Santos, General
Manager
Tel 201-227-8877
Fax 201-227-7135

Whatman, Inc.
9 Bridewell Pl.
Clifton, NJ 07014

Founded 1958
Total employees 170
Annual sales $20 million
Industries Biotechnology,
Test and Measurement

Growth Openings in past
year 20; percentage
growth 13%
Contact
Louis Metts, President/
CEO
Tel 201-773-5800
Fax 201-472-6949

**White Storage and
Retrieval Systems, Inc.**
30 Boright Ave.
Kenilworth, NJ 07033

Founded 1946
Total employees 450
Annual sales $56 million
Industries Computer
Hardware, Computer
Software, Factory
Automation
Growth Openings in past
year 49; percentage
growth 12%
Contact
Donald Weiss, President/
CEO
Tel 908-272-6700
Fax 908-272-5920

WindSoft, Inc.
66 Ford Rd.
Denville, NJ 07834

Founded 1985
Total employees 80
Annual sales $13 million
Industries Computer
Hardware, Computer
Software
Growth Openings in past
year 20; percentage
growth 33%
Contact
Rami Shatz, President
Tel 201-586-4400
Fax 201-586-9045

**Wire Pro, Inc., Garry
Electronics**
23 Front St.
Salem, NJ 08079

Founded 1978
Total employees 300
Annual sales $29 million
Industry Subassemblies
and Components
Growth Openings in past
year 50; percentage
growth 20%
Contact
Gerald Eddis, President
Tel 609-935-7603
Fax 609-935-0102

Xpedite Systems, Inc.
446 Hwy. 35
Eatontown, NJ 07724

Founded 1988
Total employees 150
Annual sales $20 million
Industries Computer
Software,
Telecommunications
Growth Openings in past
year 50; percentage
growth 50%
Contact
Roy Andersen, President/
CEO
Tel 908-389-3900
Fax 908-389-8823

New Mexico

**Applied Research
Associates, Inc.**
4300 San Mateo
Northeast, Suite A220
Albuquerque, NM 87110

Founded 1980
Total employees 197
Annual sales $21 million
Industries Defense,
Environmental,
Manufacturing Equipment
Growth Openings in past
year 50; percentage
growth 34%
Contact
Jim Eddings, Corporate
Operations Officer
Tel 505-883-3636
Fax 505-883-3673

Bell Group, Inc.
6901 Washington
Northeast
Albuquerque, NM 87109

Founded 1944
Total employees 250
Annual sales $31 million
Industry Holding
Companies
Growth Openings in past
year 35; percentage
growth 16%
Contact
Hugh Bell, President
Tel 505-345-8511
Fax 505-344-9671

Bohannan-Huston, Inc.
7500 Jefferson Northeast
Albuquerque, NM 87109

Founded 1959
Total employees 110
Industry Computer
Software
Growth Openings in past
year 15; percentage
growth 15%
Contact
Larry Huston, Chief
Executive Officer
Tel 505-823-1000
Fax 505-821-0892

Lasertechnics, Inc.
5500 Wilshire Ave.
Northeast
Albuquerque, NM 87113

Founded 1981
Total employees 62
Annual sales $6.7 million
Industries Computer
Hardware, Factory
Automation, Holding
Companies,
Subassemblies and
Components
Growth Openings in past
year 17; percentage
growth 37%
Contact
Eugene A. Bourque,
President/CFO
Tel 505-822-1123
Fax 505-821-2213

**Plant Genetic
Engineering Laboratory**
New Mexico State
University, PO Box 3GL
Las Cruces, NM 88003

Founded 1983
Total employees 30
Industries Biotechnology,
Chemicals
Growth Openings in past
year 15; percentage
growth 100%
Contact
Dr. John Kemp, Ph.D.,
Director/Lead Scientist
Tel 505-646-5453
Fax 505-646-5975

Re/Spec, Inc.
4775 Indian School Rd.
Northeast, Suite 300
Albuquerque, NM 87110

Founded 1969
Total employees 105

Annual sales $8.2 million
Industries Computer
Hardware, Environmental
Growth Openings in past
year 25; percentage
growth 31%
Contact
William E. Coons,
Chairman of the Board
Tel 505-268-2661
Fax 505-268-0040

Tech Reps, Inc.
5000 Marble Ave.
Northeast, Suite 222
Albuquerque, NM 87110

Founded 1974
Total employees 172
Annual sales $19 million
Industries Computer
Software, Environmental
Growth Openings in past
year 32; percentage
growth 22%
Contact
Donald Tiano, President
Tel 505-266-5678
Fax 505-260-1163

Vivigen, Inc.
2000 Vivigen Way
Santa Fe, NM 87505

Founded 1981
Total employees 160
Annual sales $17 million
Industry Medical
Growth Openings in past
year 15; percentage
growth 10%
Contact
David H. Lockwood, Ph.D.,
Site Manager
Tel 505-438-1111
Fax 505-438-1120

New York

ABB Air Preheater, Inc.
Andover Rd., PO Box 372
Wellsville, NY 14895

Founded 1925
Total employees 645
Annual sales $99 million
Industries Energy,
Environmental, Factory
Automation,
Manufacturing Equipment

Growth Openings in past
year 13; percentage
growth 2%
Contact
Edward J. Bysiek,
President
Tel 716-593-2700
Fax 716-593-2721

Alpine Group, Inc.
1790 Broadway, 15th Floor
New York, NY 10019

Founded 1957
Total employees 375
Annual sales $6.3 million
Industry Holding
Companies
Growth Openings in past
year 75; percentage
growth 25%
Contact
Steven S. Elbaum,
COB/CEO
Tel 212-757-3333
Fax 212-757-3423

Altana, Inc.
60 Baylis Rd.
Melville, NY 11747

Founded 1963
Total employees 450
Annual sales $100 million
Industry Pharmaceuticals
Growth Openings in past
year 49; percentage
growth 12%
Contact
Rolf Rahnstorf, President
Tel 516-454-7677

**American Reagent
Laboratories, Inc.**
1 Luitpold Dr.
Shirley, NY 11967

Founded 1946
Total employees 230
Industry Pharmaceuticals
Growth Openings in past
year 30; percentage
growth 15%
Contact
Ralf Lange, President
Tel 516-924-4000
Fax 516-924-1731

**American Standards
Testing Bureau, Inc.**
40 Water St.
New York, NY 10004

Founded 1916
Total employees 490

Annual sales $85 million
Industries Holding
Companies, Test and
Measurement
Growth Openings in past
year 79; percentage
growth 19%
Contact
D.J. Meloy, Director of
Personnel
Tel 212-943-3160
Fax 212-825-2250

**American White Cross
Labs, Inc.**
40 Nardozzi Pl.
New Rochelle, NY 10802

Founded 1913
Total employees 450
Annual sales $35 million
Industry Medical
Growth Openings in past
year 150; percentage
growth 50%
Contact
Richard Orentzel,
President
Tel 914-632-3045
Fax 914-632-3071

AMG Industries, Inc.
53 Luzerne Rd.
Glens Falls, NY 12801

Founded 1974
Total employees 85
Annual sales $8 million
Industry Environmental
Growth Openings in past
year 20; percentage
growth 30%
Contact
James Griffin, Controller
Tel 518-793-3404
Fax 518-793-3496

AMS
55 Maple Ave.
Rockville Centre, NY
11570

Founded 1975
Total employees 55
Annual sales $6.3 million
Industry Computer
Software
Growth Openings in past
year 15; percentage
growth 37%
Contact
Ms. Judy Wilson, Vice
President/General
Manager
Tel 516-764-5953
Fax 516-764-6524

**Applied Business
Technology Corp.**
361 Broadway
New York, NY 10013

Founded 1981
Total employees 150
Annual sales $17 million
Industry Computer
Software
Growth Openings in past
year 20; percentage
growth 15%
Contact
Christopher Murray,
President/CEO
Tel 212-219-8945
Fax 212-219-3597

**Applied Digital Data
Systems, Inc.**
100 Marcus Blvd., PO Box
18001
Hauppauge, NY 11788

Founded 1969
Total employees 525
Annual sales $86 million
Industry Computer
Hardware
Growth Openings in past
year 25; percentage
growth 5%
Contact
Steve Green, Director of
Human Resources and
Administ
Tel 516-342-7400
Fax 516-342-7378

**Astec America, Inc., ENI
Division**
100 Highpower Rd.
Rochester, NY 14623

Founded 1947
Total employees 350
Annual sales $37 million
Industry Subassemblies
and Components
Growth Openings in past
year 20; percentage
growth 6%
Contact
Ms. Sheila Farrell,
Manager of Human
Resources
Tel 716-427-8300
Fax 716-427-7839

ATC Environmental, Inc.
104 East 25th St., 10th
Floor
New York, NY 10010

Founded 1982
Total employees 400

Annual sales $16.5 million
Industries Environmental,
Holding Companies
Growth Openings in past
year 200; percentage
growth 100%
Contact
Morry F. Rubin, President/
CEO/Treasurer
Tel 212-353-8280
Fax 212-353-8306

Audiosears Corp.
2 South St.
Stamford, NY 12167

Founded 1956
Total employees 150
Annual sales $6.8 million
Industry
Telecommunications
Growth Openings in past
year 20; percentage
growth 15%
Contact
David Hartwell, President
Tel 607-652-7305
Fax 607-652-3653

Augat, Inc., LRC Division
901 South Ave.
Horseheads, NY 14845

Founded 1965
Total employees 337
Industry Subassemblies
and Components
Growth Openings in past
year 37; percentage
growth 12%
Contact
Ms. Marcel P. Joseph,
Chairman of the Board/
CEO
Tel 607-739-3844
Fax 607-739-0106

Belmay, Inc.
200 Corporate Blvd. South
Yonkers, NY 10701

Founded 1932
Total employees 195
Annual sales $27.5 million
Industry Chemicals
Growth Openings in past
year 24; percentage
growth 14%
Contact
Alan Kesten, President
Tel 914-376-1515
Fax 914-376-1784

Besicorp Group, Inc.
1151 Flatbush Rd.
Kingston, NY 12401

Founded 1976
Total employees 71
Annual sales $18.97
million
Industries Energy,
Holding Companies
Growth Openings in past
year 21; percentage
growth 42%
Contact
Michael F. Zinn, COB/
President
Tel 914-336-7700
Fax 914-336-7172

Bio-Technology General Corp.
1250 Broadway, 20th Fl.
New York, NY 10001

Founded 1980
Total employees 140
Annual sales $6 million
Industries Biotechnology,
Chemicals,
Pharmaceuticals
Growth Openings in past
year 20; percentage
growth 16%
Contact
Dr. Sim Fass, President/
CEO
Tel 212-239-0450
Fax 212-239-0502

CBORD Group, Inc.
61 Brown Rd.
Ithaca, NY 14850

Founded 1975
Total employees 176
Annual sales $20 million
Industry Computer
Software
Growth Openings in past
year 64; percentage
growth 57%
Contact
John E. Alexander,
President
Tel 607-257-2410
Fax 607-257-1902

Century Business Credit Corp.
119 West 40th St., 10th
Floor
New York, NY 10018

Founded 1894
Total employees 125
Annual sales $14 million

Industry Holding
Companies
Growth Openings in past
year 15; percentage
growth 13%
Contact
Andrew Tanabaum,
President
Tel 212-703-3500

Charles Ross & Son Co.
710 Old Willets Path
Hauppauge, NY 11788

Founded 1846
Total employees 150
Annual sales $25 million
Industry Test and
Measurement
Growth Openings in past
year 20; percentage
growth 15%
Contact
Ron Reid, Executive Vice
President
Tel 516-234-0500
Fax 516-234-0691

Conmed Corp.
310 Broad St.
Utica, NY 13501

Founded 1971
Total employees 450
Annual sales $53.6 million
Industries Holding
Companies, Medical,
Subassemblies and
Components
Growth Openings in past
year 49; percentage
growth 12%
Contact
Eugene Corasanti,
COB/President
Tel 315-797-8375
Fax 315-797-0321

Crellin, Inc.
87 Center St.
Chatham, NY 12037

Founded 1984
Total employees 900
Annual sales $98 million
Industry Manufacturing
Equipment
Growth Openings in past
year 97; percentage
growth 12%
Contact
Dean West, Director of
Human Resources
Tel 518-392-2000
Fax 518-392-2022

Curative Technologies, Inc.
14 Research Way, Box
9052
East Setauket, NY 11733

Founded 1987
Total employees 375
Annual sales $31.27
million
Industries Biotechnology,
Medical, Pharmaceuticals
Growth Openings in past
year 75; percentage
growth 25%
Contact
Russell B. Whitman,
President
Tel 516-689-7000
Fax 516-689-7067

Danbury Pharmacal, Inc.
1033 Stoneleigh Ave., PO
Box 990
Carmel, NY 10512

Founded 1931
Total employees 765
Industry Pharmaceuticals
Growth Openings in past
year 64; percentage
growth 9%
Contact
Paul Kirkwood, VP of
Human Resources
Tel 914-225-1700
Fax 914-225-1763

Deltown Specialties
1712 Deltown Plaza
Fraser, NY 13753

Founded 1968
Total employees 106
Annual sales $10 million
Industry Biotechnology
Growth Openings in past
year 16; percentage
growth 17%
Contact
Simon Kooyman,
President
Tel 607-746-3082
Fax 607-746-2710

Design Strategy Corp.
600 Third Ave., 23rd Floor
New York, NY 10016

Founded 1978
Total employees 135
Annual sales $15 million
Industries Computer
Hardware, Computer
Software

Growth Openings in past year 65; percentage growth 92%
Contact
Ken Jordan, Managing Director
Tel 212-370-0392
Fax 212-949-9781

Dieknowlogist, Inc.
127 West 25th St.
New York, NY 10001

Founded 1975
Total employees 50
Annual sales $1 million
Industry Photonics
Growth Openings in past year 25; percentage growth 100%
Contact
Anthony Galatie, Sales Manager
Tel 212-989-5959
Fax 212-691-0692

Dynamic Decisions, Inc.
53 Murray St.
New York, NY 10007

Founded 1978
Total employees 93
Annual sales $17.0 million
Industries Computer Hardware, Computer Software
Growth Openings in past year 25; percentage growth 36%
Contact
Peter Phame, President
Tel 212-227-9888
Fax 212-227-9610

Eagle Comtronics, Inc.
4562 Waterhouse Rd.
Clay, NY 13041

Founded 1975
Total employees 800
Industry Telecommunications
Growth Openings in past year 199; percentage growth 33%
Contact
William Devendorf, President
Tel 315-622-3402
Fax 315-622-3800

Eder Associates
4805 Forest Ave.
Locust Valley, NY 11560

Founded 1970
Total employees 160
Annual sales $17 million
Industry Environmental
Growth Openings in past year 75; percentage growth 88%
Contact
Leonard J. Eder, President/CEO
Tel 516-671-8440
Fax 516-671-3349

Electronic Technology Group, Inc.
315 North Main St.
Jamestown, NY 14701

Founded 1987
Total employees 220
Annual sales $16 million
Industry Holding Companies
Growth Openings in past year 20; percentage growth 10%
Contact
Frank Costanzo, COB/CEO
Tel 716-488-9699
Fax 716-483-5107

Emisphere Technologies, Inc.
15 Skyline Dr.
Hawthorne, NY 10532

Founded 1986
Total employees 62
Industry Medical
Growth Openings in past year 20; percentage growth 47%
Contact
Dr. Michael L. Goldberg, COB/President/CEO
Tel 914-347-2220
Fax 914-347-2498

Enable Software, Inc.
Northway Ten Executive Park
Ballston Lake, NY 12019

Founded 1983
Total employees 150
Annual sales $17 million
Industries Computer Software, Holding Companies

Growth Openings in past year 20; percentage growth 15%
Contact
Donald J. Payne, President/CEO
Tel 518-877-8600
Fax 518-877-5225

Excel Technology, Inc.
45 Adams Ave.
Hauppauge, NY 11788

Founded 1988
Total employees 175
Annual sales $19.17 million
Industries Factory Automation, Holding Companies, Medical, Photonics
Growth Openings in past year 55; percentage growth 45%
Contact
Challasree Rama Rao, Ph.D., COB/CEO
Tel 516-273-6900
Fax 516-273-6958

FAME Software Corp.
Wall St. Plaza, 77 Water St., 9th Floor
New York, NY 10005

Founded 1975
Total employees 50
Industry Computer Software
Growth Openings in past year 20; percentage growth 66%
Contact
Joe Weisbord, President
Tel 212-898-7800
Fax 212-742-8956

Fusion Systems Group, Inc.
225 Broadway, 24th Fl.
New York, NY 10007

Founded 1988
Total employees 120
Annual sales $15 million
Industry Computer Software
Growth Openings in past year 25; percentage growth 26%
Contact
Henry Wyszomierski, President
Tel 212-285-8001
Fax 212-285-8705

Gorham Clark, Inc.
17 State St.
New York, NY 10004
Founded 1990
Total employees 80
Annual sales $5 million
Industry Computer
Software
Growth Openings in past
year 15; percentage
growth 23%
Contact
John Vlcek, President
Tel 212-809-4050
Fax 212-480-1293

G.W. Lisk Co., Inc.
2 South St.
Clifton Springs, NY 14432
Founded 1949
Total employees 350
Industries Holding
Companies,
Subassemblies and
Components, Test and
Measurement,
Transportation
Growth Openings in past
year 49; percentage
growth 16%
Contact
I.A. Morris, President
Tel 315-462-2611
Fax 315-462-7661

**Hansford Manufacturing
Corp.**
3111 South Winton Rd.
Rochester, NY 14623
Founded 1920
Total employees 200
Annual sales $25 million
Industries Computer
Software, Factory
Automation,
Manufacturing
Equipment, Test and
Measurement
Growth Openings in past
year 15; percentage
growth 8%
Contact
D. Farberman, Director of
Human Resources
Tel 716-427-0660
Fax 716-427-8610

Hertz Technolgy Group
325 Fifth Ave.
New York, NY 10016
Founded 1982
Total employees 35

Annual sales $4.9 million
Industry Holding
Companies
Growth Openings in past
year 15; percentage
growth 75%
Contact
Eli Hertz, President
Tel 212-684-4141
Fax 212-684-3658

Hipotronics, Inc.
Rte. 22, PO Box 414
Brewster, NY 10509
Founded 1962
Total employees 192
Annual sales $27 million
Industries Factory
Automation,
Subassemblies and
Components, Test and
Measurement
Growth Openings in past
year 26; percentage
growth 15%
Contact
Thomas Pluff, COB/CEO
Tel 914-279-8091
Fax 914-279-2467

Hi-Tech Ceramics, Inc.
PO Box 788
Alfred, NY 14802
Founded 1981
Total employees 80
Annual sales $11 million
Industries Advanced
Materials, Subassemblies
and Components
Growth Openings in past
year 17; percentage
growth 26%
Contact
Ms. Diane Kelly, Director
of Human Resources
Tel 607-587-9146
Fax 607-587-8770

**Inchape, Inc., ETL
Testing Laboratories,
Inc.**
Route 11, Industrial Park
Cortland, NY 13045
Founded 1896
Total employees 330
Industries Manufacturing
Equipment,
Subassemblies and
Components, Test and
Measurement
Growth Openings in past
year 30; percentage
growth 10%

Contact
Paul Smith, VP of Human
Resources
Tel 607-753-6711
Fax 607-756-9891

Instinet Corp.
757 3rd Ave.
New York, NY 10017
Founded 1969
Total employees 250
Annual sales $41 million
Industry Computer
Hardware
Growth Openings in past
year 50; percentage
growth 25%
Contact
Michael Sanderson, Chief
Executive Officer
Tel 212-310-9500
Fax 212-935-2131

Interflo Technologies
19 Clay St.
Brooklyn, NY 11222
Founded 1964
Total employees 200
Industries Advanced
Materials, Chemicals,
Defense, Environmental,
Manufacturing
Equipment, Medical, Test
and Measurement
Growth Openings in past
year 50; percentage
growth 33%
Contact
Irving M. Wolbrom,
President
Tel 718-389-2860
Fax 718-389-2474

**International Imaging
Materials, Inc.**
310 Commerce Dr.
Amherst, NY 14228
Founded 1983
Total employees 500
Annual sales $48 million
Industry Computer
Hardware
Growth Openings in past
year 199; percentage
growth 66%
Contact
Michael Drennan, VP of
Finance
Tel 716-691-6333
Fax 716-691-3395

IPC Information Systems, Inc.
88 Pine St., 14th Floor
New York, NY 10005

Founded 1961
Total employees 700
Annual sales $96 million
Industry
Telecommunications
Growth Openings in past year 97; percentage growth 16%
Contact
Peter Kleinknecht, President
Tel 212-825-9060
Fax 212-344-5106

Ithaca Peripherals Inc.
20 Bomax Dr.
Ithaca, NY 14850

Founded 1983
Total employees 75
Annual sales $12 million
Industry Computer Hardware
Growth Openings in past year 25; percentage growth 50%
Contact
Seth M. Lukash, COB/CEO
Tel 607-257-8901
Fax 607-257-8922

JYACC, Inc.
116 John St.
New York, NY 10038

Founded 1978
Total employees 225
Industry Computer Software
Growth Openings in past year 25; percentage growth 12%
Contact
Ms. Annette Cappola, VP of Human Resources
Tel 212-267-7722
Fax 212-608-6753

Keystone Electronics Corp.
31-07 20th Rd.
Astoria, NY 11105

Founded 1943
Total employees 102
Annual sales $9.9 million
Industry Subassemblies and Components

Growth Openings in past year 22; percentage growth 27%
Contact
Richard David, President/CEO
Tel 718-956-8900
Fax 718-956-9040

Liberty Brokerage, Inc.
77 Water St., 12th Fl.
New York, NY 10005

Founded 1986
Total employees 250
Industry Holding Companies
Growth Openings in past year 50; percentage growth 25%
Contact
Thomas M. Wendel, President
Tel 212-574-1776
Fax 212-574-1988

Magnetic Technologies Corp.
770 Linden Ave.
Rochester, NY 14625

Founded 1969
Total employees 150
Annual sales $14 million
Industries Computer Hardware, Manufacturing Equipment, Subassemblies and Components
Growth Openings in past year 70; percentage growth 87%
Contact
Gordon McNeil, President
Tel 716-385-8711
Fax 716-385-5625

MapInfo Corp.
1 Global View
Troy, NY 12180

Founded 1986
Total employees 180
Annual sales $20 million
Industry Computer Software
Growth Openings in past year 55; percentage growth 44%
Contact
Brian D. Owen, President/CEO
Tel 518-285-6000
Fax 518-285-6060

Market Vision Corp.
40 Rector St., 18th Fl.
New York, NY 10006

Founded 1982
Total employees 70
Annual sales $8.1 million
Industry Computer Software
Growth Openings in past year 15; percentage growth 27%
Contact
Tom Wendell, Chief Executive Officer
Tel 212-227-1610
Fax 212-233-1430

Medsonic, Inc.
1938 New Hwy.
Farmingdale, NY 11735

Founded 1955
Total employees 70
Annual sales $3.5 million
Industries Environmental, Factory Automation, Test and Measurement
Growth Openings in past year 21; percentage growth 42%
Contact
Michael Juliano, President
Tel 516-694-9555
Fax 516-694-9412

Merit Electronic Design Co., Ltd.
190 Rodeo Dr.
Edgewood, NY 11717

Founded 1977
Total employees 85
Annual sales $5 million
Industry Subassemblies and Components
Growth Openings in past year 25; percentage growth 41%
Contact
Emmanuel Intoci, President
Tel 516-667-9699
Fax 516-667-9853

Metrosonics, Inc.
PO Box 23075
Rochester, NY 14692

Founded 1973
Total employees 100
Industries Environmental, Test and Measurement
Growth Openings in past year 20; percentage growth 25%

Contact
Al Stolberg, President
Tel 716-334-7300
Fax 716-334-2635

Micro Bio-Medics, Inc.
846 Pelham Pkwy.
Pelham Manor, NY 10803
Founded 1971
Total employees 225
Annual sales $73.95
 million
Industries Chemicals,
 Holding Companies,
 Medical, Test and
 Measurement
Growth Openings in past
 year 35; percentage
 growth 18%
Contact
Bruce Haber, COB/
 President
Tel 914-738-8400
Fax 914-738-9538

Microbank Software, Inc.
80 Broad St.
New York, NY 10004
Founded 1984
Total employees 95
Annual sales $11 million
Industry Computer
 Software
Growth Openings in past
 year 32; percentage
 growth 50%
Contact
Brian Twibell, Chief
 Executive Officer
Tel 212-363-5600
Fax 212-363-5891

Microwave Data Systems
175 Science Pkwy.
Rochester, NY 14620
Founded 1985
Total employees 153
Annual sales $19 million
Industry
 Telecommunications
Growth Openings in past
 year 43; percentage
 growth 39%
Contact
Paul Jacobs, President
Tel 716-242-9600
Fax 716-242-9620

Moog Controls, Inc.
300 Jamison Rd., PO Box
 3000
East Aurora, NY 14052
Founded 1988
Total employees 275
Annual sales $32 million
Industries Factory
 Automation,
 Subassemblies and
 Components, Test and
 Measurement
Growth Openings in past
 year 14; percentage
 growth 5%
Contact
Jan Reicis, Human
 Resources Manager
Tel 716-655-3000
Fax 716-655-1803

NAI Technologies, Inc.
60 Plant Ave.
Hauppauge, NY 11788
Founded 1954
Total employees 535
Annual sales $67 million
Industries Computer
 Hardware, Holding
 Companies,
 Telecommunications
Growth Openings in past
 year 82; percentage
 growth 18%
Contact
Len Stanton, Director of
 Corporate Human
 Resources
Tel 516-582-6500
Fax 516-582-8652

**Novo Nordisk of North
America, Inc.**
405 Lexington Ave., Suite
 6200
New York, NY 10017
Founded 1981
Total employees 858
Annual sales $263.71
 million
Industry Holding
 Companies
Growth Openings in past
 year 137; percentage
 growth 19%
Contact
Kurt Anker Nielsen,
 Chairman of the Board
Tel 212-867-0123
Fax 212-867-0298

**OBG Technical Services,
Inc.**
5000 Brittonfield Pkwy.,
 PO Box 5240
Syracuse, NY 13220
Founded 1981
Total employees 100
Annual sales $18 million
Industry Environmental
Growth Openings in past
 year 18; percentage
 growth 21%
Contact
Terry L. Brown, PE,
 President
Tel 315-437-6400
Fax 315-437-9800

Oncogene Science, Inc.
106 Charles Lindbergh
 Blvd.
Uniondale, NY 11553
Founded 1983
Total employees 130
Annual sales $11 million
Industries Biotechnology,
 Chemicals, Medical
Growth Openings in past
 year 18; percentage
 growth 16%
Contact
Gary Frashier, President/
 CEO
Tel 516-222-0023
Fax 516-222-0114

**Oneida Research
Services, Inc.**
One Halsey Rd.
Whitesboro, NY 13492
Founded 1977
Total employees 130
Annual sales $15 million
Industries Chemicals,
 Pharmaceuticals,
 Subassemblies and
 Components, Test and
 Measurement
Growth Openings in past
 year 24; percentage
 growth 22%
Contact
Dr. Lee Schrader, Director
 of Human Resources
Tel 315-736-5480
Fax 315-736-9321

OP-TECH Environmental Services, Inc.
5000 Brittonfield Pkwy.,
PO Box 2158
Syracuse, NY 13220

Founded 1976
Total employees 90
Annual sales $5 million
Industry Environmental
Growth Openings in past year 40; percentage growth 80%
Contact
Richard L. Elander, President
Tel 315-463-1643
Fax 315-463-9764

Par Pharmaceutical, Inc.
1 Ram Ridge Rd.
Spring Valley, NY 10977

Founded 1978
Total employees 410
Annual sales $75 million
Industry Pharmaceuticals
Growth Openings in past year 120; percentage growth 41%
Contact
George L. Leisher, HR, Administration and Investor Relation
Tel 914-425-7100
Fax 914-425-7907

PCB Piezotronics, Inc.
3425 Walden Ave.
Depew, NY 14043

Founded 1967
Total employees 230
Industries Subassemblies and Components, Test and Measurement, Transportation
Growth Openings in past year 30; percentage growth 15%
Contact
James Lally, President
Tel 716-684-0001
Fax 716-684-0987

Performance Technologies, Inc.
315 Science Pkwy.
Rochester, NY 14620

Founded 1981
Total employees 170
Industries Computer Hardware, Computer Software, Holding Companies
Growth Openings in past year 20; percentage growth 13%
Contact
John Slusser, President/COO
Tel 716-256-0200
Fax 716-256-0791

Periphonics Corp.
4000 Veterans Memorial Hwy.
Bohemia, NY 11716

Founded 1970
Total employees 305
Industry Computer Hardware
Growth Openings in past year 33; percentage growth 12%
Contact
Ms. Janet Anderson, Director of Human Resources
Tel 516-467-0500
Fax 516-737-8520

Philips Broadband Networks, Inc.
100 Fairgrounds Dr.
Manlius, NY 13104

Founded 1988
Total employees 600
Annual sales $82 million
Industries Manufacturing Equipment, Photonics, Telecommunications
Growth Openings in past year 50; percentage growth 9%
Contact
Chet Wilk, Manager of Human Resources
Tel 315-682-9105
Fax 315-682-9005

Positron Industries, Inc.
56 Pine St., 8th Floor
New York, NY 10005

Founded 1978
Total employees 300
Annual sales $35 million
Industries Medical, Subassemblies and Components, Test and Measurement, Telecommunications
Growth Openings in past year 20; percentage growth 7%

Contact
Art Swift, Regional Manager
Tel 212-797-1300
Fax 212-797-5164

Regeneron Pharmaceuticals, Inc.
777 Old Saw Mill River Rd.
Tarrytown, NY 10591

Founded 1988
Total employees 260
Industry Pharmaceuticals
Growth Openings in past year 69; percentage growth 36%
Contact
Dr. Leonard Schleifer, MD, P, CEO/President
Tel 914-347-7000
Fax 914-347-2113

Renco Electronics, Inc.
60 Jeffryn Blvd. East
Deer Park, NY 11729

Founded 1955
Total employees 325
Industry Subassemblies and Components
Growth Openings in past year 125; percentage growth 62%
Contact
Bruce A. Rensing, President/CEO
Tel 516-586-5566
Fax 516-586-5562

RVSI
425 Rabro Dr. East
Hauppauge, NY 11788

Founded 1977
Total employees 110
Annual sales $13 million
Industry Factory Automation
Growth Openings in past year 45; percentage growth 69%
Contact
Pat V. Costa, COB/President/CEO
Tel 516-273-9700
Fax 516-273-1167

Sensis Corp.
5793 Widewaters Pkwy.
De Witt, NY 13214

Founded 1985
Total employees 110

Annual sales $11 million
Industries Defense,
Manufacturing
Equipment, Test and
Measurement,
Transportation
Growth Openings in past
year 55; percentage
growth 100%
Contact
Ms. Peggy Dudarchik,
Director of Human
Resources
Tel 315-445-0550
Fax 315-445-9401

**Sevenson Environmental
Services, Inc.**
2749 Lockport Rd.
Niagara Falls, NY 14302

Founded 1977
Total employees 172
Annual sales $69.04
million
Industries Environmental,
Holding Companies
Growth Openings in past
year 16; percentage
growth 10%
Contact
Michael A. Elia, President/
CEO
Tel 716-284-0431

**Signal Transformer Co.,
Inc.**
500 Bayview Ave.
Inwood, NY 11696

Founded 1953
Total employees 550
Annual sales $25 million
Industry Subassemblies
and Components
Growth Openings in past
year 50; percentage
growth 10%
Contact
Brian Smith, Controller/
CFO
Tel 516-239-5777
Fax 516-239-7208

SSAC, Inc.
PO Box 1000
Baldwinsville, NY 13027

Founded 1967
Total employees 250
Industries Subassemblies
and Components, Test
and Measurement
Growth Openings in past
year 19; percentage
growth 8%

Contact
Charles Meigel, General
Manager
Tel 315-638-1300
Fax 315-638-0333

**Standard Data
Corporation**
440 Ninth Ave.
New York, NY 10001

Founded 1959
Total employees 140
Annual sales $16 million
Industry Computer
Software
Growth Openings in past
year 15; percentage
growth 12%
Contact
Mark W. Iobst, President
Tel 212-564-4433
Fax 212-564-4751

**Standard Microsystems
Corporation**
80 Arkay Dr.
Hauppauge, NY 11788

Founded 1971
Total employees 675
Annual sales $250.7
million
Industry Holding
Companies
Growth Openings in past
year 67; percentage
growth 11%
Contact
Ernest W. Sern, VP of
Human Resource
Tel 516-273-3100
Fax 516-273-5550

**Sterling Software, Inc.,
Eastern Operations**
Rt. 26 North, Beeches
Technical Campus
Rome, NY 13440

Founded 1982
Total employees 45
Annual sales $5.2 million
Industry Computer
Software
Growth Openings in past
year 15; percentage
growth 50%
Contact
Dr. Gerald Plant, Ph.D.,
Vice President
Tel 315-336-0500
Fax 315-336-4455

STS Duotek, Inc.
7500 West Henrietta Rd.,
PO Box 349
Rush, NY 14543

Founded 1978
Total employees 110
Industry Biotechnology
Growth Openings in past
year 25; percentage
growth 29%
Contact
Richard Whitbourne, Chief
Executive Officer
Tel 716-533-1672
Fax 716-533-1796

**Superior Printing Ink
Co., Inc.**
70 Bethune St.
New York, NY 10014

Founded 1918
Total employees 590
Annual sales $75 million
Industries Chemicals,
Holding Companies
Growth Openings in past
year 34; percentage
growth 6%
Contact
Jeffrey Simons, Chief
Executive Officer
Tel 212-741-3600
Fax 212-633-8283

TDC Electronics, Inc.
222-15 Northern Blvd.
Bayside, NY 11361

Founded 1902
Total employees 56
Annual sales $6.5 million
Industry Transportation
Growth Openings in past
year 36; percentage
growth 180%
Contact
Alex Rothchild, Managing
Director
Tel 718-225-2118
Fax 718-225-7580

**Telecom Services
Limited (U.S.), Inc.**
50 Broad St., 20th Floor
New York, NY 10004

Founded 1986
Total employees 70
Annual sales $9.6 million
Industries Computer
Software, Holding
Companies,
Telecommunications

Growth Openings in past year 20; percentage growth 40%
Contact
Alan Maltz, President
Tel 212-248-2000
Fax 212-248-4500

Teleport Communications Group
1 World Trade Ctr., Suite 5121
New York, NY 10048

Founded 1984
Total employees 575
Annual sales $79 million
Industries Photonics, Telecommunications
Growth Openings in past year 150; percentage growth 35%
Contact
William Baldwin, VP of Administration
Tel 212-478-8000
Fax 212-478-4910

TelTech Corp., Consulting Division
39 Broadway
New York, NY 10006

Founded 1973
Total employees 350
Annual sales $28 million
Industries Computer Hardware, Computer Software, Telecommunications
Growth Openings in past year 150; percentage growth 75%
Contact
Jonathan Gross, President
Tel 212-514-5440
Fax 212-514-5504

United Biomedical, Inc.
25 Davids Dr.
Hauppauge, NY 11788

Founded 1983
Total employees 100
Annual sales $13 million
Industries Biotechnology, Pharmaceuticals
Growth Openings in past year 40; percentage growth 66%
Contact
Ms. Carol Hodkin, Personnel Manager
Tel 516-273-2828
Fax 516-273-1717

Vicon Fiberoptics, Inc.
90 Secor Ln.
Pelham Manor, NY 10803

Founded 1968
Total employees 40
Annual sales $1.5 million
Industries Medical, Photonics
Growth Openings in past year 15; percentage growth 60%
Contact
Leonard Scrivo, President
Tel 914-738-5006

Welch Allyn, Inc., Inspection Systems Division
4619 Jordan Rd.
Skaneateles Falls, NY 13153

Founded 1950
Total employees 140
Annual sales $17 million
Industry Factory Automation
Growth Openings in past year 15; percentage growth 12%
Contact
Richard A. Kokosa, Division Manager
Tel 315-685-8969
Fax 315-685-7905

Young & Franklin Inc.
942 Old Liverpool Rd.
Liverpool, NY 13088

Founded 1918
Total employees 160
Annual sales $15 million
Industries Holding Companies, Subassemblies and Components
Growth Openings in past year 60; percentage growth 60%
Contact
Ms. Carol Hawkins, Personnel Manager
Tel 315-457-3110
Fax 315-457-9204

North Carolina

AAI
1206 North 23rd St.
Wilmington, NC 28405

Founded 1979
Total employees 400
Annual sales $55 million
Industry Pharmaceuticals
Growth Openings in past year 50; percentage growth 14%
Contact
Dr. Fred D. Sancilio, President
Tel 910-763-4536
Fax 910-251-6755

Accudyne, Inc.
5800 McHines Pl.
Raleigh, NC 27604

Founded 1990
Total employees 95
Annual sales $9.2 million
Industry Subassemblies and Components
Growth Openings in past year 45; percentage growth 90%
Contact
Bill Prior, President/CEO
Tel 919-872-0100
Fax 919-876-6385

Alba-Waldensian, Inc.
201 Saint Germain Ave. Southwest, PO Box 100
Valdese, NC 28690

Founded 1899
Total employees 900
Annual sales $40 million
Industry Holding Companies
Growth Openings in past year 43; percentage growth 5%
Contact
Warren Nesbit, VP of Human Resources
Tel 704-874-2191
Fax 704-879-6595

BroadBand Technologies, Inc.
4024 Stirrup Creek Dr., PO Box 13737
Research Triangle Park, NC 27709

Founded 1988
Total employees 249
Annual sales $5.3 million

Industry
Telecommunications
Growth Openings in past
year 99; percentage
growth 66%
Contact
Salim Bhatia, President
Tel 919-544-0015
Fax 919-544-3459

Captive-Aire Systems, Inc.
112 Wheaton Dr.
Youngsville, NC 27596

Founded 1980
Total employees 200
Annual sales $28 million
Industries Energy,
Subassemblies and
Components
Growth Openings in past
year 40; percentage
growth 25%
Contact
Robert Luddy, President
Tel 919-554-2414
Fax 919-554-1227

Communication Cable, Inc.
1335 2nd Ave., PO Box 729
Siler City, NC 27344

Founded 1984
Total employees 400
Annual sales $47 million
Industries Holding
Companies,
Subassemblies and
Components
Growth Openings in past
year 20; percentage
growth 5%
Contact
James R. Fore, COB/
President
Tel 919-663-2629
Fax 919-663-2297

Cree Research, Inc.
2810 Meridian Pkwy.,
Suite 176
Durham, NC 27713

Founded 1987
Total employees 65
Annual sales $6.32 million
Industries Photonics,
Subassemblies and
Components
Growth Openings in past
year 25; percentage
growth 62%

Contact
Eric Hunter, President
Tel 919-361-5709
Fax 919-361-2358

Embrex, Inc.
PO Box 13989
Research Triangle Park,
NC 27709

Founded 1985
Total employees 80
Industries Biotechnology,
Pharmaceuticals
Growth Openings in past
year 30; percentage
growth 60%
Contact
Ms. Helen J. Makarezyk,
Personnel Supervisor
Tel 919-941-5185
Fax 919-941-5186

Eutectic Electronics, Inc.
8608 Jersey Ct.
Raleigh, NC 27613

Founded 1980
Total employees 110
Annual sales $13 million
Industries Manufacturing
Equipment, Medical,
Subassemblies and
Components
Growth Openings in past
year 25; percentage
growth 29%
Contact
Charles Watts, President
Tel 919-782-3000
Fax 919-782-9113

FMC Corp., Lithium Division
449 North Cox Rd., PO
Box 3925
Gastonia, NC 28054

Founded 1948
Total employees 650
Annual sales $130 million
Industries Advanced
Materials, Chemicals,
Pharmaceuticals
Growth Openings in past
year 19; percentage
growth 3%
Contact
T.K. Johnson, Manager of
Human Resources
Tel 704-868-5300
Fax 704-868-5370

GBA Systems
8818 U.S. Hwy. 421 North
Colfax, NC 27235

Founded 1975
Total employees 56
Annual sales $8.6 million
Industry Computer
Software
Growth Openings in past
year 15; percentage
growth 36%
Contact
Gary N. Brown, President
Tel 919-668-4555
Fax 919-668-9576

Glenayre Technologies, Inc.
4201 Congress St., Suite 455
Charlotte, NC 28209

Founded 1963
Total employees 900
Annual sales $100 million
Industry
Telecommunications
Growth Openings in past
year 97; percentage
growth 12%
Contact
Ms. Beverly Cox, Director
of Corporate Human
Resources
Tel 704-553-0038
Fax 704-553-7878

Greer Laboratories, Inc.
PO Box 800
Lenoir, NC 28645

Founded 1904
Total employees 150
Annual sales $20 million
Industry Pharmaceuticals
Growth Openings in past
year 20; percentage
growth 15%
Contact
Ms. Linda Housand,
Personnel Manager
Tel 704-754-5327
Fax 704-754-5320

High Point Chemical Corp.
243 Woodbine, PO Box 2316
High Point, NC 27260

Founded 1945
Total employees 175
Annual sales $24 million
Industries Advanced
Materials, Chemicals

Growth Openings in past year 19; percentage growth 12%
Contact
R. Morton, Manager of Human Resources
Tel 910-884-2214
Fax 910-884-5039

HydroLogic, Inc.
14 South Park Square, Suite 500
Asheville, NC 28801

Founded 1986
Total employees 250
Annual sales $18 million
Industries Biotechnology, Chemicals, Environmental, Holding Companies
Growth Openings in past year 120; percentage growth 92%
Contact
Thomas R. Barr, President
Tel 704-258-3746
Fax 704-258-3973

Joy Energy Systems, Inc.
11900 West Hall Dr.
Charlotte, NC 28278

Founded 1968
Total employees 100
Industry Environmental
Growth Openings in past year 35; percentage growth 53%
Contact
Rod Tarr, Personnel Manager
Tel 704-587-8000
Fax 704-587-8030

Keiltex Industries, Inc.
PO Box 19042
Charlotte, NC 28219

Founded 1978
Total employees 150
Annual sales $17 million
Industries Computer Software, Factory Automation
Growth Openings in past year 100; percentage growth 200%
Contact
Hans Keilhack, President
Tel 704-359-8400
Fax 704-359-8324

Knowledge Systems Corp.
114 MacKenan Dr.
Cary, NC 27511

Founded 1986
Total employees 52
Industry Computer Software
Growth Openings in past year 19; percentage growth 57%
Contact
Reed Phillips, President
Tel 919-481-4000
Fax 919-460-9044

Kyocera Engineered Ceramics, Inc.
PO Box 678
Mountain Home, NC 28758

Founded 1985
Total employees 250
Industry Advanced Materials
Growth Openings in past year 19; percentage growth 8%
Contact
Michael Lashford, President
Tel 704-693-0241
Fax 704-692-1340

Morganite, Inc.
One Morganite Dr.
Dunn, NC 28334

Founded 1964
Total employees 700
Annual sales $65 million
Industry Subassemblies and Components
Growth Openings in past year 97; percentage growth 16%
Contact
Bruce Muller, President
Tel 910-892-8081
Fax 910-892-9600

MTS Systems Corp., SINTECH Division
PO Box 14226
Research Triangle Park, NC 27709

Founded 1982
Total employees 50
Annual sales $6.3 million
Industry Factory Automation

Growth Openings in past year 15; percentage growth 42%
Contact
Rashid N. Khan, Vice President/General Manager
Tel 919-677-1610
Fax 919-677-2480

Newton Instrument Co., Inc.
111 East A St.
Butner, NC 27509

Founded 1949
Total employees 220
Industry Energy
Growth Openings in past year 40; percentage growth 22%
Contact
Walter Newton, President
Tel 919-575-6426
Fax 919-575-4708

Novo Nordisk Biochem, Inc.
1003 State Rd.
Franklinton, NC 27525

Founded 1978
Total employees 201
Annual sales $19 million
Industry Biotechnology
Growth Openings in past year 104; percentage growth 107%
Contact
Ms. Joanne Steiner, Human Resources Manager
Tel 919-494-2014
Fax 919-494-5465

Pharmacia, Inc.
PO Box 597
Clayton, NC 27520

Founded 1984
Total employees 170
Industry Pharmaceuticals
Growth Openings in past year 20; percentage growth 13%
Contact
Ed Hargrove, Corporate Director of Human Resources
Tel 919-553-3831
Fax 919-553-3601

Q+E Software
5540 Centerview Dr., Suite 324
Raleigh, NC 27606

Founded 1986
Total employees 120
Annual sales $7.2 million
Industry Computer Software
Growth Openings in past year 90; percentage growth 300%
Contact
Frank Salmonese, Director of Operations
Tel 919-859-2220
Fax 919-859-9334

Rao Enterprises, Inc.
PO Box 13501
Research Triangle Park, NC 27709

Founded 1985
Total employees 100
Annual sales $5 million
Industries Chemicals, Environmental
Growth Openings in past year 50; percentage growth 100%
Contact
Dr. T.K. Rao, President
Tel 910-544-5857
Fax 910-544-5091

Rhone-Poulenc, Inc., Latex and Specialty Polymers Division
207 Telegraph Dr.
Gastonia, NC 28056

Founded 1972
Total employees 160
Industry Advanced Materials
Growth Openings in past year 25; percentage growth 18%
Contact
Barry W. Perry, Vice President/General Manager
Tel 704-865-7451
Fax 704-865-4919

Roechling Engineered Plastics
Hwy. 321 North, PO Box 2729
Gastonia, NC 28053

Founded 1983
Total employees 50
Annual sales $7.4 million

Industries Advanced Materials, Manufacturing Equipment
Growth Openings in past year 15; percentage growth 42%
Contact
Lewis Carter, General Manager
Tel 704-922-7814
Fax 704-922-7651

Schaefer Systems International, Inc.
10021 Westlake Dr., PO Box 7009
Charlotte, NC 28241

Founded 1985
Total employees 85
Annual sales $10 million
Industries Environmental, Factory Automation
Growth Openings in past year 35; percentage growth 70%
Contact
Arnold Heuzen, President
Tel 704-588-2150
Fax 704-588-1862

Seer Technologies, Inc.
8000 Regency Pkwy.
Cary, NC 27511

Founded 1990
Total employees 450
Annual sales $50 million
Industry Computer Software
Growth Openings in past year 150; percentage growth 50%
Contact
Gene Bedell, President
Tel 919-380-5000
Fax 919-469-1910

Southern Optical Co.
1909 North Church St., PO Box 21328
Greensboro, NC 27405

Founded 1947
Total employees 500
Annual sales $50 million
Industries Medical, Photonics, Test and Measurement
Growth Openings in past year 50; percentage growth 11%

Contact
Thomas R. Sloan, COB/CEO
Tel 910-272-8146
Fax 919-274-6232

Sumitomo Electric Fiber Optics Corp.
78 Alexander Dr., PO Box 13445
Research Triangle Park, NC 27709

Founded 1983
Total employees 500
Industries Manufacturing Equipment, Photonics, Telecommunications
Growth Openings in past year 100; percentage growth 25%
Contact
T. Nagao, President
Tel 919-541-8100
Fax 919-541-8265

Textron, Inc., Townsend Division
5250-77 Center Dr., Suite 300
Charlotte, NC 28217

Founded 1920
Total employees 750
Annual sales $73 million
Industries Factory Automation, Subassemblies and Components
Growth Openings in past year 50; percentage growth 7%
Contact
Robert P. Ross, President
Tel 704-525-8003
Fax 704-525-8565

Trion, Inc.
101 McNeill Rd., PO Box 760
Sanford, NC 27331

Founded 1947
Total employees 332
Annual sales $33.7 million
Industries Environmental, Factory Automation
Growth Openings in past year 19; percentage growth 6%
Contact
Michael P. Womble, Director of Human Resources
Tel 919-775-2201
Fax 919-774-8771

Virtus Corp.
117 Edinburgh South,
Suite 204
Cary, NC 27511

Founded 1990
Total employees 30
Industry Computer
Software
Growth Openings in past
year 15; percentage
growth 100%
Contact
David A. Smith, President
Tel 919-467-9700
Fax 919-460-4530

**Wandel & Goltermann
Technologies, Inc.**
1030 Swabia Ct.
Research Triangle Park,
NC 27709

Founded 1966
Total employees 220
Industries Factory
Automation,
Subassemblies and
Components, Test and
Measurement
Growth Openings in past
year 20; percentage
growth 10%
Contact
Matt Weitz, Personnel
Manager
Tel 919-941-5730
Fax 919-941-5751

**Wesson, Taylor, Wells &
Associates, Inc.**
PO Box 12274
Research Triangle Park,
NC 27709

Founded 1985
Total employees 175
Industries Computer
Hardware, Computer
Software,
Telecommunications
Growth Openings in past
year 25; percentage
growth 16%
Contact
Jim Wesson, Senior VP of
Field Support
Tel 919-941-0081

North Dakota

Fargo Assembly Co.
1402 43rd St. Northwest
Fargo, ND 58102

Founded 1975
Total employees 150
Industry Subassemblies
and Components
Growth Openings in past
year 50; percentage
growth 50%
Contact
Ron Bergan, Chief
Executive Officer
Tel 701-281-0331
Fax 701-281-0625

Great Plains Software
1701 Southwest 38th St.
Fargo, ND 58103

Founded 1980
Total employees 600
Annual sales $69 million
Industry Computer
Software
Growth Openings in past
year 280; percentage
growth 87%
Contact
Ms. Jodi Uecker-Rust,
Director of Operations
Tel 701-281-0550
Fax 701-281-3171

Ohio

ADB-ALNACO, Inc.
977 Gahanna Pkwy.
Columbus, OH 43230

Founded 1978
Total employees 139
Annual sales $13 million
Industries Energy,
Subassemblies and
Components,
Transportation
Growth Openings in past
year 52; percentage
growth 59%
Contact
Steve Rauch, Operations
Manager
Tel 614-861-1304
Fax 614-864-2069

**Allied Color Industries,
Inc.**
800 Ken Mar Industrial
Pkwy.
Cleveland, OH 44147

Founded 1967
Total employees 100
Annual sales $21 million
Industry Chemicals
Growth Openings in past
year 15; percentage
growth 17%
Contact
George Chase, Chief
Operating Manager
Tel 216-526-0230
Fax 216-526-3183

**Allied Mineral Products,
Inc.**
2700 Scioto Pkwy.
Columbus, OH 43221

Founded 1960
Total employees 150
Industry Advanced
Materials
Growth Openings in past
year 20; percentage
growth 15%
Contact
John Tabor, COB/
President
Tel 614-876-0244
Fax 614-876-0981

Allwaste Recycling, Inc.
2300 West Third St.
Cleveland, OH 44113

Founded 1896
Total employees 338
Industry Advanced
Materials
Growth Openings in past
year 23; percentage
growth 7%
Contact
Steven B. Bowles,
President
Tel 216-621-4181
Fax 216-621-9543

AMRESCO, Inc.
30175 Solon Industrial
Pkwy.
Solon, OH 44139

Founded 1976
Total employees 125
Annual sales $12 million
Industries Advanced
Materials, Biotechnology,
Chemicals, Medical

Growth Openings in past
year 30; percentage
growth 31%
Contact
Ms. Nancy Foster,
Personnel Director
Tel 216-349-1199
Fax 216-349-1182

Antenna Specialists Co.
30500 Bruce Industrial
Pkwy.
Solon, OH 44139

Founded 1953
Total employees 400
Annual sales $55 million
Industries Subassemblies
and Components,
Telecommunications
Growth Openings in past
year 20; percentage
growth 5%
Contact
Ms. Susan VanDale,
Director of Personnel
Tel 216-349-8400
Fax 216-349-8407

Arnco Corp.
860 Garden St.
Elyria, OH 44035

Founded 1985
Total employees 150
Annual sales $16 million
Industries Advanced
Materials, Photonics
Growth Openings in past
year 55; percentage
growth 57%
Contact
Robert F. Smith, President
Tel 216-322-1000
Fax 216-323-7111

Automatic Feed Co.
476 East Riverview Ave.
Napoleon, OH 43545

Founded 1948
Total employees 104
Annual sales $22.5 million
Industry Factory
Automation
Growth Openings in past
year 19; percentage
growth 22%
Contact
Kim Beck, President/CEO
Tel 419-592-0050
Fax 419-592-8590

Bliss-Salem, Inc.
530 South Ellsworth Ave.
Salem, OH 44460

Founded 1857
Total employees 240
Annual sales $30 million
Industries Computer
Hardware, Factory
Automation,
Manufacturing
Equipment, Test and
Measurement
Growth Openings in past
year 30; percentage
growth 14%
Contact
Michael Zugay, President
Tel 216-337-3444
Fax 216-337-7067

Cables To Go, Inc.
1501 Webster St.
Dayton, OH 45404

Founded 1985
Total employees 130
Annual sales $10 million
Industries Photonics,
Subassemblies and
Components,
Telecommunications
Growth Openings in past
year 45; percentage
growth 52%
Contact
Jeff Hyman, President
Tel 513-224-8646
Fax 800-331-2841

Cole-Layer-Trumble Co.
3199 Klepinger Rd.
Dayton, OH 45406

Founded 1938
Total employees 400
Annual sales $20 million
Industry Computer
Software
Growth Openings in past
year 50; percentage
growth 14%
Contact
Bruce F. Nagel, President
Tel 513-276-5261
Fax 513-278-3711

Cyberex, Inc.
7171 Industrial Park Blvd.
Mentor, OH 44060

Founded 1968
Total employees 120
Annual sales $16 million

Industries Energy,
Subassemblies and
Components
Growth Openings in past
year 20; percentage
growth 20%
Contact
Gus Stevens, President/
COO
Tel 216-946-1783
Fax 216-946-5963

Desktop Displays, Inc.
32333 Aurora Rd.
Solon, OH 44139

Founded 1992
Total employees 30
Annual sales $4.9 million
Industry Computer
Hardware
Growth Openings in past
year 25; percentage
growth 500%
Contact
D.J. Chou, President
Tel 216-349-3866
Fax 216-349-1554

Digital Technology, Inc.
2300 Edwin C. Moses
Blvd.
Dayton, OH 45408

Founded 1985
Total employees 90
Annual sales $10 million
Industries Factory
Automation,
Telecommunications
Growth Openings in past
year 20; percentage
growth 28%
Contact
Ms. Bev Bodine, Director
of Personnel
Tel 513-443-0412
Fax 513-226-0511

**Diversey Water
Technology, Inc.**
7145 Pine St., PO Box
200
Chagrin Falls, OH 44022

Founded 1915
Total employees 400
Annual sales $87 million
Industry Chemicals
Growth Openings in past
year 90; percentage
growth 29%

Contact
Richard Fruit, Vice
President/General
Manager
Tel 216-247-5000

Eaton Corp., Forge Division
1550 Marion Agosta Rd.
Marion, OH 43302

Founded 1953
Total employees 435
Annual sales $64 million
Industry Advanced
Materials
Growth Openings in past
year 13; percentage
growth 3%
Contact
Donald Keeler, Human
Resources Manager
Tel 614-383-2111
Fax 614-382-6202

Environmental Enterprises, Inc.
10163 Cincinnati Dayton
Rd.
Cincinnati, OH 45241

Founded 1976
Total employees 180
Annual sales $16 million
Industry Environmental
Growth Openings in past
year 34; percentage
growth 23%
Contact
Daniel McCabe, President
Tel 513-772-2818
Fax 513-782-8950

Essef Corp.
220 Park Dr.
Chardon, OH 44024

Founded 1955
Total employees 780
Annual sales $99 million
Industry Holding
Companies
Growth Openings in past
year 78; percentage
growth 11%
Contact
John O. Milliken, VP of
Corporate Development
Tel 216-286-2200
Fax 216-286-2206

Forma Scientific, Inc.
Millcreek Rd., PO Box 649
Marietta, OH 45750

Founded 1953
Total employees 450
Annual sales $50 million
Industries Medical,
Subassemblies and
Components, Test and
Measurement
Growth Openings in past
year 22; percentage
growth 5%
Contact
Craig Piersall, Senior VP
of Human Resources
Tel 614-373-4763
Fax 614-373-6770

General Data Co., Inc.
420 Wards Rd.
Loveland, OH 45140

Founded 1980
Total employees 100
Annual sales $16 million
Industries Computer
Hardware, Computer
Software
Growth Openings in past
year 40; percentage
growth 66%
Contact
Peter Wenzel, President
Tel 513-576-0002
Fax 513-576-9857

Globe Products Inc.
5051 Kitridge Rd.
Dayton, OH 45424

Founded 1919
Total employees 156
Annual sales $15 million
Industry Manufacturing
Equipment
Growth Openings in past
year 41; percentage
growth 35%
Contact
W. Patrick Winton,
President
Tel 513-233-0233
Fax 513-233-5290

Green Manufacturing, Inc.
1032 South Maple St., PO
Box 408
Bowling Green, OH 43402

Founded 1952
Total employees 150
Annual sales $7 million

Industry Subassemblies
and Components
Growth Openings in past
year 20; percentage
growth 15%
Contact
Jeff Snook, President
Tel 419-352-9484
Fax 419-354-2087

Gusher Pumps, Inc.
1212 Streng St.
Cincinnati, OH 45223

Founded 1950
Total employees 125
Annual sales $10 million
Industries Factory
Automation,
Subassemblies and
Components
Growth Openings in past
year 25; percentage
growth 25%
Contact
Thomas Ruthman,
President
Tel 513-559-1900
Fax 513-559-0035

Hickok Electrical Instrument Co.
10514 Dupont Ave.
Cleveland, OH 44108

Founded 1908
Total employees 200
Annual sales $16 million
Industries Factory
Automation, Holding
Companies, Test and
Measurement,
Transportation
Growth Openings in past
year 50; percentage
growth 33%
Contact
Robert L. Purcell,
Chairman of the Board
Tel 216-541-8060
Fax 216-761-9879

Hohman Plating and Manufacturing, Inc.
814 Hillrose Ave.
Dayton, OH 45404

Founded 1917
Total employees 125
Annual sales $11 million
Industries Advanced
Materials, Manufacturing
Equipment
Growth Openings in past
year 25; percentage
growth 25%

Contact
Bernard C. Stupp,
President
Tel 513-228-2191
Fax 513-228-5171

**Industrial Powder
Coatings, Inc.**
202 Republic St.
Norwalk, OH 44857

Founded 1976
Total employees 800
Industry Advanced
Materials
Growth Openings in past
year 199; percentage
growth 33%
Contact
Robert M. Warner,
President/CEO
Tel 419-668-4436
Fax 419-663-0218

ITT A-C Pump
1150 Tennesee Ave.
Cincinnati, OH 45229

Founded 1970
Total employees 380
Industries Environmental,
Subassemblies and
Components
Growth Openings in past
year 50; percentage
growth 15%
Contact
Farley Houston, Personnel
Manager
Tel 513-482-2500
Fax 513-482-2569

LaserMike, Inc.
6060 Executive Blvd.
Dayton, OH 45424

Founded 1972
Total employees 150
Annual sales $14 million
Industry Photonics
Growth Openings in past
year 25; percentage
growth 20%
Contact
Paul McNeil, Controller
Tel 513-233-9935
Fax 513-233-7284

Laurel Industries, Inc.
30000 Chagrin Blvd.
Cleveland, OH 44124

Founded 1983
Total employees 50

Industry Advanced
Materials
Growth Openings in past
year 20; percentage
growth 66%
Contact
C. Walder Parke,
President
Tel 216-831-5747
Fax 216-831-8479

LCI International
4650 Lakehurst Ct.
Dublin, OH 43017

Founded 1983
Total employees 650
Annual sales $260 million
Industry
Telecommunications
Growth Openings in past
year 49; percentage
growth 8%
Contact
Tom Wynne, President
Tel 614-798-6000
Fax 614-798-6088

LDA Systems, Inc.
6650 West Snowville Rd.
Brecksville, OH 44141

Founded 1979
Total employees 120
Industry Computer
Software
Growth Openings in past
year 20; percentage
growth 20%
Contact
Steve Sweetnich,
President
Tel 216-838-8200
Fax 216-838-4144

Macola, Inc.
333 East Center St.
Marion, OH 43302

Founded 1971
Total employees 160
Annual sales $18 million
Industry Computer
Software
Growth Openings in past
year 30; percentage
growth 23%
Contact
Bruce Hollinger, President
Tel 614-382-5999
Fax 614-382-0239

Markwith Tool, Inc.
5263 Sebring Warner Rd.
Greenville, OH 45331

Founded 1890
Total employees 18
Annual sales $2.2 million
Industry Factory
Automation
Growth Openings in past
year 16; percentage
growth 800%
Contact
Merlin Miller, President
Tel 513-548-6808

M.K. Morse Co.
PO Box 8677
Canton, OH 44711

Founded 1964
Total employees 250
Industries Advanced
Materials, Factory
Automation
Growth Openings in past
year 50; percentage
growth 25%
Contact
James T. Batchelder,
President
Tel 216-453-8187
Fax 216-453-1111

Motoman, Inc.
805 Liberty Ln.
West Carrollton, OH 45449

Founded 1989
Total employees 125
Industry Factory
Automation
Growth Openings in past
year 25; percentage
growth 25%
Contact
Philip Monnin, CEO/
President
Tel 513-847-3300
Fax 513-847-6277

**Nashbar & Associates,
Inc.**
4111 Simon Rd.
Youngstown, OH 44512

Founded 1974
Total employees 300
Industry Holding
Companies
Growth Openings in past
year 20; percentage
growth 7%

Contact
Arni Nashbar, COB/
  Founder
Tel 216-788-8832
Fax 216-782-2856

**Owens-Corning
Fiberglas Science and
Technology Center**
2790 Columbus Rd., Rte.
  16
Granville, OH 43023

Founded 1969
Total employees 475
Industries Advanced
  Materials, Chemicals
Growth Openings in past
  year 23; percentage
  growth 5%
Contact
Dr. Sharell Mikesell, VP of
  Technology
Tel 614-587-0610
Fax 614-587-7255

**Parker Hannifin Corp.,
Parflex Division**
1300 North Freedom St.
Ravenna, OH 44266

Founded 1973
Total employees 475
Annual sales $46 million
Industries Subassemblies
  and Components, Test
  and Measurement
Growth Openings in past
  year 23; percentage
  growth 5%
Contact
Robert Pizzuro, Human
  Resources Manager
Tel 216-296-2871
Fax 216-296-8433

**Parker Hannifin Corp.,
Tube Fittings Division**
3885 Gateway Blvd.
Columbus, OH 43228

Founded 1938
Total employees 750
Annual sales $73 million
Industries Factory
  Automation,
  Subassemblies and
  Components
Growth Openings in past
  year 50; percentage
  growth 7%
Contact
Wayne Pinkstaff,
  Personnel Manager
Tel 614-279-7070
Fax 614-279-7685

**Pharos Technologies,
Inc.**
8118 Corporate Way, Suite
  200
Mason, OH 45040

Founded 1987
Total employees 65
Annual sales $7.5 million
Industry Computer
  Software
Growth Openings in past
  year 20; percentage
  growth 44%
Contact
Robert Beech, President/
  COB
Tel 513-573-7100
Fax 513-573-7110

Prentke Romich Co.
1022 Heyl Rd.
Wooster, OH 44691

Founded 1966
Total employees 150
Annual sales $14 million
Industry Medical
Growth Openings in past
  year 15; percentage
  growth 11%
Contact
Ms. Sharon Romich,
  President
Tel 216-262-1984
Fax 216-263-4829

Pressco Technology, Inc.
29200 Aurora Rd.
Cleveland, OH 44139

Founded 1966
Total employees 130
Annual sales $15 million
Industry Factory
  Automation
Growth Openings in past
  year 20; percentage
  growth 18%
Contact
Don W. Cochran,
  President
Tel 216-498-2600
Fax 216-498-2615

**R.D. Zande &
Associates, Ltd.**
1237 Dublin Rd.
Columbus, OH 43215

Founded 1968
Total employees 160
Annual sales $12 million
Industry Environmental

Growth Openings in past
  year 42; percentage
  growth 35%
Contact
Richard D. Zande,
  CEO/President
Tel 614-486-4383
Fax 614-486-4387

**Roxane Laboratories,
Inc.**
PO Box 16532
Columbus, OH 43216

Founded 1886
Total employees 550
Annual sales $75 million
Industry Pharmaceuticals
Growth Openings in past
  year 100; percentage
  growth 22%
Contact
Gerald C. Wojta, President
Tel 614-276-4000
Fax 614-274-0974

Schweizer Dipple, Inc.
3380 West 137th St.
Cleveland, OH 44111

Founded 1934
Total employees 80
Annual sales $9 million
Industry Manufacturing
  Equipment
Growth Openings in past
  year 15; percentage
  growth 23%
Contact
Lynn Ulrich, Controller
Tel 216-252-7666
Fax 216-252-4544

**Simpson Industries, Inc.,
Troy Operations**
2001 Corporate Dr.
Troy, OH 45373

Founded 1985
Total employees 170
Annual sales $16 million
Industry Subassemblies
  and Components
Growth Openings in past
  year 20; percentage
  growth 13%
Contact
Roy Parrott, President/
  CEO
Tel 513-339-2677
Fax 513-339-2680

Steris Corp.
9450 Pineneedle Dr.
Mentor, OH 44060

Founded 1985
Total employees 200
Annual sales $12.94
million
Industries Chemicals,
Medical
Growth Openings in past
year 50; percentage
growth 33%
Contact
Bill R. Sanford, President
Tel 216-354-2600
Fax 216-639-4457

**Sterling Software, Inc.,
Network Services
Division**
4600 Lakehurst Ct., PO
Box 7160
Dublin, OH 43017

Founded 1975
Total employees 270
Annual sales $37 million
Industries Computer
Hardware, Computer
Software,
Telecommunications
Growth Openings in past
year 70; percentage
growth 35%
Contact
Richard Needles, Director
of Human Resources
Tel 614-793-7000
Fax 614-793-7092

**Symix Computer
Systems Inc.**
2800 Corporate Exchange
Dr.
Columbus, OH 43231

Founded 1979
Total employees 280
Annual sales $22.4 million
Industry Computer
Software
Growth Openings in past
year 30; percentage
growth 12%
Contact
Doug Foust, Human
Resources Manager
Tel 614-523-7000
Fax 614-895-2504

Synthetic Products Co.
1000 Wayside Rd.
Cleveland, OH 44110

Founded 1917
Total employees 350

Annual sales $100 million
Industry Advanced
Materials
Growth Openings in past
year 79; percentage
growth 29%
Contact
Tom Jennings, President
Tel 216-531-6010
Fax 216-283-5331

**Systems Research
Laboratories, Inc.,
Defense Electronics
Systems Division**
2800 Indian Ripple Rd.
Dayton, OH 45440

Founded 1982
Total employees 800
Annual sales $66 million
Industries Computer
Hardware, Transportation
Growth Openings in past
year 300; percentage
growth 60%
Contact
Robert Lupini, Vice
President
Tel 513-427-7471
Fax 513-427-0205

Systran Corp.
4126 Linden Ave.
Dayton, OH 45432

Founded 1977
Total employees 80
Annual sales $9.2 million
Industries Computer
Software,
Telecommunications
Growth Openings in past
year 20; percentage
growth 33%
Contact
W. Lynn Trainor, President
Tel 513-252-5601
Fax 513-258-2729

Tastemaker
1199 Edison Dr.
Cincinnati, OH 45216

Founded 1931
Total employees 480
Annual sales $100 million
Industry Chemicals
Growth Openings in past
year 80; percentage
growth 20%
Contact
Ms. Terri Bonar-Stewart,
VP of Human Resources
Tel 513-948-8000
Fax 513-948-5607

**Teledyne Industries, Inc.,
Teledyne Princeton**
PO Box 246
Canal Winchester, OH
43110

Founded 1961
Total employees 83
Annual sales $10 million
Industry Factory
Automation
Growth Openings in past
year 29; percentage
growth 53%
Contact
Larry Burton, General
Manager
Tel 614-837-9096
Fax 614-837-2105

**Tuthill Corp., Hansen
Coupling Division**
1000 West Bagley Rd.
Berea, OH 44017

Founded 1915
Total employees 200
Annual sales $20 million
Industry Factory
Automation
Growth Openings in past
year 30; percentage
growth 17%
Contact
John Weston, President
Tel 216-826-1115
Fax 216-826-0115

**Universal Vision
Systems, Inc.**
12241 North Rock Hill Rd.
Alliance, OH 44601

Founded 1991
Total employees 108
Annual sales $8 million
Industry Photonics
Growth Openings in past
year 48; percentage
growth 80%
Contact
Chris Zamagias, General
Manager/Senior Vice
President
Tel 216-823-0600
Fax 216-823-0602

Wahl Refractories, Inc.
South State Rte. 19, PO
Box 530
Fremont, OH 43420

Founded 1919
Total employees 80
Annual sales $10 million

Industry Advanced
Materials
Growth Openings in past
year 30; percentage
growth 60%
Contact
Daniel W. Lease,
President
Tel 419-334-2658
Fax 419-334-9445

**WIL Research
Laboratories, Inc.**
1407 George Rd.
Ashland, OH 44805

Founded 1933
Total employees 130
Annual sales $8 million
Industry Pharmaceuticals
Growth Openings in past
year 25; percentage
growth 23%
Contact
Dr. Joe Holson, President
Tel 419-289-8700
Fax 419-289-3650

Will-Burt Co.
169 South Main St.
Orrville, OH 44667

Founded 1918
Total employees 300
Annual sales $23 million
Industries Holding
Companies,
Manufacturing Equipment
Growth Openings in past
year 50; percentage
growth 20%
Contact
Jack Bednarowski,
Director of Human
Resources
Tel 216-682-7015
Fax 216-684-1190

Oklahoma

AMETECH, Inc.
1813 Southeast 25th St.,
PO Box 36118
Oklahoma City, OK 73129

Founded 1967
Total employees 140
Annual sales $15.92
million
Industry Holding
Companies

Growth Openings in past
year 20; percentage
growth 16%
Contact
Carl B. Anderson, Jr.,
COB/CEO
Tel 405-677-8781
Fax 405-672-1781

Central Plastics Co.
PO Box 3129
Shawnee, OK 74801

Founded 1955
Total employees 265
Annual sales $25 million
Industries Factory
Automation,
Subassemblies and
Components
Growth Openings in past
year 45; percentage
growth 20%
Contact
Ms. Jerri Webb, Personnel
Manager
Tel 405-273-6302
Fax 800-733-5993

**Coburn Optical
Industries, Inc.**
4606 South Garnett Rd.
Tulsa, OK 74146

Founded 1951
Total employees 425
Industries Manufacturing
Equipment, Photonics
Growth Openings in past
year 74; percentage
growth 21%
Contact
Tom Walden, VP of
Human Resources
Tel 918-665-1815
Fax 918-665-1821

**Eagle-Picher Industries,
Inc., Eagle-Picher
Research Laboratory**
200 9th Ave. Northeast,
PO Box 1090
Miami, OK 74354

Founded 1957
Total employees 200
Annual sales $43 million
Industries Chemicals,
Environmental,
Manufacturing
Equipment,
Subassemblies and
Components
Growth Openings in past
year 35; percentage
growth 21%

Contact
Carl Holmes, Personnel
Manager
Tel 918-542-1801
Fax 918-542-3223

**Educational
Development Corp.**
PO Box 470663
Tulsa, OK 74147

Founded 1965
Total employees 55
Annual sales $6.3 million
Industry Computer
Software
Growth Openings in past
year 17; percentage
growth 44%
Contact
Curtis Fossett, Controller
Tel 918-622-4522
Fax 918-663-4509

Erlanger Tubular Corp.
5610 Bird Creek Ave.
Catoosa, OK 74015

Founded 1986
Total employees 210
Annual sales $24 million
Industries Energy,
Subassemblies and
Components
Growth Openings in past
year 100; percentage
growth 90%
Contact
Rick Carter, Vice
President/General
Manager
Tel 918-266-3970
Fax 918-266-6116

Governair
4841 North Sewell
Oklahoma City, OK 73118

Founded 1937
Total employees 180
Annual sales $24 million
Industry Energy
Growth Openings in past
year 15; percentage
growth 9%
Contact
Ms. Lee Young, Director of
Personnel
Tel 405-525-6546
Fax 405-528-4724

Hathaway Corp., Motion Control Division
10827 East Marshall
Tulsa, OK 74116

Founded 1971
Total employees 55
Industry Subassemblies and Components
Growth Openings in past year 22; percentage growth 66%
Contact
David Richards, President
Tel 918-438-7800
Fax 918-438-7629

Innovative Computing Corp.
4300 Highline Blvd.
Oklahoma City, OK 73108

Founded 1969
Total employees 225
Industry Computer Software
Growth Openings in past year 25; percentage growth 12%
Contact
Bill Trousdale, Vice President/General Manager
Tel 405-949-9070
Fax 405-947-7921

KF Industries, Inc.
1500 Southeast 89th St., PO Box 95249
Oklahoma City, OK 73149

Founded 1874
Total employees 320
Annual sales $31 million
Industries Energy, Subassemblies and Components
Growth Openings in past year 37; percentage growth 13%
Contact
James G. Smith, Human Resources Manager
Tel 405-631-1533
Fax 405-631-5034

LB&M Associates, Inc.
211 Southwest A Ave.
Lawton, OK 73501

Founded 1982
Total employees 220
Industries Computer Hardware, Defense, Environmental, Transportation

Growth Openings in past year 50; percentage growth 29%
Contact
Rudy Alverrado, Chief Executive Officer
Tel 405-355-1471
Fax 405-357-9360

Nordam Group, Manufacturing Division
510 South Lansing
Tulsa, OK 74120

Founded 1969
Total employees 175
Annual sales $20 million
Industry Transportation
Growth Openings in past year 25; percentage growth 16%
Contact
Dale Kunze, Senior Vice President/General Manager
Tel 918-587-4105
Fax 918-583-2604

Nordam Group, Transparency Division
822 East 6th St.
Tulsa, OK 74120

Founded 1969
Total employees 115
Industries Manufacturing Equipment, Transportation
Growth Openings in past year 35; percentage growth 43%
Contact
Robert Hart, General Manager
Tel 918-587-4105
Fax 918-560-5669

Oregon

Advanced Power Technology, Inc.
405 Southwest Columbia St.
Bend, OR 97702

Founded 1984
Total employees 150
Annual sales $15 million
Industry Subassemblies and Components

Growth Openings in past year 35; percentage growth 30%
Contact
Patrick Sireta, President/CEO
Tel 503-382-8028
Fax 503-388-0364

Analogy, Inc.
9205 Southwest Gemini Dr., PO Box 1669
Beaverton, OR 97005

Founded 1985
Total employees 125
Annual sales $14 million
Industry Computer Software
Growth Openings in past year 35; percentage growth 38%
Contact
Terrence Rixford, VP of Finance and Administration
Tel 503-626-9700
Fax 503-643-3361

Cedarapids, Inc., El-Jay Division
86470 Franklin Blvd., PO Box 607
Eugene, OR 97440

Founded 1947
Total employees 230
Annual sales $25 million
Industry Manufacturing Equipment
Growth Openings in past year 39; percentage growth 20%
Contact
Ms. Joan Hampton, Personnel Manager
Tel 503-726-6541
Fax 503-741-0687

Claremont Technology Group
1600 Northwest Compton Dr., Suite 210
Beaverton, OR 97006

Founded 1989
Total employees 150
Annual sales $17 million
Industries Computer Hardware, Computer Software
Growth Openings in past year 30; percentage growth 25%

Contact
Steven L. Darrow, COB/
  President/CEO
Tel 503-690-4000
Fax 503-690-4005

CSMI, Inc.
PO Box 10087
Portland, OR 97210

Founded 1963
Total employees 140
Annual sales $17 million
Industries Factory
  Automation,
  Manufacturing Equipment
Growth Openings in past
  year 85; percentage
  growth 154%
Contact
Bill Griffiths, President
Tel 503-224-7128
Fax 503-224-4029

DecTron Products
2601 Crestview Dr.
Newberg, OR 97132

Founded 1983
Total employees 600
Annual sales $100 million
Industry Medical
Growth Openings in past
  year 50; percentage
  growth 9%
Contact
G.K. Austin, II, President
Tel 503-538-7450
Fax 503-538-8021

ECS Composites
3560 Rogue River Hwy.,
  PO Box 188
Grants Pass, OR 97526

Founded 1955
Total employees 125
Annual sales $7.5 million
Industries Advanced
  Materials, Factory
  Automation
Growth Openings in past
  year 19; percentage
  growth 17%
Contact
Jerry Slover, Manager of
  Personnel
Tel 503-476-8871
Fax 503-474-2479

Epitope, Inc.
8505 Southwest Creekside
  Pl.
Beaverton, OR 97005

Founded 1979
Total employees 140
Annual sales $3 million
Industries Biotechnology,
  Holding Companies,
  Medical
Growth Openings in past
  year 20; percentage
  growth 16%
Contact
Dr. Adolph J. Ferro, Ph.D.,
  President/CEO
Tel 503-641-6115
Fax 503-643-2781

Fiserv EFT
4550 Southwest Macadam
  Ave.
Portland, OR 97201

Founded 1956
Total employees 132
Annual sales $21 million
Industry Computer
  Hardware
Growth Openings in past
  year 72; percentage
  growth 120%
Contact
Ms. Dinah Ladizinski,
  Chief Operating Officer
Tel 503-224-9110
Fax 503-274-6700

Flight Dynamics
16600 Southwest 72nd St.
Portland, OR 97224

Founded 1979
Total employees 105
Industries Defense, Test
  and Measurement,
  Transportation
Growth Openings in past
  year 21; percentage
  growth 25%
Contact
John P. Desmond,
  President/CEO
Tel 503-684-5384
Fax 503-684-0169

INFOCUS SYSTEMS, Inc.
7770 South West Mohawk
  St.
Tualatin, OR 97062

Founded 1986
Total employees 185
Annual sales $62.5 million

Industry
  Telecommunications
Growth Openings in past
  year 45; percentage
  growth 32%
Contact
Steven R. Hix, COB/CEO
Tel 503-692-4968
Fax 503-692-4476

**Lattice Semiconductor
Corp.**
5555 Northeast Moore Ct.
Hillsboro, OR 97124

Founded 1983
Total employees 365
Annual sales $103 million
Industry Subassemblies
  and Components
Growth Openings in past
  year 165; percentage
  growth 82%
Contact
Cyrus Tsui, COB/CEO/
  President
Tel 503-681-0118
Fax 503-681-0347

Leupold & Stevens, Inc.
14400 Northwest Pkwy.
Beaverton, OR 97006

Founded 1907
Total employees 470
Annual sales $52 million
Industries Defense,
  Factory Automation,
  Photonics, Test and
  Measurement
Growth Openings in past
  year 31; percentage
  growth 7%
Contact
James Giles, VP of
  Human Resources
Tel 503-646-9171
Fax 503-526-1471

Logic Modeling Corp.
PO Box 310
Beaverton, OR 97075

Founded 1984
Total employees 250
Annual sales $35 million
Industry Computer
  Software
Growth Openings in past
  year 50; percentage
  growth 25%
Contact
Jim Higgs, VP of Human
  Resources
Tel 503-690-6900
Fax 503-690-6906

Now Software, Inc.
921 Southwest
  Washington St., Suite
  500
Portland, OR 97205

Founded 1990
Total employees 60
Industry Computer
  Software
Growth Openings in past
  year 30; percentage
  growth 100%
Contact
Stephen Saltzman,
  President
Tel 503-274-2800
Fax 503-274-0670

Photon Kinetics, Inc.
9405 Southwest Gemini
  Dr.
Beaverton, OR 97005

Founded 1979
Total employees 125
Annual sales $15 million
Industries Computer
  Software, Factory
  Automation, Test and
  Measurement
Growth Openings in past
  year 16; percentage
  growth 14%
Contact
Gene White, President
Tel 503-644-1960
Fax 503-526-4700

Point Control Co.
PO Box 2709
Eugene, OR 97402

Founded 1983
Total employees 98
Annual sales $11 million
Industry Computer
  Software
Growth Openings in past
  year 18; percentage
  growth 22%
Contact
Jerry Blakely, President
Tel 503-344-4470
Fax 503-342-8277

**Poorman-Douglas
Medical Systems**
9700 Southwest Nimbus
  Ave.
Beaverton, OR 97005

Founded 1968
Total employees 80
Annual sales $9.2 million

Industry Computer
  Software
Growth Openings in past
  year 15; percentage
  growth 23%
Contact
John Douglas, President
Tel 503-526-7700
Fax 503-526-7702

**Praegitzer Industries,
Inc.**
1270 Monmouth Cutoff
Dallas, OR 97338

Founded 1981
Total employees 800
Annual sales $78 million
Industry Subassemblies
  and Components
Growth Openings in past
  year 199; percentage
  growth 33%
Contact
Robert L. Praegitzer,
  President
Tel 503-623-9273
Fax 503-623-2303

Precision Interconnect
16640 Southwest 72nd
  Ave.
Portland, OR 97224

Founded 1972
Total employees 500
Annual sales $25 million
Industries Subassemblies
  and Components,
  Telecommunications
Growth Openings in past
  year 38; percentage
  growth 8%
Contact
Ms. Holly Borden,
  Personnel Manager
Tel 503-620-9400
Fax 503-620-7131

Protocol Systems, Inc.
8500 Southwest Creekside
  Pl.
Beaverton, OR 97005

Founded 1986
Total employees 240
Annual sales $29 million
Industry Medical
Growth Openings in past
  year 28; percentage
  growth 13%
Contact
Allen Oyler, Director of
  Human Resources
Tel 503-526-8500
Fax 503-526-4200

Siltec Corp.
PO Box 7748
Salem, OR 97303

Founded 1969
Total employees 625
Annual sales $61 million
Industry Subassemblies
  and Components
Growth Openings in past
  year 25; percentage
  growth 4%
Contact
Ms. Judy Nix, Director of
  Human Resources
Tel 503-371-0041

**Summit Information
Systems Corp.**
850 Southwest 35th St.,
  PO Box 3003
Corvallis, OR 97339

Founded 1980
Total employees 170
Annual sales $19 million
Industry Computer
  Software
Growth Openings in past
  year 30; percentage
  growth 21%
Contact
Ms. Susan Dunham,
  Personnel Manager
Tel 503-758-5888
Fax 503-758-8438

Supra Corp.
7101 Supra Dr. Southwest
Albany, OR 97321

Founded 1985
Total employees 120
Annual sales $30 million
Industries Computer
  Hardware,
  Telecommunications
Growth Openings in past
  year 30; percentage
  growth 33%
Contact
John Wiley, President
Tel 503-967-2400
Fax 503-967-2401

**Timberline Software
Corp.**
PO Box 728
Beaverton, OR 97075

Founded 1971
Total employees 224
Annual sales $14.9 million
Industry Computer
  Software

Growth Openings in past year 31; percentage growth 16%
Contact
John Gorman, President/CEO
Tel 503-626-6775
Fax 503-641-7498

Pennsylvania

Accu-Form, Inc.
5800 Bundy Dr.
Erie, PA 16509

Founded 1974
Total employees 90
Annual sales $9.8 million
Industry Manufacturing Equipment
Growth Openings in past year 30; percentage growth 50%
Contact
Richard Brooks, President
Tel 814-825-5800
Fax 814-825-5496

Accu-Sort Systems, Inc.
511 School House Rd.
Telford, PA 18969

Founded 1971
Total employees 360
Annual sales $35 million
Industry Computer Hardware
Growth Openings in past year 60; percentage growth 20%
Contact
Albert Wurz, President
Tel 215-723-0981
Fax 215-723-1515

Adhesives Research, Inc.
West of I-83 Rte. 216
Glen Rock, PA 17327

Founded 1960
Total employees 214
Annual sales $50 million
Industry Advanced Materials
Growth Openings in past year 64; percentage growth 42%
Contact
Erwin W. Huber, COB/President/Owner
Tel 717-235-7979
Fax 717-235-8320

AEG Automation Systems Corp.
PO Box 490
Pittsburgh, PA 15230

Founded 1982
Total employees 390
Industry Factory Automation
Growth Openings in past year 90; percentage growth 30%
Contact
David Armstrong, President/CEO
Tel 412-747-7100
Fax 412-747-7180

Allegheny Powder Metallurgy, Inc.
Rte. 950 South, PO Box 376
Falls Creek, PA 15840

Founded 1981
Total employees 50
Annual sales $6 million
Industries Factory Automation, Subassemblies and Components
Growth Openings in past year 18; percentage growth 56%
Contact
F.G. Grieneisen, President
Tel 814-371-0184
Fax 814-371-4640

American Auto-Matrix, Inc.
One Technology Dr.
Export, PA 15632

Founded 1979
Total employees 65
Annual sales $7.7 million
Industries Computer Hardware, Energy, Factory Automation, Test and Measurement
Growth Openings in past year 15; percentage growth 30%
Contact
Peter Hefferen, President
Tel 412-733-2000
Fax 412-327-6124

Amiable Technologies, Inc.
Scott Plaza Two, Suite 625
Philadelphia, PA 19113

Founded 1988
Total employees 45

Annual sales $4 million
Industry Computer Software
Growth Openings in past year 20; percentage growth 80%
Contact
Jim Chang, President
Tel 610-521-6300
Fax 610-521-0111

Applied Concepts, Inc.
400 Commerce Blvd.
Lawrence, PA 15055

Founded 1985
Total employees 25
Industry Factory Automation
Growth Openings in past year 15; percentage growth 150%
Contact
Dr. H.K. Wrigley, President
Tel 412-745-5028
Fax 412-745-9408

Aquatech International Corp.
1 Four Coins Dr., PO Box 150
Canonsburg, PA 15317

Founded 1981
Total employees 100
Industry Environmental
Growth Openings in past year 28; percentage growth 38%
Contact
Venkee Sharma, President
Tel 412-746-5300
Fax 412-746-5359

Astea International
100 High Point Dr.
Chalfont, PA 18914

Founded 1979
Total employees 200
Annual sales $23 million
Industry Computer Software
Growth Openings in past year 40; percentage growth 25%
Contact
Zach Bergreen, President/CEO
Tel 215-822-8888
Fax 215-997-9060

Axel Johnson Metals, Inc.
215 Welsh Pool Rd.
Exton, PA 19341

Founded 1984
Total employees 121
Industries Advanced
Materials, Manufacturing
Equipment
Growth Openings in past
year 41; percentage
growth 51%
Contact
Ms. Betty J. Dare, Director
of Human Resources
Tel 610-363-0330
Fax 610-524-1567

Aydin Corp., Vector Division
47 Friends Ln., PO Box 328
Newtown, PA 18940

Founded 1969
Total employees 320
Annual sales $44 million
Industries Computer
Hardware,
Telecommunications
Growth Openings in past
year 19; percentage
growth 6%
Contact
Denis Gimbel, Manager of
Administration
Tel 215-968-4271
Fax 215-968-3214

Bacharach, Inc.
625 Alpha Dr.
Pittsburgh, PA 15238

Founded 1909
Total employees 323
Annual sales $38 million
Industries Factory
Automation, Holding
Companies, Test and
Measurement
Growth Openings in past
year 16; percentage
growth 5%
Contact
Mrs. Linda May, Human
Resources Coordinator
Tel 412-963-2000
Fax 412-963-2091

Baker Environmental, Inc.
420 Rouser Rd.
Coraopolis, PA 15108

Founded 1981
Total employees 265

Annual sales $18 million
Industry Environmental
Growth Openings in past
year 85; percentage
growth 47%
Contact
Andrew P. Pajak,
President
Tel 412-269-6000
Fax 412-269-6097

Bentley Systems, Inc.
690 Pennsylvania Dr.
Exton, PA 19341

Founded 1984
Total employees 125
Industry Computer
Software
Growth Openings in past
year 60; percentage
growth 92%
Contact
Keith Bentley, President
Tel 610-458-5000
Fax 610-458-1060

Berk-Tek, Inc.
132 White Oak Rd.
New Holland, PA 17557

Founded 1961
Total employees 400
Annual sales $77.5 million
Industries Photonics,
Subassemblies and
Components
Growth Openings in past
year 50; percentage
growth 14%
Contact
Dennis Baughman, Human
Relations Director
Tel 717-354-6200
Fax 717-354-7944

Biocontrol Technology, Inc.
300 Indian Springs Rd.
Indiana, PA 15701

Founded 1972
Total employees 45
Industry Medical
Growth Openings in past
year 33; percentage
growth 275%
Contact
David L. Purdy, President
Tel 412-349-1811
Fax 412-349-8610

Biodecision, Inc.
5900 Penn Ave.
Pittsburgh, PA 15206

Founded 1971
Total employees 130
Annual sales $6 million
Industry Holding
Companies
Growth Openings in past
year 30; percentage
growth 30%
Contact
Edward McGolugh,
Director of Human
Resources
Tel 412-363-3300
Fax 412-362-5783

Cabot Medical Corp.
2021 Cabot Blvd.
Langhorne, PA 19047

Founded 1983
Total employees 350
Annual sales $69.56
million
Industries Holding
Companies, Medical
Growth Openings in past
year 100; percentage
growth 40%
Contact
Warren G. Wood, COB/
CEO
Tel 215-752-8300
Fax 215-750-0161

Caldon, Inc.
2857 Banksville Rd.
Pittsburgh, PA 15216

Founded 1987
Total employees 25
Annual sales $2 million
Industry Test and
Measurement
Growth Openings in past
year 16; percentage
growth 177%
Contact
Calvin R. Hastings,
President/CEO
Tel 412-341-9920
Fax 412-341-9951

Cegelec, Inc.
490 Lapp Rd.
Malvern, PA 19355

Founded 1980
Total employees 350
Annual sales $70 million
Industries Factory
Automation, Test and
Measurement

Growth Openings in past year 340; percentage growth 3400%
Contact
Jack Ladden, President/ CEO
Tel 610-651-0707
Fax 610-651-0717

Cephalon, Inc.
145 Brandywine Pkwy.
West Chester, PA 19380

Founded 1987
Total employees 200
Annual sales $16.9 million
Industry Pharmaceuticals
Growth Openings in past year 100; percentage growth 100%
Contact
Dr. Frank Baldino, Ph.D., President
Tel 610-344-0200
Fax 610-344-0065

CFM Technologies, Inc.
1380 Enterprise Dr.
West Chester, PA 19380

Founded 1984
Total employees 120
Annual sales $13 million
Industries Energy, Manufacturing Equipment
Growth Openings in past year 60; percentage growth 100%
Contact
Roger Carolin, President
Tel 610-696-8300
Fax 610-696-8309

Commonwealth Communication, Inc.
256 North Sherman St.
Wilkes-Barre, PA 18702

Founded 1979
Total employees 245
Annual sales $18.6 million
Industry Telecommunications
Growth Openings in past year 115; percentage growth 88%
Contact
John C. Balan, Executive Vice President
Tel 717-820-5000
Fax 717-820-5135

Component Technology Corp.
3409 West 14th St.
Erie, PA 16505

Founded 1982
Total employees 220
Annual sales $30 million
Industries Holding Companies, Subassemblies and Components
Growth Openings in past year 50; percentage growth 29%
Contact
Ms. Barbara Przestelski, Personnel Manager
Tel 814-838-1971
Fax 814-833-8961

DXI, Inc.
200 High Tower Blvd., Suite 202
Pittsburgh, PA 15205

Founded 1987
Total employees 57
Industry Computer Software
Growth Openings in past year 20; percentage growth 54%
Contact
Robert Ryan, President
Tel 412-788-2466
Fax 412-788-4230

Echo Data Services, Inc.
15 East Uwchlan Ave., Marsh Creek Corporate Ctr.
Exton, PA 19341

Founded 1983
Total employees 50
Industry Telecommunications
Growth Openings in past year 20; percentage growth 66%
Contact
Stephen R. Roberts, President
Tel 610-363-2400
Fax 610-363-2421

Ecogen, Inc.
2005 Cabot Blvd. West
Langhorne, PA 19047

Founded 1983
Total employees 150
Annual sales $4.3 million
Industry Biotechnology

Growth Openings in past year 70; percentage growth 87%
Contact
James P. Reilly, Jr., President/CEO
Tel 215-757-1590
Fax 215-757-2956

Efector, Inc.
805 Springdale Dr.
Exton, PA 19341

Founded 1985
Total employees 70
Annual sales $6.8 million
Industries Subassemblies and Components, Test and Measurement
Growth Openings in past year 20; percentage growth 40%
Contact
Vincent McMahon, President
Tel 610-524-2000
Fax 610-524-2010

Electronic Technology Systems, Inc.
12th St., Schreiber Industrial Park
New Kensington, PA 15068

Founded 1984
Total employees 87
Annual sales $8.1 million
Industries Subassemblies and Components, Test and Measurement
Growth Openings in past year 17; percentage growth 24%
Contact
Ron Walko, President
Tel 412-335-1300
Fax 412-335-2450

Enertec, Inc.
811 West 5th St.
Lansdale, PA 19446

Founded 1977
Total employees 50
Annual sales $6.2 million
Industries Computer Hardware, Computer Software, Environmental
Growth Openings in past year 15; percentage growth 42%
Contact
R.C. Whiffen, President
Tel 215-362-0966
Fax 215-362-2404

Extrude Hone Corp.
8075 Pennsylvania Ave.,
PO Box 527
Irwin, PA 15642

Founded 1966
Total employees 150
Annual sales $50 million
Industries Factory
Automation, Holding
Companies,
Manufacturing Equipment
Growth Openings in past
year 30; percentage
growth 25%
Contact
C. Gary Dinsel, VP of
Operations
Tel 412-863-5900
Fax 412-863-8759

FASTECH, Inc.
450 Parkway Dr.
Broomall, PA 19008

Founded 1982
Total employees 95
Annual sales $8 million
Industry Computer
Software
Growth Openings in past
year 40; percentage
growth 72%
Contact
Richard Hirsh, President
Tel 610-565-3405
Fax 610-544-3695

Flight Systems, Inc.
Hempt Rd., PO Box 25
Mechanicsburg, PA 17055

Founded 1968
Total employees 100
Annual sales $8 million
Industries Subassemblies
and Components, Test
and Measurement
Growth Openings in past
year 20; percentage
growth 25%
Contact
Robert Shaffner, President
Tel 717-697-0333
Fax 717-697-5350

**Fluid Energy Processing
and Equipment Co.**
PO Box 200
Hatfield, PA 19440

Founded 1955
Total employees 100
Annual sales $15 million
Industries Chemicals,
Holding Companies

Growth Openings in past
year 35; percentage
growth 53%
Contact
Peter Zielinski, President
Tel 215-368-2510
Fax 215-368-6235

**Foerster Instruments,
Inc.**
140 Industry Dr.
Pittsburgh, PA 15275

Founded 1978
Total employees 50
Annual sales $10 million
Industries Factory
Automation,
Manufacturing Equipment
Growth Openings in past
year 17; percentage
growth 51%
Contact
William Kitson, General
Manager
Tel 412-788-8976
Fax 412-788-8984

Fore Systems, Inc.
174 Thorn Hill Rd.
Warrendale, PA 15086

Founded 1990
Total employees 100
Annual sales $14 million
Industry
Telecommunications
Growth Openings in past
year 70; percentage
growth 233%
Contact
Eric Cooper, President
Tel 412-772-6600
Fax 412-772-6500

GAI Consultants, Inc.
570 Beatty Rd.
Monroeville, PA 15146

Founded 1958
Total employees 447
Annual sales $20 million
Industries Energy,
Environmental
Growth Openings in past
year 14; percentage
growth 3%
Contact
Anthony M. DiGioia, Jr.,
President
Tel 412-856-6400
Fax 412-856-4970

Gentex Corp.
PO Box 315
Carbondale, PA 18407

Founded 1932
Total employees 850
Annual sales $70 million
Industries Advanced
Materials, Holding
Companies, Photonics,
Transportation
Growth Openings in past
year 49; percentage
growth 6%
Contact
P. Satia, Personnel
Manager
Tel 717-282-3550
Fax 717-282-8555

GMIS Inc.
5 Country View Rd.
Malvern, PA 19355

Founded 1983
Total employees 170
Annual sales $10.5 million
Industry Computer
Software
Growth Openings in past
year 50; percentage
growth 41%
Contact
Thomas R. Owens,
President/CEO
Tel 610-296-3838
Fax 610-640-9876

**Greenwich
Pharmaceuticals, Inc.**
501 Office Center Dr.
Fort Washington, PA
19034

Founded 1979
Total employees 72
Industry Biotechnology
Growth Openings in past
year 30; percentage
growth 71%
Contact
Edwin R. Thompson,
President
Tel 215-540-9500
Fax 215-540-9696

GSI
1380 Old Freeport Rd.
Pittsburgh, PA 15238

Founded 1972
Total employees 200
Annual sales $22 million
Industry Computer
Software

Growth Openings in past year 25; percentage growth 14%
Contact
Ms. Pati Henderson, Personnel Director
Tel 412-963-6770
Fax 412-963-6779

Halmar Robicon Group
100 Sagamore Hill Rd.
Pittsburgh, PA 15239

Founded 1964
Total employees 300
Annual sales $40 million
Industries Energy, Test and Measurement
Growth Openings in past year 33; percentage growth 12%
Contact
James G. Peterson, VP of Human Resources
Tel 412-327-7000
Fax 412-733-8093

Hercon Laboratories Corp.
PO Box 786
York, PA 17405

Founded 1985
Total employees 70
Annual sales $7.7 million
Industry Medical
Growth Openings in past year 15; percentage growth 27%
Contact
Robert D. Speiser, President
Tel 717-764-1191
Fax 717-764-5395

Hull Corporation
3535 Davisville Rd.
Hatboro, PA 19040

Founded 1952
Total employees 150
Annual sales $10 million
Industries Energy, Factory Automation, Subassemblies and Components
Growth Openings in past year 35; percentage growth 30%
Contact
Bernard Kashmer, Executive Vice President
Tel 215-672-7800
Fax 215-672-7807

Integrated Circuit Systems, Inc.
2435 Blvd. of the Generals
Valley Forge, PA 19482

Founded 1976
Total employees 245
Annual sales $74.91 million
Industries Holding Companies, Subassemblies and Components
Growth Openings in past year 60; percentage growth 32%
Contact
Edward Arnold, President
Tel 610-630-5300
Fax 610-630-5399

InterDigital Communications Corp.
2200 Renaissance Blvd., Suite 105
King of Prussia, PA 19406

Founded 1972
Total employees 228
Annual sales $43 million
Industries Manufacturing Equipment, Telecommunications
Growth Openings in past year 50; percentage growth 28%
Contact
Ms. Christine Taunton, Manager of Human Resources
Tel 610-278-7800
Fax 610-278-6801

International Communication Materials, Inc.
Rte. 119 South, PO Box 716
Connellsville, PA 15425

Founded 1978
Total employees 150
Annual sales $35 million
Industry Computer Hardware
Growth Openings in past year 23; percentage growth 18%
Contact
Ms. Paula Price, Controller
Tel 412-628-1014
Fax 412-628-1214

International Computaprint Corp.
475 Virginia Dr.
Fort Washington, PA 19034

Founded 1962
Total employees 875
Annual sales $45 million
Industry Computer Hardware
Growth Openings in past year 18; percentage growth 2%
Contact
Darryl Fisher, Chief Executive Officer
Tel 215-641-6000
Fax 215-641-6227

Invotech Manufacturing Co.
17 University Dr.
Lemont Furnace, PA 15456

Founded 1988
Total employees 40
Annual sales $4 million
Industry Manufacturing Equipment
Growth Openings in past year 25; percentage growth 166%
Contact
Alan Kirk, President
Tel 412-437-8020
Fax 412-437-8048

Iroquois Tool Systems, Inc.
101 Loomis St.
North East, PA 16428

Founded 1975
Total employees 90
Industry Manufacturing Equipment
Growth Openings in past year 20; percentage growth 28%
Contact
Martin Haas, President
Tel 814-725-8726
Fax 814-725-5805

ISS, Comptek
1610 Linden Ave.
Erie, PA 16505

Founded 1985
Total employees 75
Annual sales $6 million
Industry Subassemblies and Components

Growth Openings in past year 19; percentage growth 33%
Contact
Mark Hamel, Chief Operating Officer
Tel 814-838-8660
Fax 814-833-3219

ITS Corporation
375 Valley Brook Rd.
Mc Murray, PA 15317

Founded 1982
Total employees 150
Industry Telecommunications
Growth Openings in past year 39; percentage growth 35%
Contact
Edward Tucker, Manager of Human Resources/ Facilities Ma
Tel 412-941-1500
Fax 412-941-4603

JWS Delavau Co., Inc.
2140 Germantown Ave.
Philadelphia, PA 19122

Founded 1847
Total employees 160
Annual sales $13 million
Industry Pharmaceuticals
Growth Openings in past year 60; percentage growth 60%
Contact
Richard Leff, President
Tel 215-235-1100
Fax 215-235-2202

Kensey Nash Corporation
55 East Uwchlan Ave., Suite 204
Exton, PA 19341

Founded 1984
Total employees 32
Industry Medical
Growth Openings in past year 15; percentage growth 88%
Contact
David Anderson, President
Tel 610-524-0188
Fax 610-524-0265

Kipin Industries, Inc.
513 Green Garden Rd.
Aliquippa, PA 15001

Founded 1979
Total employees 100

Annual sales $3 million
Industry Environmental
Growth Openings in past year 40; percentage growth 66%
Contact
Peter Kipin, President
Tel 412-495-6200
Fax 412-495-2219

Koppel Steel Corp.
PO Box 750
Beaver Falls, PA 15010

Founded 1988
Total employees 571
Industries Advanced Materials, Subassemblies and Components
Growth Openings in past year 129; percentage growth 29%
Contact
James Barger, Manager of Human Resources
Tel 412-843-7100
Fax 412-847-4071

Lancaster Laboratories, Inc.
2425 New Holland Pike
Lancaster, PA 17601

Founded 1961
Total employees 490
Annual sales $26 million
Industries Biotechnology, Chemicals, Environmental, Pharmaceuticals
Growth Openings in past year 28; percentage growth 6%
Contact
Dr. Earl H. Hess, Ph.D., President/CEO
Tel 717-656-2301
Fax 717-656-2681

Laser Drive, Inc.
5465 William Flynn Hwy.
Gibsonia, PA 15044

Founded 1976
Total employees 65
Annual sales $6.3 million
Industries Photonics, Subassemblies and Components
Growth Openings in past year 15; percentage growth 30%
Contact
Tony Pavlik, President
Tel 412-443-7688
Fax 412-444-6430

Latronics Corp.
1001 Lloyd Ave.
Latrobe, PA 15650

Founded 1958
Total employees 175
Industries Advanced Materials, Subassemblies and Components
Growth Openings in past year 45; percentage growth 34%
Contact
Joel Smolka, General Manager
Tel 412-539-1626
Fax 412-539-2540

Lemmon Co.
650 Cathill Rd.
Sellersville, PA 18960

Founded 1945
Total employees 437
Annual sales $185 million
Industry Pharmaceuticals
Growth Openings in past year 37; percentage growth 9%
Contact
William Fletcher, President
Tel 215-256-8400
Fax 215-256-7855

Littlewood, Shain & Co.
123 Summit Dr.
Exton, PA 19341

Founded 1977
Total employees 70
Annual sales $8.1 million
Industry Computer Software
Growth Openings in past year 15; percentage growth 27%
Contact
John Shain, President
Tel 610-524-0400
Fax 610-524-1032

LNP Engineering Plastics, Inc.
475 Creamery Way
Exton, PA 19341

Founded 1945
Total employees 626
Industry Advanced Materials
Growth Openings in past year 25; percentage growth 4%

Contact
Robert Kirkpatrick,
Manager of Employee
Relations
Tel 610-363-4500
Fax 610-363-4749

**Mastech Systems
Corporation**
2090 Greentree Rd.
Pittsburgh, PA 15220

Founded 1986
Total employees 750
Industry Computer
Software
Growth Openings in past
year 349; percentage
growth 87%
Contact
Sunil Wadhwani, Director
Tel 412-279-6400
Fax 412-279-6870

Medrad, Inc.
271 Kappa Dr.
Pittsburgh, PA 15238

Founded 1964
Total employees 752
Annual sales $67.4 million
Industry Medical
Growth Openings in past
year 121; percentage
growth 19%
Contact
Martin J. Resick, Director
of Human Resources
Tel 412-967-9700
Fax 412-963-8536

**Michael Baker Jr., Inc.,
Transportation Division**
420 Rouser Rd.
Coraopolis, PA 15108

Founded 1946
Total employees 382
Annual sales $35 million
Industries Energy,
Transportation
Growth Openings in past
year 41; percentage
growth 12%
Contact
John Hayward, Senior
Vice President/General
Manager
Tel 412-269-6000

Microbac Labs, Inc.
4721 McKnight Rd.
Pittsburgh, PA 15237

Founded 1890
Total employees 200

Annual sales $21 million
Industries Environmental,
Holding Companies,
Medical
Growth Openings in past
year 50; percentage
growth 33%
Contact
Warne Boyce, CEO/COB
Tel 412-369-9900
Fax 412-931-0473

**Molded Fiber Glass
Companies, Union City
Division**
55 Fourth Ave.
Union City, PA 16438

Founded 1948
Total employees 300
Annual sales $12 million
Industries Advanced
Materials, Environmental,
Manufacturing
Equipment,
Transportation
Growth Openings in past
year 100; percentage
growth 50%
Contact
Gerald Bender, President
Tel 814-438-3841
Fax 814-438-2284

National Draeger, Inc.
101 Technology Dr., PO
Box 120
Pittsburgh, PA 15230

Founded 1977
Total employees 250
Industries Medical, Test
and Measurement
Growth Openings in past
year 50; percentage
growth 25%
Contact
Henning Oetjen, President
Tel 412-787-8383
Fax 412-787-2207

**Neose Pharmaceuticals,
Inc.**
102 Witmere Rd.
Horsham, PA 19044

Founded 1990
Total employees 35
Annual sales $4.8 million
Industries Chemicals,
Pharmaceuticals
Growth Openings in past
year 20; percentage
growth 133%

Contact
Dennis H. Langer, MD, JD,
President/CEO
Tel 215-441-5890
Fax 215-441-5896

Omnicomp, Inc.
220 Regent Ct., Suite E
State College, PA 16801

Founded 1981
Total employees 26
Annual sales $1 million
Industry Computer
Software
Growth Openings in past
year 15; percentage
growth 136%
Contact
Ms. Jennine Vahoviak,
Senior Account Manager
Tel 814-238-4181
Fax 814-238-4673

**Oppenheimer Precision
Products**
173 Centennial Plaza
Horsham, PA 19044

Founded 1971
Total employees 190
Annual sales $19 million
Industry Transportation
Growth Openings in past
year 15; percentage
growth 8%
Contact
Ms. Barbara Carver,
Personnel Manager
Tel 215-674-9100
Fax 215-674-0423

**Pakco Industrial
Ceramics, Inc.**
55 Hillview Ave.
Latrobe, PA 15650

Founded 1980
Total employees 100
Annual sales $15 million
Industry Advanced
Materials
Growth Openings in past
year 25; percentage
growth 33%
Contact
Ms. Marylou Hamachu,
Personnel Manager
Tel 412-539-6000
Fax 412-539-6070

Parker Hannifin Corp., Daedal Division
Sandy Hill Rd., PO Box 500
Harrison City, PA 15636

Founded 1969
Total employees 135
Annual sales $14 million
Industry Photonics
Growth Openings in past year 35; percentage growth 35%
Contact
Robert Rebich, General Manager
Tel 412-744-4451
Fax 412-744-7626

PCS Technologies, Inc.
4250 Wissahickon Ave.
Philadelphia, PA 19129

Founded 1980
Total employees 45
Annual sales $5 million
Industries Computer Hardware, Computer Software
Growth Openings in past year 16; percentage growth 55%
Contact
Howard Weiss, Chief Executive Officer
Tel 215-226-2220
Fax 215-226-2339

Peak Technical Services, Inc.
3424 William Penn Hwy.
Pittsburgh, PA 15235

Founded 1967
Total employees 650
Industries Chemicals, Energy, Holding Companies
Growth Openings in past year 49; percentage growth 8%
Contact
Joe Salvucci, President
Tel 412-825-3900
Fax 412-825-3339

Peripheral Dynamics Inc.
5150 Campus Dr.
Plymouth Meeting, PA 19462

Founded 1969
Total employees 80
Annual sales $13 million
Industry Computer Hardware

Growth Openings in past year 15; percentage growth 23%
Contact
Chuck Walsh, Controller
Tel 610-825-7090
Fax 610-834-7708

PHB Polymeric
8152 West Ridge Rd.
Fairview, PA 16415

Founded 1984
Total employees 75
Annual sales $4 million
Industry Manufacturing Equipment
Growth Openings in past year 25; percentage growth 50%
Contact
William Hilbert, Sr., President/CEO
Tel 814-474-2683
Fax 814-474-5868

Phoenix Microwave Corp.
100 Emlen Way
Telford, PA 18969

Founded 1987
Total employees 71
Annual sales $6.9 million
Industries Subassemblies and Components, Telecommunications
Growth Openings in past year 18; percentage growth 33%
Contact
Gus Kamnitsis, President
Tel 215-723-6011
Fax 215-723-6015

Precision Tube Co.
287 Wissahickon Ave.
North Wales, PA 19454

Founded 1932
Total employees 178
Annual sales $17 million
Industries Holding Companies, Manufacturing Equipment, Subassemblies and Components
Growth Openings in past year 28; percentage growth 18%
Contact
H.E. Passmore, CEO/President
Tel 215-699-5801
Fax 215-699-0761

PSC, Inc.
5525 Swamp Rd.
Fountainville, PA 18923

Founded 1982
Total employees 288
Annual sales $35.9 million
Industries Computer Hardware, Factory Automation
Growth Openings in past year 48; percentage growth 20%
Contact
Benny R. Tafoya, VP of Product Development
Tel 215-249-3300
Fax 215-249-0580

Quad Systems Corp.
2 Electronic Dr.
Horsham, PA 19044

Founded 1981
Total employees 185
Annual sales $34.77 million
Industries Factory Automation, Manufacturing Equipment
Growth Openings in past year 35; percentage growth 23%
Contact
Tony Drury, Chief Financial Officer
Tel 215-657-6202
Fax 215-657-5013

R.E. Wright Associates, Inc.
3240 Schoolhouse Rd.
Middletown, PA 17057

Founded 1975
Total employees 170
Annual sales $20 million
Industry Environmental
Growth Openings in past year 30; percentage growth 21%
Contact
Richard E. Wright, President
Tel 717-944-5501
Fax 717-944-5642

Reality Technologies, Inc.
2200 Renaissance Blvd., Siute 401
King of Prussia, PA 19406

Founded 1987
Total employees 80
Annual sales $10 million

Industry Computer Software
Growth Openings in past year 20; percentage growth 33%
Contact
Mark Goldstein, President/ CEO
Tel 610-277-7600
Fax 610-278-6115

Red Lion Controls
20 Willow Springs Cir.
York, PA 17402

Founded 1975
Total employees 180
Annual sales $24 million
Industries Photonics, Subassemblies and Components, Test and Measurement
Growth Openings in past year 30; percentage growth 20%
Contact
Lester Goodman, President
Tel 717-767-6961
Fax 717-764-0839

Resco Products, Inc.
PO Box 108
Norristown, PA 19404

Founded 1945
Total employees 570
Annual sales $66 million
Industries Advanced Materials, Holding Companies
Growth Openings in past year 70; percentage growth 14%
Contact
W.T. Tredennick, President
Tel 610-279-5010
Fax 610-279-6070

Respironics, Inc.
1001 Murry Ridge Dr.
Murrysville, PA 15668

Founded 1979
Total employees 415
Annual sales $69.3 million
Industries Medical, Test and Measurement
Growth Openings in past year 115; percentage growth 38%
Contact
Gerald McGinnis, President/CEO
Tel 412-733-0200
Fax 412-733-0299

Seitz Technical Products, Inc.
111C Newark Rd., PO Box 338
Avondale, PA 19311

Founded 1982
Total employees 33
Industries Computer Hardware, Telecommunications
Growth Openings in past year 18; percentage growth 120%
Contact
John R. Seitz, President
Tel 610-268-2228
Fax 610-268-2229

Skelly and Loy, Inc.
2601 North Front St.
Harrisburg, PA 17110

Founded 1969
Total employees 180
Annual sales $13 million
Industry Environmental
Growth Openings in past year 35; percentage growth 24%
Contact
Ms. Sandi Loy, Executive VP of Marketing
Tel 717-232-0593
Fax 717-232-1799

Soft-Switch, Inc.
640 Lee Rd.
Wayne, PA 19087

Founded 1979
Total employees 275
Annual sales $40 million
Industries Computer Software, Telecommunications
Growth Openings in past year 50; percentage growth 22%
Contact
Michael D. Zisman, President/CEO
Tel 610-640-9600
Fax 610-640-7550

Spang & Co., Magnetics Division
PO Box 391
Butler, PA 16003

Founded 1949
Total employees 650
Annual sales $60 million
Industry Subassemblies and Components

Growth Openings in past year 25; percentage growth 4%
Contact
Robert K. Brown, Human Resources Manager
Tel 412-282-8282
Fax 412-282-6955

Spirax Sarco, Inc.
1951 Glenwood St. Southwest, PO Box 119
Allentown, PA 18105

Founded 1913
Total employees 400
Annual sales $39 million
Industries Subassemblies and Components, Test and Measurement
Growth Openings in past year 20; percentage growth 5%
Contact
John D. Nicholas, President
Tel 610-797-5830
Fax 610-433-1346

St. Marys Carbon Co.
State St.
Saint Marys, PA 15857

Founded 1939
Total employees 183
Annual sales $22 million
Industries Holding Companies, Subassemblies and Components
Growth Openings in past year 22; percentage growth 13%
Contact
Jim Zwald, Personnel Manager
Tel 814-781-7333
Fax 814-834-9201

STV Group, Inc.
11 Robinson St., PO Box 459
Pottstown, PA 19464

Founded 1968
Total employees 960
Annual sales $75.8 million
Industries Environmental, Manufacturing Equipment
Growth Openings in past year 88; percentage growth 10%

Contact
William Rex, Vice
  President
Tel 610-326-4600
Fax 610-326-2718

Suckle Corp.
733 Davis St.
Scranton, PA 18505

Founded 1945
Total employees 300
Annual sales $32 million
Industry Manufacturing
  Equipment
Growth Openings in past
  year 150; percentage
  growth 100%
Contact
James Castellino,
  President
Tel 717-346-3871
Fax 717-346-1612

**SunGard Recovery
Services, Inc.**
1285 Drummer Ln.
Wayne, PA 19087

Founded 1975
Total employees 333
Annual sales $94.7 million
Industry Computer
  Hardware
Growth Openings in past
  year 33; percentage
  growth 11%
Contact
Ms. Karen Bilinski, VP of
  Human Resources
Tel 610-341-8700
Fax 610-341-8739

**Svedala Industries, Inc.,
Grinding Division**
240 Arch St., PO Box
  15-312
York, PA 17405

Founded 1983
Total employees 250
Annual sales $100 million
Industries Advanced
  Materials, Energy,
  Factory Automation,
  Manufacturing Equipment
Growth Openings in past
  year 50; percentage
  growth 25%
Contact
Andy Benco, General
  Manager of the Grinding
  Divion
Tel 717-843-8671
Fax 717-845-5154

**Swanson Analysis
Systems, Inc.**
Johnson Rd., PO Box 65
Houston, PA 15342

Founded 1970
Total employees 175
Annual sales $20 million
Industry Computer
  Software
Growth Openings in past
  year 28; percentage
  growth 19%
Contact
Peter J. Smith, Chief
  Executive Officer
Tel 412-746-3304
Fax 412-746-9494

Synergistech, Inc.
637 Lowther Rd.
Lewisberry, PA 17339

Founded 1981
Total employees 26
Industries Factory
  Automation,
  Manufacturing Equipment
Growth Openings in past
  year 19; percentage
  growth 271%
Contact
Edward J. Paukovits, Jr.,
  Chief Executive Officer
Tel 717-938-9323
Fax 717-938-9364

Tartan Laboratories, Inc.
300 Oxford Dr.
Monroeville, PA 15146

Founded 1981
Total employees 91
Industry Computer
  Software
Growth Openings in past
  year 21; percentage
  growth 30%
Contact
Stephen McMahon, VP of
  Finance
Tel 412-856-3600
Fax 412-856-3636

T.B. Wood's
440 North 5th Ave.
Chambersburg, PA 17201

Founded 1857
Total employees 400
Industries Energy,
  Subassemblies and
  Components, Test and
  Measurement

Growth Openings in past
  year 23; percentage
  growth 6%
Contact
Michael Hurt, President/
  CEO
Tel 717-264-7161
Fax 717-264-6420

**Thoren Caging Systems,
Inc.**
PO Box 586
Hazelton, PA 18201

Founded 1978
Total employees 55
Industries Biotechnology,
  Medical
Growth Openings in past
  year 40; percentage
  growth 266%
Contact
William Thomas, President
Tel 717-455-5041
Fax 717-454-3500

**Tollgrade
Communications, Inc.**
493 Nixon Rd.
Cheswick, PA 15024

Founded 1986
Total employees 70
Annual sales $4.8 million
Industry Computer
  Hardware
Growth Openings in past
  year 22; percentage
  growth 45%
Contact
Rocky Flaminio, Vice
  Chairman/Chief
  Technology Officer
Tel 412-274-2156
Fax 412-274-8014

Transarc Corporation
Gulf Tower, 707 Grant St.
Pittsburgh, PA 15219

Founded 1989
Total employees 200
Annual sales $23 million
Industry Computer
  Software
Growth Openings in past
  year 50; percentage
  growth 33%
Contact
Alfred Z. Spector,
  President/CEO
Tel 412-338-4400
Fax 412-338-4404

Triangle Circuits of Pittsburgh, Inc.
931 3rd St.
Oakmont, PA 15139

Founded 1979
Total employees 180
Annual sales $17 million
Industry Subassemblies and Components
Growth Openings in past year 15; percentage growth 9%
Contact
Michael D'Ambrosio, President
Tel 412-828-5322
Fax 412-828-5803

U.S. Bioscience, Inc.
100 Front St.
Conshohocken, PA 19428

Founded 1987
Total employees 162
Annual sales $2.36 million
Industries Medical, Pharmaceuticals
Growth Openings in past year 42; percentage growth 35%
Contact
H. Charles Ford, III, VP of Human Resources
Tel 610-832-0570
Fax 610-832-4500

U.S. Filter, Inc.
181 Thorn Hill Rd.
Warrendale, PA 15086

Founded 1950
Total employees 110
Annual sales $11 million
Industry Environmental
Growth Openings in past year 25; percentage growth 29%
Contact
Andy Seidel, Vice President/General Manager
Tel 412-772-0044
Fax 412-772-1360

Vertex Inc.
1041 Old Cassatt Rd.
Berwyn, PA 19312

Founded 1976
Total employees 120
Annual sales $13 million
Industry Computer Software

Growth Openings in past year 28; percentage growth 30%
Contact
Bill Boyer, Controller
Tel 610-640-4200
Fax 610-640-1207

VIR, Inc.
105-C James Way
Southampton, PA 18966

Founded 1979
Total employees 65
Annual sales $8.9 million
Industries Computer Hardware, Holding Companies, Subassemblies and Components, Telecommunications
Growth Openings in past year 21; percentage growth 47%
Contact
Alex Rabey, President
Tel 215-364-8866
Fax 215-364-0920

Westinghouse Electric Corp., Distribution and Control Business Unit
875 Greentree Rd., 5 Park Way Ctr.
Pittsburgh, PA 15220

Founded 1886
Total employees 400
Annual sales $36 million
Industries Energy, Photonics, Subassemblies and Components, Test and Measurement, Telecommunications
Growth Openings in past year 50; percentage growth 14%
Contact
J.L. Becherer, Vice President/General Manager
Tel 412-937-6100
Fax 412-937-6357

X-Mark Industries, Inc.
2001 North Main St.
Washington, PA 15301

Founded 1967
Total employees 100
Annual sales $5 million
Industry Manufacturing Equipment

Growth Openings in past year 25; percentage growth 33%
Contact
Robert F. Kastelic, President
Tel 412-228-7373
Fax 412-228-2122

Zynaxis, Inc.
371 Phoenixville Pike
Malvern, PA 19355

Founded 1987
Total employees 60
Industries Biotechnology, Medical
Growth Openings in past year 26; percentage growth 76%
Contact
Ms. Theresa Doyle, Manager of Human Resources
Tel 610-889-2200
Fax 610-889-2222

Puerto Rico

Hewlett-Packard Co., Puerto Rico Division
Hwy. 110 North, Kilometer 5.1
Aguadilla, PR 00603

Founded 1980
Total employees 500
Annual sales $82 million
Industry Computer Hardware
Growth Openings in past year 100; percentage growth 25%
Contact
Jerry L. Harmon, General Manager
Tel 809-890-6000
Fax 809-882-6262

Telecom Solutions Puerto Rico, Inc.
Industrial Park, Bldg. 7, PO Box 1046
Aguada, PR 00602

Founded 1979
Total employees 179
Industries Computer Hardware, Subassemblies and Components, Test and Measurement

Growth Openings in past year 21; percentage growth 13%
Contact
Nick Barreto, General Manager
Tel 809-868-3535
Fax 809-868-4466

Rhode Island

American Power Conversion Corp.
132 Fairgrounds Rd., PO Box 278
West Kingston, RI 02892

Founded 1981
Total employees 730
Annual sales $157 million
Industries Computer Software, Energy, Subassemblies and Components
Growth Openings in past year 169; percentage growth 30%
Contact
Rodger B. Dowdell, Jr., President/CEO
Tel 401-789-5735
Fax 401-789-3710

Cherry Semiconductor Corp.
2000 South County Trail
East Greenwich, RI 02818

Founded 1972
Total employees 550
Annual sales $57 million
Industry Subassemblies and Components
Growth Openings in past year 149; percentage growth 37%
Contact
Alfred S. Budnick, President
Tel 401-885-3600
Fax 401-885-5786

Comtec Information Systems, Inc.
53 John St.
Cumberland, RI 02864

Founded 1959
Total employees 120
Annual sales $19 million
Industry Computer Hardware

Growth Openings in past year 20; percentage growth 20%
Contact
Alfred J. Petteruti, President
Tel 401-724-8500
Fax 401-724-0296

CytoTherapeutics, Inc.
2 Richmond St.
Providence, RI 02903

Founded 1989
Total employees 70
Industry Biotechnology
Growth Openings in past year 15; percentage growth 27%
Contact
Seth A. Rudnick, MD, Chief Executive Officer
Tel 401-272-3310

Daly & Wolcott, Inc.
141 James P. Murphy Hwy.
West Warwick, RI 02893

Founded 1977
Total employees 100
Annual sales $11 million
Industries Computer Hardware, Computer Software
Growth Openings in past year 20; percentage growth 25%
Contact
Terrance J. Daly, President/Founder
Tel 401-823-8400
Fax 401-823-7268

Early Cloud and Co.
Aquidneck Industrial Park
Newport, RI 02840

Founded 1981
Total employees 165
Annual sales $18 million
Industries Computer Hardware, Computer Software
Growth Openings in past year 40; percentage growth 32%
Contact
Bob Pardini, Director of Human Resources
Tel 401-849-0500
Fax 401-849-1190

EG&G Sealol, Industrial Division
50 Sharpe Dr.
Cranston, RI 02920

Founded 1935
Total employees 300
Industry Subassemblies and Components
Growth Openings in past year 100; percentage growth 50%
Contact
Michael Galluccio, General Manager
Tel 401-463-8700
Fax 401-463-6198

Electronic Book Technologies, Inc.
One Richmond Sq.
Providence, RI 02906

Founded 1989
Total employees 74
Annual sales $8.5 million
Industry Computer Software
Growth Openings in past year 41; percentage growth 124%
Contact
Lou Reynolds, President
Tel 401-421-9550
Fax 401-421-9551

Environmental Science Services, Inc.
532 Atwells Ave.
Providence, RI 02909

Founded 1981
Total employees 75
Annual sales $8.0 million
Industries Environmental, Holding Companies
Growth Openings in past year 25; percentage growth 50%
Contact
Ken Dreyer, President
Tel 401-421-0398
Fax 401-421-5731

Hibbitt, Karlsson & Sorensen, Inc.
1080 Main St.
Pawtucket, RI 02860

Founded 1978
Total employees 85
Industry Computer Software
Growth Openings in past year 35; percentage growth 70%

Contact
David Hibbitt, President
Tel 401-727-4200
Fax 401-727-4208

NEPTCO, Inc.
PO Box 2323
Pawtucket, RI 02861

Founded 1953
Total employees 420
Annual sales $62 million
Industry Advanced
Materials
Growth Openings in past
year 20; percentage
growth 5%
Contact
Guy Marini, President
Tel 401-722-5500
Fax 401-722-6378

Network Solutions, Inc.
475 Kilvert St.
Warwick, RI 02886

Founded 1976
Total employees 120
Annual sales $6.8 million
Industries Computer
Hardware, Computer
Software
Growth Openings in past
year 39; percentage
growth 48%
Contact
Richard Hawkins,
President/CEO
Tel 401-732-9000
Fax 401-732-9009

**Popper Precision
Instruments, Inc.**
Jenckes Hill Rd.
Lincoln, RI 02865

Founded 1948
Total employees 65
Annual sales $7.1 million
Industries Medical, Test
and Measurement
Growth Openings in past
year 15; percentage
growth 30%
Contact
Walter L. Popper,
President
Tel 401-334-3600
Fax 401-334-0567

**Promptus
Communications, Inc.**
207 Highpoint Ave.,
Portsmouth Business
Park
Portsmouth, RI 02871

Founded 1989
Total employees 55
Industry
Telecommunications
Growth Openings in past
year 20; percentage
growth 57%
Contact
Aurelio Lucci, President
Tel 401-683-6100
Fax 401-683-6105

**Science Applications
International Corp.,
Ocean, Science, and
Technology Division**
221 Third St.
Newport, RI 02840

Founded 1979
Total employees 120
Annual sales $22 million
Industries Defense,
Environmental,
Transportation
Growth Openings in past
year 70; percentage
growth 140%
Contact
Dave Pearson, Division
Manager
Tel 401-847-4210
Fax 401-849-1585

**Systems Engineering
Associates Corp.**
221 Third St.
Newport, RI 02840

Founded 1981
Total employees 75
Industries Computer
Software, Defense
Growth Openings in past
year 47; percentage
growth 167%
Contact
Michael G. Fisk, President
Tel 401-847-2260
Fax 401-841-5860

**Toray Plastics America,
Inc.**
50 Belver Ave.
North Kingstown, RI 02852

Founded 1972
Total employees 475
Annual sales $70 million

Industry Advanced
Materials
Growth Openings in past
year 124; percentage
growth 35%
Contact
Harvey Greenhalgh,
Director of Human
Resources
Tel 401-294-4511
Fax 401-294-2154

UltraCision, Inc.
25 Thurber Blvd.
Smithfield, RI 02917

Founded 1988
Total employees 80
Annual sales $8.8 million
Industry Medical
Growth Openings in past
year 30; percentage
growth 60%
Contact
Thomas W. Davison, Ph.D,
President
Tel 401-232-7660
Fax 401-232-7664

**Visiting Nurses
Association of Rhode
Island**
100 Medway St.
Providence, RI 02906

Founded 1900
Total employees 520
Annual sales $25 million
Industry Holding
Companies
Growth Openings in past
year 169; percentage
growth 48%
Contact
Ms. Jane A. Mackenzie,
President
Tel 401-444-9770
Fax 401-444-9782

South Carolina

Ambac International, Inc.
PO Box 85
Columbia, SC 29202

Founded 1986
Total employees 425
Industries Holding
Companies,
Subassemblies and
Components

Growth Openings in past year 25; percentage growth 6%
Contact
Ms. Glenda Thompson-Norton, VP of Human Resources
Tel 803-735-1400
Fax 803-735-2163

AT&T Global Information Solutions, Workstation Products Division
7240 Moorefield Hwy.
Liberty, SC 29657

Founded 1984
Total employees 900
Industries Computer Hardware, Computer Software
Growth Openings in past year 97; percentage growth 12%
Contact
Michael Morrissey, Vice President
Tel 803-843-1500
Fax 803-843-1595

Compact Air Products, Inc.
PO Box 499
Westminster, SC 29693

Founded 1974
Total employees 150
Industry Factory Automation
Growth Openings in past year 45; percentage growth 42%
Contact
Ms. Marge Putnam, Personnel Director
Tel 803-647-9521
Fax 803-647-9574

Computer Dynamics, Inc.
105 South Main St.
Greer, SC 29650

Founded 1981
Total employees 100
Annual sales $10 million
Industry Computer Hardware
Growth Openings in past year 20; percentage growth 25%
Contact
Kurt Priester, President
Tel 803-877-7471
Fax 803-879-2030

Crown Metro Aerospace
315 Echelon Rd., Donaldson Ctr., PO Box 5695
Greenville, SC 29606

Founded 1983
Total employees 105
Annual sales $20 million
Industry Advanced Materials
Growth Openings in past year 25; percentage growth 31%
Contact
Ms. Lynne Nichols, Human Resources Manager
Tel 803-277-1870
Fax 803-277-3244

Datastream Systems, Inc.
1200 Woodruff Rd., Suite C40
Greenville, SC 29607

Founded 1982
Total employees 72
Annual sales $5 million
Industry Computer Software
Growth Openings in past year 16; percentage growth 28%
Contact
Larry Blackwell, President
Tel 803-297-6775
Fax 803-627-7227

Hardwicke Chemical, Inc.
2114 Larry Jeffers Rd.
Elgin, SC 29045

Founded 1967
Total employees 200
Industries Advanced Materials, Chemicals
Growth Openings in past year 25; percentage growth 14%
Contact
Charles E. Marble, General Manager
Tel 803-438-3471
Fax 803-438-4497

JM Smith Corp.
PO Box 1779
Spartanburg, SC 29304

Founded 1944
Total employees 365
Industry Holding Companies

Growth Openings in past year 64; percentage growth 21%
Contact
Henry Dale Smith, Chief Executive Officer
Tel 803-582-1216

Phoenix Medical Technology, Inc.
Hwy. 521 West, PO Box 346
Andrews, SC 29510

Founded 1978
Total employees 300
Annual sales $12.1 million
Industries Medical, Test and Measurement
Growth Openings in past year 20; percentage growth 7%
Contact
Roger Hughes, Personnel Manager
Tel 803-221-5100
Fax 803-221-5201

Talley Metals Technology, Inc.
PO Box 2498
Hartsville, SC 29550

Founded 1984
Total employees 175
Annual sales $26 million
Industry Advanced Materials
Growth Openings in past year 15; percentage growth 9%
Contact
Donald Bailey, President/CEO
Tel 803-335-7540
Fax 803-335-7593

Teleco, Inc.
430 Woodruff Rd., Suite 300
Greenville, SC 29607

Founded 1981
Total employees 98
Industry Holding Companies
Growth Openings in past year 43; percentage growth 78%
Contact
William M. Rogers, President
Tel 803-297-4400
Fax 803-297-9983

Zeus Industrial Products, Inc.
501 Blvd. St., PO Box 2167
Orangeburg, SC 29116

Founded 1966
Total employees 330
Annual sales $32 million
Industries Manufacturing Equipment, Medical, Subassemblies and Components
Growth Openings in past year 30; percentage growth 10%
Contact
Ms. Cheryl Lynch, Human Resources Manager
Tel 803-531-2174
Fax 803-533-5694

South Dakota

Daktronics, Inc.
331 32nd Ave., PO Box 5128
Brookings, SD 57006

Founded 1968
Total employees 525
Industries Computer Hardware, Holding Companies, Photonics, Test and Measurement
Growth Openings in past year 99; percentage growth 23%
Contact
Ms. Carla Gatzke, Personnel Manager
Tel 605-697-4000
Fax 605-697-4700

Tennessee

ABB Environmental Systems
Centerpoint Plaza, 1400 Centerpoint Blvd.
Knoxville, TN 37932

Founded 1984
Total employees 315
Annual sales $33 million
Industry Environmental

Growth Openings in past year 15; percentage growth 5%
Contact
Woodrow France, VP of Human Resources
Tel 615-693-7550
Fax 615-694-5203

Allen & Hoshall, Inc.
2430 Poplar Ave.
Memphis, TN 38112

Founded 1915
Total employees 175
Annual sales $19 million
Industries Defense, Manufacturing Equipment
Growth Openings in past year 15; percentage growth 9%
Contact
Thomas E. Needham, PE, President
Tel 901-327-8222
Fax 901-324-7154

AZO, Inc.
4445 Malone Rd.
Memphis, TN 38118

Founded 1978
Total employees 90
Annual sales $11 million
Industry Factory Automation
Growth Openings in past year 20; percentage growth 28%
Contact
Robert Moore, President
Tel 901-794-9480
Fax 901-794-9934

Barge, Waggoner, Sumner & Cannon, Inc.
162 Third Ave. North
Nashville, TN 37201

Founded 1955
Total employees 390
Annual sales $26.3 million
Industry Environmental
Growth Openings in past year 36; percentage growth 10%
Contact
Jack L. Wood, President
Tel 615-254-1500
Fax 615-255-6572

Cedar Chemical Corp.
5100 Poplar Ave., Suite 2414
Memphis, TN 38137

Founded 1985
Total employees 600
Annual sales $100 million
Industry Chemicals
Growth Openings in past year 100; percentage growth 20%
Contact
Zwi Waldman, President
Tel 901-685-5348
Fax 901-684-5398

Chattem, Inc.
1715 West 38th St.
Chattanooga, TN 37409

Founded 1866
Total employees 370
Annual sales $110 million
Industry Holding Companies
Growth Openings in past year 18; percentage growth 5%
Contact
Zan Guerry, President/ COB
Tel 615-821-4571
Fax 615-821-0395

Control Technology
PO Box 59003
Knoxville, TN 37950

Founded 1980
Total employees 80
Industry Factory Automation
Growth Openings in past year 20; percentage growth 33%
Contact
Mark Medley, President
Tel 615-584-0440
Fax 615-584-5720

CTI, Inc.
810 Innovation Dr., PO Box 22999
Knoxville, TN 37933

Founded 1984
Total employees 220
Annual sales $24 million
Industries Holding Companies, Medical
Growth Openings in past year 20; percentage growth 10%

Contact
Ms. Kathy Coleman, VP of
Human Resources
Tel 615-966-7539
Fax 615-966-8955

**Cubic Corp., Precision
Systems Division**
1308 South Washington
St., PO Box 821
Tullahoma, TN 37388

Founded 1912
Total employees 169
Annual sales $19 million
Industries Photonics,
Transportation
Growth Openings in past
year 49; percentage
growth 40%
Contact
Ms. Carolyn Mitchell,
Human Resources
Administrator
Tel 615-455-8524
Fax 615-455-0699

**Environmental Systems
Corp.**
200 Tech Center Dr.
Knoxville, TN 37912

Founded 1969
Total employees 120
Industries Computer
Hardware, Computer
Software, Environmental,
Test and Measurement
Growth Openings in past
year 20; percentage
growth 20%
Contact
Mark Margetts, President
Tel 615-688-7900
Fax 615-687-8977

Envoy Corp.
15 Century Blvd., Suite
600
Nashville, TN 37214

Founded 1981
Total employees 267
Annual sales $35 million
Industry Computer
Software
Growth Openings in past
year 67; percentage
growth 33%
Contact
Don Foutch, VP of
Finance/CFO
Tel 615-885-3700
Fax 615-889-9955

**Jefferson-Pilot Data
Services, Inc.**
785 Crossover Ln., Suite
141
Memphis, TN 38117

Founded 1969
Total employees 242
Annual sales $27.5 million
Industries Computer
Hardware, Computer
Software
Growth Openings in past
year 20; percentage
growth 9%
Contact
Ms. Birgirt Ziedler,
Personnel Director
Tel 901-762-8000
Fax 901-762-8038

Micro Craft, Inc.
PO Box 370
Tullahoma, TN 37388

Founded 1958
Total employees 430
Annual sales $33 million
Industries Factory
Automation, Holding
Companies,
Manufacturing Equipment
Growth Openings in past
year 29; percentage
growth 7%
Contact
Dan J. Marcum, President
Tel 615-455-2664
Fax 615-455-7060

PAI Corp.
116 Milan Way
Oak Ridge, TN 37830

Founded 1983
Total employees 300
Annual sales $10 million
Industry Environmental
Growth Openings in past
year 250; percentage
growth 500%
Contact
Doan L. Phung, President
Tel 615-483-0666
Fax 615-481-0003

**Precision Products of
Tennessee, Inc.**
724 Central Ave., PO Box
516
Springfield, TN 37172

Founded 1986
Total employees 96

Industries Factory
Automation,
Manufacturing Equipment
Growth Openings in past
year 16; percentage
growth 20%
Contact
George Cheran,
Administrative Manager
Tel 615-384-2501
Fax 615-384-2397

**Science Applications
International Corp.,
Environmental
Compliance Group**
800 Oak Ridge Tpke.
Oak Ridge, TN 37831

Founded 1972
Total employees 460
Annual sales $49 million
Industry Environmental
Growth Openings in past
year 109; percentage
growth 31%
Contact
Barry Goss, Group Senior
Vice President
Tel 615-482-9031
Fax 615-482-7257

Steward, Inc.
PO Box 510
Chattanooga, TN 37401

Founded 1876
Total employees 300
Annual sales $20 million
Industry Advanced
Materials
Growth Openings in past
year 50; percentage
growth 20%
Contact
Lee Atchley, Manager of
Personnel
Tel 615-867-4100
Fax 615-867-4102

**Wright Medical
Technology, Inc.**
5677 Airline Rd.
Arlington, TN 38002

Founded 1977
Total employees 530
Annual sales $58 million
Industry Medical
Growth Openings in past
year 70; percentage
growth 15%

Contact
Herbert W. Korthoff,
COB/CEO
Tel 901-867-9971
Fax 901-867-8249

Texas

ABB Control, Inc.
1206 Hatton Rd.
Wichita Falls, TX 76302

Founded 1975
Total employees 105
Annual sales $35 million
Industry Subassemblies
and Components
Growth Openings in past
year 21; percentage
growth 25%
Contact
Ms. Shari Carpenter,
Manager of Human
Resources
Tel 817-761-3232
Fax 817-761-3202

**Accu Tech International,
Inc.**
2550 North Loop West,
Suite 111
Houston, TX 77092

Founded 1988
Total employees 54
Industry Computer
Software
Growth Openings in past
year 18; percentage
growth 50%
Contact
Ben Guzzetta, President
Tel 713-688-9614
Fax 713-688-5306

**Air Products and
Chemicals, Inc., Silicon
Materials Services
Division**
2985 Market St.
Garland, TX 75041

Founded 1981
Total employees 70
Annual sales $6.8 million
Industry Subassemblies
and Components
Growth Openings in past
year 20; percentage
growth 40%

Contact
Charles MacGregor,
General Manager
Tel 214-271-8506
Fax 214-271-1375

**Allen Telecom Group,
Decibel Products
Division**
3184 Quebec St.
Dallas, TX 75356

Founded 1947
Total employees 550
Annual sales $65 million
Industries Subassemblies
and Components,
Telecommunications
Growth Openings in past
year 50; percentage
growth 10%
Contact
Dr. Peter Mailandt,
President
Tel 214-631-0310
Fax 214-631-4706

ALLUS Technology Corp.
12611 Jones Rd.
Houston, TX 77070

Founded 1979
Total employees 90
Industry Computer
Hardware
Growth Openings in past
year 60; percentage
growth 200%
Contact
Ms. Betty Seabaugh,
President
Tel 713-894-4455
Fax 713-894-6709

Altai, Inc.
624 Six Flags Dr., Suite
150
Arlington, TX 76011

Founded 1979
Total employees 100
Annual sales $9.5 million
Industries Computer
Hardware, Computer
Software
Growth Openings in past
year 20; percentage
growth 25%
Contact
James P. Williams,
President/CEO
Tel 817-640-8911
Fax 817-633-4449

American BioMed, Inc.
PO Box 8429
The Woodlands, TX 77387

Founded 1984
Total employees 70
Industries Holding
Companies, Medical,
Pharmaceuticals
Growth Openings in past
year 20; percentage
growth 40%
Contact
Dave Summers, Ph.D.,
Chairman of the Board
Tel 713-367-3895
Fax 713-367-3212

**American Ecology
Corporation**
5333 Westeimer Rd., Suite
#1000
Houston, TX 77056

Founded 1983
Total employees 350
Annual sales $71 million
Industry Environmental
Growth Openings in past
year 130; percentage
growth 59%
Contact
Harry J. Phillips, Jr., Chief
Executive Officer
Tel 713-624-1900
Fax 713-624-1999

**American Medical
Electronics, Inc.**
250 East Arapaho Rd.
Richardson, TX 75081

Founded 1982
Total employees 300
Annual sales $39.29
million
Industry Medical
Growth Openings in past
year 70; percentage
growth 30%
Contact
Ms. LaVonne Chimbel, VP
of Human Resources
Tel 214-918-8400
Fax 214-918-8490

American Ref-Fuel Co.
PO Box 3151
Houston, TX 77253

Founded 1971
Total employees 385
Industry Energy
Growth Openings in past
year 45; percentage
growth 13%

Contact
Sean Burke, Director of
Human Resources
Tel 713-531-4233
Fax 713-584-4696

Amtech Corp.
17304 Preston Rd.
Dallas, TX 75252

Founded 1983
Total employees 300
Annual sales $37 million
Industry Factory
Automation
Growth Openings in past
year 100; percentage
growth 50%
Contact
G. Russel Mortenson,
President/CEO
Tel 214-733-6600
Fax 214-733-6699

Anago, Inc.
7524 Mosier View Ct.
Fort Worth, TX 76118

Founded 1978
Total employees 900
Industry Medical
Growth Openings in past
year 248; percentage
growth 38%
Contact
Andrew Pryor, Human
Resources Coordinator
Tel 817-284-1345
Fax 817-284-0767

Antrim Corp.
101 East Park Blvd., 12th
Fl.
Plano, TX 75074

Founded 1982
Total employees 173
Annual sales $20 million
Industries Computer
Hardware, Computer
Software
Growth Openings in past
year 29; percentage
growth 20%
Contact
Richard Brink, COB/CEO
Tel 214-422-1022
Fax 214-516-3460

**Argo Data Resource
Corp.**
12770 Coit Rd., Suite 600
Dallas, TX 75251

Founded 1980
Total employees 65

Annual sales $12 million
Industry Computer
Software
Growth Openings in past
year 15; percentage
growth 30%
Contact
Max Martin, President
Tel 214-386-4949
Fax 214-991-1214

Astro International Corp.
100 Park Ave.
League City, TX 77573

Founded 1973
Total employees 100
Annual sales $11 million
Industries Environmental,
Test and Measurement
Growth Openings in past
year 25; percentage
growth 33%
Contact
Ms. Susan Boyd,
Personnel Manager
Tel 713-332-2484
Fax 713-554-6795

**Austin Semiconductor,
Inc.**
8701 Cross Park Dr.
Austin, TX 78754

Founded 1988
Total employees 93
Annual sales $9.0 million
Industry Subassemblies
and Components
Growth Openings in past
year 33; percentage
growth 55%
Contact
Roger C. Minard,
President/CEO
Tel 512-339-1188
Fax 512-339-6641

**Austin-American
Technology**
12201 Technology Blvd.
Austin, TX 78727

Founded 1986
Total employees 30
Annual sales $3.7 million
Industries Factory
Automation,
Manufacturing Equipment
Growth Openings in past
year 20; percentage
growth 200%

Contact
Robert Simon, Financial
Controller
Tel 512-335-6400
Fax 512-335-5753

**Benchmarq
Microelectronics, Inc.**
2611 Westgrove, Suite 109
Carrollton, TX 75006

Founded 1989
Total employees 135
Industry Subassemblies
and Components
Growth Openings in past
year 50; percentage
growth 58%
Contact
Derrell Coker, President
Tel 214-407-0011
Fax 214-407-9845

BGRS, Inc.
10440 Windfern Rd.
Houston, TX 77064

Founded 1976
Total employees 70
Annual sales $7.4 million
Industries Environmental,
Factory Automation,
Subassemblies and
Components
Growth Openings in past
year 20; percentage
growth 40%
Contact
Frank Cmajdalka,
President
Tel 713-890-6862
Fax 713-890-7949

BSG Corp.
11 Greenway Plaza, Suite
900
Houston, TX 77046

Founded 1987
Total employees 400
Industries Computer
Hardware, Computer
Software
Growth Openings in past
year 200; percentage
growth 100%
Contact
Steven Papermaster,
COB/CEO
Tel 713-965-9000
Fax 713-993-9249

Caprock Manufacturing, Inc.
2303 120th St.
Lubbock, TX 79423

Founded 1983
Total employees 155
Annual sales $7.9 million
Industry Manufacturing
Equipment
Growth Openings in past
year 15; percentage
growth 10%
Contact
Ms. Gwen Messer,
Personnel Manager
Tel 806-745-6454
Fax 806-745-9441

Champion Technologies, Inc.
3355 West Alabama, Suite
400
Houston, TX 77098

Founded 1950
Total employees 400
Industries Advanced
Materials, Chemicals
Growth Openings in past
year 50; percentage
growth 14%
Contact
Charles Hainebach, Group
President
Tel 713-627-3303
Fax 713-623-8083

Clif Mock Co., Inc.
Johnson Rd., FM 2854,
PO Box 1159
Conroe, TX 77305

Founded 1978
Total employees 100
Annual sales $11 million
Industries Factory
Automation, Test and
Measurement
Growth Openings in past
year 20; percentage
growth 25%
Contact
James H. Miller, President
Tel 409-588-1171
Fax 409-588-1783

Cogniseis Development, Inc.
2401 Portsmouth St.
Houston, TX 77098

Founded 1987
Total employees 225
Annual sales $26 million

Industry Computer
Software
Growth Openings in past
year 75; percentage
growth 50%
Contact
Pat Poe, COB/President
Tel 713-526-3273
Fax 713-630-3968

Columbia Scientific Industries Corp.
11950 Jollyville Rd., PO
Box 203190
Austin, TX 78720

Founded 1968
Total employees 120
Annual sales $15 million
Industries Environmental,
Test and Measurement,
Telecommunications
Growth Openings in past
year 45; percentage
growth 60%
Contact
Gerald C. Phillips, COB/
President
Tel 512-258-5191
Fax 512-258-5004

Competitive Technologies, Inc.
2901 Wilcrest, Suite 600
Houston, TX 77042

Founded 1987
Total employees 95
Annual sales $11 million
Industry Computer
Software
Growth Openings in past
year 40; percentage
growth 72%
Contact
Jim Yasinski, General
Manager
Tel 713-954-2900
Fax 713-954-2999

Comtec Automated Solutions
10000 Old Katy Rd., Suite
150
Houston, TX 77055

Founded 1992
Total employees 45
Annual sales $7.4 million
Industry Computer
Hardware
Growth Openings in past
year 35; percentage
growth 350%

Contact
Ms Deborah Denison,
President
Tel 713-935-3666
Fax 713-935-3650

Control Systems International, Inc.
1625 West Crosby Rd.
Carrollton, TX 75006

Founded 1965
Total employees 250
Annual sales $41 million
Industries Computer
Hardware, Energy
Growth Openings in past
year 29; percentage
growth 13%
Contact
Wayne Stevenson,
President/CEO
Tel 214-323-1111
Fax 214-242-0026

Cooperative Computing, Inc.
6207 Bee Cave Rd.
Austin, TX 78746

Founded 1976
Total employees 240
Industry Computer
Software
Growth Openings in past
year 65; percentage
growth 37%
Contact
Phillip Waters, Director of
Human Resources
Tel 512-328-2300
Fax 512-328-6461

C-Power Companies, Inc.
2007-B Industrial Ln.
Rockwall, TX 75087

Founded 1986
Total employees 400
Annual sales $53 million
Industries Energy,
Manufacturing
Equipment, Test and
Measurement
Growth Openings in past
year 125; percentage
growth 45%
Contact
Ms. Dee Goleman,
Director of Human
Resources
Tel 214-771-4303
Fax 214-771-0462

Crystal Semiconductor Corp.
PO Box 17847
Austin, TX 78760

Founded 1984
Total employees 370
Annual sales $100 million
Industry Subassemblies and Components
Growth Openings in past year 130; percentage growth 54%
Contact
John McGovern, VP of Finance
Tel 512-445-7222
Fax 512-445-7581

Cuplex, Inc.
1500 East Hwy. 66
Garland, TX 75040

Founded 1973
Total employees 435
Annual sales $42 million
Industry Subassemblies and Components
Growth Openings in past year 85; percentage growth 24%
Contact
Ron Ryno, President
Tel 214-276-0333
Fax 214-276-3401

Cyrix Corp.
2703 North Central Expwy.
Richardson, TX 75080

Founded 1988
Total employees 210
Annual sales $34 million
Industries Computer Hardware, Subassemblies and Components
Growth Openings in past year 95; percentage growth 82%
Contact
Ms. Margaret Quinn, Director of Human Resources
Tel 214-994-8387
Fax 214-699-9857

Cyten Circuit Design, Inc.
11601 North Plano Rd., Suite 118
Dallas, TX 75243

Founded 1987
Total employees 35
Annual sales $3.4 million

Industry Subassemblies and Components
Growth Openings in past year 15; percentage growth 75%
Contact
E. Winkelmann, President
Tel 214-341-1069
Fax 214-341-1173

DacEasy, Inc.
17950 Preston Rd., Suite 800
Dallas, TX 75252

Founded 1985
Total employees 260
Industry Computer Software
Growth Openings in past year 89; percentage growth 52%
Contact
Ms. Carrie Ferrer, Manager of Personnel and Benefits
Tel 214-248-0305
Fax 214-248-8349

Docucon, Inc.
7461 Callaghan Rd., Suite 200
San Antonio, TX 78229

Founded 1986
Total employees 250
Annual sales $12 million
Industry Computer Hardware
Growth Openings in past year 130; percentage growth 108%
Contact
Ms. Alice Hopkins, Personnel Manager
Tel 210-525-9221
Fax 210-525-0507

DPC&A OGRE Partners, Ltd.
6510 Abrams Rd., Suite 410
Dallas, TX 75231

Founded 1978
Total employees 40
Annual sales $4.6 million
Industry Computer Software
Growth Openings in past year 15; percentage growth 60%

Contact
Bruce Roden, General Partner
Tel 214-349-6900
Fax 214-343-9699

DPT Laboratories, Inc.
307 East Josephine
San Antonio, TX 78215

Founded 1938
Total employees 250
Annual sales $34 million
Industry Pharmaceuticals
Growth Openings in past year 74; percentage growth 42%
Contact
Ms. Elizabeth Olivia, Director of Human Resources
Tel 210-223-3281
Fax 210-224-6505

Ecom-Elite Computer Consultants
10333 Northwest Frwy., Suite 414
Houston, TX 77092

Founded 1978
Total employees 135
Annual sales $22 million
Industries Computer Hardware, Computer Software
Growth Openings in past year 25; percentage growth 22%
Contact
Wayne Holtkamp, President
Tel 713-686-9740
Fax 713-686-9454

EGC Corp.
11718 McGallion, PO Box 16080
Houston, TX 77076

Founded 1959
Total employees 350
Industries Advanced Materials, Factory Automation, Manufacturing Equipment, Subassemblies and Components
Growth Openings in past year 23; percentage growth 7%
Contact
John Ostroot, President
Tel 713-447-8611
Fax 713-931-2201

Energy BioSystems Corp.
3608 Research Forrest Dr., B7
The Woodlands, TX 77381

Founded 1989
Total employees 35
Industry Environmental
Growth Openings in past year 28; percentage growth 400%
Contact
John H. Webb, President/CEO
Tel 713-364-6100
Fax 713-364-6110

Epcon Industrial Systems, Inc.
PO Box 7060
The Woodlands, TX 77387

Founded 1976
Total employees 50
Industry Environmental
Growth Openings in past year 15; percentage growth 42%
Contact
Aziz Jamaluddin, President
Tel 409-273-1774
Fax 409-273-4600

Evolutionary Technologies, Inc.
1101 Capital of Texas Hwy., Building I
Austin, TX 78746

Founded 1991
Total employees 43
Annual sales $4.9 million
Industry Computer Software
Growth Openings in past year 23; percentage growth 115%
Contact
Dr. Katherine Hammer, President
Tel 512-327-6994
Fax 512-327-6117

Eyesys Laboratories, Inc.
2776 Bingle Rd.
Houston, TX 77055

Founded 1986
Total employees 44
Annual sales $7.8 million
Industry Medical
Growth Openings in past year 19; percentage growth 76%

Contact
Joe Wakil, President
Tel 713-465-1921
Fax 713-465-2418

FSSL, Inc.
525 Julie Rivers Dr.
Sugar Land, TX 77478

Founded 1985
Total employees 100
Annual sales $8.4 million
Industries Manufacturing Equipment, Subassemblies and Components, Test and Measurement
Growth Openings in past year 40; percentage growth 66%
Contact
Robert A. Mintz, General Manager
Tel 713-240-1122
Fax 713-240-0951

FutureSoft Engineering, Inc.
12012 Wickchester, Suite 600
Houston, TX 77079

Founded 1982
Total employees 65
Annual sales $7.5 million
Industry Computer Software
Growth Openings in past year 15; percentage growth 30%
Contact
Tim Farrell, Chief Executive Officer
Tel 713-496-9400
Fax 713-496-1090

FWT, Inc.
PO Box 8597
Fort Worth, TX 76124

Founded 1959
Total employees 80
Annual sales $11 million
Industry Telecommunications
Growth Openings in past year 26; percentage growth 48%
Contact
T. Moore, President
Tel 817-457-3060
Fax 817-429-6010

GB Tech, Inc.
PO Box 580427
Houston, TX 77258

Founded 1985
Total employees 153
Industries Computer Hardware, Computer Software
Growth Openings in past year 73; percentage growth 91%
Contact
Gale E. Burkett, COB/CEO
Tel 713-333-3703
Fax 713-333-3745

Genosys Biotechnology, Inc.
8701-A New Trails Dr.
The Woodlands, TX 77381

Founded 1987
Total employees 50
Annual sales $4.8 million
Industries Biotechnology, Chemicals
Growth Openings in past year 16; percentage growth 47%
Contact
Tim McGrath, President
Tel 713-363-3693
Fax 713-363-2212

G.H. Flow Automation
9303 Sam Houston Pkwy.
Houston, TX 77099

Founded 1970
Total employees 100
Annual sales $11 million
Industries Factory Automation, Test and Measurement
Growth Openings in past year 45; percentage growth 81%
Contact
Neil Duarte, President/CEO
Tel 713-272-0404
Fax 713-272-2272

Grant TFW, Inc.
363 North Sam Houston Pkwy. East, Suite 1660
Houston, TX 77060

Founded 1953
Total employees 750
Industries Energy, Manufacturing Equipment, Subassemblies and Components

Growth Openings in past
year 56; percentage
growth 8%
Contact
Robert Cobb, Human
Resources Manager
Tel 713-931-0040
Fax 713-931-4535

Health Synq Corp.
1700 Alma, Suite 400
Plano, TX 75075

Founded 1968
Total employees 30
Industry Computer
Software
Growth Openings in past
year 15; percentage
growth 100%
Contact
Alan Jones, President/
CEO
Tel 214-424-8187
Fax 214-424-9708

Heath Consultants, Inc.
9030 Monroe Rd.
Houston, TX 77061

Founded 1933
Total employees 370
Annual sales $44 million
Industry Test and
Measurement
Growth Openings in past
year 25; percentage
growth 7%
Contact
Ms. Kathy Vu, Director of
Human Resources
Tel 713-947-9292
Fax 713-947-0427

H-O-H Systems, Inc.
6818 FM 2855
Katy, TX 77493

Founded 1976
Total employees 60
Annual sales $5 million
Industries Chemicals,
Environmental, Test and
Measurement
Growth Openings in past
year 20; percentage
growth 50%
Contact
Larry W. Reed, President
Tel 713-371-3333
Fax 713-371-3343

HR Industries, Inc.
1302 East Collins Blvd.
Richardson, TX 75081

Founded 1976
Total employees 152
Annual sales $15.5 million
Industries Computer
Hardware,
Subassemblies and
Components
Growth Openings in past
year 42; percentage
growth 38%
Contact
Ms. Kathleen Kolb,
Secretary/Treasurer
Tel 214-301-6620
Fax 214-699-3704

ICON Industries, Inc.
1101 Pamela Dr.
Euless, TX 76040

Founded 1979
Total employees 105
Annual sales $9.0 million
Industries Computer
Hardware,
Subassemblies and
Components
Growth Openings in past
year 19; percentage
growth 22%
Contact
Robert E. Kunkle,
President
Tel 817-283-5361
Fax 817-571-4281

Ideal Learning, Inc.
8505 Freeport Pkwy., Suite
360
Irving, TX 75063

Founded 1982
Total employees 85
Annual sales $4 million
Industry Computer
Software
Growth Openings in past
year 43; percentage
growth 102%
Contact
Gary D. Volding,
President/COB
Tel 214-929-4201
Fax 214-929-6691

**Institute of Biosciences
& Technology**
2121 West Holcombe
Blvd.
Houston, TX 77030

Founded 1991
Total employees 110

Annual sales $10 million
Industry Biotechnology
Growth Openings in past
year 65; percentage
growth 144%
Contact
Dr. Robert D. Wells, Ph.D.,
Director
Tel 713-677-7700
Fax 713-677-7725

Intelect, Inc.
1100 Executive Dr.
Richardson, TX 75081

Founded 1964
Total employees 165
Annual sales $19 million
Industry Transportation
Growth Openings in past
year 24; percentage
growth 17%
Contact
Ms. Lucille Moore,
President
Tel 214-437-1888
Fax 214-437-9041

**Intercontinental
Manufacturing Co.**
1200 North Glennbrook Dr.
Garland, TX 75040

Founded 1949
Total employees 550
Annual sales $59 million
Industries Defense,
Transportation
Growth Openings in past
year 50; percentage
growth 10%
Contact
Don Steppe, President
Tel 214-276-5131
Fax 214-272-3845

**Intermedics Orthopedics,
Inc.**
1300C East Anderson Ln.,
Bldg. C
Austin, TX 78752

Founded 1982
Total employees 600
Annual sales $66 million
Industry Medical
Growth Openings in past
year 100; percentage
growth 20%
Contact
Gerry Marlar, President
Tel 512-835-1971
Fax 512-835-6014

International Bio-Medical, Inc.
8508 Cross Park Dr.
Austin, TX 78754

Founded 1958
Total employees 70
Annual sales $7.7 million
Industry Holding
Companies
Growth Openings in past
year 17; percentage
growth 32%
Contact
A.J. Segars, President/
CEO
Tel 512-873-0033
Fax 512-873-9090

International Retail Systems Inc.
150 West Carpenter Frwy.
Irving, TX 75039

Founded 1986
Total employees 140
Annual sales $4.66 million
Industry Holding
Companies
Growth Openings in past
year 100; percentage
growth 250%
Contact
Dwight J. Romanica,
President/CEO
Tel 214-541-1600
Fax 214-541-1155

InterVoice, Inc.
17811 Waterview Pkwy.
Dallas, TX 75252

Founded 1983
Total employees 300
Annual sales $45 million
Industries Computer
Hardware, Computer
Software,
Telecommunications
Growth Openings in past
year 50; percentage
growth 20%
Contact
Daniel D. Hammond,
COB/CEO
Tel 214-669-3988
Fax 214-907-1079

IRI International, Inc.
PO Box 1101
Pampa, TX 79065

Founded 1985
Total employees 450
Annual sales $48 million

Industries Advanced
Materials, Energy,
Manufacturing Equipment
Growth Openings in past
year 49; percentage
growth 12%
Contact
R.F. Hupp, VP of
Administration
Tel 806-665-3701
Fax 806-665-3216

i2 Technologies, Inc.
1603 LBJ Frwy., Suite 780
Dallas, TX 75234

Founded 1988
Total employees 45
Annual sales $5 million
Industry Computer
Software
Growth Openings in past
year 22; percentage
growth 95%
Contact
Sarjiv Sidhu, President
Tel 214-620-2100
Fax 214-484-8110

Kent Electronics Corp.
7433 Harwin Dr.
Houston, TX 77036

Founded 1963
Total employees 800
Annual sales $155 million
Industry Holding
Companies
Growth Openings in past
year 199; percentage
growth 33%
Contact
James Corporran,
President
Tel 713-780-7770
Fax 713-978-5898

Kodak Health Imaging Systems, Inc.
2929 North Central
Express, Suite 101
Richardson, TX 75080

Founded 1985
Total employees 150
Annual sales $16 million
Industries Computer
Software, Medical
Growth Openings in past
year 50; percentage
growth 50%
Contact
Ms. Cathy Burzik, CEO/
President
Tel 214-994-1200
Fax 214-994-1310

Lacerte Software Corp.
4835 LBJ Frwy., 10th Fl.
Dallas, TX 75244

Founded 1978
Total employees 150
Industry Computer
Software
Growth Openings in past
year 25; percentage
growth 20%
Contact
Larry Lacerte, President
Tel 214-490-8500
Fax 214-770-8689

LanOptics Inc.
13748 Neutron
Dallas, TX 75244

Founded 1990
Total employees 100
Annual sales $20 million
Industries Computer
Software,
Telecommunications
Growth Openings in past
year 50; percentage
growth 100%
Contact
Ed Grace, President
Tel 214-392-0647
Fax 214-385-0723

Lars Industries, Inc.
2220 West Peter Smith St.
Fort Worth, TX 76102

Founded 1976
Total employees 70
Annual sales $6.8 million
Industry Subassemblies
and Components
Growth Openings in past
year 15; percentage
growth 27%
Contact
Weldon Johnson,
President
Tel 817-332-3672
Fax 817-877-4009

Lear Data Info-Services, Inc.
5910 North Central Expwy.
Dallas, TX 75206

Founded 1965
Total employees 90
Industry Computer
Software
Growth Openings in past
year 15; percentage
growth 20%

Contact
Bruce Smith, Chief
  Executive Officer
Tel 214-360-9008
Fax 214-363-1384

**Learmonth & Burchett
Management Systems**
1800 West Loop South,
  Suite 1800
Houston, TX 77027

Founded 1988
Total employees 400
Annual sales $44 million
Industries Computer
  Hardware, Computer
  Software
Growth Openings in past
  year 50; percentage
  growth 14%
Contact
John Bantleman,
  President/CEO
Tel 713-623-0414
Fax 713-623-4955

Magflux Corp.
1101 East Walnut
Garland, TX 75040

Founded 1976
Total employees 75
Annual sales $8.0 million
Industries Energy,
  Subassemblies and
  Components
Growth Openings in past
  year 25; percentage
  growth 50%
Contact
C. Glynn Davis, President
Tel 214-272-8572
Fax 214-272-6897

**Marvel Communications
Corporation**
6000D Old Hemphill Rd.
Fort Worth, TX 76134

Founded 1974
Total employees 75
Industry
  Telecommunications
Growth Openings in past
  year 35; percentage
  growth 87%
Contact
Ms. Sheila Simmons,
  Secretary/Treasurer
Tel 817-568-0177
Fax 817-293-4441

**McDonald Technologies
International, Inc.**
2434 McIver Ln.
Carrollton, TX 75006

Founded 1986
Total employees 45
Annual sales $5 million
Industry Subassemblies
  and Components
Growth Openings in past
  year 25; percentage
  growth 125%
Contact
Pip Sivakumar, President
Tel 214-243-6767
Fax 214-241-2643

Medical Technology, Inc.
2601 Pinewood Dr.
Grand Prairie, TX 75051

Founded 1982
Total employees 95
Annual sales $9 million
Industry Medical
Growth Openings in past
  year 17; percentage
  growth 21%
Contact
Gary Bledsoe, President/
  CEO
Tel 214-647-0884
Fax 214-660-5495

**Merlin Software
Services, Inc.**
1420 Presidential Dr.
Richardson, TX 75081

Founded 1981
Total employees 100
Industry
  Telecommunications
Growth Openings in past
  year 50; percentage
  growth 100%
Contact
Paul Voss, President
Tel 214-235-9551
Fax 214-235-9586

**Microwave Networks,
Inc.**
10795 Rockley Rd.
Houston, TX 77099

Founded 1982
Total employees 250
Annual sales $34 million
Industry
  Telecommunications
Growth Openings in past
  year 74; percentage
  growth 42%

Contact
A.W. Epley, III, COB/
  President
Tel 713-495-7123
Fax 713-879-4728

Mouser Electronics
2401 Hwy. 287 North
Mansfield, TX 76063

Founded 1964
Total employees 350
Annual sales $34 million
Industries Energy,
  Photonics,
  Subassemblies and
  Components, Test and
  Measurement,
  Telecommunications
Growth Openings in past
  year 49; percentage
  growth 16%
Contact
Glenn L. Smith, President
Tel 817-483-4422
Fax 817-483-0931

National Instruments
6504 Bridge Point Pkwy.
Austin, TX 78730

Founded 1976
Total employees 700
Annual sales $110 million
Industries Computer
  Hardware, Computer
  Software, Subassemblies
  and Components, Test
  and Measurement,
  Telecommunications
Growth Openings in past
  year 97; percentage
  growth 16%
Contact
Tom Dalton, Human
  Resource Officer
Tel 512-794-0100
Fax 512-794-8411

N-Viro Recovery, Inc.
20515 State Hwy. 249,
  Suite 380
Houston, TX 77070

Founded 1990
Total employees 55
Annual sales $5.8 million
Industry Holding
  Companies
Growth Openings in past
  year 50; percentage
  growth 1000%

Contact
Gerry Runolfson,
President/CEO
Tel 713-370-6700
Fax 713-370-9292

**Operational
Technologies Corp.**
4100 North West Loop
410, Suite 230
San Antonio, TX 78229

Founded 1986
Total employees 180
Annual sales $9.5 million
Industries Defense,
Environmental, Holding
Companies,
Subassemblies and
Components
Growth Openings in past
year 35; percentage
growth 24%
Contact
Max Navarro, President
Tel 210-731-0000
Fax 210-731-0008

Origin Systems, Inc.
12940 Research Blvd.
Austin, TX 78750

Founded 1983
Total employees 225
Industry Computer
Software
Growth Openings in past
year 60; percentage
growth 36%
Contact
Dallas Snell, Executive
VP/General Manager
Tel 512-335-5200
Fax 512-331-9558

Parker Technology, Inc.
4501 South County Rd.,
1310
Odessa, TX 79765

Founded 1954
Total employees 75
Annual sales $3 million
Industries Energy,
Subassemblies and
Components
Growth Openings in past
year 25; percentage
growth 50%
Contact
Joe Brown, Operations
Manager
Tel 915-563-2236
Fax 915-561-9406

PDX, Inc.
101 Jim Wright Frwy.
South, Suite 200
Fort Worth, TX 76108

Founded 1983
Total employees 105
Annual sales $12 million
Industry Holding
Companies
Growth Openings in past
year 40; percentage
growth 61%
Contact
Ken Hill, President
Tel 817-246-6760
Fax 817-246-0131

Powell-Esco Co.
3200 Frontage Rd.
Greenville, TX 75401

Founded 1947
Total employees 85
Annual sales $8.3 million
Industries Energy,
Subassemblies and
Components, Test and
Measurement
Growth Openings in past
year 31; percentage
growth 57%
Contact
Glenn D. Auer, President
Tel 903-455-6234
Fax 903-455-3807

Power Computing Co.
1930 HiLine Dr.
Dallas, TX 75207

Founded 1963
Total employees 300
Annual sales $50 million
Industries Computer
Hardware, Computer
Software
Growth Openings in past
year 37; percentage
growth 14%
Contact
Robert A. Andrews, Vice
President/General
Manager
Tel 214-655-8822
Fax 214-655-8836

Pure Data, Inc.
1740 South I-35, Suite 140
Carrollton, TX 75006

Founded 1979
Total employees 100
Industries Computer
Hardware, Computer
Software

Growth Openings in past
year 24; percentage
growth 31%
Contact
Ms. Jan Griffin, Operating
Manager
Tel 214-242-2040
Fax 214-242-9487

**Radiation Systems, Inc.,
Universal Antennas
Division**
900 Alpha Dr., Suite 410
Richardson, TX 75081

Founded 1977
Total employees 100
Annual sales $13 million
Industry
Telecommunications
Growth Openings in past
year 35; percentage
growth 53%
Contact
Kenneth D. Kruse,
President
Tel 214-690-8865
Fax 214-644-6322

RF Monolithics, Inc.
4441 Sigma Rd.
Dallas, TX 75244

Founded 1979
Total employees 175
Annual sales $24 million
Industries Subassemblies
and Components,
Telecommunications
Growth Openings in past
year 55; percentage
growth 45%
Contact
Gary A. Andersen,
President/CEO
Tel 214-233-2903
Fax 214-387-8148

Rochester Gauges, Inc.
11616 Harry Hines Blvd.
Dallas, TX 75229

Founded 1957
Total employees 400
Industries Subassemblies
and Components, Test
and Measurement
Growth Openings in past
year 50; percentage
growth 14%
Contact
Sam Sims, Personnel
Manager
Tel 214-241-2161
Fax 214-620-1403

**Satis Vacuum Industries,
Optovision U.S.A.**
10510 Olympic Dr.
Dallas, TX 75220

Founded 1990
Total employees 50
Industry Subassemblies
and Components
Growth Openings in past
year 20; percentage
growth 66%
Contact
Peter Zuccarelli, President
Tel 214-351-1155
Fax 214-357-2004

**Scientific and
Engineering Software,
Inc.**
4301 Westbank Dr., Bldg.
A
Austin, TX 78746

Founded 1971
Total employees 75
Industries Computer
Hardware, Computer
Software
Growth Openings in past
year 25; percentage
growth 50%
Contact
Dr. Doug Neuse, VP of
Development
Tel 512-328-5544
Fax 512-327-6646

Sematech, Inc.
2706 Montopolis Dr.
Austin, TX 78741

Founded 1988
Total employees 700
Industry Subassemblies
and Components
Growth Openings in past
year 122; percentage
growth 21%
Contact
William J. Spencer, Chief
Executive Officer
Tel 512-356-3500
Fax 512-356-3083

Solvay Interox
3333 Richmond Ave.
Houston, TX 77098

Founded 1979
Total employees 250
Annual sales $100 million
Industry Chemicals
Growth Openings in past
year 50; percentage
growth 25%

Contact
Rene DeGreve, Executive
Vice President
Tel 713-525-6500
Fax 713-524-9032

Solvay Minerals Co.
3333 Richmand Ave.
Houston, TX 77098

Founded 1981
Total employees 446
Industry Chemicals
Growth Openings in past
year 69; percentage
growth 18%
Contact
David R. Delling, President
Tel 713-525-6800

**Southwestern Bell
Telecommmunications,
Inc.**
1651 North Collins Blvd.
Richardson, TX 75080

Founded 1982
Total employees 850
Annual sales $110 million
Industry
Telecommunications
Growth Openings in past
year 63; percentage
growth 8%
Contact
Steven Carter, President/
CEO
Tel 214-994-8800
Fax 214-907-5704

**Specialized Waste
Systems, Inc.**
1273 Sheffield
Houston, TX 77015

Founded 1985
Total employees 40
Annual sales $2.1 million
Industry Environmental
Growth Openings in past
year 17; percentage
growth 73%
Contact
Leigh Parker, Assistant
General Manager
Tel 713-455-7799
Fax 713-455-7789

Star Tel, Inc.
1200 Briarcrest Dr.
Bryan, TX 77802

Founded 1981
Total employees 35
Annual sales $4.8 million

Industry
Telecommunications
Growth Openings in past
year 15; percentage
growth 75%
Contact
Phillip Stephenson,
President
Tel 409-821-2830

**Starkey Laboratories,
Omni Hearing Systems
Division**
3418 Midcourt Rd.
Carrollton, TX 75006

Founded 1982
Total employees 116
Industry Medical
Growth Openings in past
year 41; percentage
growth 54%
Contact
Larry Myers, General
Manager
Tel 214-934-2961
Fax 214-991-7864

**Stemco Inc., Truck
Products Division**
PO Box 1989
Longview, TX 75606

Founded 1951
Total employees 500
Annual sales $48 million
Industries Subassemblies
and Components, Test
and Measurement,
Transportation
Growth Openings in past
year 24; percentage
growth 5%
Contact
Doug Buck, VP of
Personnel
Tel 903-758-9981
Fax 903-232-3508

**Sterling Information
Group, Inc.**
PO Box 161148
Austin, TX 78716

Founded 1985
Total employees 42
Annual sales $4.8 million
Industry Computer
Software
Growth Openings in past
year 17; percentage
growth 68%
Contact
Chip Wolfe, President
Tel 512-327-0090
Fax 512-327-0197

**Sterling Software, Inc.,
Banking Systems
Division**
15301 Dallas Pkwy., Suite
400
Dallas, TX 75248

Founded 1976
Total employees 70
Annual sales $8.1 million
Industry Computer
Software
Growth Openings in past
year 15; percentage
growth 27%
Contact
Mark Alexander, Senior
Vice President/Controller
Tel 214-788-2580
Fax 214-788-1049

Surgimedics, Inc.
2828 North Crescent
Ridge Dr.
The Woodlands, TX 77381

Founded 1969
Total employees 200
Annual sales $22 million
Industry Holding
Companies
Growth Openings in past
year 35; percentage
growth 21%
Contact
Ms. Sherry Darden,
Personnel Manager
Tel 713-363-4949
Fax 713-292-1269

Syntron, Inc.
17200 Park Row
Houston, TX 77084

Founded 1973
Total employees 180
Annual sales $20 million
Industries Computer
Software, Test and
Measurement,
Transportation
Growth Openings in past
year 30; percentage
growth 20%
Contact
Mike Kahn, Human
Resources Manager
Tel 713-579-7700
Fax 713-579-7505

Tecnol, Inc.
7201 Industrial Park Blvd.
Fort Worth, TX 76180

Founded 1976
Total employees 850

Annual sales $93 million
Industry Holding
Companies
Growth Openings in past
year 248; percentage
growth 41%
Contact
Ms. DeLania Truly, VP of
Corporate
Communications and
Human
Tel 817-581-6424
Fax 817-581-9354

**Teknekron Infoswitch
Corp.**
4425 Cambridge Rd.
Fort Worth, TX 76155

Founded 1983
Total employees 125
Industries Computer
Software,
Telecommunications
Growth Openings in past
year 21; percentage
growth 20%
Contact
Michael J. Tamer,
President
Tel 817-267-3025
Fax 817-571-9464

Telecom Corp.
1545 West Mockingbird
Ln., Suite 7000
Dallas, TX 75235

Founded 1958
Total employees 305
Annual sales $63 million
Industry Holding
Companies
Growth Openings in past
year 23; percentage
growth 8%
Contact
Lawrence Schumann,
President/CEO/COB
Tel 214-638-0638
Fax 214-638-7043

**Teledyne Brown
Engineering, Control
Applications**
3401 Shiloh Rd.
Garland, TX 75041

Founded 1936
Total employees 59
Annual sales $7.0 million
Industries Computer
Hardware, Energy, Test
and Measurement,
Telecommunications

Growth Openings in past
year 17; percentage
growth 40%
Contact
Jonathan Whitcomb,
Division Manager
Tel 214-271-2561
Fax 214-278-1440

**Tescorp Seismic
Products, Inc.**
6209 Windfern Rd.
Houston, TX 77040

Founded 1981
Total employees 150
Annual sales $14 million
Industry Subassemblies
and Components
Growth Openings in past
year 30; percentage
growth 25%
Contact
Don Fussell, President
Tel 713-462-6608
Fax 713-460-1633

Tessco Group, Inc.
300 Industrial Ave.
Georgetown, TX 78626

Founded 1977
Total employees 270
Annual sales $19 million
Industries Subassemblies
and Components, Test
and Measurement
Growth Openings in past
year 29; percentage
growth 12%
Contact
Rand Mueller, President/
CEO
Tel 512-863-8742
Fax 512-863-0002

Texas Hydraulics
PO Box 1067
Temple, TX 76503

Founded 1968
Total employees 180
Annual sales $17 million
Industry Subassemblies
and Components
Growth Openings in past
year 60; percentage
growth 50%
Contact
Nick Petelski, President
Tel 817-778-4701
Fax 817-774-9940

Tivoli Systems, Inc.
6034 West Courtyard Dr.,
Suite 210
Austin, TX 78730

Founded 1989
Total employees 110
Annual sales $12 million
Industry Computer
Software
Growth Openings in past
year 20; percentage
growth 22%
Contact
Frank Moss, President/
CEO
Tel 512-794-9070
Fax 512-794-0623

TN Technologies, Inc.
PO Box 800
Round Rock, TX 78680

Founded 1957
Total employees 250
Annual sales $33 million
Industries Energy,
Environmental, Factory
Automation, Test and
Measurement
Growth Openings in past
year 19; percentage
growth 8%
Contact
Ms. Lynette Caldwell,
Personnel Administrator
Tel 512-388-9100
Fax 512-388-9200

Vertex Communications Corp.
2600 Longview St., PO
Box 1277
Kilgore, TX 75662

Founded 1973
Total employees 450
Annual sales $49 million
Industries Holding
Companies,
Telecommunications
Growth Openings in past
year 59; percentage
growth 15%
Contact
J. Rex Vardeman,
President
Tel 903-984-0555
Fax 903-984-1826

VLSI Packaging Corp.
1161 Executive Dr. West
Richardson, TX 75081

Founded 1984
Total employees 100

Industries Defense,
Subassemblies and
Components, Test and
Measurement
Growth Openings in past
year 20; percentage
growth 25%
Contact
Rolf Haberecht, Chief
Executive Officer
Tel 214-437-5506
Fax 214-644-1286

Utah

Applied Manufacturing Technology, Inc.
1176 South 1480 West
Orem, UT 84058

Founded 1989
Total employees 105
Industries Manufacturing
Equipment,
Subassemblies and
Components
Growth Openings in past
year 35; percentage
growth 50%
Contact
Jim Trent, President/CEO
Tel 801-224-3700
Fax 801-224-3744

Ballard Medical Products
12050 Lone Peak Pkwy.
Draper, UT 84020

Founded 1978
Total employees 500
Annual sales $38 million
Industry Medical
Growth Openings in past
year 20; percentage
growth 4%
Contact
Ms. Geri Stelling, Director
of Personnel
Tel 801-572-6800
Fax 801-572-6999

Campbell Scientific, Inc.
PO Box 551
Logan, UT 84321

Founded 1974
Total employees 148
Annual sales $17 million
Industries Computer
Hardware, Energy,
Factory Automation, Test
and Measurement

Growth Openings in past
year 15; percentage
growth 11%
Contact
Roger D. Ellis, Assistant
Treasurer
Tel 801-753-2342
Fax 801-752-3268

CUSA, Inc.
969 East 4800 South
Salt Lake City, UT 84117

Founded 1977
Total employees 120
Annual sales $9.2 million
Industry Computer
Software
Growth Openings in past
year 40; percentage
growth 50%
Contact
Gary Leavitt, President
Tel 801-263-1840
Fax 801-265-3222

Datachem Laboratories, Inc.
960 West Levoy Dr.
Salt Lake City, UT 84123

Founded 1971
Total employees 215
Annual sales $22 million
Industry Environmental
Growth Openings in past
year 15; percentage
growth 7%
Contact
James Nelson, President
Tel 801-266-7700
Fax 801-268-9992

DHI Computing Service, Inc.
1525 West 820 North, PO
Box 51427
Provo, UT 84603

Founded 1954
Total employees 200
Annual sales $25 million
Industries Computer
Hardware, Computer
Software, Holding
Companies
Growth Openings in past
year 20; percentage
growth 11%
Contact
Bliss H. Crandall,
President
Tel 801-373-8518

Dynix, Inc.
400 West Dynix Dr.
Provo, UT 84604

Founded 1983
Total employees 620
Annual sales $71 million
Industry Computer
Software
Growth Openings in past
year 174; percentage
growth 39%
Contact
Paul Sybrowsky, President
Tel 801-223-5200
Fax 801-373-1889

EFI Electronics Corp.
2415 South 2300 West
Salt Lake City, UT 84119

Founded 1979
Total employees 160
Annual sales $15.5 million
Industry Subassemblies
and Components
Growth Openings in past
year 45; percentage
growth 39%
Contact
Scott Nelson, President
Tel 801-977-9009
Fax 801-977-0200

**EIMCO Process
Equipment Co.**
669 West 2nd South, PO
Box 300
Salt Lake City, UT 84101

Founded 1906
Total employees 800
Annual sales $85 million
Industries Environmental,
Subassemblies and
Components, Test and
Measurement
Growth Openings in past
year 99; percentage
growth 14%
Contact
Dean Smith, President
Tel 801-526-2000
Fax 801-526-2425

**Hyclone Laboratories,
Inc.**
1725 South Hyclone Rd.
Logan, UT 84321

Founded 1975
Total employees 220
Annual sales $28 million
Industries Biotechnology,
Medical

Growth Openings in past
year 20; percentage
growth 10%
Contact
Greg Cox, Personnel
Manager
Tel 801-753-4584
Fax 801-753-4589

**Macrotech Fluid Sealing,
Inc., Polyseal Division**
1754 West 500 South
Salt Lake City, UT 84104

Founded 1974
Total employees 190
Annual sales $18 million
Industry Subassemblies
and Components
Growth Openings in past
year 60; percentage
growth 46%
Contact
David Norton, Personnel
Director
Tel 801-973-9171
Fax 801-973-9188

Megahertz Corp.
4505 South Wasatch Blvd.
Salt Lake City, UT 84124

Founded 1985
Total employees 430
Annual sales $80 million
Industry
Telecommunications
Growth Openings in past
year 270; percentage
growth 168%
Contact
Spencer Kirk, President
Tel 801-272-6000
Fax 801-272-6077

**NPS Pharmaceuticals,
Inc.**
420 Chipeta Way
Salt Lake City, UT 84105

Founded 1986
Total employees 55
Industry Pharmaceuticals
Growth Openings in past
year 30; percentage
growth 120%
Contact
Hunter Jackson, Ph.D.,
COB/CEO
Tel 801-583-4939
Fax 801-583-4961

Oldham Associates, Inc.
500 West 1200 South
Orem, UT 84058

Founded 1960
Total employees 239
Annual sales $27 million
Industry Holding
Companies
Growth Openings in past
year 54; percentage
growth 29%
Contact
Ms. Joanne Froelich,
President
Tel 801-226-2984
Fax 801-226-8438

**RAM Manufacturing Co.,
Inc.**
3172 East Deseret Dr.
South
Saint George, UT 84770

Founded 1975
Total employees 100
Annual sales $9.7 million
Industry Subassemblies
and Components
Growth Openings in past
year 17; percentage
growth 20%
Contact
Raymond Ganowsky,
President
Tel 801-673-4603
Fax 801-673-8239

San Juan Assembly, Inc.
378 West 500 North, Suite
33-8
Blanding, UT 84511

Founded 1987
Total employees 60
Annual sales $4.8 million
Industry Subassemblies
and Components
Growth Openings in past
year 20; percentage
growth 50%
Contact
Donnet Williams,
Accounting Manager
Tel 801-678-3255
Fax 801-678-2812

System Connection, Inc.
PO Box 50540
Provo, UT 84605

Founded 1986
Total employees 120
Annual sales $20 million

Industries Computer
Hardware,
Subassemblies and
Components
Growth Openings in past
year 20; percentage
growth 20%
Contact
Richard McCloskey, Jr.,
President/CEO
Tel 801-373-9800
Fax 801-373-9847

Theratech, Inc.
417 Wakara Way, Suite
100
Salt Lake City, UT 84108

Founded 1985
Total employees 125
Annual sales $2.56 million
Industries Medical,
Pharmaceuticals
Growth Openings in past
year 35; percentage
growth 38%
Contact
Dr. Dinesh Patel, Ph.D.,
President/CEO
Tel 801-583-6028
Fax 801-583-6042

**Utah Medical Products,
Inc.**
7043 South 300 West
Midvale, UT 84047

Founded 1978
Total employees 400
Annual sales $44 million
Industries Medical,
Subassemblies and
Components
Growth Openings in past
year 43; percentage
growth 12%
Contact
Ms. Iris McClure, Director
of Human Resources
Tel 801-566-1200
Fax 801-566-2062

Vermont

A&M Software, Inc.
77 Hegeman Ave.
Winooski, VT 05446

Founded 1982
Total employees 37
Annual sales $2 million

Industry Computer
Software
Growth Openings in past
year 18; percentage
growth 94%
Contact
Rick Fletcher, Office
Manager
Tel 802-655-4522
Fax 802-655-3307

Arnold Edwards Corp.
1608 Troy Ave.
Colchester, VT 05446

Founded 1963
Total employees 40
Annual sales $3 million
Industries Energy,
Manufacturing Equipment
Growth Openings in past
year 32; percentage
growth 400%
Contact
Andrew J. Edwards,
President
Tel 802-655-2533
Fax 802-655-0659

**Arrowsmith Shelburne,
Inc.**
2085 Shelburne Rd.
Shelburne, VT 05482

Founded 1974
Total employees 65
Annual sales $6.3 million
Industry Subassemblies
and Components
Growth Openings in past
year 15; percentage
growth 30%
Contact
Ms. Barb Noel, Human
Resources Manager
Tel 802-985-8621
Fax 802-985-1042

**Bennington Iron Works,
Inc.**
PO Box 798
Bennington, VT 05201

Founded 1968
Total employees 85
Annual sales $15 million
Industry Manufacturing
Equipment
Growth Openings in past
year 20; percentage
growth 30%
Contact
Curtis Morin, President
Tel 802-442-3145
Fax 802-447-3440

Bio-Tek Instruments, Inc.
Highland Industrial Park,
PO Box 998
Winooski, VT 05404

Founded 1965
Total employees 220
Annual sales $22 million
Industries Factory
Automation, Test and
Measurement
Growth Openings in past
year 29; percentage
growth 15%
Contact
Ms. Kathleen Gilpin,
Director of M.I.S. and
Human Resources
Tel 802-655-4040
Fax 802-655-7941

Carris Reels, Inc.
PO Box 696
Rutland, VT 05702

Founded 1956
Total employees 600
Annual sales $75 million
Industry Factory
Automation
Growth Openings in past
year 24; percentage
growth 4%
Contact
William Carris, President
Tel 802-773-9111

**Courtaulds Aerospace,
Inc., Performance
Composites Division**
6 Shields Dr.
Bennington, VT 05201

Founded 1979
Total employees 95
Annual sales $6 million
Industries Medical,
Subassemblies and
Components,
Telecommunications,
Transportation
Growth Openings in past
year 15; percentage
growth 18%
Contact
Daniel J. Maneely, General
Manager
Tel 802-442-9964
Fax 802-447-3642

IDX Systems Corp.
1400 Shelburne Rd., PO
Box 1070
Burlington, VT 05402

Founded 1969
Total employees 950

Annual sales $92 million
Industries Computer
Software, Holding
Companies
Growth Openings in past
year 145; percentage
growth 18%
Contact
Dean Haller, Director of
Human Resources
Tel 802-862-1022
Fax 802-862-6848

**Nexus Custom
Electronics**
Prospect St., PO Box 250
Brandon, VT 05733

Founded 1986
Total employees 110
Annual sales $15 million
Industries Subassemblies
and Components, Test
and Measurement
Growth Openings in past
year 60; percentage
growth 120%
Contact
Frank Simons, President
Tel 802-247-6811
Fax 802-247-3946

Springer-Miller, Inc.
Mountain Rd., PO Box
1547
Stowe, VT 05672

Founded 1982
Total employees 65
Annual sales $7.5 million
Industry Computer
Software
Growth Openings in past
year 45; percentage
growth 225%
Contact
John Springer-Miller,
President
Tel 802-253-4335

Virginia

ACS, Inc.
1807 Michael Farady Ct.
Reston, VA 22009

Founded 1973
Total employees 72
Annual sales $10 million
Industries Computer
Hardware, Computer
Software

Growth Openings in past
year 22; percentage
growth 44%
Contact
Ben A. Spaisman, COB/
CEO
Tel 703-742-9798
Fax 703-742-3774

**Advanced
Communication
Systems, Inc.**
1900 North Beauregard
St., Suite 300
Alexandria, VA 22311

Founded 1987
Total employees 187
Annual sales $20 million
Industries Defense,
Telecommunications
Growth Openings in past
year 62; percentage
growth 49%
Contact
George Robinson,
President
Tel 703-553-4389
Fax 703-820-8435

**Advanced Engineering &
Management Associates,
Aerospace and
Education Division**
1755 Jefferson Davis
Hwy., Suite 800
Arlington, VA 22202

Founded 1993
Total employees 60
Annual sales $6.9 million
Industry Computer
Software
Growth Openings in past
year 30; percentage
growth 100%
Contact
Rich Sadala, Vice
President/General
Manager
Tel 703-412-7188

**Advanced Engineering &
Research Associates**
2361 Jefferson Davis
Hwy., Suite 1120
Arlington, VA 22202

Founded 1988
Total employees 150
Annual sales $7.6 million
Industries Computer
Hardware, Energy,
Holding Companies,
Manufacturing Equipment

Growth Openings in past
year 70; percentage
growth 87%
Contact
Ned Daffan, President/
CEO
Tel 703-415-1790
Fax 703-415-1059

**Advanced Technology
Systems, Inc.**
800 Follin Ln., Suite 270
Vienna, VA 22180

Founded 1978
Total employees 350
Annual sales $18.1 million
Industries Computer
Hardware, Computer
Software
Growth Openings in past
year 100; percentage
growth 40%
Contact
Ms. Elsie Love, Personnel
Manager
Tel 703-242-0030
Fax 703-242-5220

Aerofin Corp.
4621 Murray Pl., PO Box
10819
Lynchburg, VA 24506

Founded 1923
Total employees 208
Industry Energy
Growth Openings in past
year 23; percentage
growth 12%
Contact
Jeffrey Dearing, Director of
Human Resources
Tel 804-845-7081
Fax 804-528-6242

**American
Communications Co.**
14200 Park Meadow Dr.
Chantilly, VA 22021

Founded 1975
Total employees 300
Annual sales $21 million
Industries Computer
Hardware,
Telecommunications
Growth Openings in past
year 50; percentage
growth 20%
Contact
Donald Kirk, Vice
President
Tel 703-968-6300
Fax 703-968-5151

American Systems Corp.
PO Box 10810
Chantilly, VA 22021

Founded 1975
Total employees 750
Annual sales $80 million
Industry Holding
Companies
Growth Openings in past
year 125; percentage
growth 20%
Contact
Thomas H. Curran,
President/CEO
Tel 703-968-6300
Fax 703-968-5151

Autometric, Inc.
5301 Shawnee Rd.
Alexandria, VA 22312

Founded 1957
Total employees 229
Annual sales $27 million
Industries Defense,
Holding Companies
Growth Openings in past
year 53; percentage
growth 30%
Contact
Ms. Wendy Harrison,
Director of Human
Resources
Tel 703-658-4000
Fax 703-658-4021

BDS, Inc.
105 Carpenter Dr.
Sterling, VA 22170

Founded 1983
Total employees 80
Annual sales $27 million
Industry Computer
Hardware
Growth Openings in past
year 27; percentage
growth 50%
Contact
Paul Collins, President
Tel 703-742-0800
Fax 703-481-8727

Betac International Corp.
2001 North Beauregard St.
Alexandria, VA 22311

Founded 1977
Total employees 215
Annual sales $23 million
Industry Defense

Growth Openings in past
year 15; percentage
growth 7%
Contact
Malcolm S. MacNichol,
Personnel Director
Tel 703-824-3100
Fax 703-824-0333

C-CUBED Corporation
5252 Cherokee Ave., Suite
400
Alexandria, VA 22312

Founded 1974
Total employees 260
Annual sales $17 million
Industries Computer
Hardware, Defense,
Telecommunications
Growth Openings in past
year 60; percentage
growth 30%
Contact
Ms. Susan Darke,
Manager of Human
Resources
Tel 703-658-9685
Fax 703-658-9689

**Coherent
Communications
Systems Corp.**
44084 Riverside Pkwy.
Lansdowne, VA 22075

Founded 1968
Total employees 125
Annual sales $17 million
Industries Subassemblies
and Components,
Telecommunications
Growth Openings in past
year 25; percentage
growth 25%
Contact
Daniel L. McGinnis,
President/COO
Tel 703-729-6400
Fax 703-729-6152

**Coleman Research
Corp., Washington
Division**
9302 Lee Hwy, Suite 800
Fairfax, VA 22031

Founded 1980
Total employees 85
Annual sales $9.1 million

Industries Defense,
Transportation
Growth Openings in past
year 18; percentage
growth 26%
Contact
Alan D. Stern, Vice
President/General
Manager
Tel 703-934-7800
Fax 703-934-7810

**Computer Based
Systems, Inc.**
2750 Prosperity Ave.,
Suite 300
Fairfax, VA 22031

Founded 1978
Total employees 650
Annual sales $30 million
Industries Computer
Hardware, Computer
Software
Growth Openings in past
year 150; percentage
growth 30%
Contact
Ms. Barbara Glover,
Director of Administration
Tel 703-849-8080
Fax 703-849-1763

Comsearch
11720 Sunrise Valley Dr.
Reston, VA 22091

Founded 1977
Total employees 176
Annual sales $14 million
Industry
Telecommunications
Growth Openings in past
year 32; percentage
growth 22%
Contact
Harry L. Stemple, Chief
Executive Officer
Tel 703-620-6300
Fax 703-476-2697

COR, Inc.
105 North Virginia Ave.
Falls Church, VA 22046

Founded 1979
Total employees 225

Annual sales $12 million
Industries Defense,
Manufacturing
Equipment,
Telecommunications
Growth Openings in past
year 75; percentage
growth 50%
Contact
Pham Chopra, Chief
Executive Officer
Tel 703-534-0011
Fax 703-534-6655

DataFocus, Inc.
12450 Fair Lakes Cir.,
Suite 400
Fairfax, VA 22033

Founded 1981
Total employees 50
Annual sales $8.2 million
Industries Computer
Hardware, Computer
Software, Test and
Measurement
Growth Openings in past
year 24; percentage
growth 92%
Contact
Patrick B. Higbie,
President
Tel 703-631-6770
Fax 703-818-1532

Datatel, Inc.
4375 Fair Lakes Ct.
Fairfax, VA 22033

Founded 1968
Total employees 170
Annual sales $26 million
Industry Computer
Software
Growth Openings in past
year 25; percentage
growth 17%
Contact
Ms. Ginger Piercy, VP of
Finance
Tel 703-968-9000
Fax 703-968-4625

DCS Corp.
1330 Braddock Pl.
Alexandria, VA 22314

Founded 1977
Total employees 287
Annual sales $24 million
Industries Defense,
Manufacturing
Equipment,
Subassemblies and
Components

Growth Openings in past
year 22; percentage
growth 8%
Contact
James T. Wood, President
Tel 703-683-8430
Fax 703-684-7229

Delex Systems, Inc.
1953 Gallows Rd., Suite
700
Vienna, VA 22182

Founded 1968
Total employees 265
Annual sales $19.8 million
Industries Defense,
Transportation
Growth Openings in past
year 15; percentage
growth 6%
Contact
Ms. Susan Klein, Director
of Human Resources
Tel 703-734-8300
Fax 703-734-9303

Deltek Systems, Inc.
8280 Greensboro Dr.
Mc Lean, VA 22102

Founded 1983
Total employees 150
Annual sales $18 million
Industry Computer
Software
Growth Openings in past
year 25; percentage
growth 20%
Contact
Ken de Laski, President
Tel 703-734-8606
Fax 703-734-0346

Dewberry & Davis
8401 Arlington Blvd.
Fairfax, VA 22031

Founded 1959
Total employees 992
Industry Manufacturing
Equipment
Growth Openings in past
year 39; percentage
growth 4%
Contact
Richard Renner, Assistant
Director of Human
Resources
Tel 703-849-0100
Fax 703-849-0118

Dual, Inc.
2101 Wilson Blvd., Suite
600
Arlington, VA 22201

Founded 1983
Total employees 260
Annual sales $18 million
Industries Manufacturing
Equipment,
Subassemblies and
Components
Growth Openings in past
year 20; percentage
growth 8%
Contact
Ms. Nancy Streeter,
Director of Administration
Tel 703-527-3500
Fax 703-527-0829

**Dunham-Bush, Inc.,
Compressurized Air
Conditioning Division**
101 Burgess Rd.
Harrisonburg, VA 22801

Founded 1968
Total employees 575
Annual sales $60 million
Industry Energy
Growth Openings in past
year 23; percentage
growth 4%
Contact
Steve Riddleberger,
Personnel Manager
Tel 703-434-0711
Fax 703-434-4010

Edunetics Corp.
1600 Wilson Blvd., Suite
710
Arlington, VA 22209

Founded 1984
Total employees 130
Annual sales $5 million
Industry Computer
Software
Growth Openings in past
year 50; percentage
growth 62%
Contact
Benjamin Chen, President/
CEO
Tel 703-243-2602
Fax 703-243-2606

**Electronic
Instrumentation and
Technology, Inc.**
108 Carpenter Dr.
Sterling, VA 20164

Founded 1977
Total employees 143

Annual sales $14 million
Industry Subassemblies
and Components
Growth Openings in past
year 31; percentage
growth 27%
Contact
Joe May, President
Tel 703-478-0700
Fax 703-478-0291

**Electronic Warfare
Associates, Inc.**
13873 Park Center Rd.
Herndon, VA 22017

Founded 1977
Total employees 285
Annual sales $30 million
Industry Defense
Growth Openings in past
year 65; percentage
growth 29%
Contact
Carl N. Guerreri, President
Tel 703-904-5700
Fax 703-904-5779

**Engineering Research
Associates, Inc.**
1595 Springhill Rd.
Vienna, VA 22182

Founded 1977
Total employees 350
Industry Computer
Software
Growth Openings in past
year 49; percentage
growth 16%
Contact
Pat Flanagan, Director of
Personnel
Tel 703-734-8800
Fax 703-734-8862

ENSCO, Inc.
5400 Port Royal Rd.
Springfield, VA 22151

Founded 1969
Total employees 400
Annual sales $34 million
Industry Holding
Companies
Growth Openings in past
year 20; percentage
growth 5%
Contact
Ms. Joanne McDonald, VP
of Human Resources and
Administration
Tel 703-321-9000
Fax 703-321-4529

**Environmental
Protection Systems, Inc.**
3800 Concord Pkwy., Suite
2100
Chantilly, VA 22021

Founded 1973
Total employees 110
Annual sales $11 million
Industries Chemicals,
Environmental
Growth Openings in past
year 18; percentage
growth 19%
Contact
Arnie Kalm, President
Tel 703-631-2411
Fax 703-631-9855

Erni Components, Inc.
520 Southlake Blvd.
Richmond, VA 23236

Founded 1965
Total employees 100
Annual sales $15 million
Industry Computer
Hardware
Growth Openings in past
year 45; percentage
growth 81%
Contact
Willi Rau, President
Tel 804-794-6367
Fax 804-379-2109

FiberCom, Inc.
3353 Orange Ave.
Roanoke, VA 24012

Founded 1982
Total employees 220
Industries Photonics,
Telecommunications
Growth Openings in past
year 20; percentage
growth 10%
Contact
Ms. Lacy Carter, Human
Resources Manager
Tel 703-342-6700
Fax 703-342-5961

**Fuentez Systems
Concepts, Inc.**
11781 Lee Jackson Hwy.,
Suite 700
Fairfax, VA 22033

Founded 1983
Total employees 80
Annual sales $5.5 million
Industries Computer
Hardware, Computer
Software, Defense,
Manufacturing Equipment

Growth Openings in past
year 35; percentage
growth 77%
Contact
Ms. Espeticion T. Fuentez,
COB/President
Tel 703-273-1447
Fax 703-273-2972

Genetics & IVF Institute
3020 Javier Rd.
Fairfax, VA 22031

Founded 1984
Total employees 210
Annual sales $20 million
Industry Biotechnology
Growth Openings in past
year 29; percentage
growth 16%
Contact
Joseph D. Schulman, MD,
COB/CEO
Tel 703-698-7355
Fax 703-698-3963

Global Associates, Ltd.
2300 Clarendon Blvd.,
Suite 205
Arlington, VA 22201

Founded 1986
Total employees 85
Annual sales $9.1 million
Industries Computer
Hardware, Defense,
Manufacturing
Equipment,
Telecommunications
Growth Openings in past
year 25; percentage
growth 41%
Contact
Ms. Jeannette Mullens,
Manager of Human
Resources
Tel 703-351-5660
Fax 703-351-5650

Globalink, Inc.
9302 Lee Hwy., 12th Fl.
Fairfax, VA 22031

Founded 1990
Total employees 50
Annual sales $4.0 million
Industry Computer
Software
Growth Openings in past
year 15; percentage
growth 42%
Contact
Dominic Laiti, President
Tel 703-273-5600
Fax 703-273-3866

Information Management Consultants, Inc.
7915 Westpark Dr.
Mc Lean, VA 22102

Founded 1981
Total employees 175
Annual sales $12 million
Industry Computer
Software
Growth Openings in past
year 15; percentage
growth 9%
Contact
Sudhakar Shenoy,
President
Tel 703-893-3100
Fax 703-893-3489

Interlog, Inc.
5109 Leesburg Pike, Suite
400
Falls Church, VA 22041

Founded 1983
Total employees 140
Annual sales $8 million
Industries Computer
Software, Defense,
Manufacturing Equipment
Growth Openings in past
year 20; percentage
growth 16%
Contact
John Brown, Jr., President
Tel 703-845-8441
Fax 703-845-9443

JIL Systems, Inc.
1213 Jefferson Davis
Hwy., Gateway #4, Suite
1000
Arlington, VA 22202

Founded 1985
Total employees 110
Annual sales $18 million
Industries Computer
Hardware, Computer
Software, Defense,
Manufacturing Equipment
Growth Openings in past
year 60; percentage
growth 120%
Contact
Tony Nelson, Chief
Executive Officer
Tel 703-979-0430
Fax 703-979-0640

JWK International Corp.
7617 Little River Tpke.,
Suite 1000
Annandale, VA 22003

Founded 1973
Total employees 300

Industries Defense,
Manufacturing Equipment
Growth Openings in past
year 100; percentage
growth 50%
Contact
Ms. Jean Munson,
Administrator
Tel 703-750-0500
Fax 703-256-1986

Lydall, Inc., Southern Products Division
3021 Vernon Rd.
Richmond, VA 23228

Founded 1879
Total employees 110
Annual sales $16 million
Industries Advanced
Materials, Factory
Automation
Growth Openings in past
year 18; percentage
growth 19%
Contact
Raymond J. Lanzi,
Division President
Tel 804-266-9611
Fax 804-266-3875

Maida Development Co.
20 Libby St., PO Box 3529
Hampton, VA 23663

Founded 1947
Total employees 350
Annual sales $24 million
Industry Subassemblies
and Components
Growth Openings in past
year 100; percentage
growth 40%
Contact
Donald H. Merritt,
President
Tel 804-723-0785
Fax 804-722-1194

Metters Industries, Inc.
8200 Greensboro Dr.
Mc Lean, VA 22102

Founded 1981
Total employees 450
Annual sales $43 million
Industry Defense
Growth Openings in past
year 49; percentage
growth 12%
Contact
Samuel Metters, Chief
Executive Officer
Tel 703-821-3300
Fax 703-821-3996

Michael Baker Jr., Inc., Civil and Water Resources Division
3601 Eisenhower Ave.
Alexandria, VA 22304

Founded 1946
Total employees 440
Annual sales $28 million
Industries Computer
Software, Environmental,
Manufacturing
Equipment,
Telecommunications
Growth Openings in past
year 190; percentage
growth 76%
Contact
Edward Wiley, Senior Vice
President/General
Manager
Tel 703-960-8800
Fax 703-960-9125

Microdyne Corp.
207 South Peyton St.
Alexandria, VA 22314

Founded 1968
Total employees 500
Annual sales $73 million
Industries Computer
Hardware,
Telecommunications
Growth Openings in past
year 38; percentage
growth 8%
Contact
Paul Sinclair, Director of
Human Resources
Tel 703-739-0500
Fax 703-739-0558

NCI Information Systems, Inc.
8260 Greensboro Dr.,
Suite 400
Mc Lean, VA 22102

Founded 1986
Total employees 230
Annual sales $26 million
Industry Computer
Software
Growth Openings in past
year 120; percentage
growth 109%
Contact
Ms. Kathy Kander, Human
Resources Manager
Tel 703-903-0325
Fax 703-903-9750

Netrix Corp.
13595 Dulles Technology Dr.
Herndon, VA 22071

Founded 1985
Total employees 192
Annual sales $23.4 million
Industry
Telecommunications
Growth Openings in past year 38; percentage growth 24%
Contact
Charles W. Stein, President
Tel 703-742-6000
Fax 703-742-4048

Network Solutions, Inc.
505 Huntmar Park Dr.
Herndon, VA 22070

Founded 1979
Total employees 400
Annual sales $49 million
Industries Computer Hardware, Computer Software, Holding Companies
Growth Openings in past year 23; percentage growth 6%
Contact
Ms. Karyn Trader, Director of Human Resources
Tel 703-742-0400
Fax 703-742-4837

Newbridge Networks, Inc.
593 Herndon Pkwy., Suite 200
Herndon, VA 22070

Founded 1986
Total employees 400
Annual sales $166 million
Industries Computer Software, Photonics, Subassemblies and Components, Telecommunications
Growth Openings in past year 100; percentage growth 33%
Contact
F. Michael Pascoe, President
Tel 703-834-3600
Fax 703-471-7080

PSI International, Inc.
10306 Eaton Pl., Suite 400
Fairfax, VA 22030

Founded 1983
Total employees 250
Annual sales $41 million
Industries Computer Hardware, Computer Software, Defense
Growth Openings in past year 50; percentage growth 25%
Contact
Dr. Elizabeth Pan, Ph.D., Chief Executive Officer
Tel 703-352-8700
Fax 703-352-8236

Quality Systems, Inc.
4000 Legato Rd., Suite 1100
Fairfax, VA 22033

Founded 1981
Total employees 301
Annual sales $24.2 million
Industries Computer Hardware, Computer Software
Growth Openings in past year 106; percentage growth 54%
Contact
Robert C. Dehaven, Chief Executice Officer
Tel 703-352-9200
Fax 703-352-9216

Resource Applications, Inc.
2980 Fairview Park Dr., Suite 1000
Falls Church, VA 22042

Founded 1979
Total employees 150
Annual sales $12 million
Industry Environmental
Growth Openings in past year 30; percentage growth 25%
Contact
Ms. Deborah Monte, Director of Human Resources
Tel 703-698-2000
Fax 703-698-2030

Resource Consultants, Inc.
1960 Gallows Rd.
Vienna, VA 22128

Founded 1979
Total employees 800

Annual sales $86 million
Industry Defense
Growth Openings in past year 99; percentage growth 14%
Contact
Ronald S. Newlan, President
Tel 703-893-6120
Fax 703-893-0917

Riverbend Group, Inc.
1430 Spring Hill Rd., Suite 600
Mc Lean, VA 22102

Founded 1983
Total employees 50
Annual sales $8.2 million
Industry Computer Hardware
Growth Openings in past year 20; percentage growth 66%
Contact
Ms. Becky Millis, Director of Human Resources
Tel 703-883-0616
Fax 703-893-9858

Science & Technology Corp.
101 Research Dr.
Hampton, VA 23666

Founded 1979
Total employees 325
Industries Computer Software, Environmental, Holding Companies, Photonics, Transportation
Growth Openings in past year 125; percentage growth 62%
Contact
Dr. Ardash Deepak, President
Tel 804-865-1894
Fax 804-865-1294

Software AG of North America, Inc.
11190 Sunrise Valley Dr.
Reston, VA 22091

Founded 1972
Total employees 760
Annual sales $88 million
Industry Computer Software
Growth Openings in past year 44; percentage growth 6%

Contact
William Cripe, VP of
Human Resources
Tel 703-860-5050
Fax 703-391-6975

**Sumitomo Machinery
Corp. of America**
4200 Holland Blvd.
Chesapeake, VA 23323

Founded 1965
Total employees 247
Industries Energy,
Subassemblies and
Components
Growth Openings in past
year 47; percentage
growth 23%
Contact
John Cali, VP of
Operations
Tel 804-485-3355
Fax 804-487-3193

**Super Radiator Coils,
Ltd.**
451 Southlake Blvd.
Richmond, VA 23235

Founded 1928
Total employees 100
Annual sales $14 million
Industry Energy
Growth Openings in past
year 25; percentage
growth 33%
Contact
Jon Holt, President
Tel 804-794-2887
Fax 804-379-2118

SWL Inc.
1900 Gallows Rd.
Vienna, VA 22182

Founded 1964
Total employees 350
Annual sales $36 million
Industries Computer
Hardware, Defense,
Manufacturing
Equipment,
Subassemblies and
Components
Growth Openings in past
year 49; percentage
growth 16%
Contact
Ms. Arlene Rimson,
Human Resource
Director
Tel 703-506-5000
Fax 703-506-0585

**Systems Research and
Applications Corp.**
2000 15th St. North
Arlington, VA 22201

Founded 1978
Total employees 830
Annual sales $66 million
Industries Manufacturing
Equipment,
Telecommunications
Growth Openings in past
year 109; percentage
growth 15%
Contact
Jerry Yates, VP of
Administration
Tel 703-558-4700
Fax 703-558-4788

Titan Systems Group
1900 Campus Commons
Dr.
Reston, VA 22091

Founded 1981
Total employees 300
Annual sales $32 million
Industries Computer
Hardware, Manufacturing
Equipment
Growth Openings in past
year 75; percentage
growth 33%
Contact
Ed Knauf, President
Tel 703-883-9200
Fax 703-821-3351

TYX Corp.
1851 Alexander Bell Dr.
Reston, VA 22091

Founded 1982
Total employees 40
Annual sales $4 million
Industry Computer
Software
Growth Openings in past
year 15; percentage
growth 60%
Contact
Narayanan
Ramachrandran,
President
Tel 703-264-1080
Fax 703-264-1090

Universal Dynamics, Inc.
13600 Dabney Rd.
Woodbridge, VA 22191

Founded 1957
Total employees 170
Annual sales $20 million

Industries Factory
Automation,
Manufacturing
Equipment, Test and
Measurement
Growth Openings in past
year 20; percentage
growth 13%
Contact
Donald Rainville, President
Tel 703-491-2191
Fax 703-690-6535

**Universal Systems
Incorporated**
4350 Fairlakes Ct., Suite
200
Fairfax, VA 22033

Founded 1989
Total employees 300
Annual sales $30 million
Industry Computer
Hardware
Growth Openings in past
year 50; percentage
growth 20%
Contact
Robert E. LaRose,
President/CEO
Tel 703-222-2840
Fax 703-222-0543

Valcom, Inc.
1111 Industry Ave.
Roanoke, VA 24013

Founded 1977
Total employees 250
Annual sales $34 million
Industry
Telecommunications
Growth Openings in past
year 50; percentage
growth 25%
Contact
Ms. Linda Bishop, Human
Resources Administrator
Tel 703-982-3900
Fax 703-982-7032

Vigyan, Inc.
30 Research Dr.
Hampton, VA 23666

Founded 1979
Total employees 170
Annual sales $11 million
Industry Transportation
Growth Openings in past
year 40; percentage
growth 30%
Contact
S.C. Mehrotra, President
Tel 804-865-1400
Fax 804-865-8177

Virginia Transformer Corp.
220 Glade View Dr.
Northeast
Roanoke, VA 24012

Founded 1971
Total employees 160
Annual sales $21 million
Industry Energy
Growth Openings in past
year 20; percentage
growth 14%
Contact
Prab Jain, President
Tel 703-345-9892
Fax 703-342-7694

Zimmerman Associates, Inc.
8229 Boone Blvd., Suite 200
Vienna, VA 22182

Founded 1977
Total employees 170
Annual sales $10 million
Industry Holding
Companies
Growth Openings in past
year 20; percentage
growth 13%
Contact
Paul E. Jones, CEO/
President
Tel 703-883-0506
Fax 703-886-0526

Washington

Active Voice Corp.
2901 3rd Ave., Suite 500
Seattle, WA 98121

Founded 1983
Total employees 125
Annual sales $18.5 million
Industry Computer
Software
Growth Openings in past
year 25; percentage
growth 25%
Contact
Ms. Debra Faulkner,
Personnel and Facilities
Manager
Tel 206-441-4700
Fax 206-441-4784

Adonis Corp.
6742 185th Ave.
Northeast, Suite 150
Redmond, WA 98052

Founded 1988
Total employees 47
Annual sales $4 million
Industries Computer
Hardware, Computer
Software
Growth Openings in past
year 23; percentage
growth 95%
Contact
Tom Young, Personnel
Manager
Tel 206-881-8251
Fax 206-869-0252

Advanced Digital Information Corp.
14737 Northeast 87th St.,
PO Box 97057
Redmond, WA 98073

Founded 1983
Total employees 95
Annual sales $15 million
Industries Computer
Hardware, Computer
Software
Growth Openings in past
year 30; percentage
growth 46%
Contact
Ms. Pauline Dempsey, VP
of Human Resources
Tel 206-881-8004
Fax 206-881-2296

Asymetrix Corp.
110-110th Ave., Suite 700
Bellevue, WA 98004

Founded 1985
Total employees 200
Annual sales $23 million
Industry Computer
Software
Growth Openings in past
year 100; percentage
growth 100%
Contact
Paul Allen, President
Tel 206-462-0501
Fax 206-455-3071

Augat Communications Group, Inc.
23315 66th Ave. South
Kent, WA 98032

Founded 1976
Total employees 225

Industries Photonics,
Telecommunications
Growth Openings in past
year 75; percentage
growth 50%
Contact
Larry Buffington, President
Tel 206-854-9802
Fax 206-813-1001

Bright Star Technology, Inc.
40 Lake Bellevue Dr.,
Suite 350
Bellevue, WA 98005

Founded 1987
Total employees 30
Annual sales $3.4 million
Industry Computer
Software
Growth Openings in past
year 21; percentage
growth 233%
Contact
Al Higginson, President
Tel 206-451-3697
Fax 206-454-1062

Cascade Design Automation Corp.
3650 131st Ave. Southeast
Bellevue, WA 98006

Founded 1991
Total employees 85
Annual sales $13 million
Industry Computer
Software
Growth Openings in past
year 20; percentage
growth 30%
Contact
Ms. Lee Frazer, Director of
Personnel
Tel 206-643-0200
Fax 206-649-7600

Cellpro, Inc.
22322 20th Ave.
Southeast, Suite 100
Bothell, WA 98021

Founded 1989
Total employees 112
Annual sales $1.73 million
Industry Biotechnology
Growth Openings in past
year 42; percentage
growth 60%
Contact
Richard D. Murdock,
President
Tel 206-485-7644
Fax 206-485-4787

Darius Technology, Inc.
22028 26th Ave. Southeast
Bothell, WA 98021

Founded 1990
Total employees 25
Annual sales $40 million
Industry Computer
  Hardware
Growth Openings in past
  year 18; percentage
  growth 257%
Contact
Glen Griffin, President/
  CEO
Tel 206-483-8889
Fax 206-486-2577

Datacom Technologies, Inc.
11001 31st Pl. West
Everett, WA 98204

Founded 1981
Total employees 90
Annual sales $11 million
Industries Computer
  Hardware, Factory
  Automation,
  Telecommunications
Growth Openings in past
  year 25; percentage
  growth 38%
Contact
Val Durham, President
Tel 206-355-0590
Fax 206-290-1600

Emcon Northwest, Inc.
18912 North Creek Pkwy.,
  Suite 100
Bothell, WA 98011

Founded 1974
Total employees 275
Industry Environmental
Growth Openings in past
  year 64; percentage
  growth 30%
Contact
Ms. Cecilia Simonis,
  Director of Human
  Resources
Tel 206-485-5000
Fax 206-486-9766

Fleck Co., Inc.
3410 A St. Southeast
Auburn, WA 98002

Founded 1967
Total employees 130
Industry Manufacturing
  Equipment

Growth Openings in past
  year 40; percentage
  growth 44%
Contact
Mrs. Darlene Locken,
  Personnel Manager
Tel 206-833-5900
Fax 206-833-2245

FourGen Software, Inc.
115 Northeast 100th St.
Seattle, WA 98125

Founded 1983
Total employees 90
Annual sales $10 million
Industry Computer
  Software
Growth Openings in past
  year 15; percentage
  growth 20%
Contact
Gary Gagliardi, President
Tel 206-522-0055
Fax 206-522-0053

Hathaway Corp., Systems Northwest Division
7661 South 180th St.
Kent, WA 98032

Founded 1961
Total employees 75
Annual sales $9.4 million
Industry Factory
  Automation
Growth Openings in past
  year 20; percentage
  growth 36%
Contact
Robert Sodergren,
  President
Tel 206-251-0211
Fax 206-251-0113

IC Designs
12020 113th Ave.
  Northeast
Kirkland, WA 98034

Founded 1985
Total employees 40
Industry Subassemblies
  and Components
Growth Openings in past
  year 20; percentage
  growth 100%
Contact
Dr. John Q. Torode,
  President
Tel 206-821-9202
Fax 206-820-8959

ICOS Corp.
22021 20th Ave. Southeast
Bothell, WA 98021

Founded 1989
Total employees 160
Industry Pharmaceuticals
Growth Openings in past
  year 60; percentage
  growth 60%
Contact
George Rathmann,
  COB/CEO
Tel 206-485-1900
Fax 206-485-1911

Immunex Corp.
51 University St.
Seattle, WA 98101

Founded 1981
Total employees 611
Annual sales $95.31
  million
Industry Biotechnology
Growth Openings in past
  year 80; percentage
  growth 15%
Contact
Ms. Anita Williamson,
  Human Resources
  Director
Tel 206-587-0430
Fax 206-587-0606

IMRE Corp.
401 Queen Anne Ave.
  North
Seattle, WA 98109

Founded 1981
Total employees 60
Annual sales $4 million
Industry Medical
Growth Openings in past
  year 15; percentage
  growth 33%
Contact
Ms. Lois H. Yoshida,
  VP/Chief Administrative
  Officer
Tel 206-298-9400
Fax 206-298-9494

InControl, Inc.
6675 185th Ave. Northeast
Redmond, WA 98052

Founded 1990
Total employees 70
Industry Medical
Growth Openings in past
  year 30; percentage
  growth 75%

Contact
Ms. Kay Hannah,
Administrator
Tel 206-861-9800
Fax 206-861-9301

**Index Sensors &
Controls, Inc.**
13205 South East 30th St.
Bellevue, WA 98005

Founded 1976
Total employees 75
Annual sales $7.3 million
Industries Subassemblies
and Components, Test
and Measurement
Growth Openings in past
year 37; percentage
growth 97%
Contact
Robert Champoux,
Co-President
Tel 206-746-4049
Fax 206-747-8902

Interlinq Software Corp.
10210 Northeast Points
Dr., Suite 400
Kirkland, WA 98033

Founded 1982
Total employees 150
Annual sales $15.15
million
Industry Computer
Software
Growth Openings in past
year 24; percentage
growth 19%
Contact
Ms. Sandra Daubenspeck,
Human Resources
Manager
Tel 206-827-1112
Fax 206-827-0927

Itron, Inc.
2818 North Sullivan Rd.
Spokane, WA 99215

Founded 1977
Total employees 577
Annual sales $88.6 million
Industries Computer
Hardware,
Telecommunications
Growth Openings in past
year 23; percentage
growth 4%
Contact
Johnny Humphreys,
President/CEO
Tel 509-924-9900
Fax 509-928-1465

**Johnson Matthey
Electronics, Inc.**
East 15128 Euclid Ave.
Spokane, WA 99216

Founded 1961
Total employees 460
Industries Advanced
Materials, Manufacturing
Equipment,
Subassemblies and
Components
Growth Openings in past
year 175; percentage
growth 61%
Contact
Geoff Wild, General
Manager
Tel 509-924-2200
Fax 509-922-8617

**MathSoft, Inc., Statistical
Sciences Division**
1700 Westlake Ave. North,
Suite 500
Seattle, WA 98109

Founded 1987
Total employees 60
Annual sales $3.4 million
Industry Computer
Software
Growth Openings in past
year 20; percentage
growth 50%
Contact
Matt Schiltz, General
Manager
Tel 206-283-8802
Fax 206-283-8691

Microrim, Inc.
15395 Southeast 30th Pl.
Bellevue, WA 98007

Founded 1981
Total employees 100
Annual sales $11 million
Industry Computer
Software
Growth Openings in past
year 30; percentage
growth 42%
Contact
Art Miller, CEO/President
Tel 206-649-9500
Fax 206-649-2792

Northwest Alloys, Inc.
1560A Marble Valley Rd.
Addy, WA 99101

Founded 1888
Total employees 400
Industry Advanced
Materials

Growth Openings in past
year 50; percentage
growth 14%
Contact
E.L. Sandman, Plant
Manager
Tel 509-935-3300
Fax 509-935-3211

Pacific Circuits, Inc.
17550 Northeast 67th Ct.
Redmond, WA 98052

Founded 1978
Total employees 290
Annual sales $20 million
Industry Subassemblies
and Components
Growth Openings in past
year 29; percentage
growth 11%
Contact
L.O. Coley, President
Tel 206-883-7575
Fax 206-882-1268

**Pacific Western
Services, Inc.**
3594 Northwest Byron St.,
Suite 202
Silverdale, WA 98383

Founded 1984
Total employees 85
Industries Computer
Hardware,
Environmental,
Telecommunications
Growth Openings in past
year 30; percentage
growth 54%
Contact
Ms. Naomi K. Pursel,
President
Tel 206-692-2602
Fax 206-692-5917

Panlabs, Inc.
11804 North Creek Pkwy.
South
Bothell, WA 98011

Founded 1970
Total employees 400
Annual sales $25 million
Industry Holding
Companies
Growth Openings in past
year 30; percentage
growth 8%
Contact
Nicholas Dykstra, VP of
Finance and
Administration
Tel 206-487-8200
Fax 206-487-3787

Quinton Instrument Co.
2121 Terry Ave.
Seattle, WA 98121

Founded 1961
Total employees 750
Annual sales $82 million
Industries Medical,
 Telecommunications
Growth Openings in past
 year 36; percentage
 growth 5%
Contact
Ed Schnebele, Director of
 Personnel
Tel 206-223-7373
Fax 206-223-8465

Raima Corp.
1605 Northwest
 Sammamish Rd.
Issaquah, WA 98027

Founded 1982
Total employees 90
Annual sales $8.1 million
Industry Computer
 Software
Growth Openings in past
 year 20; percentage
 growth 28%
Contact
J. Robert Newton,
 President
Tel 206-557-0200
Fax 206-557-5200

Saros Corp.
10900 Northeast 8th St.,
 Suite 700
Bellevue, WA 98004

Founded 1986
Total employees 102
Annual sales $11 million
Industry Computer
 Software
Growth Openings in past
 year 42; percentage
 growth 70%
Contact
Wayne Carpenter,
 President/CEO
Tel 206-646-1066
Fax 206-462-0879

SeaMED Corp.
11810 North Creek Pkwy.
 North
Bothell, WA 98011

Founded 1976
Total employees 105
Annual sales $11 million
Industry Medical

Growth Openings in past
 year 25; percentage
 growth 31%
Contact
Robert W. Berg, President/
 CEO
Tel 206-485-3399
Fax 206-487-1736

Spry, Inc.
316 Occidental Ave. South
Seattle, WA 98104

Founded 1987
Total employees 30
Annual sales $6 million
Industry Computer
 Software
Growth Openings in past
 year 15; percentage
 growth 100%
Contact
David Pool, President
Tel 206-447-0300
Fax 206-447-9008

**Statpower Technologies
Corp.**
200 14th St., PO Box
 1850
Blaine, WA 98230

Founded 1988
Total employees 50
Annual sales $6.7 million
Industry Energy
Growth Openings in past
 year 21; percentage
 growth 72%
Contact
Ms. Kelli O'Keefe, Director
 of Personnel
Tel 800-668-0003

Traveling Software, Inc.
18702 North Creek Pkwy.
Bothell, WA 98011

Founded 1982
Total employees 120
Annual sales $13 million
Industry Computer
 Software
Growth Openings in past
 year 24; percentage
 growth 25%
Contact
Jonathan Scott, President/
 COO
Tel 206-483-8088
Fax 206-487-1284

**Walker, Richer and
Quinn, Inc.**
2815 Eastlake Ave. East
Seattle, WA 98102

Founded 1981
Total employees 250
Annual sales $40 million
Industry Computer
 Software
Growth Openings in past
 year 50; percentage
 growth 25%
Contact
Ms. Char Harrington,
 Personnel Director
Tel 206-324-0350
Fax 206-322-8151

ZymoGenetics, Inc.
4225 Roosevelt Way
 Northeast
Seattle, WA 98105

Founded 1981
Total employees 180
Annual sales $17 million
Industry Biotechnology
Growth Openings in past
 year 60; percentage
 growth 50%
Contact
Dr. Bruce Carter, Ph.D.,
 President
Tel 206-547-8080
Fax 206-548-2329

**ZyzaTech Water
Systems, Inc.**
6705 South 216th St.
Kent, WA 98032

Founded 1970
Total employees 40
Annual sales $2 million
Industry Environmental
Growth Openings in past
 year 20; percentage
 growth 100%
Contact
Emanuel Anato, President
Tel 206-395-2200
Fax 206-395-2363

West Virginia

**Wheeling Corrugating
Co.**
1134 Market St.
Wheeling, WV 26003

Founded 1968
Total employees 375

Annual sales $214 million
Industry Advanced
Materials
Growth Openings in past
year 25; percentage
growth 7%
Contact
J.G. Bronchik, General
Manager of Corporate
Personnel
Tel 304-234-2400
Fax 304-234-2678

Wisconsin

**ABB Industrial Systems,
Inc.**
16250 West Glendale Dr.
New Berlin, WI 53151

Founded 1985
Total employees 375
Annual sales $44 million
Industries Manufacturing
Equipment, Test and
Measurement
Growth Openings in past
year 25; percentage
growth 7%
Contact
Ms. Cindy Allmand,
Manager of Human
Resources
Tel 414-785-3200
Fax 414-785-0397

ABB Robotics, Inc.
2487 South Commerce Dr.
New Berlin, WI 53151

Founded 1984
Total employees 400
Annual sales $50 million
Industry Factory
Automation
Growth Openings in past
year 50; percentage
growth 14%
Contact
Richard Armbrust,
President
Tel 414-785-3400
Fax 414-785-0342

**Aldrich Chemical Co.,
Inc.**
1001 West Saint Paul
Ave., PO Box 355
Milwaukee, WI 53201

Founded 1951
Total employees 800

Annual sales $170 million
Industries Biotechnology,
Chemicals
Growth Openings in past
year 46; percentage
growth 6%
Contact
Dr. Jai Nagarkatti,
President
Tel 414-273-3850
Fax 414-273-4979

**AMETEK, Inc., Plymouth
Products Division**
502 Indiana Ave.
Sheboygan, WI 53081

Founded 1967
Total employees 300
Industries Factory
Automation,
Subassemblies and
Components, Test and
Measurement
Growth Openings in past
year 50; percentage
growth 20%
Contact
Ed Knauf, Jr., Vice
President/General
Manager
Tel 414-457-9435
Fax 414-457-6652

**Automating Peripherals,
Inc.**
310 North Wilson Ave.
Hartford, WI 53027

Founded 1981
Total employees 40
Annual sales $4.6 million
Industry Computer
Software
Growth Openings in past
year 15; percentage
growth 60%
Contact
Luis Garcia, President
Tel 414-673-6815
Fax 414-673-2650

**Best Power Technology,
Inc.**
PO Box 280
Necedah, WI 54646

Founded 1977
Total employees 825
Annual sales $132.64
million
Industry Energy
Growth Openings in past
year 120; percentage
growth 17%

Contact
William Paul, Chairman of
the Board/President/CEO
Tel 608-565-7200
Fax 608-565-2221

Catalyst USA, Inc.
1971 Washington St.
Grafton, WI 53024

Founded 1979
Total employees 120
Annual sales $13 million
Industries Computer
Hardware, Computer
Software
Growth Openings in past
year 60; percentage
growth 100%
Contact
John McGinnis, President
Tel 414-377-9400
Fax 414-377-6263

**Chris Hansens
Laboratory, Inc.**
9015 West Maple St.
Milwaukee, WI 53214

Founded 1965
Total employees 234
Annual sales $25 million
Industry Biotechnology
Growth Openings in past
year 34; percentage
growth 17%
Contact
Ms. Debra K. Kessler, VP
of Finance and
Administration
Tel 414-476-3630
Fax 414-259-9399

**Effective Management
Systems, Inc.**
12000 West Park Pl.
Milwaukee, WI 53224

Founded 1978
Total employees 150
Industries Computer
Software, Holding
Companies
Growth Openings in past
year 25; percentage
growth 20%
Contact
Michael Dunham,
President
Tel 414-359-9800
Fax 414-359-9011

Electronic Cable Specialists, Inc.
5300 West Franklin Dr.
Franklin, WI 53132

Founded 1984
Total employees 115
Annual sales $10 million
Industry Subassemblies and Components
Growth Openings in past year 35; percentage growth 43%
Contact
Paul J. Smyczek, President
Tel 414-421-5300
Fax 414-421-5301

Electronic Theatre Control, Inc.
3030 Laura Ln.
Middleton, WI 53562

Founded 1975
Total employees 120
Annual sales $16 million
Industry Energy
Growth Openings in past year 25; percentage growth 26%
Contact
Fred Foster, President
Tel 608-831-4116
Fax 608-836-1736

FMS/Magnacraft
4200 North Holton St.
Milwaukee, WI 53212

Founded 1964
Total employees 180
Industry Computer Hardware
Growth Openings in past year 30; percentage growth 20%
Contact
Charles Bucolt, President/ Owner
Tel 414-332-8466
Fax 414-332-5231

Fulton Performance Products, Inc.
50 Indianhead Dr., PO Box 8
Mosinee, WI 54455

Founded 1988
Total employees 190
Industry Subassemblies and Components
Growth Openings in past year 15; percentage growth 8%

Contact
Tom Rudasics, President
Tel 715-693-1700
Fax 715-693-1799

Generac Corp.
Hwy. 59 and Hillside Rd.
Waukesha, WI 53187

Founded 1959
Total employees 500
Annual sales $48 million
Industry Subassemblies and Components
Growth Openings in past year 100; percentage growth 25%
Contact
R. Kern, President
Tel 414-544-4811
Fax 414-544-4851

Graef, Anhalt, Schloemer & Associates, Inc., Public Works Division
345 North 95th St.
Milwaukee, WI 53226

Founded 1961
Total employees 250
Annual sales $14.5 million
Industry Environmental
Growth Openings in past year 29; percentage growth 13%
Contact
Bruce Lammi, VP of Personnel
Tel 414-259-1500
Fax 414-259-0037

Great Lakes Instruments, Inc.
8855 North 55th St.
Milwaukee, WI 53223

Founded 1970
Total employees 236
Industries Environmental, Test and Measurement
Growth Openings in past year 36; percentage growth 18%
Contact
Ms. Sandie Nowak, Director of Personnel
Tel 414-355-3601
Fax 414-355-8346

Husco International, Inc.
PO Box 257
Waukesha, WI 53187

Founded 1946
Total employees 280

Annual sales $70 million
Industry Subassemblies and Components
Growth Openings in past year 19; percentage growth 7%
Contact
Martin Lombardi, VP of Human Resources
Tel 414-547-0261
Fax 414-547-5978

Kaul-Tronics, Inc.
1140 Sextonville Rd.
Richland Center, WI 53581

Founded 1980
Total employees 230
Industry Telecommunications
Growth Openings in past year 45; percentage growth 24%
Contact
John R. Kaul, Chief Executive Officer
Tel 608-647-8902
Fax 608-647-7394

Lanson Industries, Inc.
S82 W18717 Gemini Dr., PO Box 906
Muskego, WI 53150

Founded 1970
Total employees 145
Annual sales $18 million
Industries Factory Automation, Test and Measurement
Growth Openings in past year 20; percentage growth 16%
Contact
Ms. Janet McGraw, Corporate Secretary/ Treasurer/Personnel
Tel 414-679-0045
Fax 414-679-2505

Lunar Corp.
313 West Beltline Hwy.
Madison, WI 53713

Founded 1978
Total employees 100
Annual sales $24.5 million
Industry Medical
Growth Openings in past year 15; percentage growth 17%
Contact
Ms. Ann Trainor, Human Resources Manager
Tel 608-274-2663
Fax 608-274-5374

McHugh, Freeman & Associates, Inc.
20975 Swenson Dr., Suite 400
Waukesha, WI 53186

Founded 1975
Total employees 75
Annual sales $8.7 million
Industries Computer Software, Factory Automation
Growth Openings in past year 25; percentage growth 50%
Contact
Ritch Durheim, Senior Vice President
Tel 414-798-8600
Fax 414-798-8619

Medical Advances, Inc.
10431 West Watertown Plank Rd., PO Box 26425
Milwaukee, WI 53226

Founded 1985
Total employees 63
Annual sales $14 million
Industries Medical, Subassemblies and Components
Growth Openings in past year 18; percentage growth 40%
Contact
Ms. Kim Rkoepsel, Human Resources Manager
Tel 414-258-3808
Fax 414-258-4931

Milwaukee Gear Co.
5150 North Port Washington Rd.
Milwaukee, WI 53217

Founded 1918
Total employees 150
Annual sales $14 million
Industry Subassemblies and Components
Growth Openings in past year 50; percentage growth 50%
Contact
Tim Sukow, Personnel Manager
Tel 414-962-3532
Fax 414-962-2774

Modern Machine Works, Inc.
5355 South Kirkwood Ave.
Cudahy, WI 53110

Founded 1930
Total employees 220
Annual sales $23 million
Industry Manufacturing Equipment
Growth Openings in past year 50; percentage growth 29%
Contact
Brian Manske, Personnel Director
Tel 414-744-5900
Fax 414-744-0718

Mox-Med, Inc.
2316 West Wisconsin St.
Portage, WI 53901

Founded 1970
Total employees 120
Industries Manufacturing Equipment, Medical
Growth Openings in past year 20; percentage growth 20%
Contact
James D. Perkins, President/COO
Tel 608-742-8541
Fax 608-742-3179

Plastic Engineered Components, Inc.
2665 South Moorland Rd., Suite 210
New Berlin, WI 53151

Founded 1981
Total employees 900
Annual sales $78 million
Industry Holding Companies
Growth Openings in past year 97; percentage growth 12%
Contact
Edward Mentzer, President/CEO
Tel 414-782-2610
Fax 414-782-5143

Promega Corp.
2800 Woods Hollow Rd.
Madison, WI 53711

Founded 1977
Total employees 353
Annual sales $35 million
Industries Biotechnology, Chemicals, Medical

Growth Openings in past year 84; percentage growth 31%
Contact
William A. Linton, President
Tel 608-274-4330
Fax 608-277-2516

Rice Lake Weighing Systems, Inc.
230 West Coleman St.
Rice Lake, WI 54868

Founded 1946
Total employees 270
Industries Manufacturing Equipment, Test and Measurement
Growth Openings in past year 45; percentage growth 20%
Contact
James Conn, VP of Marketing
Tel 715-234-9171
Fax 715-234-6967

SNC Manufacturing Co., Inc.
101 West Waukau Ave.
Oshkosh, WI 54901

Founded 1946
Total employees 600
Annual sales $24 million
Industries Subassemblies and Components, Telecommunications
Growth Openings in past year 280; percentage growth 87%
Contact
Dan Roth, Human Resource Manager
Tel 414-231-7370
Fax 414-231-1090

Spacesaver Corp.
1450 Janesville Ave.
Fort Atkinson, WI 53538

Founded 1969
Total employees 325
Annual sales $30 million
Industry Factory Automation
Growth Openings in past year 75; percentage growth 30%
Contact
Jon Dahle, Personnel Manager
Tel 414-563-6362
Fax 414-563-2702

Strand Associates, Inc.
910 West Wingra Dr.
Madison, WI 53715

Founded 1946
Total employees 123
Annual sales $13 million
Industries Environmental,
Manufacturing Equipment
Growth Openings in past
year 23; percentage
growth 23%
Contact
Ted Richards, President
Tel 608-251-4843
Fax 608-251-8655

**Strategic Data Systems,
Inc.**
PO Box 819
Sheboygan, WI 53082

Founded 1981
Total employees 250
Annual sales $17.5 million
Industries Computer
Software, Holding
Companies
Growth Openings in past
year 29; percentage
growth 13%
Contact
Stuart Warrington, COB/
CEO
Tel 414-459-7999
Fax 414-459-9123

**TDS Computing
Services, Inc.**
301 South Westfield Rd.
Madison, WI 53705

Founded 1976
Total employees 265

Annual sales $25 million
Industry Computer
Software
Growth Openings in past
year 15; percentage
growth 6%
Contact
Larry Skrenes, President
Tel 608-845-4600
Fax 608-845-4613

Versa Technologies, Inc.
9301 Washington Ave., PO
Box 085012
Racine, WI 53408

Founded 1960
Total employees 570
Annual sales $52.85
million
Industry Holding
Companies
Growth Openings in past
year 33; percentage
growth 6%
Contact
Edward V. Surek, Director
of Human Resources
Tel 414-886-1174
Fax 414-886-4614

**Waukesha Fluid
Handling**
611 Sugar Creek Rd.
Delavan, WI 53115

Founded 1984
Total employees 407
Annual sales $39 million
Industry Subassemblies
and Components

Growth Openings in past
year 82; percentage
growth 25%
Contact
William Kowaleski, Director
of Human Resources
Tel 414-728-1900
Fax 800-252-5045

**Wausau Financial
Systems, Inc.**
1103 Grand Ave.
Schofield, WI 54476

Founded 1974
Total employees 95
Annual sales $11 million
Industry Computer
Software
Growth Openings in past
year 21; percentage
growth 28%
Contact
P. Monsos, Vice President
Tel 715-359-0427
Fax 715-359-9762

**Wisconsin Automated
Machinery Corp.**
123 Jackson St., PO Box
3008
Oshkosh, WI 54903

Founded 1954
Total employees 120
Annual sales $16 million
Industry Holding
Companies
Growth Openings in past
year 20; percentage
growth 20%
Contact
Paul Ehrlich, President
Tel 414-231-4100
Fax 414-231-8166

Indexes

In the preceding part of *Peterson's Hidden Job Market 1995*, company profiles appear alphabetically within each state, providing a geographic directory of the fastest-growing small technology companies in the United States. To make your search for the right job opportunity even easier, this section features three indexes.

The first, the **Industry Index**, lists all companies in this book according to the industry or industries in which they are active, along with their state abbreviation and the page number of their detailed description. Because of the diversity of opportunities offered by high-tech companies, you might find the kind of position you are looking for in more than one area. Don't limit your possibilities!

The second index, the **Company Index**, lists all companies in *Peterson's Hidden Job Market 1995* alphabetically, giving their state abbreviation and the page number on which their detailed description appears.

The final index, the **Metropolitan Area Index**, lists companies alphabetically within the country's major metropolitan areas. Areas usually span several cities and/or states and are defined by the dominant metropolitan area. For instance, Florence, Kentucky would be found under "Cincinnati" because Cincinnati dominates this particular metropolitan area.

INDUSTRY INDEX

Advanced Materials

3M Superabrasive and Microfinishing Systems Department, 133
AAR Manufacturing Corp., Cadillac Manufacturing Division, 123
Ablestik Laboratories, 23
Adhesives Research, Inc., 169
Allied Mineral Products, Inc., 159
Allwaste Recycling, Inc., 159
Alucobond Technologies, Inc., 134
American Colloid Co., Inc., 82
Auburn Foundry, Inc., 90
Bay Resins, Inc., 99
BP Chemicals Inc., Filon Products, 95
Ceramichrome, Inc., 95
C.P. Hall Co., 84
Crown Metro Aerospace, 182
Dexter Corp., Automotive Division, 138
Eaton Corp., Forge Division, 161
Ensolite, Inc., 91
Fil-Tec, Inc., 101
Gates Formed-Fibre Products, Inc., 98
Industrial Powder Coatings, Inc., 162
Johnson and Johnston Associates, Inc., 138
Kyocera Engineered Ceramics, Inc., 157
Laurel Industries, Inc., 162
LNP Engineering Plastics, Inc., 174
MACSTEEL, 125
Maine Poly, Inc., 98
Nelco Products, Inc., 48
NEPTCO, Inc., 181
Northwest Alloys, Inc., 208

Pakco Industrial Ceramics, Inc., 175
P.D. George & Co., 136
Pre Finish Metals Incorporated, 88
Rhone-Poulenc, Inc., Latex and Specialty Polymers Division, 158
RTP Company, 132
Steward, Inc., 184
Superior Graphite Co., 89
Synthetic Products Co., 164
Talley Metals Technology, Inc., 182
Toray Plastics America, Inc., 181
Universal Super Abrasive, Inc., 127
Wahl Refractories, Inc., 164
Wesgo, Duramic, 145
Wheeling Corrugating Co., 209

Biotechnology

Alltech, Inc., 24
American Red Cross, Jerome H. Holland Laboratory for the Biomedical Sciences, 98
BASF Bioresearch Corp., 107
Biomatrix, Inc., 140
Cellpro, Inc., 206
Cell Genesys, Inc., 30
Chris Hansens Laboratory, Inc., 210
Creative Biomolecules, Inc., 110
CytoTherapeutics, Inc., 180
Deltown Specialties, 148
Ecogen, Inc., 171
Genetics & IVF Institute, 202
Genetic Therapy, Inc., 101

Greenwich Pharmaceuticals, Inc., 172
Immunex Corp., 207
ImmunoGen, Inc., 113
Institute of Biosciences & Technology, 190
Liposome Co., Inc., 143
Liposome Technology, Inc., 43
Mitotix, Inc., 115
Molecular Devices Corp., 47
Novo Nordisk Biochem, Inc., 157
Pathology Associates, Inc., 103
Pharmingen, Inc., 51
Procept, Inc., 118
Scantibodies Laboratories, Inc., 55
STS Duotek, Inc., 154
ZymoGenetics, Inc., 209

Chemicals

Aldrich Chemical Co., Inc., 25
AlliedSignal Inc., AlliedSignal Research and Technology, 82
Allied Color Industries, Inc., 159
Anderson Chemical Co., 128
Belmay, Inc., 147
CDR Pigments and Dispersions, 95
Cedar Chemical Corp., 183
Champion Technologies, Inc., 187
ChemDesign Corp., 108
Chemical Products Corp., 78
Chemtool, Inc., Metalcote, 84
Ciba-Geigy Corp., Pigments Division, 70

Diversey Water
Technology, Inc., 160
EcoScience Corp., 111
Furane Products Co., 37
Genosys Biotechnology,
Inc., 189
Hammond Lead Products,
Inc., 92
Hardwicke Chemical,
Inc., 182
Hauser Chemical
Research, Inc., 63
High Point Chemical
Corp., 156
Lion Industries, Inc., 21
Novabiochem, 49
Nutrite Corp., 98
Owens-Corning Fiberglas
Science and Technology
Center, 163
Penta Manufacturing
Co., 144
Plant Genetic Engineering
Laboratory, 146
Rohm Tech, Inc., Specialty
Chemicals Division, 119
Solvay Interox, 194
Solvay Minerals Co., 194
Tastemaker, 164
Troy Corp., 144
Velsicol Chemical
Corp., 89

Computer Hardware

Accu-Sort Systems,
Inc., 20
Advanced Input
Devices, 81
Advanced Management
Technologies, 24
Advantage Memory
Corp., 24
Akashic Memories
Corporation, 24
ALLUS Technology
Corp., 185
Alpha Systems Lab,
Inc., 25
American Ink Jet
Corp., 106
AmeriData, Inc., 128
Applied Digital Data
Systems, Inc., 147
Artecon, Inc., 26
BDS, Inc., 200
BellSouth Information
Systems, 77

Bohdan Associates,
Inc., 100
BORIS Systems, Inc., 124
C-Cube Microsystems
Corp., 29
Ciber, Inc., 62
CMD Technology, Inc., 31
Command Systems,
Inc., 67
Computersmith, Inc., 138
Computer Dynamics,
Inc., 182
Computer Intelligence
InfoCorp, 32
Comtec Automated
Solutions, 187
Comtec Information
Systems, Inc., 180
Connect Computer
Co., 129
Cornerstone Imaging,
Inc., 32
C. Centennial, Inc., 108
CTX International, Inc., 32
Darius Technology,
Inc., 207
Datapro Information
Services Group, 141
Data Storage Marketing,
Inc., 63
Dauphin Technology,
Inc., 85
Denon America, Inc., 141
Desktop Displays,
Inc., 160
Desktop Sales, Inc., 85
Dialogic Corp., 142
Diamond Computer
Systems, Inc., 34
Diamond Flower
Instruments, Inc., 34
Docucon, Inc., 188
ECCS, Inc., 142
Educational Resources, 85
ENCAD, Inc., 35
Erni Components,
Inc., 202
Esselte Meto, 142
FCS Computing Services,
Inc., 85
Federal Data Corp., 101
FileTek, Inc., 101
First International
Computer of America,
Inc., 36
FIserv EFT, 167
FMS/Magnacraft, 211
Fora, Inc., 37
Genoa Systems Corp., 37

George Risk Industries,
Inc., 137
Golden Ribbon, Inc., 63
Granite Communications,
Inc., 138
Hazelet & Erdal, Inc., 95
Hewlett-Packard Co.,
Puerto Rico Division, 179
Howtek, Inc., 138
Inforite Corp., 40
Instinet Corp., 150
Integral Peripherals,
Inc., 63
International
Communication
Materials, Inc., 173
International Computaprint
Corp., 173
International Imaging
Materials, Inc., 150
International Management
Systems, Inc., 41
IRIS Graphics, Inc., 114
Ithaca Peripherals
Inc., 151
Jackson Laboratory, 98
Kingston Technology
Corp., 42
Kronos, Inc., 114
LaserByte Corporation, 43
Melita International
Corporation, 80
MicroNet Technology,
Inc., 46
Micropublication Systems,
Inc., 46
Micro Express, Inc., 46
Micro Solutions Computer
Products, Inc., 87
Nashua Precision
Technologies, 87
NBI, Inc., 64
New Horizons Computer
Learning Center, 49
Orchid Technology, 50
Peripheral Dynamics
Inc., 176
Periphonics Corp., 153
Philips LMS, 64
Pinnacle Micro, Inc., 51
Printek, Inc., 126
Printrak International,
Inc., 52
Raster Graphics, Inc., 53
Rhetorex, Inc., 54
Riverbend Group, Inc., 204
Siemens Nixdorf Printing
Systems, 75
Sigma Game, Inc., 137

Computer Software

Holding Companies

Manufacturing Equipment

Medical

Ballard Medical
Products, 196
Becton Dickinson
Diagnostic Instrument
Systems, 99
Biocontrol Technology,
Inc., 170
bioMerieux Vitek, Inc., 134
Bio-Plexus, Inc., 67
BioSource International,
Inc., 28
Biotrack, Inc., 28
Boston Biomedica,
Inc., 107
B. Braun Medical, Inc.,
Cardiovascular
Division, 129
Cabot Medical Corp., 170
Cardiometrics, Inc., 29
Centrix, Inc., 67
Cerplex, Inc., 30
ChemTrack, Inc., 30
CliniCom, Inc., 62
Collagen Corp., 31
Corvita Corp., 72
C.R. Bard, Inc.,
Electrophysiology
Division, 110
Cryomedical Sciences,
Inc., 100
CTI, Inc., 183
Dako Corp., 33
DecTron Products, 167
Dentsply International Inc.,
LD Caulk Division, 71
Devices for Vascular
Intervention, Inc., 34
Diametrics Medical
Inc., 130
Electromedics, Inc., 63
Emisphere Technologies,
Inc., 149
Empi, Inc., 130
Epitope, Inc., 167
Eyesys Laboratories,
Inc., 189
Genica Pharmaceuticals
Corp., 112
Gen-Probe, Inc., 37
Gerardo International,
Inc., 73
Hercon Laboratories
Corp., 173
Hyclone Laboratories,
Inc., 197
ICN Biomedicals, Inc.,
Diagnostics Division, 39
Immunomedics, Inc., 142
IMRE Corp., 207

InControl, Inc., 207
Infrasonics, Inc., 40
Intermedics Orthopedics,
Inc., 190
Isomedix Inc., 143
Kensey Nash
Corporation, 174
Kodak Health Imaging
Systems, Inc., 191
Lake Region
Manufacturing Co.,
Inc., 130
Lorad Corp., 68
Lunar Corp., 211
Mallinckrodt Sensor
Systems, Inc., 126
Medical Devices, Inc., 131
Medical Parameters,
Inc., 115
Medical Technology,
Inc., 192
MEDIQ Mobile X-Ray
Services, Inc., 115
MediTek Health Corp., 74
Medrad, Inc., 175
Mentor Corp., 45
Mentor O&O, Inc., 115
Microbac Labs, Inc., 175
Microgenics Corp., 46
Mitek Surgical Products,
Inc., 115
Mox-Med, Inc., 212
Noise Cancellation
Technologies, Inc., 69
Olicon Imaging Systems,
Inc., 96
Oncogene Science,
Inc., 152
Pacific Device, Inc., 50
Possis Medical, Inc., 131
Prentke Romich Co., 163
Promega Corp., 212
Protocol Systems,
Inc., 168
Pyxis Corp., 52
Quidel Corp., 53
Schneider (USA) Inc, 132
SeaMED Corp., 209
Sequana Therapeutics,
Inc., 55
Specialty Laboratories,
Inc., 56
Staodyn, Inc., 65
Starkey Laboratories,
Omni Hearing Systems
Division, 194
Steris Corp., 164
Sunrise Medical Inc.,
Quickie Designs, 57

Sutter Corporation, 58
Symbiosis Corporation, 76
Tech Pak, Inc., 120
Terrapin Technologies,
Inc., 59
Thermoscan, Inc., 59
Thoren Caging Systems,
Inc., 178
Tomtec Imaging Systems,
Inc., 65
Tri-Tronics, Inc., 22
UltraCision, Inc., 181
Ventritex, Inc., 60
Veratex Corp., 128
VISX, Inc., 61
Vital Signs, Inc., 145
Vivigen, Inc., 146
Wright Medical
Technology, Inc., 184
Xenometrix, Inc., 66
Zoll Medical
Corporation, 123
Zynaxis, Inc., 179

Pharmaceuticals

AAI, 117
Agouron Pharmaceuticals,
Inc., 24
Alexion Pharmaceuticals,
Inc., 66
Alliance Pharmaceutical
Corp., 25
Alpha-Beta Technology,
Inc., 105
Altana, Inc., 146
A.L. Laboratories, Inc.,
Animal Health
Division, 140
Ambico, Inc., 93
American BioMed,
Inc., 185
American Reagent
Laboratories, Inc., 146
Amylin Pharmaceuticals,
Inc., 25
ANGUS Chemical Co., 82
Astra USA, Inc., 106
Athena Neurosciences,
Inc., 27
AutoImmune, Inc., 107
Baxa Corp., 62
Biogen, Inc., 107
Bio-Technology General
Corp., 148
Bock Pharmacal Co., 134
Boehringer Mannheim
Pharmaceuticals, 99

Photonics

Subassemblies and Components

Accutron, Inc., 66
ACTEL Corp., 23
Advanced Cable
  Technologies, Inc., 105
Advanced Electronics,
  Inc., 105
Advanced Hardware
  Architecture Corp., 81
Advanced Power
  Technology, Inc., 166
Advanced Technology
  Materials, Inc., 66
Aegis, Inc., 105
Air Products and
  Chemicals, Inc., Silicon
  Materials Services
  Division, 185
Allegheny Powder
  Metallurgy, Inc., 169
Alliance Semiconductor
  Corp., 25
Allomatic Products Co., 90
Alps Electric (U.S.A.),
  Inc., 25
Altera Corp., 25
Ambac International,
  Inc., 181
American Power
  Conversion Corp., 180
American Superconductor
  Corp., 106
Anadigics, Inc., 140
Antec, Inc., 25
Applied Manufacturing
  Technology, Inc., 196
Applied Micro Circuits
  Corp., 26
Arrowsmith Shelburne,
  Inc., 198
ASC, 136
Assembly Solutions,
  Inc., 137
Astec America, Inc., ENI
  Division, 147
Augat, Inc., LRC
  Division, 147
Ault, Inc., 129
AuraVision Corp., 28
Austin Semiconductor,
  Inc., 186
A.W. Industries, Inc., 71
Babcock & Wilcox Co.,
  Struthers Thermo-
  Flood, 22
Benchmarq
  Microelectronics,
  Inc., 186
Bergen Cable
  Technologies, Inc., 140

Berk-Tek, Inc., 170
BGRS, Inc., 186
B.H. Electronics, Inc., 129
Bowles Fluidics Corp., 100
Brake Parts, Inc., 83
Brooktree Corp., 29
Burgess-Norton
  Manufacturing Co., 83
Captive-Aire Systems,
  Inc., 156
CDR Manufacturing,
  Inc., 95
Celeritek, Inc., 30
Central Plastics Co., 165
Cherokee International,
  Inc., 30
Cherry Semiconductor
  Corp., 180
Circuit Systems, Inc., 84
Clary Corp., 30
C-MAC of America,
  Inc., 72
C&M Corp., 67
Colder Products Co., 129
Cold Heading Co., 124
Columbia Technical
  Services, 109
Comair Rotron, Inc., 31
Communication Cable,
  Inc., 156
Component Technology
  Corp., 171
Conelec of Florida, Inc., 72
Conmed Corp., 148
Continental Circuits
  Corp., 20
Contract Assembly,
  Inc., 109
Conversion Devices,
  Inc., 109
Cree Research, Inc., 156
Crispaire Corp., 78
Crystal Semiconductor
  Corp., 188
Cuplex, Inc., 188
Cyberex, Inc., 160
Cyrix Corp., 188
Cyten Circuit Design,
  Inc., 188
DATAMAX Corp., 73
DCS Corp., 201
Dearborn Wire & Cable
  L.P., 85
Decatur Cylinders, Inc., 19
Design Circuits, Inc., 110
Destiny Technology
  Corp., 34

Dexter Corp., Dexter
  Electronic Materials
  Division, 34
Distron Corp., 110
Dual, Inc., 201
Dynaco Corporation, 20
Eagle-Picher Industries,
  Inc., Eagle-Picher
  Research
  Laboratory, 165
Eaton Corp., Torque
  Control Products, 124
EFI Electronics Corp., 197
EGC Corp., 188
EG&G Sealol, Industrial
  Division, 180
Electronic Cable
  Specialists, Inc., 211
Electronic Instrumentation
  and Technology, Inc., 201
Electronic Solutions, 35
Electronic Systems
  Products, Inc., 79
ELMA Electronic Inc., 35
Erlanger Tubular
  Corp., 165
Eutectic Electronics,
  Inc., 156
Everest Electronic
  Equipment, Inc., 36
Excalibur Extrusions,
  Inc., 36
Exsil, Inc., 36
EZ Form Cable Corp., 68
Fargo Assembly Co., 159
Fiberspar, Inc., 111
Fluoroware, Inc., 130
Fotel, Inc., 85
Fulton Performance
  Products, Inc., 211
GCA Group, Inc., 95
Generac Corp., 211
Grant TFW, Inc., 189
Great Bend Industries, 94
Green Manufacturing,
  Inc., 161
Gusher Pumps, Inc., 161
Hash-Tech, Inc., 38
Hathaway Corp., Motion
  Control Division, 166
Hibbing Electronics
  Corp., 130
Hi-Tech Ceramics,
  Inc., 150
Homaco, Inc., 86
HR Industries, Inc., 190
Hull Corporation, 173
Husco International,
  Inc., 211

Hydraulic Components
Industries, 137
ICON Industries, Inc., 190
IC Designs, 207
Innovex, Inc., 130
Integrated Circuit Systems,
Inc., 173
Interlink Electronics
Corp., 40
International Circuits and
Components, Inc., 41
ISE Labs, Inc., 41
ISS, Comptek, 173
ITT A-C Pump, 162
JFW Industries, Inc., 92
Jideco of Bardstown,
Inc., 96
Johanson Dielectrics,
Inc., 42
Johnson Matthey
Electronics, Inc., 208
Kalmus and Associates,
Inc., 86
Kavlico Corp., 42
Keystone Electronics
Corp., 151
KF Industries, Inc., 166
Kobe Precision, Inc., 42
Kopin Corp., 114
Koppel Steel Corp., 174
Lanxide Corp., 71
Lars Industries, Inc., 191
Laser Drive, Inc., 174
Lasertechnics, Inc., 146
Latronics Corp., 174
Lattice Semiconductor
Corp., 167
L.E.A. Dynatech, Inc., 73
LoDan Electronics, Inc., 86
Macrotech Fluid Sealing,
Inc., Polyseal
Division, 197
Macrotech Fluid Sealing,
Inc., Selastomer
Division, 86
Magflux Corp., 192
Magnetec Corp., 69
Magnetek Power
Technologies Systems,
Inc., 44
Magnetic Metals
Corp., 144
Magnetic Technologies
Corp., 151
Maida Development
Co., 203
Maxwell Laboratories,
Inc., 44

McDonald Technologies
International, Inc., 192
Medical Advances,
Inc., 212
Merit Electronic Design
Co., Ltd., 151
Metform, Inc., 87
Micron Custom
Manufacturing Services,
Inc., 82
Microsemi Corp.,
Scottsdale Division, 21
Milbank Manufacturing
Co., 135
Milwaukee Gear Co., 212
Mod-Tap Corp., 116
Mohawk, Cable Design
Technology, 116
Morganite, Inc., 157
M & W Pump Corp., 74
Natel Engineering Co.,
Inc., 47
National Magnetics Co., 96
National Magnetics
Corp., 47
nCHIP, Inc., 48
Netra Corp., 48
Nidec-Power General, 116
Nooter/Eriksen
Cogeneration Systems,
Inc., 135
Nortech Systems, Inc., 131
Northern Technologies,
Ltd., 116
NTI, 64
OKI America, Inc., OKI
Semiconductor
Group, 49
Operational Technologies
Corp., 193
Pacific Circuits, Inc., 208
PAGG Corp., 117
Paradigm Technology,
Inc., 50
Paragon, Inc., 50
Parker Hannifin Corp.,
Tube Fittings
Division, 163
Parker Technology,
Inc., 193
Patapsco Designs,
Inc., 103
Paul-Munroe Engineering
International, Inc., 51
Peak Electronics, Inc., 69
Polygon Co., 92
Praegitzer Industries,
Inc., 168
Precision Tube Co., 176

QMC Technologies,
Inc., 131
Qualitronics, Inc., 118
Quality Manufacturing Co.,
Inc., 96
RAM Manufacturing Co.,
Inc., 197
Renco Electronics,
Inc., 153
Reptron Electronics, Inc.,
K-Byte Division, 75
Riverside Electronics,
Ltd., 132
Rockwell International
Suspension Systems
Co., 127
RWA, Inc., 119
Ryan Electronics Products,
Inc., 75
St. Marys Carbon Co., 177
Sanmina Corp., 55
San Juan Assembly,
Inc., 197
SANYO Video
Components.] Corp., 55
Satis Vacuum Industries,
Optovision U.S.A., 194
Schott Corp., 132
Sematech, Inc., 194
SHURflo Pump
Manufacturing Co., 56
Siemon Co., 70
Sierra, Inc., 88
Sierra Semiconductor
Corp., 56
Signal Transformer Co.,
Inc., 154
Siltec Corp., 168
Simpson Industries, Inc.,
Bluffton Operations, 92
Simpson Industries, Inc.,
Gladwin Division, 127
Simpson Industries, Inc.,
Troy Operations, 163
Smartflex Systems,
Inc., 56
SMT East Corp., 120
South Bay Circuits,
Inc., 56
Spang & Co., Magnetics
Division, 177
Springfield Press and
Machine Co., Inc., 98
Startech Innovations,
Inc., 76
Sumitomo Machinery
Corp. of America, 205
Surya Electronics, Inc., 89
SWL Inc., 205

Telecommunications

ST Microwave (California)
Corp., 57
Sumitomo Electric Fiber
Optics Corp., 158
Summa Four, Inc., 140
Supra Corp., 168
Synernetics Inc., 120
Synetics Corp., 120
Syntellect, Inc., 21
Systems Research and
Applications Corp., 205
Systran Corp., 164
Teknekron Infoswitch
Corp., 195
Telebit Corp., 58
Telecom Services Limited
(U.S.), Inc., 154
Teledyne Brown
Engineering, Control
Applications, 195
Teleglobe
Communications,
Inc., 121
Teleport Communications
Group, 155
TeleSciences C O
Systems, Inc., 144
TelTech Corp., Consulting
Division, 155
Telular Group L.P., 89
TIW Systems, Inc., 59
Tom Snyder
Productions, 121
Trak Microwave Corp., 76
Tricord Systems, Inc., 133
T&R Communications,
Inc., 58
Unex Corp., 122
U.S. Robotics, Inc., 89
Valcom, Inc., 205
Vari-L Co., Inc., 65
Vertex Communications
Corp., 196
ViaSat, Inc., 60
VideoServer, Inc., 122
VIR, Inc., 179
VME Microsystems
International Corp., 20
VMX, Inc., 61
Voysys, Inc., 61
Walker Equipment
Corp., 81
Wellfleet Communications,
Inc., 122
Wesson, Taylor, Wells &
Associates, Inc., 159
Western Multiplex
Corp., 61

Westinghouse Electric
Corp., Distribution and
Control Business
Unit, 179
Wireless Access, Inc., 61
XDB Systems, Inc., 105
Xircom, Inc., 61
Xpedite Systems, Inc., 145
Xylogics, Inc., 123
Xyplex, Inc., 123
Zoom Telephonics,
Inc., 123
ZyXEL USA, 62

Test and Measurement

ABB Industrial Systems,
Inc., 20
ABB Power Plant Controls,
Inc., 66
Advanced Membrane
Technology, Inc., 24
Alltech Associates, Inc., 82
American Auto-Matrix,
Inc., 169
American Computer and
Electronics Corp., 98
American Standards
Testing Bureau, Inc., 146
AMETEK, Inc., Plymouth
Products Division, 210
Andrulis Research
Corp., 99
Applied Measurement
Systems, Inc., 71
Applied Power, Inc., Barry
Controls Division, 106
Aquatec Water Systems,
Inc., 26
Arizona Instrument
Corp., 20
Astro International
Corp., 186
Asymtek, 27
ATI Orion Research, 106
Bacharach, Inc., 170
Balboa Instruments,
Inc., 28
Baldor Motion Products
Group, 129
Baxter Diagnostics, Inc.,
Burdick & Jackson
Division, 124
Becton Dickinson
Microbiology
Systems, 99
Biosystems, Inc., 67

Bio-Tek Instruments,
Inc., 198
BI, Inc., 62
Bliss-Salem, Inc., 160
Bruker Instruments,
Inc., 108
Caldon, Inc., 170
Campbell Scientific,
Inc., 196
Cegelec, Inc., 170
Charles Ross & Son
Co., 148
Clif Mock Co., Inc., 187
Commercial Testing &
Engineering Co., 84
Compliance Corp., 100
Compressor Controls
Corp., 93
Corpane Industries,
Inc., 95
C-Power Companies,
Inc., 187
Custom Products, Inc., 95
Daktronics, Inc., 183
DataFocus, Inc., 201
Delta Design, Inc., 33
Denver Instrument Co., 63
Desalination Systems,
Inc., 33
Detroit Edge Tool Co., 124
Dialight Corp., 141
Dwyer Instruments,
Inc., 91
Dynamic Instruments,
Inc., 35
Efector, Inc., 171
EIMCO Process
Equipment Co., 197
Electronic Controls Co., 82
Electronic Technology
Systems, Inc., 171
EnergyLine Systems,
Inc., 36
Environmental Systems
Corp., 184
Environmental
Technologies Group,
Inc., 101
Enviroplan, Inc., 142
Figgie International Inc.,
Interstate Engineering
Division, 36
Fire-Lite Alarms, Inc., 68
Flight Systems, Inc., 172
Forma Scientific, Inc., 161
FSSL, Inc., 189
GaSonics International,
Inc., 37
Gentex Corp., 125

Geo-Centers, Inc., 112
G.H. Flow Automation, 189
Great Lakes Instruments, Inc., 211
Halmar Robicon Group, 173
Hansford Manufacturing Corp., 150
Harris Environmental Systems, Inc., 112
HBM, Inc., 112
Heath Consultants, Inc., 190
Hipotronics, Inc., 150
H-O-H Systems, Inc., 190
IDC Engineering, 95
Inchape, Inc., ETL Testing Laboratories, Inc., 150
Index Sensors & Controls, Inc., 208
Ingold Electrodes, Inc., 113
Interflo Technologies, 150
Isco, Inc., Environmental Division, 137
John Brown, Inc., Brown Machine Division, 125
Keithley Instruments, Inc., Data Acquisition Division, 114
Kip, Inc., 68
K-Tron International, Inc., 143
Lanson Industries, Inc., 211
Leupold & Stevens, Inc., 167
Mamac Systems, Inc., 130
Medical Graphics Corp., 131
Medsonic, Inc., 151
Metrosonics, Inc., 151
Micrel Semiconductor, Inc., 45
Micro Bio-Medics, Inc., 152
Milton Roy Company, Liquid Metronics Division, 115
Moog Controls, Inc., 152
Mosler, Inc., Electronic Systems Division, 144
Nartron Corp., 126
National Draeger, Inc., 175
Network General Corp., 48
Nexus Custom Electronics, 199
Nunc, Inc., 87
Nutramax Products, Inc., 117

Oneida Research Services, Inc., 152
Optical Engineering, Inc., 50
Osmonics, Inc., 131
Otsuka Electronics USA, Inc., 64
Parker Hannifin Corp., Parflex Division, 163
Parker Hannifin Corp., Racor Division, 50
Patterson Pump Co., 80
PerSeptive Biosystems, Inc., 117
PHD, Inc., 92
Phoenix Controls Corp., 117
Phoenix Medical Technology, Inc., 182
Photon Kinetics, Inc., 168
Popper Precision Instruments, Inc., 181
Powell-Esco Co., 193
Quantum Group, Inc., 52
Raytek, Inc., 54
Red Lion Controls, 177
Reliance Motion Control, Inc., 131
Respironics, Inc., 177
Rice Lake Weighing Systems, Inc., 212
Rochester Gauges, Inc., 193
R. Howard Strasbaugh, Inc., 53
Siemens Medical Systems, Inc., Oncology Care Systems, 56
Slope Meter Co., 132
Southern Optical Co., 158
Spirax Sarco, Inc., 177
SSAC, Inc., 154
Statek Corp., 57
T.B. Wood's, 178
Telecom Solutions Puerto Rico, Inc., 179
Tessco Group, Inc., 195
Thermedics, Inc., 121
TN Technologies, Inc., 196
Turck Inc., 133
Tylan General, 59
UDT Sensors, Inc., 60
Unisyn Technologies, Inc., 60
Universal Dynamics, Inc., 205
VLSI Packaging Corp., 196

Wandel & Goltermann Technologies, Inc., 159
Whatman, Inc., 145
X-Rite, Inc., 128
Yokogawa Corp. of America, 81
Zymark Corp., 123

Transportation

3M, Verification and Optical Systems Project, 133
Active Noise and Vibration Technologies, Inc., 20
ADB-ALNACO, Inc., 159
AEL Industries, Inc., Cross Systems Division, 77
Aero Corp., 71
Alinabal Holdings, Corp., 66
Applied Research Corp., 99
Ashtech, Inc., 27
Ayres Corp., 77
Blackstone Manufacturing Co., Inc., 83
Brunswick Corp., Intellitec Division, 83
Cambridge Systematics, Inc., 108
Coleman Research Corp., Washington Division, 200
Courtaulds Aerospace, Inc., Performance Composites Division, 198
Crestview Aerospace Corp., 72
Cubic Corp., Precision Systems Division, 184
Delex Systems, Inc., 201
Digicourse, Inc., 97
DME Corp., 73
Electro Pneumatic Corp., 35
Flight Dynamics, 167
Frasca International, Inc., 86
GEC-Marconi Materials, 37
General Engineering Services, Inc., 79
General Sciences Corp., 101
Gentex Corp., 172
Grote Industries, Inc., 91
G.W. Lisk Co., Inc., 150
Gyration, Inc., 38

COMPANY INDEX

3M Superabrasive and Microfinishing Systems Department (MN), 133

3M, Verification and Optical Systems Project (MN), 133

AAI (NC), 155

AAR Manufacturing Corp., Cadillac Manufacturing Division (MI), 123

ABB Air Preheater, Inc. (NY), 146

ABB Control, Inc. (TX), 185

ABB Environmental Systems (TN), 183

ABB Industrial Systems, Inc. (WI), 210

ABB Power Plant Controls, Inc. (CT), 66

ABB Robotics, Inc. (WI), 210

ABB Systems Control Co., Inc. (CA), 22

Ablestik Laboratories (CA), 23

Abra Cadabra Software, Inc. (FL), 71

Access Health Marketing, Inc. (CA), 23

Access Industries, Inc., American Stair-Glide Division (MO), 134

Accolade, Inc. (CA), 23

Accom, Inc. (CA), 23

Accudyne, Inc. (NC), 155

Accu-Form, Inc. (PA), 169

Accu-Sort Systems, Inc. (PA), 169

Accutron, Inc. (CT), 66

Accu Tech International, Inc. (TX), 185

ACIUS, Inc. (CA), 23

ACS Communications, Inc. (CA), 23

ACS, Inc. (VA), 199

ACTEL Corp. (CA), 23

Active Noise and Vibration Technologies, Inc. (AZ), 20

Active Voice Corp. (WA), 206

Activision, Inc. (CA), 23

Acucobol, Inc. (CA), 23

ADB-ALNACO, Inc. (OH), 159

Addison Product Co. (FL), 71

Adhesives Research, Inc. (PA), 169

Adobe Systems, Inc. (CA), 23

Adonis Corp. (WA), 206

ADRA Systems, Inc. (MA), 105

Adtran, Inc. (AL), 19

Advanced Cable Technologies, Inc. (MA), 105

Advanced Communication Systems, Inc. (VA), 199

Advanced Computer Communications (CA), 23

Advanced Digital Information Corp. (WA), 206

Advanced Electronics, Inc. (MA), 105

Advanced Engineering & Management Associates, Aerospace and Education Division (VA), 199

Advanced Engineering & Research Associates (VA), 199

Advanced Hardware Architecture Corp. (ID), 81

Advanced Input Devices (ID), 81

Advanced Management Technologies (CA), 24

Advanced Membrane Technology, Inc. (CA), 24

Advanced NMR Systems, Inc. (MA), 105

Advanced Power Technology, Inc. (OR), 166

Advanced Technology (CA), 24

Advanced Technology Materials, Inc. (CT), 66

Advanced Technology Systems, Inc. (VA), 199

Advanced Tissue Sciences, Inc. (CA), 24

Advantage Memory Corp. (CA), 24

Advent Software, Inc. (CA), 24

Aegis, Inc. (MA), 105

AEG Automation Systems Corp. (PA), 169

AEL Industries, Inc., Cross Systems Division (GA), 77

Aerofin Corp. (VA), 199

Aero Corp. (FL), 71

AER Energy Resources, Inc. (GA), 77

Aetrium, Inc. (MN), 128

Affymax N.V. (CA), 24

Agency Management Services, Inc. (MA), 105

Agouron Pharmaceuticals, Inc. (CA), 24

Aguirre Engineers, Inc. (CO), 62

AimTech Corp. (NH), 137

Air Products and Chemicals, Inc., Silicon Materials Services Division (TX), 185

Akashic Memories Corporation (CA), 24

ALANTEC (CA), 24

Alba-Waldensian, Inc. (NC), 155

Aldrich Chemical Co., Inc. (WI), 210

Alexander Batteries (IA), 92

Alexion Pharmaceuticals, Inc. (CT), 66

METROPOLITAN AREA INDEX

AKRON
Parker Hannifin Corp.,
Parflex Division
(OH), 163

ALBANY-SCHENECTADY
Enable Software, Inc.
(NY), 149
MapInfo Corp. (NY), 151

ALBANY, GA
Ayres Corp. (GA), 77

ALBUQUERQUE
Applied Research
Associates, Inc.
(NM), 145
Bell Group, Inc. (NM), 145
Bohannan-Huston, Inc.
(NM), 146
Lasertechnics, Inc.
(NM), 146
Re/Spec, Inc. (NM), 146
Tech Reps, Inc. (NM), 146

ALLENTOWN-BETHLEHEM, PA-NJ
St. Marys Carbon Co.
(PA), 177
Spirax Sarco, Inc.
(PA), 177

ANAHEIM-SANTA ANA
Advantage Memory Corp.
(CA), 24
Alpha Systems Lab, Inc.
(CA), 25
American Turnkey (CA), 25
Amtec Engineering Corp.
(CA), 25

Aquatec Water Systems,
Inc. (CA), 26
ASI Systems International,
Inc. (CA), 27
Balboa Instruments, Inc.
(CA), 28
Catalina Marketing Corp.
(CA), 29
Cerplex, Inc. (CA), 30
Cherokee International,
Inc. (CA), 30
CMD Technology, Inc.
(CA), 31
CMSI, Inc. (CA), 31
Dainippon Screen
Engineering of America,
Inc. (CA), 33
Energy & Environmental
Research Corp. (CA), 36
Everest Electronic
Equipment, Inc. (CA), 36
Excalibur Extrusions, Inc.
(CA), 36
Figgie International Inc.,
Interstate Engineering
Division (CA), 36
ICN Biomedicals, Inc.,
Diagnostics Division
(CA), 39
Information Management
Associates, Inc. (CA), 40
International Circuits and
Components, Inc.
(CA), 41
Kingston Technology Corp.
(CA), 42
Label-Aire, Inc. (CA), 43
Lantronix Corp. (CA), 43
Ling Electronics, Inc.
(CA), 43
Megatool, Inc. (CA), 45
MetroLaser (CA), 45
MicroNet Technology, Inc.
(CA), 46
Micro Express, Inc.
(CA), 46
Nano Pulse Industries, Inc.
(CA), 47
Nelco Products, Inc.
(CA), 48

NetSoft (CA), 48
New Horizons Computer
Learning Center (CA), 49
Paul-Munroe Engineering
International, Inc.
(CA), 51
PDA Engineering (CA), 51
Pinnacle Micro, Inc.
(CA), 51
Platinum Software Corp.
(CA), 51
Printrak International, Inc.
(CA), 52
RAD Network Devices,
Inc. (CA), 53
Rainbow Technologies,
Inc. (CA), 53
Satellite Technology
Management, Inc.
(CA), 55
SHURflo Pump
Manufacturing Co.
(CA), 56
Smartflex Systems, Inc.
(CA), 56
Smith Micro Software, Inc.
(CA), 56
Sparta, Inc. (CA), 56
Statek Corp. (CA), 57
State Of The Art, Inc.
(CA), 57
Sync Research, Inc.
(CA), 58
Triconex Corp. (CA), 59
Unisyn Technologies, Inc.
(CA), 60
Virgin Interactive
Entertainment (CA), 61
Wonderware Corp.
(CA), 61
ZyXEL USA (CA), 62

ANN ARBOR
Arbor Technologies, Inc.
(MI), 123
Automated Analysis Corp.
(MI), 124

Horiba Instruments,
Automation Division
(MI), 125
Information Transfer
Systems, Inc. (MI), 125
John Brown, Inc., Brown
Machine Division
(MI), 125
Mallinckrodt Sensor
Systems, Inc. (MI), 126

APPLETON-OSHKOSH

SNC Manufacturing Co.,
Inc. (WI), 212
Spacesaver Corp.
(WI), 212
Wisconsin Automated
Machinery Corp.
(WI), 213

ASHEVILLE

HydroLogic, Inc. (NC), 157

ATHENS

Rhone Merieux, Inc.
(GA), 80

ATLANTA

Advanced Hardware
Architecture Corp.
(ID), 81
Advanced Input Devices
(ID), 81
AEL Industries, Inc., Cross
Systems Division
(GA), 77
AER Energy Resources,
Inc. (GA), 77
Atlanta Group Systems,
Inc. (GA), 77
AVL Scientific Corp.
(GA), 77
BellSouth Information
Systems (GA), 77
Brock Control Systems,
Inc. (GA), 78
Chemical Products Corp.
(GA), 78
Comprehensive Computer
Consulting, Inc. (GA), 78
Crispaire Corp. (GA), 78
CytRx Corp. (GA), 78
DayStar Digital, Inc.
(GA), 78

DISC ACCESS Products
Group, Inc. (GA), 78
Dolphin Networks, Inc.
(GA), 78
Dynamic Resources, Inc.
(GA), 78
EcoTek Laboratory
Services, Inc. (GA), 78
Electronic Systems
Products, Inc. (GA), 79
ENCORE Systems, Inc.
(GA), 79
General Engineering
Services, Inc. (GA), 79
Harbinger*EDI Services,
Inc. (GA), 79
IMNET, Inc. (GA), 79
Industrial Computer Corp.
(GA), 79
IQ Software Corporation
(GA), 79
KASEWORKS, Inc.
(GA), 79
KnowledgeWare, Inc.
(GA), 79
Mayo Chemical Co., Inc.
(GA), 79
Melita International
Corporation (GA), 80
Norton Construction
Products (GA), 80
Patterson Pump Co.
(GA), 80
PCC Airfoils, Inc. (GA), 80
Phillips & Brooks/Gladwin,
Inc. (GA), 80
RealCom Office
Communications, Inc.
(GA), 80
Royal Oak Enterprises,
Inc. (GA), 80
SofNet, Inc. (GA), 80
Softlab, Inc. (GA), 80
Solvay Pharmaceuticals
(GA), 80
Stockholder Systems, Inc.
(GA), 81
System Builder Corp.
(GA), 81
System Works, Inc.
(GA), 81
Waste Abatement
Technology (GA), 81
Westinghouse
Remediation Services,
Inc. (GA), 81
World Travel Partners
(GA), 81

Yokogawa Corp. of
America (GA), 81

AURORA-ELGIN

Burgess-Norton
Manufacturing Co.
(IL), 83
Educational Resources
(IL), 85

AUSTIN

Austin-American
Technology (TX), 186
Austin Semiconductor, Inc.
(TX), 186
Columbia Scientific
Industries Corp.
(TX), 187
Cooperative Computing,
Inc. (TX), 187
Crystal Semiconductor
Corp. (TX), 188
Evolutionary Technologies,
Inc. (TX), 189
Intermedics Orthopedics,
Inc. (TX), 190
International Bio-Medical,
Inc. (TX), 191
National Instruments
(TX), 192
Origin Systems, Inc.
(TX), 193
Scientific and Engineering
Software, Inc. (TX), 194
Sematech, Inc. (TX), 194
Sterling Information Group,
Inc. (TX), 194
Tessco Group, Inc.
(TX), 195
Tivoli Systems, Inc.
(TX), 196
TN Technologies, Inc.
(TX), 196

BALTIMORE

American Urethane, Inc.
(MD), 99
Becton Dickinson
Diagnostic Instrument
Systems (MD), 99
Becton Dickinson
Microbiology Systems
(MD), 99
Bowles Fluidics Corp.
(MD), 100

Spectrum Associates, Inc. (MA), 120
Steinbrecher Corp. (MA), 120
Synernetics Inc. (MA), 120
Synetics Corp. (MA), 120
Systems Group, Inc. (MA), 120
System Resources Corp. (MA), 120
Technology Integration, Inc. (MA), 121
Tech Pak, Inc. (MA), 120
Teleglobe Communications, Inc. (MA), 121
Telor Ophthalmic Pharmaceutical, Inc. (MA), 121
TERC (MA), 121
Thermedics, Inc. (MA), 121
Thermo Environmental Instruments, Inc. (MA), 121
Tom Snyder Productions (MA), 121
TRC Environmental Corp. (MA), 121
Unex Corp. (MA), 122
Vanasse Hangen Bustlin, Inc. (MA), 122
Vertex Pharmaceuticals, Inc. (MA), 122
Vicor Corp. (MA), 122
VideoServer, Inc. (MA), 122
Viewlogic Systems, Inc. (MA), 122
Visibility Inc. (MA), 122
Vision-Sciences, Inc. (MA), 122
VMARK Software, Inc. (MA), 122
Wellfleet Communications, Inc. (MA), 122
XLI Corp. (MA), 123
Xylogics, Inc. (MA), 123
Xyplex, Inc. (MA), 123
Zoll Medical Corporation (MA), 123
Zoom Telephonics, Inc. (MA), 123
Zymark Corp. (MA), 123

BOULDER-LONGMONT
BI, Inc. (CO), 62
CliniCom, Inc. (CO), 62

Data Storage Marketing, Inc. (CO), 63
Golden Ribbon, Inc. (CO), 63
Hauser Chemical Research, Inc. (CO), 63
Integral Peripherals, Inc. (CO), 63
Johnson Engineering Corp. (CO), 64
Micro Decisionware, Inc. (CO), 64
NBI, Inc. (CO), 64
S.M. Stoller Corp. (CO), 65
Somatogen, Inc. (CO), 65
Soricon Corp. (CO), 65
Staodyn, Inc. (CO), 65
Synergen, Inc. (CO), 65
Xenometrix, Inc. (CO), 66
XVT Software, Inc. (CO), 66

BREMERTON
Pacific Western Services, Inc. (WA), 208

BRIDGEPORT-STAMFORD-NORWALK
Advanced Technology Materials, Inc. (CT), 66
Applied Information for Marketing, Inc. (CT), 67
Centrix, Inc. (CT), 67
Food Automation Service Techniques, Inc. (CT), 68
IMRS Inc. (CT), 68
Lorad Corp. (CT), 68
Micrognosis, Inc. (CT), 69
Noise Cancellation Technologies, Inc. (CT), 69
Numetrix, Inc. (CT), 69
Photronics, Inc. (CT), 69
Revelation Technologies, Inc. (CT), 70
Siemon Co. (CT), 70
TranSwitch Corp. (CT), 70
Voltarc Technologies, Inc. (CT), 70
Zeitech, Inc. (CT), 70

BRYAN-COLLEGE STATION
Star Tel, Inc. (TX), 194

BUFFALO
International Imaging Materials, Inc. (NY), 150
Moog Controls, Inc. (NY), 152
PCB Piezotronics, Inc. (NY), 153

BURLINGTON
A&M Software, Inc. (VT), 198
Arnold Edwards Corp. (VT), 198
Arrowsmith Shelburne, Inc. (VT), 198
Bennington Iron Works, Inc. (VT), 198
Bio-Tek Instruments, Inc. (VT), 198
Carris Reels, Inc. (VT), 198
Courtaulds Aerospace, Inc., Performance Composites Division (VT), 198
IDX Systems Corp. (VT), 198
Nexus Custom Electronics (VT), 199
Springer-Miller, Inc. (VT), 199

CANTON
M.K. Morse Co. (OH), 162
Universal Vision Systems, Inc. (OH), 164
Wahl Refractories, Inc. (OH), 164
Will-Burt Co. (OH), 165
WIL Research Laboratories, Inc. (OH), 165

CEDAR RAPIDS
Norand Corp. (IA), 93
Parsons Technology (IA), 93
Source Data Systems, Inc. (IA), 93

CHAMPAIGN-URBANA-RANTOUL
Construction Engineering Research Laboratories (IL), 84

Daily & Associates Engineers, Inc. (IL), 84
Frasca International, Inc. (IL), 86
Nashua Precision Technologies (IL), 87
Wolfram Research, Inc. (IL), 90

CHARLOTTE-GASTONIA, NC-SC

FMC Corp., Lithium Division (NC), 156
Glenayre Technologies, Inc. (NC), 156
Greer Laboratories, Inc. (NC), 156
Joy Energy Systems, Inc. (NC), 157
Keiltex Industries, Inc. (NC), 157
Rhone-Poulenc, Inc., Latex and Specialty Polymers Division (NC), 158
Roechling Engineered Plastics (NC), 158
Schaefer Systems International, Inc. (NC), 158
Textron, Inc., Townsend Division (NC), 158
Trion, Inc. (NC), 158

CHATTANOOGA, TN-GA

Chattem, Inc. (TN), 183
Steward, Inc. (TN), 184
Walker Equipment Corp. (GA), 81

CHICAGO

Alfred Benesch & Co. (IL), 82
AlliedSignal Inc., AlliedSignal Research and Technology (IL), 82
Allied Products Corp., Verson Corp. (IL), 82
Allomatic Products Co. (IN), 90
American Colloid Co., Inc. (IL), 82
ANGUS Chemical Co. (IL), 82

Application Engineering Corp. (IL), 83
Applied Systems, Inc. (IL), 83
BACG, Inc. (IL), 83
Barrett Industrial Trucks, Inc. (IL), 83
Blackstone Manufacturing Co., Inc. (IL), 83
Brake Parts, Inc. (IL), 83
Brunswick Corp., Intellitec Division (IL), 83
Cara Corp. (IL), 83
Chemtool, Inc., Metalcote (IL), 84
Chicago Miniature Lamp, Inc. (IL), 84
Circuit Systems, Inc. (IL), 84
Clean Air Engineering (IL), 84
Commercial Testing & Engineering Co. (IL), 84
C.P. Hall Co. (IL), 84
Darome Teleconferencing, Inc. (IL), 84
Dauphin Technology, Inc. (IL), 85
Dearborn Wire & Cable L.P. (IL), 85
Delphi Information Systems, Inc. (IL), 85
Desktop Sales, Inc. (IL), 85
Enterprise Systems, Inc. (IL), 85
Envirodyne Engineers, Inc. (IL), 85
Fansteel, Inc., Escast Division (IL), 85
FCS Computing Services, Inc. (IL), 85
Fotel, Inc. (IL), 85
Greenbrier & Russel, Inc. (IL), 86
Homaco, Inc. (IL), 86
Indeck Energy Services, Inc. (IL), 86
Internet Systems Corp. (IL), 86
Kalmus and Associates, Inc. (IL), 86
LoDan Electronics, Inc. (IL), 86
Macrotech Fluid Sealing, Inc., Selastomer Division (IL), 86
Marketing Information Systems, Inc. (IL), 86

Medicus Systems Corporation (IL), 87
Metform, Inc. (IL), 87
Micro Solutions Computer Products, Inc. (IL), 87
Mid-West Automation Systems, Inc. (IL), 87
Mostardi-Platt Associates, Inc. (IL), 87
MultiMedia Communication Systems (IL), 87
Nissan Forklift Corp. (IL), 87
Nunc, Inc. (IL), 87
Platinum Technology, Inc. (IL), 87
Polyfoam Packers Corp. (IL), 88
Pre Finish Metals Incorporated (IL), 88
Rauland-Borg Corp. (IL), 88
Resource Information Management Systems, Inc. (IL), 88
Seaquist Dispensing (IL), 88
Siemens Medical Systems, Inc., Nuclear Medicine Group (IL), 88
Sierra, Inc. (IL), 88
SoloPak Pharmaceuticals, Inc. (IL), 88
Speedfam Corp., Machine Tool Group (IL), 88
SunGard Investment Systems, Inc. (IL), 89
Superior Graphite Co. (IL), 89
Surya Electronics, Inc. (IL), 89
Systems and Programming Resources, Inc. (IL), 89
Telular Group L.P. (IL), 89
THK America, Inc. (IL), 89
Total Control Products, Inc. (IL), 89
U.S. Robotics, Inc. (IL), 89
Vapor Mark IV, Transportation Products Group (IL), 89
Velsicol Chemical Corp. (IL), 89
Viktron Technologies, Inc., Electronics Support Systems Division (IL), 90
Wes-Tech Automation Systems, Inc. (IL), 90

Wizdom Systems, Inc.
(IL), 90
Zenith Controls, Inc.
(IL), 90

CINCINNATI

BP Chemicals Inc., Filon
Products (KY), 95
CDR Manufacturing, Inc.
(KY), 95
CDR Pigments and
Dispersions (KY), 95
Ceramichrome, Inc.
(KY), 95
Environmental Enterprises,
Inc. (OH), 161
General Data Co., Inc.
(OH), 161
Gusher Pumps, Inc.
(OH), 161
ITT A-C Pump (OH), 162
Pharos Technologies, Inc.
(OH), 163
Prentke Romich Co.
(OH), 163
Tastemaker (OH), 164

CLARKSVILLE-HOPKINSVILLE, TN-KY

White Hydraulics, Inc.
(KY), 97

CLEVELAND

Allied Color Industries, Inc.
(OH), 159
Allwaste Recycling, Inc.
(OH), 159
AMRESCO, Inc. (OH), 159
Antenna Specialists Co.
(OH), 160
Cyberex, Inc. (OH), 160
Desktop Displays, Inc.
(OH), 160
Diversey Water
Technology, Inc.
(OH), 160
Eaton Corp., Forge
Division (OH), 161
Essef Corp. (OH), 161
Hickok Electrical
Instrument Co. (OH), 161
Laurel Industries, Inc.
(OH), 162
LDA Systems, Inc.
(OH), 162

Macola, Inc. (OH), 162
Markwith Tool, Inc.
(OH), 162
Pressco Technology, Inc.
(OH), 163
Schweizer Dipple, Inc.
(OH), 163
Steris Corp. (OH), 164
Synthetic Products Co.
(OH), 164
Tuthill Corp., Hansen
Coupling Division
(OH), 164

COLORADO-SPRINGS

NSR Information, Inc.
(CO), 64
NTI (CO), 64
Omnipoint Corp. (CO), 64
Philips LMS (CO), 64
Polydyne International,
Inc. (CO), 65
RUST Geotech Inc.
(CO), 65

COLUMBIA, MO

Datastorm Technologies,
Inc. (MO), 135

COLUMBIA, SC

Ambac International, Inc.
(SC), 181

COLUMBUS

ADB-ALNACO, Inc.
(OH), 159
Allied Mineral Products,
Inc. (OH), 159
LCI International (OH), 162
Owens-Corning Fiberglas
Science and Technology
Center (OH), 163
Parker Hannifin Corp.,
Tube Fittings Division
(OH), 163
R.D. Zande & Associates,
Ltd. (OH), 163
Roxane Laboratories, Inc.
(OH), 163
Sterling Software, Inc.,
Network Services
Division (OH), 164
Symix Computer Systems
Inc. (OH), 164

Teledyne Industries, Inc.,
Teledyne Princeton
(OH), 164

DALLAS

Air Products and
Chemicals, Inc., Silicon
Materials Services
Division (TX), 185
Allen Telecom Group,
Decibel Products
Division (TX), 185
American Medical
Electronics, Inc.
(TX), 185
Amtech Corp. (TX), 186
Antrim Corp. (TX), 186
Argo Data Resource Corp.
(TX), 186
Benchmarq
Microelectronics, Inc.
(TX), 186
Control Systems
International, Inc.
(TX), 187
C-Power Companies, Inc.
(TX), 187
Cuplex, Inc. (TX), 188
Cyrix Corp. (TX), 188
Cyten Circuit Design, Inc.
(TX), 188
DacEasy, Inc. (TX), 188
DPC&A OGRE Partners,
Ltd. (TX), 188
Health Synq Corp.
(TX), 190
HR Industries, Inc.
(TX), 190
i2 Technologies, Inc.
(TX), 191
Ideal Learning, Inc.
(TX), 190
Intelect, Inc. (TX), 190
Intercontinental
Manufacturing Co.
(TX), 190
International Retail
Systems Inc. (TX), 191
InterVoice, Inc. (TX), 191
IRI International, Inc.
(TX), 191
Kodak Health Imaging
Systems, Inc. (TX), 191
Lacerte Software Corp.
(TX), 191
LanOptics Inc. (TX), 191
Lear Data Info-Services,
Inc. (TX), 191

Unitech Engineering, Inc.
(MI), 127
United Solar Systems,
Corp. (MI), 127
Universal Super Abrasive,
Inc. (MI), 127
Variation Systems
Analysis, Inc. (MI), 128
Veratex Corp. (MI), 128
X-Ray Industries, Inc.,
X-R-I Testing Division
(MI), 128

DULUTH, MN-WI

Hibbing Electronics Corp.
(MN), 130

ELKHART-GOSHEN

Crown International, Inc.
(IN), 91
Crown Unlimited Machine,
Inc. (IN), 91

ELMIRA

Augat, Inc., LRC Division
(NY), 147

ERIE

Accu-Form, Inc. (PA), 169
Component Technology
Corp. (PA), 171
Iroquois Tool Systems, Inc.
(PA), 173
ISS, Comptek (PA), 173
Molded Fiber Glass
Companies, Union City
Division (PA), 175
PHB Polymeric (PA), 176

EUGENE-SPRINGFIELD

Cedarapids, Inc., El-Jay
Division (OR), 166
Point Control Co.
(OR), 168

EVANSVILLE, IN-KY

Service Tool & Die, Inc.
(KY), 96
Vincent Industrial Plastic,
Inc. (KY), 97

FARGO-MOORHEAD, ND-MN

Fargo Assembly Co.
(ND), 159
Great Plains Software
(ND), 159

FORT COLLINS

Otsuka Electronics USA,
Inc. (CO), 64
Wedding & Associates,
Inc. (CO), 66

FORT LAUDERDALE-HOLLYWOOD

Applied Measurement
Systems, Inc. (FL), 71
A.W. Industries, Inc.
(FL), 71
DME Corp. (FL), 73
M & W Pump Corp.
(FL), 74
TransTechnology Corp.,
Lundy Technical Center
(FL), 76
Unipower Corporation
(FL), 76

FORT WALTON BEACH

Crestview Aerospace
Corp. (FL), 72
Startech Innovations, Inc.
(FL), 76
TYBRIN Corp. (FL), 76

FORT WAYNE

Auburn Foundry, Inc.
(IN), 90
BRC Rubber Group, Inc.
(IN), 90
Corson Research, Inc.
(IN), 91
PHD, Inc. (IN), 92

FORT WORTH-ARLINGTON

Altai, Inc. (TX), 185
Anago, Inc. (TX), 186
FWT, Inc. (TX), 189
ICON Industries, Inc.
(TX), 190
Lars Industries, Inc.
(TX), 191
Marvel Communications
Corporation (TX), 192
Mouser Electronics
(TX), 192
PDX, Inc. (TX), 193
Powell-Esco Co. (TX), 193
Tecnol, Inc. (TX), 195
Teknekron Infoswitch Corp.
(TX), 195

FRESNO

Claude Laval Corp.
(CA), 30
Sunrise Medical Inc.,
Quickie Designs (CA), 57

GADSDEN

Marathon Equipment Co.
(AL), 19
M&M Chemical and
Equipment Co., Inc.
(AL), 19

GALVESTON-TEXAS CITY

Astro International Corp.
(TX), 186

GARY-HAMMOND

Hammond Lead Products,
Inc. (IN), 92

GLENS FALLS

AMG Industries, Inc.
(NY), 147

GRAND RAPIDS

Fishbeck, Thompson, Carr
& Huber, Inc. (MI), 125
Gentex Corp. (MI), 125
X-Rite, Inc. (MI), 128

GREENSBORO-WINSTON SALEM

GBA Systems (NC), 156
High Point Chemical Corp.
(NC), 156
Southern Optical Co.
(NC), 158

MADISON

Electronic Theatre Control, Inc. (WI), 211
Lunar Corp. (WI), 211
Promega Corp. (WI), 212
Rice Lake Weighing Systems, Inc. (WI), 212
Strand Associates, Inc. (WI), 213
TDS Computing Services, Inc. (WI), 213

MANCHESTER-NASHUA

AimTech Corp. (NH), 137
Assembly Solutions, Inc. (NH), 137
Coda, Inc. (NH), 138
Computersmith, Inc. (NH), 138
Cyplex Corporation (NH), 138
Granite Communications, Inc. (NH), 138
Howtek, Inc. (NH), 138
Keyfile Corp. (NH), 138
Lockheed Sanders, Inc., Avionics Division (NH), 139
Palette Systems Corp. (NH), 139
Presstek, Inc. (NH), 139
Saphikon, Inc. (NH), 139
Source Electronics Corp. (NH), 139
Summa Four, Inc. (NH), 140
Tally Systems Corp. (NH), 140
Unitrode Integrated Circuits Corp. (NH), 140

MELBOURNE-TITUSVILLE

Harris Corp., Air Traffic Control Systems Division (FL), 73
Opto Mechanik, Inc. (FL), 74
Quality Contract Manufacturing, Inc. (FL), 75
Scientific-Atlanta, Inc., Private Networks Business Division (FL), 75

Targ-It-Tronics, Inc. (FL), 76

MEMPHIS, TN-AR-MS

Allen & Hoshall, Inc. (TN), 183
AZO, Inc. (TN), 183
Cedar Chemical Corp. (TN), 183
Jefferson-Pilot Data Services, Inc. (TN), 184
Micro Craft, Inc. (TN), 184
Wright Medical Technology, Inc. (TN), 184

MIAMI-HIALEAH

Corvita Corp. (FL), 72
Equitrac Corp. (FL), 73
Hobart Brothers Co., Diversified Products Group (FL), 73
National Water Purifiers Corp. (FL), 74
Ryan Electronics Products, Inc. (FL), 75
Symbiosis Corporation (FL), 76

MIDDLESEX-SOMERSET-HUNTERDON

AMP Incorporated, Lytel Division (NJ), 140
Anadigics, Inc. (NJ), 140
Blonder-Tongue Laboratories, Inc. (NJ), 140
Computer Systems Development, Inc. (NJ), 141
Integra Life Science, Inc. (NJ), 143
Ortho Pharmaceutical Corp., Advanced Care Products Division (NJ), 144

MILWAUKEE

ABB Industrial Systems, Inc. (WI), 210
ABB Robotics, Inc. (WI), 210

Aldrich Chemical Co., Inc. (WI), 210
Automating Peripherals, Inc. (WI), 210
Best Power Technology, Inc. (WI), 210
Catalyst USA, Inc. (WI), 210
Chris Hansens Laboratory, Inc. (WI), 210
Effective Management Systems, Inc. (WI), 210
Electronic Cable Specialists, Inc. (WI), 211
FMS/Magnacraft (WI), 211
Generac Corp. (WI), 211
Graef, Anhalt, Schloemer & Associates, Inc., Public Works Division (WI), 211
Great Lakes Instruments, Inc. (WI), 211
Husco International, Inc. (WI), 211
Kaul-Tronics, Inc. (WI), 211
Lanson Industries, Inc. (WI), 211
McHugh, Freeman & Associates, Inc. (WI), 212
Medical Advances, Inc. (WI), 212
Milwaukee Gear Co. (WI), 212
Modern Machine Works, Inc. (WI), 212
Mox-Med, Inc. (WI), 212
Plastic Engineered Components, Inc. (WI), 212

MINNEAPOLIS-ST.PAUL, MN-WI

3M Superabrasive and Microfinishing Systems Department (MN), 133
3M, Verification and Optical Systems Project (MN), 133
Aetrium, Inc. (MN), 128
Americable, Inc. (MN), 128
AmeriData, Inc. (MN), 128
Anderson Chemical Co. (MN), 128
Andreasen Engineering and Manufacturing, Inc. (MN), 128
Audiotone, Inc. (MN), 128
Ault, Inc. (MN), 129

Baldor Motion Products Group (MN), 129
Barr Engineering Co. (MN), 129
Benchmark Computer Systems, Inc. (MN), 129
B.H. Electronics, Inc. (MN), 129
B. Braun Medical, Inc., Cardiovascular Division (MN), 129
Colder Products Co. (MN), 129
Computer Network Technology Corp. (MN), 129
Connect Computer Co. (MN), 129
David Mitchell & Associates, Inc. (MN), 129
Decision Systems, Inc. (MN), 130
Diametrics Medical Inc. (MN), 130
Digi International Inc. (MN), 130
Empi, Inc. (MN), 130
Fluoroware, Inc. (MN), 130
Fourth Shift Corp. (MN), 130
Health Systems Integration, Inc. (MN), 130
Innovex, Inc. (MN), 130
Lake Region Manufacturing Co., Inc. (MN), 130
Mamac Systems, Inc. (MN), 130
Medical Devices, Inc. (MN), 131
Medical Graphics Corp. (MN), 131
Milltronics Manufacturing Co. (MN), 131
Mississippi Chemical Corp. (MS), 133
Multi-Tech Systems, Inc. (MN), 131
Nortech Systems, Inc. (MN), 131
Osmonics, Inc. (MN), 131
Pace, Inc. (MN), 131
Possis Medical, Inc. (MN), 131
QMC Technologies, Inc. (MN), 131

Reliance Motion Control, Inc. (MN), 131
Remmele Engineering, Inc. (MN), 132
Research Inc., Control Systems Division (MN), 132
Riverside Electronics, Ltd. (MN), 132
RTP Company (MN), 132
St. Jude Medical, Inc. (MN), 132
Schneider (USA) Inc (MN), 132
Schott Corp. (MN), 132
Serving Software Inc. (MN), 132
Shared Resource Management, Inc. (MN), 132
Slope Meter Co. (MN), 132
Tricord Systems, Inc. (MN), 133
Turck Inc. (MN), 133
Turtle Mountain Corp. (MN), 133
Varitronic Systems, Inc. (MN), 133
VTC Inc. (MN), 133
Zercom Corp. (MN), 133

MOBILE

CPSI (AL), 19
XANTE Corp. (AL), 20

MODESTO

Parker Hannifin Corp., Racor Division (CA), 50

MONMOUTH OCEAN

Brightwork Development, Inc. (NJ), 141
Celwave RF (NJ), 141
Dialight Corp. (NJ), 141
ECCS, Inc. (NJ), 142
Osteotech, Inc. (NJ), 144
Xpedite Systems, Inc. (NJ), 145

MONTGOMERY

Thermal Components, Inc. (AL), 20

MUNCIE

Arrowhead Plastic Engineering, Inc. (IN), 90

MUSKEGON

Baxter Diagnostics, Inc., Burdick & Jackson Division (MI), 124

NASHVILLE

Barge, Waggoner, Sumner & Cannon, Inc. (TN), 183
Envoy Corp. (TN), 184
Precision Products of Tennessee, Inc. (TN), 184

NASSAU-SUFFOLK

Altana, Inc. (NY), 146
American Reagent Laboratories, Inc. (NY), 146
AMS (NY), 147
Applied Digital Data Systems, Inc. (NY), 147
Charles Ross & Son Co. (NY), 148
Curative Technologies, Inc. (NY), 148
Eder Associates (NY), 149
Excel Technology, Inc. (NY), 149
Medsonic, Inc. (NY), 151
Merit Electronic Design Co., Ltd. (NY), 151
NAI Technologies, Inc. (NY), 152
Oncogene Science, Inc. (NY), 152
Periphonics Corp. (NY), 153
Renco Electronics, Inc. (NY), 153
RVSI (NY), 153
Signal Transformer Co., Inc. (NY), 154
Standard Microsystems Corporation (NY), 154
United Biomedical, Inc. (NY), 155

NEWARK

Denon America, Inc. (NJ), 141
Dialogic Corp. (NJ), 142

Edwards and Kelcey, Inc. (NJ), 142
Enviroplan, Inc. (NJ), 142
Esselte Meto (NJ), 142
Immunomedics, Inc. (NJ), 142
Isomedix Inc. (NJ), 143
Joyce Molding Corp. (NJ), 143
KDI Triangle Electronics, Inc. (NJ), 143
Logos Corp. (NJ), 143
MICRO HealthSystems, Inc. (NJ), 144
Penta Manufacturing Co. (NJ), 144
Teleware, Inc. (NJ), 144
Troy Corp. (NJ), 144
Unified Systems Solutions (NJ), 144
Wesgo, Duramic (NJ), 145
White Storage and Retrieval Systems, Inc. (NJ), 145
WindSoft, Inc. (NJ), 145

NEW BEDFORD-FALL RIVER

Aegis, Inc. (MA), 105
Keithley Instruments, Inc., Data Acquisition Division (MA), 114
Kopin Corp. (MA), 114
Teledyne, Inc., Teledyne Rodney Metals (MA), 121

NEW HAVEN-WATERBURY

Alexion Pharmaceuticals, Inc. (CT), 66
Alinabal Holdings, Corp. (CT), 66
American Lightwave Systems, Inc. (CT), 66
CMX Systems, Inc. (CT), 67
Diversified Technologies Corporation (CT), 68
Eyelematic Manufacturing Co., Inc. (CT), 68
EZ Form Cable Corp. (CT), 68
Fire-Lite Alarms, Inc. (CT), 68
Fluidyne Ansonia, LP (CT), 68

Notifier (CT), 69
Peak Electronics, Inc. (CT), 69
SNET Cellular, Inc. (CT), 70
Tri-Tech, Inc. (CT), 70

NEW LONDON-NORWICH

DDL OMNI Engineering Corp. (CT), 68
Ortronics, Inc. (CT), 69

NEW ORLEANS

Digicourse, Inc. (LA), 97
Laitram Corp. (LA), 97

NEW YORK

Alpine Group, Inc. (NY), 146
American Standards Testing Bureau, Inc. (NY), 146
American White Cross Labs, Inc. (NY), 147
Applied Business Technology Corp. (NY), 147
ATC Environmental, Inc. (NY), 147
Audiosears Corp. (NY), 147
Belmay, Inc. (NY), 147
Besicorp Group, Inc. (NY), 148
Bio-Technology General Corp. (NY), 148
CBORD Group, Inc. (NY), 148
Century Business Credit Corp. (NY), 148
Danbury Pharmacal, Inc. (NY), 148
Deltown Specialties (NY), 148
Design Strategy Corp. (NY), 148
Dieknowlogist, Inc. (NY), 149
Dynamic Decisions, Inc. (NY), 149
Emisphere Technologies, Inc. (NY), 149
FAME Software Corp. (NY), 149

Fusion Systems Group, Inc. (NY), 149
Gorham Clark, Inc. (NY), 150
Hertz Technolgy Group (NY), 150
Hipotronics, Inc. (NY), 150
Hi-Tech Ceramics, Inc. (NY), 150
Inchape, Inc., ETL Testing Laboratories, Inc. (NY), 150
Instinet Corp. (NY), 150
Interflo Technologies (NY), 150
IPC Information Systems, Inc. (NY), 151
Ithaca Peripherals Inc. (NY), 151
JYACC, Inc. (NY), 151
Keystone Electronics Corp. (NY), 151
Liberty Brokerage, Inc. (NY), 151
Market Vision Corp. (NY), 151
Microbank Software, Inc. (NY), 152
Micro Bio-Medics, Inc. (NY), 152
Novo Nordisk of North America, Inc. (NY), 152
Par Pharmaceutical, Inc. (NY), 153
Positron Industries, Inc. (NY), 153
Regeneron Pharmaceuticals, Inc. (NY), 153
Standard Data Corporation (NY), 154
Superior Printing Ink Co., Inc. (NY), 154
TDC Electronics, Inc. (NY), 154
Telecom Services Limited (U.S.), Inc. (NY), 154
Teleport Communications Group (NY), 155
TelTech Corp., Consulting Division (NY), 155
Vicon Fiberoptics, Inc. (NY), 155

NIAGARA FALLS

Sevenson Environmental Services, Inc. (NY), 154

PHOENIX

PITTSBURGH

Alucobond Technologies, Inc. (MO), 134
Atlas, Soundolier (MO), 134
bioMerieux Vitek, Inc. (MO), 134
Bock Pharmacal Co. (MO), 134
CITATION Computer Systems, Inc. (MO), 134
Continental Cement, Inc. (MO), 134
Data Research Associates, Inc. (MO), 135
Hilco Technologies, Inc. (MO), 135
Jack Henry & Associates, Inc. (MO), 135
Jones Medical Industries, Inc. (MO), 135
K-V Pharmaceutical Co. (MO), 135
Mycotech Corporation (MT), 136
Nooter/Eriksen Cogeneration Systems, Inc. (MO), 135
OHM Corporation, Missouri Division (MO), 136
P.D. George & Co. (MO), 136
Schreiber, Grana, Yonley, Inc. (MO), 136
Sverdrup Environmental, Inc. (MO), 136

SYRACUSE

Eagle Comtronics, Inc. (NY), 149
OBG Technical Services, Inc. (NY), 152
OP-TECH Environmental Services, Inc. (NY), 153
Philips Broadband Networks, Inc. (NY), 153
Sensis Corp. (NY), 153
SSAC, Inc. (NY), 154
Welch Allyn, Inc., Inspection Systems Division (NY), 155
Young & Franklin Inc. (NY), 155

TALLAHASSEE

CMS/Data Corp. (FL), 72
PC DOCS, Inc. (FL), 74

TAMPA-ST.PETERSBURG

Abra Cadabra Software, Inc. (FL), 71
Crystal Software International-U.S., Inc. (FL), 72
Custom Cable Industries, Inc. (FL), 73
L.E.A. Dynatech, Inc. (FL), 73
Medical Technology Systems, Inc. (FL), 74
MediTek Health Corp. (FL), 74
Precisionaire, Inc. (FL), 75
Reflectone, Inc. (FL), 75
Reptron Electronics, Inc. (FL), 75
Reptron Electronics, Inc., K-Byte Division (FL), 75
Solar Plastics, Inc. (FL), 75
Technology Research Corp. (FL), 76
Trak Microwave Corp. (FL), 76
Williams Earth Sciences, Inc. (FL), 77

TOLEDO

Green Manufacturing, Inc. (OH), 161

TOPEKA

NewTek, Inc. (KS), 94

TRENTON

Crestek, Inc. (NJ), 141
EG&G Instruments, Inc. (NJ), 142
Epitaxx, Inc. (NJ), 142
Liposome Co., Inc. (NJ), 143

TUCSON

Avalon Software, Inc. (AZ), 20
Tri-Tronics, Inc. (AZ), 22
Universal Navigation Corp. (AZ), 22

TULSA

Advanced Power Technology, Inc. (OR), 166

Coburn Optical Industries, Inc. (OK), 165
Eagle-Picher Industries, Inc., Eagle-Picher Research Laboratory (OK), 165
Educational Development Corp. (OK), 165
Erlanger Tubular Corp. (OK), 165
Hathaway Corp., Motion Control Division (OK), 166
Nordam Group, Manufacturing Division (OK), 166
Nordam Group, Transparency Division (OK), 166

UTICA-ROME

Conmed Corp. (NY), 148
Crellin, Inc. (NY), 148
Oneida Research Services, Inc. (NY), 152
Sterling Software, Inc., Eastern Operations (NY), 154

VALLEJO-FAIRFIELD-NAPA

Real Time Solutions, Inc. (CA), 54

VINELAND-MILLVILLE

IGI, Inc. (NJ), 142

WASHINGTON DC-MD-VA

ACS, Inc. (VA), 199
Advanced Communication Systems, Inc. (VA), 199
Advanced Engineering & Management Associates, Aerospace and Education Division (VA), 199
Advanced Engineering & Research Associates (VA), 199
Advanced Technology Systems, Inc. (VA), 199
American Communications Co. (VA), 199

American Computer and
Electronics Corp.
(MD), 98
American Red Cross,
Jerome H. Holland
Laboratory for the
Biomedical Sciences
(MD), 98
American Systems Corp.
(VA), 200
Andrulis Research Corp.
(MD), 99
Applied Ordnance
Technology, Inc.
(MD), 99
Applied Research Corp.
(MD), 99
A&T Systems, Inc.
(MD), 98
Automated Information
Management, Inc.
(MD), 99
Autometric, Inc. (VA), 200
Bay Resins, Inc. (MD), 99
BDS, Inc. (VA), 200
Betac International Corp.
(VA), 200
BioWhittaker, Inc. (MD), 99
Boehringer Mannheim
Pharmaceuticals
(MD), 99
Bohdan Associates, Inc.
(MD), 100
C-CUBED Corporation
(VA), 200
CDA Investment
Technologies, Inc.
(MD), 100
Century Technologies, Inc.
(MD), 100
Chemonics Industries, Inc.,
Chemonics International
Consulting Division
(DC), 71
Coherent Communications
Systems Corp. (VA), 200
Coleman Research Corp.,
Washington Division
(VA), 200
COMNET Corporation
(MD), 100
Compliance Corp.
(MD), 100
Computer Based Systems,
Inc. (VA), 200
Comsearch (VA), 200
COMSYS Technical
Services, Inc. (MD), 100
COR, Inc. (VA), 200

Cryomedical Sciences, Inc.
(MD), 100
CSCI Association Group
(MD), 100
CSC Intelicom, Inc.
(MD), 100
DataFocus, Inc. (VA), 201
Datatel, Inc. (VA), 201
DCS Corp. (VA), 201
Delex Systems, Inc.
(VA), 201
Deltek Systems, Inc.
(VA), 201
Dewberry & Davis
(VA), 201
DIGICON Corp. (MD), 101
Dual, Inc. (VA), 201
Dunham-Bush, Inc.,
Compressurized Air
Conditioning Division
(VA), 201
Eagan, McAllister
Associates, Inc.
(MD), 101
Edunetics Corp. (VA), 201
Electronic Instrumentation
and Technology, Inc.
(VA), 201
Electronic Warfare
Associates, Inc.
(VA), 202
Engineering Design Group,
Inc. (DC), 71
Engineering Research
Associates, Inc.
(VA), 202
ENSCO, Inc. (VA), 202
Environmental Protection
Systems, Inc. (VA), 202
Federal Data Corp.
(MD), 101
FileTek, Inc. (MD), 101
Fuentez Systems
Concepts, Inc. (VA), 202
Futron Corp. (MD), 101
General Sciences Corp.
(MD), 101
Genetics & IVF Institute
(VA), 202
Genetic Therapy, Inc.
(MD), 101
Globalink, Inc. (VA), 202
Global Associates, Ltd.
(VA), 202
Information Management
Consultants, Inc.
(VA), 203
Information Systems and
Services, Inc. (MD), 102

Interlog, Inc. (VA), 203
International Computers &
Telecommunications, Inc.
(MD), 102
INTRAFED, Inc. (MD), 102
Jackson & Tull, Inc.,
Aerospace Division
(MD), 102
J.F. Taylor, Inc. (MD), 102
JIL Systems, Inc.
(VA), 203
JWK International Corp.
(VA), 203
Merkle Computer Systems,
Inc. (MD), 102
Metters Industries, Inc.
(VA), 203
Michael Baker Jr., Inc.,
Civil and Water
Resources Division
(VA), 203
Microdyne Corp. (VA), 203
Microlog Corporation
(MD), 102
Micronetics Design Corp.
(MD), 102
MICROS Systems, Inc.
(MD), 103
Mobile Telesystems, Inc.
(MD), 103
NCI Information Systems,
Inc. (VA), 203
Netrix Corp. (VA), 204
Network Solutions, Inc.
(VA), 204
Newbridge Networks, Inc.
(VA), 204
North American Vaccine,
Inc. (MD), 103
One Call Concepts, Inc.
(MD), 103
Orion Network Systems,
Inc. (MD), 103
Otsuka America
Pharmaceutical Inc.,
Maryland Research
Laboratories (MD), 103
Patapsco Designs, Inc.
(MD), 103
Pathology Associates, Inc.
(MD), 103
Patton Electronics Co.
(MD), 103
PSI International, Inc.
(VA), 204
Quality Systems, Inc.
(VA), 204
Racal Communications,
Inc. (MD), 104